The first five years of the Communist International
VOLUME 1

The first five years of the Communist International
VOLUME 1

Leon Trotsky

Pathfinder
NEW YORK   LONDON   MONTREAL   SYDNEY

Copyright © 1945, 1972 Pathfinder Press
Copyright renewed 1973
All rights reserved

ISBN 978-0-87348-830-3
Library of Congress Catalog Card Number 72-92701
Manufactured in the United States of America

First edition, 1945
Second edition, 1972
Twelfth printing, 2024

COVER PAINTING: Morris Louis, *Number 11*, 1961, 72 x 72 in. / 182.9 x 182.9 cm. Private collection, courtesy of Marcella Louis Brenner and The André Emmerich Gallery, Inc.

COVER DESIGN: Eric Simpson

PATHFINDER
www.pathfinderpress.com
Email: pathfinder@pathfinderpress.com

Contents

Preface   7

Author's 1924 introduction   9

I. The First World Congress
1. Manifesto of the Communist International to the workers of the world   35
2. Report on the Communist Party of the Soviet Union and the Red Army   51
3. Order of the Day Number 83 to the Red Army and Navy   57

II. From the First to the Second World Congress
4. To comrades of the Spartacus League   63
5. A creeping revolution   71
6. Great days   77
7. En route: Thoughts on the progress of the proletarian revolution   81
8. French Socialism on the eve of revolution   101
9. Jean Longuet   119
10. On the coming congress of the Comintern   131

III. The Second World Congress
11. Speech on Comrade Zinoviev's report on the role of the party   151
12. Manifesto of the Second World Congress   157

IV. From the Second to the Third World Congress
13. On the policy of the KAPD   205
14. Speech delivered at the Second World Conference of Communist Women   227
15. Letter to Comrade Monatte   235
16. Letter to Comrades Cachin and Frossard   241

17. On 'l'Humanité,' the central organ
    of the French party   247

V. The Third World Congress
18. The Red Army to the General Staff
    of the Revolution   257
19. Report on the world economic crisis and the
    new tasks of the Communist International   259
20. Summary speech   331
21. Theses of the Third World Congress
    on the international situation and
    the tasks of the Comintern   347
22. Speech on the Italian question at the Third
    Congress of the Communist International   379
23. Speech on Comrade Radek's report
    on 'Tactics of the Comintern'
    at the Third Congress   389
24. Speech on Comrade Lenin's report:
    'Tactics of the Russian Communist Party'   407

VI. From the Third to the Fourth World Congress
25. The main lesson of the Third Congress   423
26. Report on 'The Balance Sheet' of the Third
    Congress of the Communist International   429
27. Summary speech   451

Explanatory notes   461

Index   505

Preface

These two volumes of speeches and writings by Leon Trotsky document the discussions and debates of the communist movement as it grappled with the concrete questions of the fight for working-class power in the epoch of imperialist decline—class collaborationism versus revolutionary politics; the role of the trade unions; defense of the young Soviet republics; building an alliance of workers and farmers; and the rising struggles for national liberation in the colonial world.

Readers of *The First Five Years of the Communist International* will also be interested in *The Communist International in Lenin's Time*, also available from Pathfinder. The six volumes of the series that have been published so far include:

> *Lenin's Struggle for a Revolutionary International 1907–1916;*
> *The German Revolution and the Debate on Soviet Power, 1918–1919;*
> *Founding the Communist International: Proceedings and Documents of the First Congress, March 1919;*
> *Workers of the World and Oppressed Peoples, Unite! Proceedings and Documents of the Second Congress, 1920 (in two volumes);* and
> *To See the Dawn: Baku, 1920, First Congress of the Peoples of the East.*

The First Five Years of the Communist International was first published in English in 1945 by Pioneer Publishers. The second volume was added in 1953. Both volumes were translated, edited, and annotated by John G. Wright. With the exception of the illustrations in volume two, which were added in 1972, this edition is identical to the 1953 edition.

Leon Trotsky was a central leader of the October 1917 revolution in Russia. During the Soviet republic's first ten years he served as foreign minister, head of the Red Army during the civil war of 1918–20, convener of economic planning bodies, and a leader of the Communist International. Following Lenin's death in 1924, Trotsky was the principal leader of the fight to defend Lenin's revolutionary course against the anti–working class policies and actions of the growing petty-bourgeois caste whose most prominent spokesperson was Joseph Stalin. He was expelled from the Soviet Union in 1929 and assassinated in Mexico in 1940 by an agent of Stalin's secret police.

NOVEMBER 1996

Author's 1924 introduction

The half-decade of the Communist International's existence is divided into two periods by the Third World Congress. During its first two years the Comintern still remains wholly and exclusively under the aegis of the imperialist war. Revolutionary perspectives are drawn directly from the consequences of the war. It is considered virtually self-evident that the constantly rising and intensifying political ferment of the masses, growing out of the social paroxysms of the war, must lead directly to the conquest of power by the proletariat. This evaluation of the course of developments found its expression in the Manifestoes of the First and Second World Congresses which are included in this volume. The principled evaluation of the postwar situation given in these documents wholly retains its force to this day. But the tempo of development proved to be different.

War did not lead directly to the victory of the proletariat in Western Europe. It is all too obvious today just what was lacking for victory in 1919 and 1920: a revolutionary party was lacking.

Not until the powerful postwar mass ferment had already begun to ebb did young Communist parties begin to take shape, and even then only in rough outline. The March 1921 events in Germany graphically disclose the contradiction between the then-existing situation and the policy of the Communist International. Communist parties, or at least their Left Wings, impetuously seek to unleash an offensive at a time when the multimillioned proletarian masses, after the initial defeats, sullenly take stock of the postwar situation and watchfully observe the Communist parties. At the Third World Congress Lenin formulates this threatening divergence between the line of development of the masses and the tactical line of the Communist parties, and with a firm hand secures a decisive turn in the policy of the International. At the present time, when we are far enough removed from the Third Congress to appraise it correctly in retrospect, it can be said that the turn made by the Third Congress was of as great importance to the Communist International as the Brest-Litovsk turn was to the Soviet Republic. Had the Third International continued mechanically to follow the former path, one of whose stages was marked by the March events in Germany, perhaps within a year or two only splinters of Communist parties would have been left. With the Third Congress, a new stage begins: the parties take into account that they have yet to win the masses, and that an assault must be preceded by a more or less protracted period of preparatory work. There opens up the zone of the united front, that is, the tactic of fusing the masses on the basis of transitional demands. The speeches and articles in the second part of this volume are devoted to this "new stage."

This second period of the development of the Communist International, which invariably extended the influence of all its chief sections over the working masses, runs into the mighty revolutionary flood tide in Germany in the latter part of 1923. Europe is once again shaken by wild convulsions, at whose focus stands the Ruhr. The question of power is once again posed in Germany in all its nakedness and acuteness. But the bourgeoisie survived this time as well. A third chapter then opens in the development of the Communist International. The subject for the work of the Fifth World Congress is to define the main political peculiarities and tactical tasks of this new period.

Why did the German revolution fail to lead to victory? The causes for this lie wholly in tactics and not in objective conditions. We have here a truly classic example of a revolutionary situation permitted to slip by. From the moment of the Ruhr occupation, and all the more so when the bankruptcy of passive resistance became evident, it was imperative for the Communist Party to steer a firm and resolute course toward the conquest of power. Only a courageous tactical turn could have unified the German proletariat in the struggle for power. If at the Third Congress and in part of the Fourth Congress we told the German comrades: "You will win the masses only on the basis of taking a leading part in their struggle for transitional demands," then by the middle of 1923 the question became posed differently: After all that the German proletariat had gone through in recent years, it could be led into the decisive battle only in the event that it became convinced that this time the issue was posed, as the Germans say, *aufs Ganze* (i.e., that it was not a question of this or that partial task, but of the fundamental one), and that the Communist Party was ready to march into battle and was capable of securing victory. But the German Communist Party executed this turn without the necessary assurance and after an extreme delay. Both the Rights and the Lefts, despite their sharp struggle against each other, evinced up to September–October [1923] a rather fatalistic attitude toward the process of the development of the revolution. At a time when the entire objective situation demanded that the party undertake a decisive blow, the party did not act to organize the revolution but kept awaiting it. "The revolution is not made on schedule," replied the Rights and the Lefts, confusing the revolution as a whole with one of its specific stages, *i.e.*, the uprising for the seizure of power. My article, "Can the Revolution Be Made on Schedule?" was devoted to this question. This article summarizes the interminable discussions and polemics which had previously taken place. True, in the month of October a sharp break occurred in the party's policy. But it was already too late. In the course of 1923 the working masses realized or sensed that the moment of decisive struggle was approaching. However, they did not see the necessary resolution and self-confidence on the side of the Communist Party. And when the latter began its feverish preparations for an uprising, it immediately lost its balance and also its ties with the masses. Approximately the same thing happened as in the case of a rider who, after slowly approaching a high barrier, at the last moment nervously digs his spurs into the horse's flanks. Were the horse to leap over the barrier, it would in all likelihood break its legs. As matters turned out, it stopped at the barrier, and then shied aside. Such are the mechanics of the cruelest defeat of the German Communist Party and the whole International in November of last year [1923].

When a sharp shift in the reciprocal relation of forces became delineated, when the legalized fascists moved to the forefront while the Communists found themselves driven underground, some comrades hastened to announce that "we overestimated the situation; the revolution hasn't matured as yet." Naturally, nothing is simpler than this sort of strategy: first to muff the revolution and then to proclaim it as not yet mature. In reality, however, the revolution failed to lead to victory not because it generally "had not matured" but because the decisive link—

the leadership—dropped out of the chain at the decisive moment. "Our" mistake does not lie in "our" having overestimated the conditions of revolution, but in "our" having underestimated them; it lies in "our" inability to understand in time the need of an abrupt and bold tactical turn: from the struggle for the masses to—the struggle for power. "Our" mistake lies in this, that "we" continued for several weeks to repeat old banalities to the effect that "the revolution is not made on schedule," and in this way let slip all time intervals.

Did the Communist Party have the majority of the workers behind it in the latter part of last year? It is hard to say what the result would have been had we taken a poll at the time. Such questions are not decided by polls. They are decided by the dynamics of the movement. Despite the fact that a very considerable number of workers still remained in the ranks of the Social Democracy, only an insignificant minority was ready to take a hostile, and even then a rather passively hostile position toward the overturn. The majority of the Social Democratic as well as non-party workers sensed keenly the oppressive impasse of the bourgeois-democratic regime and awaited the overturn. Their complete and final trust and sympathy could have been won only in the course of the overturn itself. All the talk about the awesome strength of reaction, the many hundred thousands of the Black Reichswehr, etc., proved to be mere monstrous exaggeration, of which there was no doubt from the outset in the minds of people with revolutionary sense. Only the official Reichswehr represented a genuine force. But it was too small numerically and would have been inevitably swept away by the onset of millions.

Side by side with the masses already firmly won over by the Communist Party, far greater masses were gravitating toward it during the months of crisis, awaiting from it a signal for battle and leadership in battle. Failing to receive this, they began to move away from the Communists just as spontaneously as they had previously been streaming toward them. Precisely this explains the sharp shift in the relation of forces which enabled Seeckt to capture the field of political struggle almost without resistance. Meanwhile fatalistically inclined politicians, observing Seeckt's swift successes, proclaimed: "You see, the proletariat doesn't want to struggle." In reality, the German workers after the experience of the revolutionary half-decade did not want merely a struggle; they wanted that struggle which would at long last bring victory. Not finding the necessary leadership they avoided the struggle. Thereby they showed only that the lessons of 1918–21 had become deeply imbedded in their memory.

The German Communist Party led 3,600,000 workers to the ballot boxes. How many did it lose on the way? It is hard to answer this question. But the results of numerous partial elections to the Landtags, the municipalities and so on, testify that the Communist Party participated in the recent elections to the Reichstag in an already extremely weakened condition. And despite all this it still obtained 3,600,000 votes! "Look," we are told, "the German Communist Party is being severely criticized, and yet it represents a huge force!" But, after all, the whole gist of the matter lies in this, that 3,600,000 votes in May 1924, *i.e.*, after the spontaneous ebb of the masses, after the intrenchment of the bourgeois regime, testify that the Communist Party was the decisive force in the latter part of last year, but unfortunately this was not understood and utilized in time. Those who even today refuse to grasp that the defeat rose directly out of an underestimation, more precisely, out of a belated evaluation of last year's exceptional revolutionary situation—those who persist in so doing incur the risk of learning nothing and, therefore, of refusing to recognize the revolution a second time when it again knocks at the door.

The circumstance that the German Communist Party has drastically renovated its leading organs is quite in the order of things. The party together with the working class expected and wanted battle and hoped for victory—but was proffered instead a defeat without a battle. It is only natural that the party should turn its back on the old leadership. There is only limited significance today in the question of whether the Left Wing could have coped with the task had it been in power last year. Frankly speaking, we do not think so. We have already remarked that despite their sharp factional struggle, the Left Wing shared on the basic question—the seizure of power—the formless, semi-fatalistic, dilatory policy of the then Central Committee. But the mere fact that the Left Wing was in opposition made it the natural heir of party power after the party turned its back on the old Central Committee. At present the leadership is in the hands of the Left Wing. This is a new fact in the development of the German party. It is necessary to take this fact into account, to take it as the starting point. It is necessary to do everything possible to help the party's new leading body cope with its task. And for this it is first of all necessary to see the dangers clearly. The first possible danger might arise from an insufficiently serious attitude toward last year's defeat: an attitude that nothing out of the ordinary has happened, just a slight delay; the revolutionary situation will soon repeat itself; we proceed as before—toward the decisive assault. This is wrong! Last year's crisis signified a colossal expenditure of revolutionary energy by the proletariat. The proletariat needs time in order to digest last year's tragic defeat, a defeat without a decisive battle, a defeat without even an attempt at a decisive battle. It needs time in order to orient itself once again in a revolutionary way in an objective situation. This does not mean, of course, that a long number of years is required. But weeks will not suffice for it. And it would constitute the greatest danger if the strategic line of our German party were now to impatiently cut across the processes taking place at present in the German proletariat as a consequence of last year's defeat.

In the last analysis what decides, as we know, is economics. Those small economic successes which have been attained in the last few months by the German bourgeoisie are in themselves the inescapable result of the weakening of the revolutionary process, a certain—very superficial and shaky—strengthening of bourgeois "law and order," and so on. But the reestablishment of any kind of stable capitalist equilibrium in Germany has not been brought appreciably closer than was the case in the period from July to November of last year. At all events the road to this equilibrium traverses such mighty conflicts between labor and capital, and France obstructs the way with such difficulties, that the German proletariat is still assured a revolutionary economic foundation for an indefinitely long period ahead. However, those partial processes which occur in the foundation—either temporary aggravations or, on the contrary, temporary mitigations of the crisis and its auxiliary manifestations are in no case matters of indifference to us. If a relatively well-fed and thriving proletariat is always very sensitive even to a slight worsening of its position, then the long-suffering, long-famished and exhausted proletariat of Germany is sensitive even to the slightest improvement of its living conditions. This undoubtedly explains the strengthening—again, very unstable—of the ranks of the German Social Democracy and the trade union bureaucracy which is now manifest. Today more than ever before we are obliged to follow attentively the fluctuations in the commercial and industrial conjuncture in Germany and the way in which they are reflected in the living standards of the German worker.

It is economics that decides, but only in the last analysis. Of more direct significance are those political-psychological processes which are now taking place within the German proletariat and which likewise have an inner logic of their own. The party received 3,600,000 votes at the elections: a marvelous proletarian core! But the vacillating elements have moved away from us. Meanwhile, a direct revolutionary situation is always characterized by the flow of vacillating elements toward us. A great many worker-Social Democrats, we may assume, said to themselves during the elections: "We know perfectly well that our leaders are case-hardened scoundrels, but whom can we vote for? The Communists promised to take power, but proved unable to do it and only helped reaction.* Are we then to follow the Nazis?" And with revulsion in their hearts they cast their votes for the Social Democrats. The school of bourgeois reaction, we may hope, will quickly enough compel the German proletariat in its overwhelming majority to assimilate a revolutionary orientation, this time more definitively and firmly. It is necessary to assist this process in every way. It is necessary to speed it up. But it is altogether impossible to leap over its inevitable phases. To picture the situation as if nothing extra-

---

* This is the most telling argument of the Social-Democratic adventurers and rascals.—L.T.

ordinary has happened, as if only a slight hitch has taken place, etc., would be false to the core, and would portend the greatest blunders of a strategic order. What has taken place is no superficial stoppage, but an enormous defeat. Its meaning must be assimilated by the proletarian vanguard. Resting on this lesson, the vanguard must speed up the process of rallying the proletarian forces around the 3,600,000. The revolutionary flood tide, then the ebb, and then a new flood tide—these processes have their own inner logic and their own tempo. Revolutions not only unfold, we repeat, revolutions are organized. But it is possible to organize revolution only on the basis of its own internal evolution. To ignore the critical, watchful, skeptical moods among wide circles of the proletariat after what has happened is to head for a new defeat. A day after defeat even the best revolutionary party cannot arbitrarily call forth a new revolution, any more than the best obstetrician can call forth births every three or every five months. That last year's revolutionary birth pangs proved false ones, does not alter matters. The German proletariat must pass through a stage of restoring and gathering its forces for the new revolutionary culmination, before the Communist Party, having appraised the situation, can issue the signal for a new assault. But on the other hand, we know that no less a danger would threaten if at a new turn the Communist Party were again to fail to recognize a revolutionary situation, and thereby again prove impotent to utilize it to the end.

Two greatest lessons mark the history of the German Communist Party: March 1921 and November 1923. In the first case, the party mistook its own impatience for a mature revolutionary situation; in the second case, it was unable to recognize a mature revolutionary situation and let it slip by. These are the extreme dangers from the "left" and the "right"—these are the limits between which the policy of the proletarian party generally passes in our epoch. We shall continue to firmly hope that enriched by battles, defeats and experience the German Communist Party will succeed in the not-so-distant future in guiding its ship between the "March" Scylla and the "November" Charybdis and will secure to the German proletariat what the latter has so honestly earned: victory!

Whereas in Germany the last parliamentary elections, under the influence of last year's danger, have given the bourgeois concentration a new impulsion to the right—but within the framework of parliamentarianism and not of fascist dictatorship—throughout the rest of Europe and in America the shift of the ruling political groupings is proceeding in the direction of "conciliationism." In England and Denmark the bourgeoisie rules through the parties of the Second International. The victory of the Left Bloc in France signifies either an open or slightly masked (most likely open) participation of the Socialists in the government. Italian fascism is taking to the road of parliamentary "regulation" of its policy. In the United States the conciliationist illusions are being mobilized under the banner of the "Third Party." In Japan, the opposition parties won the elections.

When a ship loses its rudder, it is sometimes necessary to keep its left and right engines running alternately: the ship moves in zigzags, a great amount of energy is expended, but the ship keeps moving. Such at the present time is the steering device of the capitalist states of Europe. The bourgeoisie is compelled to alternate fascist and Social-Democratic methods. Fascism was and remains strongest in those countries where the proletariat came closest to power, but was unable to take it or hold it: Italy, Germany, Hungary, etc. On the contrary, conciliationist tendencies begin to gain preponderance to the extent that the bourgeoisie begins to sense less directly the threat of the proletarian overturn. While the bourgeoisie feels itself strong enough not to require the direct activities of the fascist gangs, it does not on the other hand feel strong enough to get along without a Menshevik cover.

In the era of the Fourth Congress of the Comintern, which passed entirely under the aegis of capitalist offensive and fascist reaction, we wrote that if the German revolution did not grow directly out of the situation existing at the time and did not thereby give a new direction to the entire political development of Europe, then one could with complete assurance expect the replacement of the fascist chapter by a conciliationist chapter, in particular, the coming of a labor government to power in England, and that of the Left Bloc in France. At the time this forecast seemed to some to be the sowing of . . . conciliationist illusions. There are people who succeed in being revolutionists only by keeping their eyes shut.

Let us, however, cite the verbatim quotations. In an article, "Political Perspectives," published in *Izvestia*, November 30, 1922, I polemicized against the simplified, non-Marxist, mechanistic view of political development which allegedly must fatally lead through the automatic strengthening of fascism and Communism to the victory of the proletariat. In this article it is stated:

> As far back as June 16 [1921] in my speech at a session of the enlarged ECCI I developed the idea that if revolutionary events in Europe and France did not erupt first, then the entire parliamentary-political life of France would inevitably begin crystallizing around

the axis of the "Left Bloc" in contrast to the currently dominant "National" Bloc. In the one and a half years that have elapsed the revolution has not taken place. And whoever has been following the life of France will hardly deny that—with the exception of Communists and revolutionary syndicalists—her policy is actually proceeding along the path of preparing the replacement of the National Bloc by the Left Bloc. True, France remains wholly under the aegis of capitalist offensive, of interminable threats addressed to Germany, and so on. But parallel with this there is a growing confusion among bourgeois classes, especially among the intermediate layers, who live in dread of tomorrow, who are disillusioned with the policy of "reparations," who are striving to mitigate the financial crisis by cutting down the expenditures for imperialism, who have hopes of restoring relations with Russia, etc., etc. These moods also seize a considerable section of the working class through the medium of reformist Socialists and syndicalists. Thus the continued offensive of French capitalism and French reaction in no way contradicts the fact that the French bourgeoisie is clearly preparing a new orientation for itself.

And further in the same article we wrote:

> In England the situation is no less instructive. As a result of recent elections, the domination of the liberal-conservative coalition has been replaced by purely conservative rule. An obvious step to the "right"! But, on the other hand, precisely the results of the last elections testify to the fact that bourgeois-conciliationist England has already fully prepared a new orientation for herself in the event of a further aggravation of con-

tradictions and growing difficulties (and both are inevitable). . . . Are there serious grounds for thinking that the present conservative regime will lead directly to the dictatorship of the proletariat in England? We do not see any such grounds. On the contrary, we assume that the insolvable economic, colonial and international contradictions of the British Empire today will provide considerable nourishment for the plebeian-middle class opposition in the guise of the so-called Labor Party. According to every indication, in England, more than any other country on our globe, the working class before arriving at the dictatorship will have to pass through the stage of a "labor" government in the person of the reformist-pacifist Labor Party, which at the last elections already received some four and a quarter million votes.

"But doesn't this imply that you hold the standpoint that there is a mitigation of political contradictions? But, after all, this is outright opportunism!" objected those comrades who are able to protect themselves against opportunist temptations only by turning their backs on them. As if to foresee a new temporary rise of conciliationist illusions is tantamount to sharing them to any degree whatever! It is, of course, much simpler not to foresee anything, restricting oneself to a repetition of sacrosanct formulas. But there is no need whatever to continue the dispute nowadays. Events have supplied the verification of this prognosis: we have MacDonald's government in England, the Stauning ministry in Denmark, the victory of the Left Bloc in France and the oppositional parties in Japan, while on the political horizon of the United States there looms the symbolic figure of LaFollette, a quite hopeless figure to be sure.

The elections in France supply the final verification for still another dispute: concerning the influence of the French Socialist Party. As is well known, this "party" is almost without an organization. Its official press is extremely wretched and hardly read by anybody. Proceeding from these incontestable facts some comrades were inclined to evaluate the Socialist Party as an insignificant magnitude. This consoling but false viewpoint found accidental expression even in certain official documents of the Comintern. In reality it is false to the core to evaluate the political influence of the French Socialists on the basis of their organization or the circulation of their press. The Socialist Party represents an apparatus for attracting workers into the camp of the "radical" bourgeoisie. The more backward as well as the more privileged elements of the working class have need neither for organization nor for a party press. They do not join the party or the trade unions; they vote for the Socialists and read the yellow press. The relation between the number of party members, the number of subscribers to the party press and the number of voters among the Socialists is not at all the same as among the Communists. We had occasion to express ourselves more than once on this score. Let us again adduce verbatim citations. Back on March 2, 1922, we wrote in *Pravda:*

> If we take into consideration the fact that the Communist Party numbers 130,000 members while the Socialists have 30,000 then the enormous successes of the Communist idea in France become quite obvious. However, if we take into account the relation of these figures to the numerical strength of the working class as a whole, the existence of reformist trade unions and anti-Communist tendencies within the revolution-

ary trade unions, then the question of the hegemony of the Communist Party in the workers' movement confronts us as a very difficult task, which is far from solved by our numerical preponderance over the Dissidents (Socialists). Under certain conditions the latter may prove a far more significant counter-revolutionary factor within the working class than might appear if one were to judge solely by the weakness of their organization, the insignificant circulation and ideological content of their organ, *Populaire*.

Quite recently we had occasion to return to this same question. At the beginning of this year, one of the documents referred to the Socialist Party as "moribund" and stated that only a "few workers" would vote for it, etc., etc. In this connection I wrote on January 7 of this year as follows:

> It is far too facile to speak of the French Socialist Party as moribund and to say that only "a few workers" will vote for it. This is an illusion. The French Socialist Party is an electoral organization of a considerable section of passive and semi-passive working masses. If among Communists the proportion between those who are organized and those who vote is, say, 1 to 10 or 1 to 20, then among the Socialists this proportion may prove to be 1 to 50 or 1 to 100. Our task in election campaigns consists to a large measure in splitting away a considerable section of the passive workers' mass who awaken only during elections. And in order to achieve this one must not underestimate the enemy.

The recent French elections have wholly and decisively confirmed the foregoing views. The Communists with a far stronger party organization and party press obtained considerably fewer votes than the Socialists. Even the arithmetical proportions turned out approximately as they had been tentatively indicated. . . . Nevertheless the fact that our party received about 900,000 votes represents a serious success, especially if we take into account the swift growth of our influence in the suburbs of Paris!

There is every reason to expect today that the entry of the Socialist Party into the Left Bloc and thereby its participation in the government will create favorable conditions for the growth of the political influence of the Communists, as the only party free from any sort of political obligations to the bourgeois regime.

In America the conciliationist illusions of the petty-bourgeoisie, primarily the farmers, and the petty-bourgeois illusions of the proletariat take the form of the Third Party. The latter is being mobilized at the present moment around Senator LaFollette, or, more correctly, around his name, for the Senator himself, almost 70 years old, has not yet found time to leave the ranks of the Republican Party. All this, by the way, is quite in the nature of things. But truly amazing is the position of certain leaders of the American Communist Party[1] who propose to summon the party to vote for LaFollette, hoping in this way to secure for Communists influence over the farmers. More than this, they cite the example of Russian Bolshevism which allegedly won over the peasantry by means of this sort of politics. In addition, of course, there is no lack of variations on the theme which has already lost all semblance of sense, namely, that "underestimation" of the peasantry is the

[EXPLANATORY NOTES BEGIN ON PAGE 461.]

basic trait of Menshevism. The history of Marxism and Bolshevism in Russia is first of all the history of a struggle against *Narodnikism* (Populism) and S.R.'ism. This struggle provided the premise for the fight against Menshevism and it had as its fundamental task, the task of assuring the *proletarian character of the party*. Decades of struggle against petty-bourgeois *Narodnikism* enabled Bolshevism at the decisive moment, *i.e.,* the moment of open struggle for power, to destroy the S.R.'s with a single blow, taking possession of their agrarian program and drawing the peasant masses behind the party. This political expropriation of the S.R.'s was the necessary premise for the economic expropriation of the landlords and the bourgeoisie. It is quite self-evident that the path which certain American comrades are ready to follow has nothing in common with the paths of Bolshevism. For a young and weak Communist Party, lacking in revolutionary temper, to play the role of solicitor and gatherer of "progressive voters" for the Republican Senator LaFollette is to head toward the political dissolution of the party in the petty bourgeoisie. After all, opportunism expresses itself not only in moods of gradualism but also in political impatience: it frequently seeks to reap where it has not sown, to realize successes which do not correspond to its influence. Underestimation of the basic task—the development and strengthening of the proletarian character of the party—here is the basic trait of opportunism! Insufficient faith in the powers of the proletariat is the source of the fantastic leaps in a chase after the farmers which may cost the Communist Party its head. That the Communist Party must attentively follow the needs and moods of the farmers, utilizing the current crisis politically in order to extend its influence to the countryside—this is quite self-evident. But the party cannot accompany the farmers and the petty bourgeoisie generally through all their political stages and zigzags, it cannot voluntarily pass through all the illusions and disillusions, dragging after LaFollette in order to expose him later on. In the last analysis, the mass of the farmers will follow the Communist Party into battle against the bourgeoisie only in the event that they are convinced that this party represents a force capable of tearing the power from the bourgeoisie. And the Communist Party can become such a force in action, and consequently also in the eyes of the farmers, only as the vanguard of the proletariat but never as a tail of the Third Party.

The rapidity with which a false starting position leads to the crudest political mistakes is demonstrated by a document emanating from the so-called Organizing Committee, set up in order to convene a congress of the Third Party in June for the purpose of nominating LaFollette as candidate for the post of president. The chairman of this committee is one of the leaders of the Farmer-Labor Party of the state of Minnesota; its secretary is a Communist, assigned to this work by the Communist Party. And now this Communist has lent his signature to a Manifesto which in appealing to "progressive voters" declares that the aim of the movement is to attain "national political unity"; and which, in refuting charges that the campaign is under the control of the Communists, declares that the Communists comprise an insignificant minority and that even were they to try to seize the leadership they could never succeed inasmuch as the [Farmer-Labor] "party" aims to obtain constructive legislation and not any utopias. And for these middle-class abominations the Communist Party assumes responsibility before the eyes of the working class! In the name of what? In the name of this, that the inspirers of this monstrous opportunism, who are thoroughly imbued with skepticism concerning the

American proletariat, are impatiently seeking to transfer the party's center of gravity into a farmer milieu—a milieu that is being shaken by the agrarian crisis. By underwriting, even if with reservations, the worst illusions of the petty bourgeoisie, it is not at all difficult to create for oneself the illusion of wielding influence over the petty bourgeoisie. To think that Bolshevism consists of this is to understand nothing about Bolshevism.*

It is hard to forecast how long the current phase of conciliationism will endure. But at all events, there cannot even be talk of bourgeois Europe's ability to restore economic equilibrium on the European continent, much less with the United States. In relation to the problem of reparations, to be sure, a major attempt is being made for a conciliationist solution. The coming of the Left Bloc to power in France adds strength to this attempt. But the fundamental contradiction of the entire problem still remains: in order to pay, Germany must export; in order to pay a great deal, Germany must export a great deal; but German exports are a threat to those of England and France. In order to regain the possibility of a victorious struggle on the European market, which has been extremely narrowed down, the German bourgeoisie would have to overcome gigantic internal difficulties, and this, in its turn, cannot fail to be accompanied by a new ag-

---

* The Executive Committee of the Communist International naturally rejected this policy which is so utterly false and so extremely dangerous. The decision of the ECCI was quite opportune. A few days following its adoption, Senator LaFollette came out with a rabid attack against the Communists and piously declared that he would have nothing to do with any undertaking with which these rascals, this Red spawn of Beelzebub and of Moscow, were connected. Let us hope that this lesson will not prove unfruitful so far as certain super-clever strategists are concerned.—*L.T., June 4, 1924.*

gravation of the class struggle. On the other hand, France herself has monstrous debts which she has not begun to pay. In order to begin paying, France must intensify her exports, *i.e.,* increase England's difficulties in the field of foreign trade. Meanwhile England herself has barely reached 75 percent of her pre-war exports. In the face of the basic economic, political and military problems, the conciliationist government of MacDonald discloses its bankruptcy to a far greater degree than might have been expected. Needless to say, matters will not be much better in the case of the Left Bloc government in France. Europe's impasse, now camouflaged by international and internal deals, will once again disclose itself in its revolutionary essence. Without doubt, the Communist parties will prove better prepared for that moment. The recent parliamentary elections in a number of countries show that Communism already represents a mighty historical force and that this force is growing.

MAY 20, 1924

The First World Congress

Editor's note

The First Congress convened in Moscow, March 2–6, 1919, with 51 delegates present: 35 with decisive votes representing 17 countries; 16 with consultative votes representing 16 countries. Because of the Allied blockade not all those sent arrived. Thus the Italian Socialist Party and a number of oppositional groups in France, Great Britain and America were not represented at the Congress. One of the German delegates was arrested at the German border. Others suffered great hazards and arrived only after the Congress was already in session.

The agenda was as follows:

1. The Founding of the Third International;
2. Reports from Various Countries;
3. Platform of the Congress (reporters: Eberlein, Bukharin);
4. Bourgeois Democracy and the Proletarian Dictatorship (reporters: Lenin, Rakhia);
5. The Berne Conference and Our Attitude Toward Socialist Tendencies (reporters: Platten, Zinoviev);
6. The World Situation and the Policy of the Entente (reporters: Ossinsky, Platten);
7. Manifesto (reporter: Trotsky);
8. The White Terror (reporter: Sirola);
9. Election of the Bureau, and Other Organizational Questions.

On the organizational question, the Congress favored two directing organs: an Executive Committee to be composed of representatives from Russia, Germany, Austria, Hungary, the Balkan Federation, Switzerland and Scandinavia; and a Bureau consisting of five members to be elected by the Executive Committee.

The elaboration of the statutes of the new International was laid over until the next Congress.

The Russian Bolshevik Party was represented by Lenin, Trotsky, Zinoviev, Bukharin, Chicherin and two alternates: Vorovsky and Ossinsky.

1. Manifesto of the Communist International to the workers of the world[2]

Seventy-two years ago the Communist Party proclaimed its program to the world in the form of a Manifesto written by the greatest heralds of the proletarian revolution, Karl Marx and Frederick Engels. Even at that time Communism no sooner entered the arena of struggle than it was beset by baiting, lies, hatred and persecution of the possessing classes who rightfully sensed their mortal enemy in Communism. The development of Communism during this three-quarters of a century proceeded along complex paths: side by side with periods of stormy upsurge it knew periods of decline; side by side with successes—cruel defeats. But essentially the movement proceeded along the path indicated in advance by the *Communist Manifesto*. The epoch of final, decisive struggle has come later than the apostles of the socialist revolution had expected and hoped. But it has come. We Communists, the representatives of the revolutionary proletariat of the various countries of Europe, America and Asia who have gathered in Soviet Moscow, feel and consider ourselves to be the heirs and consummators of the cause whose program was affirmed 72 years ago. Our task is to generalize the revolutionary experience of the working class, to purge the movement of the corroding admixture of opportunism and social-patriotism, to unify the efforts of all genuinely revolutionary parties of the world proletariat and thereby facilitate and hasten the victory of the Communist revolution throughout the world.

Today when Europe is covered with debris and smoking ruins, the worst pyromaniacs in history are busy seeking out the criminals responsible for the war. In their wake follow their servants—professors, members of parliament, journalists, social-patriots and other political pimps of the bourgeoisie.

For many years the Socialist movement predicted the inevitability of the imperialist war, seeing its causes in the insatiable greed of the property-owning classes of the two chief camps and, generally, of all capitalist countries. At the Basle Congress,[3] two years before the war exploded, the responsible Socialist leaders of all countries branded imperialism as bearing the guilt for the impending war, and threatened the bourgeoisie with the socialist revolution which would descend upon the bourgeoisie's head as the proletarian retribution for the crimes of militarism. Today after the experience of the last five years, after history, having laid bare the predatory appetites of Germany, is unmasking the no less criminal acts of the Allies, the state-Socialists of the Entente countries continue in the wake of their respective governments to discover the war criminal in the person of the overthrown German Kaiser. On top of this, the German social-patriots who in August

1914 proclaimed Hohenzollern's diplomatic "White Book" to be the holiest evangel of the peoples are nowadays following in the footsteps of the Entente Socialists and are with vile subservience indicting the overthrown German monarchy, which they had so slavishly served, as the chief war criminal. They thus hope to obscure their own role and at the same time to worm their way into the good graces of the conquerors. But in the light of unfolding events and diplomatic revelations, side by side with the role of the toppled dynasties—the Romanovs, the Hohenzollerns, and the Habsburgs—and of the capitalist cliques of these countries, the role of the ruling classes of France, England, Italy and the United States stands out in all its boundless criminality.

English diplomacy did not lift its visor of secrecy up to the very outbreak of war. The government of the City[4] obviously feared to reveal its intention of entering the war on the side of the Entente lest the Berlin government take fright and be compelled to eschew war. In London they wanted war. That is why they conducted themselves in such a way as to raise hopes in Berlin and Vienna that England would remain neutral, while Paris and Petrograd firmly counted on England's intervention.

Prepared by the entire course of development over a number of decades, the war was unleashed through the direct and conscious provocation of Great Britain. The British government thereby calculated on extending just enough aid to Russia and France, while they became exhausted, to exhaust England's mortal enemy, Germany. But the might of German militarism proved far too formidable and demanded of England not token but actual intervention in the war. The role of a gleeful third partner to which Great Britain, following her ancient tradition, aspired, fell to the lot of the United States.

The Washington government became all the more easily reconciled to the English blockade which one-sidedly restricted American stock market speculation in European blood, because the countries of the Entente reimbursed the American bourgeoisie with lush profits for violations of "international law." However, the Washington government was likewise constrained by the enormous military superiority of Germany to drop its fictitious neutrality. In relation to Europe as a whole the United States assumed the role which England had taken in previous wars and which she tried to take in the last war in relation to the continent, namely: weakening one camp by playing it against another, intervening in military operations only to such an extent as to guarantee her all the advantages of the situation. According to American standards of gambling, Wilson's stake was not very high, but it was the final stake, and consequently assured his winning the prize.

As a result of the war the contradictions of the capitalist system confronted mankind in the shape of pangs of hunger, exhaustion from cold, epidemics and moral savagery. This settled once and for all the academic controversy within the Socialist movement over the theory of impoverishment[5] and the gradual transition from capitalism to socialism. Statisticians and pedants of the theory that contradictions were being blunted, had for decades fished out from all the corners of the globe real or mythical facts testifying to the rising well-being of various groups and categories of the working class. The theory of mass impoverishment was regarded as buried, amid contemptuous jeers from the eunuchs of bourgeois professordom and mandarins of Socialist opportunism. At the present time this impoverishment, no longer only of a social but also of a physiological and biological kind, rises before us in all its shocking reality.

The catastrophe of the imperialist war has completely swept away all the conquests of trade union and parliamentary struggles. For this war itself was just as much a product of the internal tendencies of capitalism as were those economic agreements and parliamentary compromises which the war buried in blood and muck.

Finance capital, which plunged mankind into the abyss of war, itself underwent a catastrophic change in the course of this war. The dependency of paper money upon the material foundation of production has been completely disrupted. Progressively losing its significance as the means and regulator of capitalist commodity circulation, paper money became transformed into an instrument of requisition, of seizure and military-economic violence in general.

The debasement of paper money reflects the general mortal crisis of capitalist commodity circulation. During the decades preceding the war, free competition, as the regulator of production and distribution, had already been thrust aside in the main fields of economic life by the system of trusts and monopolies; during the course of the war the regulating-directing role was torn from the hands of these economic groups and transferred directly into the hands of military-state power. The distribution of raw materials, the utilization of Baku or Rumanian oil, Donbas coal, Ukrainian wheat, the fate of German locomotives, freight cars and automobiles, the rationing of relief for starving Europe—all these fundamental questions of the world's economic life are not being regulated by free competition, nor by associations of national and international trusts and consortiums, but by the direct application of military force, for the sake of its continued preservation. If the complete subjection of the state power to the power of finance capital had led mankind into the imperialist slaughter, then through this slaughter finance capital has succeeded in completely militarizing not only the state but also itself; and it is no longer capable of fulfilling its basic economic functions otherwise than by means of blood and iron.

The opportunists, who before the World War summoned the workers to practice moderation for the sake of gradual transition to socialism, and who during the war demanded class docility in the name of civil peace and national defense, are again demanding self-renunciation of the proletariat—this time for the purpose of overcoming the terrible consequences of the war. If these preachments were to find acceptance among the working masses, capitalist development in new, much more concentrated and monstrous forms would be restored on the bones of several generations—with the perspective of a new and inevitable world war. Fortunately for mankind this is not possible.

The state-ization of economic life, against which capitalist liberalism used to protest so much, has become an accomplished fact. There is no turning back from this fact—it is impossible to return not only to free competition but even to the domination of trusts, syndicates and other economic octopuses. Today the one and only issue is: Who shall henceforth be the bearer of state-ized production—the imperialist state or the state of the victorious proletariat?

In other words: Is all toiling mankind to become the bond slaves of victorious world cliques who, under the firm-name of the League of Nations[6] and aided by an "international" army and "international" navy, will here plunder and strangle some peoples and there cast crumbs to others, while everywhere and always shackling the proletariat—with the sole object of maintaining their own rule? Or shall the working class of Europe and of the advanced countries in other parts of the world take in hand the disrupted and ruined economy in order to assure its regeneration upon socialist principles?

It is possible to shorten the epoch of crisis through which we are living only by measures of the proletarian dictatorship which does not look back to the past, which respects neither inherited privileges nor property rights, which takes as its starting point the need of saving the starving masses; and to this end mobilizes all forces and resources, introduces universal labor conscription, establishes the regime of labor discipline in order in the course of a few years not only to thus heal the gaping wounds inflicted by war but also to raise mankind to new and unprecedented heights.

The national state which gave a mighty impulse to capitalist development has become too narrow for the further development of productive forces. This renders all the more precarious the position of small states, hemmed in by the major powers of Europe and scattered through other sections of the world. These small states, which have arisen at different times as fragments chipped from bigger ones, as so much small change in payment for various services rendered and as strategic buffers, retain their own dynasties, their own ruling cliques, their own imperialist pretensions, their own diplomatic intrigues. Prior to the war, their phantom independence rested on the selfsame thing as the equilibrium of Europe: the uninterrupted antagonism between the two imperialist camps. The war has disrupted this equilibrium. By giving at first an enormous preponderance to Germany, the war compelled the small states to seek their salvation under the magnanimous wings of German militarism. After Germany was crushed, the bourgeoisie of the small states, together with their respective patriotic "Socialists," turned their faces to the victorious Allied imperialism and began seeking guarantees for their continued independent existence in the hypocritical points of the Wilsonian program. At the same time the number of small states has increased; out of the Austro-Hungarian monarchy, out of portions of the former Czarist empire, new states[7] have been carved, which were no sooner born than they flung themselves at one another's throats over the question of state boundaries. The Allied imperialists are meanwhile preparing such combinations of small powers, both old and new, as would be bound to themselves through the hold of mutual hatreds and common impotence. While oppressing and violating the small and weak peoples, while dooming them to starvation and destruction, the Allied imperialists, like the imperialists of the Central Empire a brief while ago, do not stop talking about the right of self-determination, which is today being trampled underfoot in Europe as in all other parts of the world.

The small peoples can be assured the opportunity of free existence only by the proletarian revolution which will free the productive forces of all countries from the tentacles of the national states, unifying the peoples in closest economic collaboration on the basis of a common economic plan, and offering the weakest and smallest people an opportunity of freely and independently directing their national cultural affairs without any detriment to the unified and centralized European and world economy.

The last war, which was by and large a war for colonies, was at the same time a war conducted with the help of colonies. The colonial populations were drawn into the European war on an unprecedented scale. Indians, Negroes, Arabs and Madagascans fought on the territories of Europe—for the sake of what? For the sake of their right to continue to remain the slaves of England and France. Never before has the infamy of capitalist rule in the colonies been delineated so clearly; never before has the problem of colonial slavery been posed so sharply as it is today.

A number of open insurrections and the revolutionary ferment in all the colonies have hence arisen. In Europe itself, Ireland[8] keeps signaling through sanguinary street battles that she still remains and still feels herself to be an enslaved country. In Madagascar,[9] Annam[10] and elsewhere the troops of the bourgeois republic have more than once quelled the uprisings of colonial slaves during the war. In India the revolutionary movement has not subsided for a single day and has recently led to the greatest labor strikes in Asia, which the English government has met by ordering its armored cars into action in Bombay.

The colonial question has been thus posed in its fullest measure not only on the maps at the diplomatic congress in Paris but also within the colonies themselves. At best, Wilson's program[11] has as its task: to effect a change of labels with regard to colonial slavery. The emancipation of the colonies is conceivable only in conjunction with the emancipation of the working class in the metropolises. The workers and peasants not only of Annam, Algiers[12] and Bengal,[13] but also of Persia and Armenia,[14] will gain their opportunity of independent existence only in that hour when the workers of England and France, having overthrown Lloyd George[15] and Clemenceau,[16] will have taken state power into their own hands. Even now the struggle in the more developed colonies, while taking place only under the banner of national liberation, immediately assumes a more or less clearly defined social character. If capitalist Europe has violently dragged the most backward sections of the world into the whirlpool of capitalist relations, then socialist Europe will come to the aid of liberated colonies with her technology, her organization and her ideological influence in order to facilitate their transition to a planned and organized socialist economy.

Colonial slaves of Africa and Asia! The hour of proletarian dictatorship in Europe will strike for you as the hour of your own emancipation!

The entire bourgeois world accuses the Communists of destroying freedom and political democracy. These are lies. Upon assuming power, the proletariat merely lays bare the complete impossibility of employing the methods of bourgeois democracy and creates the conditions and forms of a new and much higher workers' democracy. The whole course of capitalist development, especially during its final imperialist epoch, has acted to undermine political democracy not only by dividing nations into two irreconcilably hostile classes, but also by condemning numerous petty-bourgeois and proletarian layers, as well as the most disinherited lowest strata of the proletariat, to economic debilitation and political impotence.

In those countries where historical development provided the opportunity, the working class has utilized the regime of political democracy in order to organize against capitalism. The same thing will likewise take place in the future in those countries where conditions for the proletarian revolution have not yet matured. But broad intermediate masses not only in the villages but also in the cities are being held back by capitalism, lagging entire epochs behind historical development.

The peasant in Bavaria[17] and Baden[18] who still cannot see beyond the spires of his village church, the small French wine producer who is being driven into bankruptcy by the large-scale capitalists who adulterate wine, and the small American farmer fleeced and cheated by bankers and Congressmen—all these social layers thrust back by capitalism away from the mainstream of development are called upon, on paper, by the regime of political democracy to assume the direction of the state. But in reality, on all the basic questions which determine the destinies of the peoples, the financial oligarchy makes the decision behind the back of parliamentary democracy. Such was previously the case on the question of war; such is now the case on the question of peace. To the extent that the financial oligarchy still bothers to obtain the sanction of parliamentary ballots for its acts of violence, there are at the disposal of the bourgeois state for obtaining the necessary results all the instruments of lies, demagogy, baiting, calumny, bribery and terror, inherited from the centuries of class slavery and multiplied by all the miracles of capitalist technology.

To demand of the proletariat that it devoutly comply with rules and regulations of political democracy in the final life-and-death combat with capitalism is like demanding of a man, fighting for his life against cutthroats, that he observe the artificial and restrictive rules of French wrestling, which the enemy introduces but fails to observe.

In this kingdom of destruction where not only the means of production and transport but also the institutions of political democracy are heaps of blood-soaked stumps, the proletariat is compelled to create its own apparatus designed first and foremost to cement the inner ties of the working class and to assure the possibility of its revolutionary intervention into the future development of mankind. This apparatus is represented by the Workers' Soviets. The old parties, the old organizations of trade unions have in the persons of their leading summits proved incapable not only of solving but even of understanding the tasks posed by the new epoch. The proletariat has created a new type of organization, a broad organization which embraces the working masses independently of trade or level of political development already attained; a flexible apparatus which permits of continual renovation and extension; and is capable of attracting into its orbit ever newer layers, opening wide its doors to the toiling layers in the city and the country who are close to the proletariat. This irreplaceable organization of working-class self-rule, this organization of its struggle for and later of its conquest of state power, has been tested in the experience of various countries and constitutes the mightiest conquest and weapon of the proletariat in our epoch.

In those countries where the toiling masses live a conscious life, Soviets of Workers', Soldiers' and Peasants' Deputies are now being built and will continue to be built. To strengthen the Soviets, to raise their authority, to counterpose them to the state apparatus of the bourgeoisie—this is today the most important task of the class-conscious and honest workers of all countries. Through the medium of Soviets the working class can save itself from the decomposition which is introduced into its midst by the hellish sufferings of war, by starvation, by the violence of the possessing classes and by the treachery of its former leaders. Through the medium of Soviets the working class will be able to come to power most surely and easily in all countries where the Soviets are able to rally the majority of the toilers. Through the medium of Soviets the working class, having conquered power, will exercise its sway over all spheres of the country's economic and cultural life, as is the case at present in Russia. The foundering of the imperialist state, from the Czarist state to the most "democratic" ones, is taking place simultaneously with the foundering of the imperialist military system. The multimillioned armies mobilized by imperialism could only be maintained so long as the proletariat remained obediently under the yoke of the bourgeoisie. The crack-up of national unity signifies the inevitable crack-up of the army. This is what happened first in Russia, then in Germany and Austria-Hungary. The same thing may be expected to occur in other imperialist countries as well. The uprising of the peasant against the landlord, of the worker against the capitalist, and of both against the monarchical or "democratic" bureaucracy, inevitably brings in its train the uprising of soldiers against the commanders and subsequently—a deep cleavage between the proletarian and bourgeois elements of the army. Imperialist war, which pitted one nation against another, has passed and is passing over into civil war which pits class against class.

The wails of the bourgeois world against civil war and against Red Terror represent the most monstrous hypocrisy yet known in the history of political struggles. There would be no civil war if the clique of exploiters who have brought mankind to the very brink of ruin did not resist every forward step of the toiling masses, if they did not organize conspiracies and assassinations, and did not summon armed assistance from without in order to maintain or restore their thievish privileges.

Civil war is imposed upon the working class by its mortal enemies. Without renouncing itself and its own future, which is the future of all mankind, the working class cannot fail to answer blow for blow.

While never provoking civil war artificially, the Communist parties seek to shorten as much as possible the duration of civil war whenever the latter does arrive with iron necessity; they seek to reduce to a minimum the number of victims and, above all, to assure victory to the proletariat. Hence flows the necessity of disarming the bourgeoisie in time, of arming the workers in time, of creating in time the Communist army to defend the workers' power and to preserve its socialist construction inviolate. Such is the Red Army of Soviet Russia which arose and exists as the bulwark of the conquests of the working class against all attacks from within and without. The Soviet Army is inseparable from the Soviet State.

Recognizing the world character of their tasks, the advanced workers have from the very first steps of the organized Socialist movement striven to unify it on an international scale. The beginnings were made in 1864 in London by the First International. The Franco-Prussian War out of which emerged the Germany of the Hohenzollerns[19] cut the ground from under the First International and at the same time gave impetus to the development of national workers' parties. As far back as 1889 these parties came together in the Congress of Paris and created the organization of the Second International. But the center of gravity of the labor movement during that period remained wholly on national soil, wholly within the framework of national states, upon the foundation of national industry, within the sphere of national parliamentarianism. The decades of reformist organizational activity gave birth to an entire generation of leaders, the majority of whom recognized in words the program of the social revolution but renounced it in deeds, becoming mired in reformism, in a docile adaptation to the bourgeois state. The opportunist character of the leading parties of the Second International has been completely disclosed; and it led to the greatest collapse in world history at a moment when the march of historic events demanded revolutionary methods of struggle from the working-class parties. If the war of 1870 dealt a blow to the First International, disclosing that there was as yet no fused mass force behind its social-revolutionary program, then the war of 1914 killed the Second International, disclosing that the mightiest organizations of the working masses were dominated by parties which had become transformed into auxiliary organs of the bourgeois state!

This applies not only to the social-patriots who have today clearly and openly gone over to the camp of the bourgeoisie, who have become the latter's favorite plenipotentiaries and trustees and the most reliable executioners of the working class; it also applies to the amorphous and unstable tendency of the Socialist Center[20] which seeks to reestablish the Second International, that is, to reestablish the narrowness, the opportunism and the revolutionary impotence of its leading summits. The Independent Party of Germany, the present majority of the Socialist Party of France, the Menshevik group of Russia, the Independent Labor Party of England and other similar groups are actually trying to fill the place which had been occupied prior to the war by the old official parties of the Second International. They come forward as hitherto with the ideas of compromise and conciliationism; with all the means at their disposal, they paralyze the energy of the proletariat, prolonging the crisis and thereby redoubling Europe's calamities. The struggle against the Socialist Center is the indispensable premise for the successful struggle against imperialism.

Sweeping aside the half-heartedness, lies and corruption of the outlived official Socialist parties, we Communists, united in the Third International, consider ourselves the direct continuators of the heroic endeavors and martyrdom of a long line of revolutionary generations from Babeuf[21]—to Karl Liebknecht[22] and Rosa Luxemburg.[23]

If the First International presaged the future course of development and indicated its paths; if the Second International gathered and organized millions of workers; then the Third International is the International of open mass action, the International of revolutionary realization, the International of the deed.

Bourgeois world order has been sufficiently lashed by Socialist criticism. The task of the International Communist Party consists in overthrowing this order and erecting in its place the edifice of the socialist order. We summon the working men and women of all countries to unite under the Communist banner which is already the banner of the first great victories.

Workers of the World—in the struggle against imperialist barbarism, against monarchy, against the privileged estates, against the bourgeois state and bourgeois property, against all kinds and forms of class or national oppression—*Unite!*

Under the banner of Workers' Soviets, under the banner of revolutionary struggle for power and the dictatorship of the proletariat, under the banner of the Third International—*Workers of the World Unite!*

2. Report on the Communist Party of the Soviet Union and the Red Army

Delivered at the first session of the First World Congress, March 2, 1919

It is clear from the report of Comrade Albert[24] that the question of the Red Guard has become "a proverb and a byword" in Germany; and if I understood him correctly, speculations anent the possible incursion of our Red Guard into the territories of Eastern Prussia cause Messrs. Ebert[25] and Scheidemann[26] to suffer nightmares during their nights of sleeplessness. On this score Comrade Albert may reassure the rulers of Germany—they have nothing to fear. Fortunately or unfortunately—and this is, of course, a matter of taste—affairs have not yet reached that stage at the present time. As regards the intervention that does threaten us, we can say boldly that today we are in a far better position than was the case last year at the conclusion of the Brest-Litovsk Treaty.[27] It is hardly necessary to dwell on this. At that time we were still wearing diapers so far as the construction of both the Red Army and the Soviet government as a whole was concerned. The Red Army was then actually called the Red Guard but this appellation has long since dropped out of circulation among us. The Red Guard was the name given the first partisan detachments, improvised groups of revolutionary workers, who burning with revolutionary zeal spread the proletarian revolution from Petrograd and Moscow throughout the country. This phase lasted until the initial clash between this Red Guard and the regular German regiments, when it became quite obvious that such improvised detachments, while able to conquer the Russian counterrevolution, were impotent before a disciplined army and in consequence could not serve as the real shield of the revolutionary Socialist Republic.

This marks a breaking-point in the attitude of the working masses toward the army, and a start in the scrapping of old methods of army organization. Under the pressure of events we proceeded to the creation of a healthy army, organized on principles dictated by military science. Now, our program calls for a "people's militia." But it is impossible even to talk of a people's militia—this demand of political democracy—in a country where the dictatorship of the proletariat is in power, for an army is always intimately bound up with the character of the reigning power. War, as old Clausewitz[28] says, is the continuation of politics by other means. The army is the instrument of war and it must therefore correspond to politics. Since the government is proletarian, therefore the army, too, must be proletarian in its social composition.

For this reason we introduced a set of rigid restrictions into the army. Since May of last year we passed from a volunteer army, from the Red Guard, to an army based on compulsory military service, but we accept into our army only workers and peasants, nonexploiters of labor.

The impossibility of seriously considering a people's militia in Russia becomes even clearer if we take into account the fact that within the boundaries of the former Czarist empire there were and are still to be found at one and the same time several armies of classes hostile to us. In the Don province there even exists a monarchist army consisting of bourgeois elements and rich Cossacks, and under the command of Cossack officers. Furthermore, in the Volga and Ural provinces there was the army of the Constituent Assembly.[29] After all, this army was also designed as a "people's army," and was so designated, but it quickly fell apart. The honorable members of the Constituent Assembly remained with empty hands. They found it necessary—entirely against their will—to leave the Volga province and to accept the hospitality of our Soviet government. Admiral Kolchak[30] simply placed the government of the Constituent Assembly under arrest and the army was converted into a monarchist army. We thus observe that in a country involved in a civil war, the army can be built only along the line of class principle; we did exactly that and we got results.

On our road we were confronted with great difficulties resulting from the question of the commanding personnel. Our primary concern, naturally, was to train Red officers from among the workers and the most advanced peasant youth. This is a job we tackled from the outset, and here at the doors of this building you can see not a few Red ensigns who will shortly enter the army as Red officers. We have quite a number of them. I don't want to specify the exact figure inasmuch as military secrets should always remain military secrets. This number, I repeat, is rather large. But we could not bide our time until Red generals arose out of our Red ensigns, inasmuch as the enemy did not extend us such a breathing spell; and we had to turn to the old commanding personnel and find capable people among these reserves; this, too, was crowned with success. Naturally, we sought our officers not amid the glittering salons of military courtesans, but we did find in more modest circles people who were quite capable and who are now helping us in the struggle against their own former colleagues. On the one side, we have the best and the most honest elements among the old officers corps, whom we surround with sensible Communists in the capacity of Commissars; and on the other, the best elements from among the soldiers, workers and peasants in the lower commanding posts. It is in this manner that we compounded our Red commanding personnel.

From the moment the Soviet Republic arose in our country, it was compelled to wage war, and is waging war to this very hour. Our front extends more than 8,000 kilometers; from the South to the North, from the East to the West—everywhere the struggle is being waged against us arms in hand and we are constrained to defend ourselves. Why, Kautsky[31] has even accused us of cultivating militarism. But it seems to me that if we wish to preserve the power in the hands of the workers, then we must show them how to use the weapons they themselves forge. We began by disarming the bourgeoisie and by arming the workers. If this bears the name of militarism, so be it. We have created our own socialist militarism and we shall not renounce it.

Our military position in August of last year was extremely precarious; not only were we caught in a ring of steel, but this ring surrounded Moscow rather tightly. Since then we have widened this ring more and more, and in the course of the last six months the Red Army has reconquered for the Soviet Republic an area not less than 700,000 square kilometers, with a population of some 42,000,000, 16 *gubernias* (provinces) with 16 large cities, the workers of which conducted and continue to conduct an energetic struggle. Even today, if you draw a straight line on the map radiating from Moscow in any direction, you will find everywhere at the front—a Russian peasant, a Russian worker standing in this cold night, gun in hand, at the frontiers of the Socialist Republic and defending it. And I can assure you that the worker-Communists who comprise the hard core of this army feel that they are not only the Guards Regiment of the Russian Socialist Republic but also the Red Army of the Third International. And if we are today given the opportunity to extend hospitality to this Socialist conference, and in this way repay our Western European brothers for their many years of friendship, then we in our turn owe this to the efforts and sacrifices of the Red Army, in which the best comrades from among the worker-Communist milieu are serving as ordinary soldiers, Red officers or Commissars, *i.e.*, as direct representatives of our party, of the Soviet Power. In every regiment, in every division they set the moral tone, that is, by their example show the Red soldiers how to fight and die for socialism. And these are not the empty words of our comrades; accompanying these words are deeds: In this struggle we have lost hundreds and thousands of our best socialist workers. I believe they have fallen not only for the Soviet Republic but also for the Third International.

And although it does not even enter our minds at present to attack Eastern Prussia—on the contrary, we would be extremely satisfied if Messrs. Ebert and Scheidemann left us in peace—one thing is nonetheless unquestionable: should the hour strike and our Western brothers call upon us for aid, we shall reply:

"We are here! We have in the meantime become skilled in the use of arms; we are ready to struggle and to die for the world revolution!"

3. Order of the Day Number 83 to the Red Army and Navy[32]

Greetings from the Communist International

In Moscow early in March the representatives of the revolutionary workers of various countries of Europe and America came together in order to establish close revolutionary collaboration among the toilers of the world in the struggle against their oppressors. This conference founded the Communist International, that is, it founded the international alliance of workers, soldiers and toiling peasants for the establishment of the World Soviet Republic which will forever put an end to enmity and wars among the peoples. At one of its sessions the Communist International adopted the following resolution of greetings to the Russian Workers' and Peasants' Red Army:

> The Congress of the Communist International sends the Red Army of Soviet Russia its heartiest greetings and extends its fullest hopes for a complete victory in the struggle against world imperialism.

This fraternal salute of the world proletariat must be made known to all the warriors of the Red Army and Navy. I hereby order the Commissars to make it publicly known to all squads, detachments, squadrons, batteries, and all ships. Every soldier of the Red Army, every sailor of the Red Navy will hear with merited pride this message of greeting from the highest and most authoritative body of the world working class. The Red Army and the Red Navy will not fail the expectations and hopes of the Communist International.

Under the Banner of the World Working Class—Forward!
Issued March 9, 1919. Moscow.

L. Trotsky,
CHAIRMAN OF THE MILITARY
REVOLUTIONARY COUNCIL
OF THE REPUBLIC;
COMMISSAR OF WAR AND
NAVAL AFFAIRS.

FIRST PUBLISHED IN *IZVESTIA*,
NO. 54, MARCH 11, 1919

II

From the First to the Second World Congress

Editor's note

The interval between the First and Second Congress covers approximately 18 months from March 7, 1919 to July 18, 1920. This was the decisive period of the Civil War in Russia marked by the liquidation of Kolchak's armies, the defeat of Denikin and the crushing of Yudenich's second offensive against Petrograd (October 1919). The military danger to Soviet Russia was, however, far from liquidated. In March 1920 Poland resumed military operations, and by May Kiev was in Polish hands. By the time the Second Congress convened, the Red Army had passed to the counter-offensive, recapturing Kiev and marching into Poland, but suffering defeat at Warsaw just as the Second Congress concluded its work (August 1920).

These eighteen months marked at the same time the period of greatest postwar ferment in Europe. A great strike wave marked by uprisings swept over Europe. On March 21, 1919, the Soviet Republic was formed in Hungary (overthrown August 1, 1919).

On April 14, 1919, after an uprising in Munich, the Bavarian Soviet Republic was established, lasting until May 1 of the same year.

On June 28, 1919, the German delegation signed the Versailles Treaty. On July 31 the Weimar Republic was inaugurated in Germany.

November of that year marked another important victory for the bourgeois counter-revolution in the electoral triumph of the National Bloc in France.

In Germany the counter-revolution first attempted to pass to an open offensive in the early part of 1920 (Kapp-Luettwitz putsch, March 12–19, 1920).

Throughout this period, however, the Communist International recorded major successes. In one country after another, sections of the world Communist movement were organized.

4. To comrades of the Spartacus League

With the greatest willingness and joy I accept the suggestion of Comrade Albert, delegate of the German Communist Party, to write a few lines for the German party press.

Having been, like all Russian Marxists, a disciple of German Socialism during my émigré existence, I participated to the best of my ability in the German party press for a number of years. With special gratification I seize this opportunity to renew my collaboration—under the existing, extremely altered conditions.

In these years the Hegelian[1] mole of history has been diligently digging his subterranean tunnels; much that had once stood firmly now lies in ruins—much that was weak, or seemingly so, has now become mighty. Moscow used to be justifiably considered the incarnation of world reaction. Today Moscow has become the meeting place for the Congress of the Third Communist International. At one time I could visit the Berlin of the Hohenzollerns only by using a false passport. (Let me retroactively apologize to the esteemed gendarmes of the Prussian monarchy, nowadays fulfilling the role of guardians of the Republic.) Today . . . incidentally, even today the gates of Berlin cannot as yet be considered open to a Russian Communist. However, I hope that for the opening of these gates, we shall not have to wait as long as we have waited up to now. There have been some changes in the German Social Democracy, too.

Comrade Albert confirms that which we never had any doubts about, namely, that the German workers are following the struggle of the Russian working class not only attentively but with fervent sympathy. Neither the unconscionable slanders of the bourgeoisie nor the most erudite criticisms of Karl Kautsky have swerved them from this sympathy.

From Kautsky we have heard that although the conquest of political power by the working class happens to be the historical task of a Social-Democratic Party, inasmuch as the Russian Communist Party has come to power not through those portals nor at the time indicated by Kautsky's prescription, the Soviet Republic must therefore be handed over for correction and reform to Kerensky,[2] Tseretelli[3] and Chernov.[4]

Kautsky's pedantic-reactionary criticism must seem the more unexpected to those German comrades who lived consciously through the period of the first Russian revolution and who read the 1905–06 articles[5] of Kautsky. At that time Kautsky (true, not without Rosa Luxemburg's beneficent influence) thoroughly understood and recognized that the Russian revolution could not be consummated by a bourgeois-democratic republic but, because of the level attained by the class struggle within the country and because of the entire international condition of capitalism, must lead to the dictatorship of the working class. Kautsky at that time wrote flatly in favor of a workers' government with a Social-Democratic majority. It did not even enter his mind to place the actual course of the class struggle in dependence upon any transitory and superficial combinations of political democracy. Kautsky then understood that the revolution would for the first time awaken the multimillioned peasant and middle-class masses; and do so, moreover, not at a single stroke, but gradually, layer by layer, so that when the decisive moment was reached in the struggle between the proletariat and the capitalist bourgeoisie, the broad peasant masses would still be found at an extremely primitive level of political development and would cast their votes for the intermediate political parties, reflecting thereby only the backwardness and the prejudices of the peasantry. Kautsky then understood that the proletariat, on arriving, by the logic of the revolution, at the conquest of power, could not arbitrarily postpone this action to an indefinite future because such an act of self-renunciation would only clear the field for the counter-revolution. Kautsky then understood that the proletariat, having taken the revolutionary power into its own hands, would not stake the fate of the revolution upon the fleeting moods of the least conscious and still unawakened masses at a given moment, but would, on the contrary, transform the entire state power concentrated in its hands into a mighty apparatus of enlightenment and organization of the most backward and most ignorant peasant masses. Kautsky understood that to pin on the Russian revolution the label, "bourgeois," and thereby delimit its tasks, would be to remain abysmally ignorant of what is occurring under the sun. He acknowledged quite correctly—together with the revolutionary Marxists of Russia and Poland—that in the event the Russian proletariat attained power before the European working class, it would have to utilize its ruling class position in order to further with every effort the extension of the proletarian revolution in Europe and throughout the whole world—if only for the sake of saving the Russian revolution by making the latter an integral part of the European revolution, and thus hastening Russia's own transition to a socialist system. At that time, all these world perspectives, permeated with the genuine spirit of the Marxist doctrine, were naturally made neither by Kautsky nor by us in any way dependent upon how or for whom the peasantry would vote in November–December 1917 during elections to the so-called Constituent Assembly.

Today when the perspectives outlined 15 years ago have become the reality, Kautsky refuses to issue a certificate of baptism to the Russian Revolution because it has not been legally certified by the political department of bourgeois democracy. An astonishing fact! What incredible debasement of Marxism! One can say with complete justification that the collapse of the Second International finds an even more odious expression in this philistine attitude of its outstanding theoretician toward the Russian Revolution than it did in the vote cast August 4, 1914, in favor of war credits.[6]

For a number of decades Kautsky promoted and defended the ideas of social revolution. Today when the revolution has come, Kautsky shies away in terror. He abjures the Soviet power in Russia, he stands hostilely opposed to the mighty movement of the Communist proletariat of Germany. Kautsky closely resembles a schoolmaster who, year in and year out, within the four walls of a stuffy schoolroom keeps repeating to his pupils a description of spring and then, in the decline of his pedagogical career, happens to stumble into the lap of nature during springtime, fails to recognize spring, is driven to frenzy (insofar as frenzy is proper to school teachers) and begins proving that the greatest disorder prevails in nature, that is, that the real spring is no spring at all for it is occurring contrary to—nature's laws. How good it is that the workers do not harken to even the most authoritative pedants, but do harken to the voice of spring.

We, the disciples of German philosophy, the disciples of Marx, remain, together with the German workers, convinced that the spring of revolution is taking place wholly in accordance with the laws of nature and at the same time the laws of Marx's theory, for Marxism is not a supra-historical kindergarten rod but the social analysis of the paths and methods of an actually unfolding historical process.

We likewise learned from Comrade Albert that the revolutionary German workers rejected those accusations which were leveled in their time against us by the selfsame Kautskyan Independent Party, which indicted us for deeming it possible to conclude the Brest-Litovsk peace with victorious German militarism. Bernstein[7] in his time circulated literary productions wherein he not only submitted to harsh judgment our having concluded peace with the Hohenzollern diplomats but also accompanied his criticism with darkest insinuations. He accused us— no more, no less—of consciously deceiving the Russian workers about the inevitability of the German revolution— solely for the purpose of covering up our intrigues with the Hohenzollern government. I refrain from referring to the fact that these "theoreticians of Marxism" who consider themselves genuine realists and sages didn't understand even a few months ago the inevitability of a social catastrophe in Germany, whereas we "utopians" had predicted it from the very first day of the war. But isn't it astounding political stupidity to proclaim the German revolution impossible, that is, to acknowledge the immutability of mighty German militarism, while at the same time demanding that the government of a weakened and exhausted country like Russia should at all costs continue waging—hand in hand with English imperialism—war against Hohenzollern? According to Bernstein and Co. we were guilty of failing to monopolize the struggle against German imperialism, and resting our hopes on the revolutionary activity of the German proletariat. But here, too, we were proved correct. Contrary to the logic of pedants and school teachers, the German working class has settled scores with the monarchy and is moving on the correct path toward the complete destruction of the rule of the bourgeoisie. Unfortunately I haven't the opportunity of ascertaining whether the English and French Bernsteins are now indicting the German working class because it is compelled to agree to a peace with Anglo-French imperialism. But we Russian Communists do not for a moment doubt that the terrible peace now being imposed by the world bandits on the German people will react completely to the damage of the ruling classes of the Entente.

Since the argument relating to the illegitimate birth of the dictatorship of the Russian working class does not exercise any great influence upon the German workers, a new argument is now being advanced in order to traduce the Russian Revolution. The Soviet government is aiming, mind you, to invade Eastern Prussia with the Red Army. We don't doubt that this fiction, too, which political charlatans are circulating in order to frighten and deceive idiots meets with no credence among German workers. It is our considered opinion that we shall fulfill our duty to the international revolution if we preserve the rule of the working class on the soil of Russia. This task demands of the Russian proletariat an enormous straining of forces and revolutionary self-sacrifice. Up to now our Red Army has successfully coped with its task. In the last six months it has liberated from the White Guard gangs an area of 700,000 square kilometers with a population of 42,000,000 souls. We confidently expect that the Workers' and Peasants' Army will not only maintain socialist power on this territory but also sweep clean those provinces of the Federated Republic where the power of the bourgeoisie is still being maintained with the assistance of foreign imperialists. As regards Germany, we consider that the task of transforming her into a socialist republic is first of all the business of the German working class. Precisely for this reason, this business is in firm and reliable hands. We send to the German proletarians our fervent greetings and ask them to believe that never have they been so close and dear to the heart of every Russian Communist as they are today, when amid incredible hardships in the struggle against traitors and turncoats, with the road dotted with lifeless bodies of their best fighters like Liebknecht and Luxemburg, they are tirelessly and courageously marching toward final victory.

MARCH 9, 1919

5. A creeping revolution[8]

The German revolution bears clear traits of similarity with the Russian. But no less instructive are its traits of dissimilarity. At the beginning of October[9] a "February" revolution took place in Germany. Two months later the German proletariat was already going through its "July days,"[10] that is, engaging in the first open clash with the bourgeois-conciliationist imperialist forces, on a new "republican" foundation. In Germany, as in our country, the July days were neither an organized uprising, nor a decisive battle spontaneous in origin. This was the first stormy manifestation, a pure manifestation of the class struggle, occurring on the soil conquered by the revolution, and this manifestation was accompanied by clashes between the vanguard detachments. In our country the experience of the July days served and aided the proletariat in further concentrating its forces in the organized preparation for the decisive battle. In Germany, after the first open revolutionary manifestation of the Spartacists was crushed and after their leaders were murdered, no breathing spell followed, not for a single day virtually. A succession of strikes, uprisings, open battles occurred in various places throughout the country. No sooner had Scheidemann's government succeeded in restoring order in the suburbs of Berlin than the valiant Guardsmen, inherited from Hohenzollern, had to rush to Stuttgart or Nuremberg. Essen, Dresden, Munich in turn become the arena of sanguinary civil war. Every new victory of Scheidemann is only the point of departure for a new uprising of Berlin workers. The revolution of the German proletariat has become protracted and creeping in character and, at first sight, this might rouse fears lest the ruling scoundrels succeed in bleeding it white, section by section, through a series of countless skirmishes. At the same time the following question seems automatically to arise: Haven't the leaders of the movement perhaps committed serious tactical blunders which threaten the entire movement with destruction?

In order to understand the German proletarian revolution one must judge it not simply by analogy with the Russian October Revolution, but by taking the internal conditions of Germany's own evolution as the starting point.

History has been so shaped that in the epoch of imperialist war the German Social Democracy proved—and this can now be stated with complete objectivity—to be the most counter-revolutionary factor in world history. The German Social Democracy, however, is not an accident; it did not fall from the skies but was created by the efforts of the German working class in the course of decades of uninterrupted construction and adaptation to conditions prevalent under the capitalist-Junker state. The party organization and the trade unions connected with it drew from the proletarian milieu the most outstanding, energetic elements, who were then molded psychologically and politically. The moment war broke out, and consequently when the moment arrived for the greatest historical test, it turned out that the official working-class organization acted and reacted not as the proletariat's organization of combat against the bourgeois state but as an auxiliary organ of the bourgeois state, designed to discipline the proletariat. The working class was paralyzed, since bearing down upon it was not only the full weight of capitalist militarism but also the apparatus of its own party. The hardships of war, its victories, its defeats, broke the paralysis of the German working class, freed it from the discipline of the official party. The latter split asunder. But the German proletariat remained without a revolutionary combat organization. History once again exhibited to the world one of its dialectic contradictions: precisely because the German working class had expended most of its energy in the previous epoch upon self-sufficient organizational construction, occupying the first place in the Second International both in party as well as trade union apparatus—precisely because of this, in a new epoch, at the moment of its transition to open revolutionary struggle for power the German working class proved to be extremely defenseless organizationally.

The Russian working class which accomplished its October Revolution was bequeathed by the previous epoch a priceless legacy in the shape of a centralized revolutionary party. The pilgrimages of the *Narodnik* (Populist) intelligentsia among the peasantry; the terrorist struggle of the *Narodovoltsi*;[11] the underground agitation of the pioneer Marxists; the revolutionary manifestation during the early years of this century, the October general strike and the barricades of 1905; the revolutionary "parliamentarianism" of the Stolypin epoch,[12] most intimately bound up with the underground movement—all this prepared a large personnel of revolutionary leaders, tempered in struggle and bound together by the unity of the social-revolutionary program.

History bequeathed nothing like this to the German working class. It is compelled not only to fight for power but to create its organization and train future leaders in the very course of this struggle. True, in the conditions of the revolutionary epoch this work of education is being done at a feverish pace, but time is nevertheless needed to accomplish it. In the absence of a centralized revolutionary party with a combat leadership whose authority is universally accepted by the working masses; in the absence of leading combat nuclei and leaders, tried in action and tested in experience throughout the various centers and regions of the proletarian movement; this movement upon breaking out into the streets became of necessity intermittent, chaotic, creeping in character. These erupting strikes, insurrections and battles represent at present the only form accessible for the purpose of openly mobilizing the forces of the German proletariat, freed from the old party's yoke; and at the same time they represent under the given conditions the sole means of educating new leaders and building the new party. It is quite self-evident that such a road calls for enormous exertions and demands countless sacrifices. But there is no choice. It is the one and only road along which the class uprising of the German proletariat can unfold till final victory.

After Bloody Sunday, January 9, 1905, when the workers of Petrograd and after them the workers throughout the country came gradually to understand the necessity of struggle and concurrently sensed how dispersed their forces were, there ensued in the land a powerful but extremely chaotic strike movement. Sages then arose to shed tears over the expenditure of energy by the Russian working class and to foretell its exhaustion and the defeat of the revolution attendant on this. In reality, however, the spontaneous, creeping strikes in the spring and summer months of 1905 were the only possible form of revolutionary mobilization and of organizational education. These strikes laid the groundwork for the great October strike and for the building of the first Soviets.

There is a certain analogy between what is now occurring in Germany and the period of the first Russian revolution I have just indicated. But the German revolutionary movement is, of course, developing on incomparably higher and mightier foundations. While the old official party has suffered complete bankruptcy and has become converted into an instrument of reaction, this naturally doesn't mean that the work accomplished by it in the preceding epoch has disappeared without a trace. The political and cultural level of the German workers, their organizational habits and capabilities are superlative. Tens and hundreds of thousands of worker-leaders, who had been absorbed during the previous epoch by the political and trade union organizations and seemingly assimilated by the latter, in reality endured the violence done to their revolutionary conscience only up to a certain point. Today in the course of partial open clashes, through the hardships of this revolutionary mobilization, in the harsh experience of this creeping revolution, tens of thousands of temporarily blinded, deceived and intimidated worker-leaders are awakening and rising to their full stature. The working class is seeking them out, just as they themselves are finding their places in the new struggle of the proletariat. If the historical assignment of Kautsky-Haase's[13] Independent Party consists in introducing vacillation among the ranks of the government party and supplying refuge for its frightened, desperate or indignant elements, then contrariwise, the stormy movement in which our Spartacist brothers-in-arms are playing such a heroic role will, as one of its effects, lead to the uninterrupted demolition from the left of the Independent Party whose best and most self-sacrificing elements are being drawn into the Communist movement.

The difficulties, the partial defeats and the great sacrifices of the German proletariat should not for a moment dishearten us. History does not offer the proletariat a choice of ways. The stubborn, unabated erupting and re-erupting, creeping revolution is clearly approaching the critical moment when, having mobilized and trained all its forces in advance for combat, the revolution will deal the class enemy the final mortal blow.

FIRST PUBLISHED IN *PRAVDA*,
NO. 85, APRIL 23, 1919

6. Great days[14]

The czars and the priests—ancient rulers of the Moscow Kremlin—we must assume, never had a premonition that within its gray walls would one day gather the representatives of the most revolutionary section of modern mankind. However, it did happen. In one of the halls of a former juridical institution, where weary ghosts of criminal statutes from Czarist codices still wander, today the delegates of the Third International sit in session. Assuredly, the mole of history did not excavate poorly beneath the Kremlin walls. . . .

This material setting of the Communist Congress is only an external expression, and affixes its seal upon the enormous changes which have occurred in the last ten or twelve years in the entire world situation.

In the era not only of the First International but also the Second, Czarist Russia was the chief bulwark of world reaction. At international Socialist Congresses the Russian revolution was represented by émigrés upon whom the majority of the opportunist leaders of European Socialism looked down with ironic condescension. These parliamentarian and trade union functionaries were filled with an unconquerable conviction that it was the lot of semi-Asiatic Russia to suffer the evils of revolution, while Europe remained assured of a gradual, painless, tranquil evolution from capitalism to socialism.

But in August 1914 the accumulated imperialist contradictions ripped to shreds the "peaceful" integument of capitalism with its parliamentarianism, with its legislated "freedoms" and its legalized prostitution, political and otherwise. From the heights of civilization mankind was cast into the abyss of shocking barbarism and sanguinary brutalization.

Despite the fact that Marxist theory had foreseen and forecast the bloody catastrophe, the social-reformist parties were caught unawares. Perspectives of peaceful development turned into lowering smoke and reeking rubbish. The opportunist leaders were able to find no other task for themselves than to summon the working masses to the defense of the bourgeois national state. On August 4, 1914, the Second International ignobly perished.

From that moment all genuine revolutionists, heirs to the spirit of Marxism, set the creation of a new International as their task—the International of irreconcilable revolutionary struggle against capitalist society. The war unleashed by imperialism knocked the entire capitalist world out of its equilibrium. All questions were starkly revealed as questions of the revolution. The old revolutionary patch-sewers brought into play all their skill in order to preserve a semblance of former hopes, old deceits, and old organization. In vain. War—not for the first time in history—turned out to be the mother of revolution. The imperialist war was the mother of the proletarian revolution.

To the Russian working class and its battle-tempered Communist Party belongs the honor of making the beginning. By its October Revolution the Russian proletariat not only swung open the Kremlin doors for the representatives of the international proletariat but also lodged the cornerstone in the edifice of the Third International.

The revolutions in Germany, Austria, Hungary, the tempestuous sweep of the Soviet movement and of civil war, sealed by the martyrdom of Karl Liebknecht and Rosa Luxemburg and many thousands of nameless heroes, have demonstrated that Europe has no roads different from Russia's. The unity of methods in the struggle for socialism, disclosed in action, guaranteed ideologically the creation of the Communist International, and at the same time rendered the convocation of the Communist Congress unpostponable.

Today this Congress convenes within the Kremlin walls. We are witnesses of and participants in one of the greatest events of world history.

The working class of the world has seized from its enemies the most impregnable fortress—the former Czarist empire. With this stronghold as its base, it is uniting its forces for the final and decisive battle.

What a joy it is to live and to fight in such times!

FIRST PUBLISHED IN
COMMUNIST INTERNATIONAL,
MAY 1919

7. En route: Thoughts on the progress of the proletarian revolution[15]

I

Once upon a time the church had a saying: "The light shineth from the East." In our generation the revolution began in the East. From Russia it passed over into Hungary, from Hungary to Bavaria and, doubtless, it will march westward through Europe. This march of events is taking place contrary to prejudices, allegedly Marxist and rather widespread among broad circles of intellectuals, and not those of Russia alone.

The revolution through which we are now living is proletarian, and the proletariat is strongest in the old capitalist countries where it is much larger numerically, better organized, more class-conscious. It is seemingly in the nature of things to expect that the revolution in Europe ought to unfold approximately along the same paths as those of capitalist development: England—the first-born capitalist country, to be followed by France, to be followed by Germany, Austria and, finally, at the bottom of the list—Russia.

It may be said that in this erroneous conception lies the original sin of Menshevism, the theoretical ground for its entire future downfall. In accordance with this "Marxism," adjusted to petty-bourgeois horizons, all the countries of Europe must, in inexorable succession, pass through two stages: the feudal-serf stage and the bourgeois-democratic stage, in order to reach socialism. According to Dan[16] and Potressov,[17] Germany in 1910 was only beginning to consummate her bourgeois-democratic revolution, in order later to prepare on this foundation the socialist revolution. Just what these gentlemen meant by "socialist revolution" they could never explain. Incidentally, they did not even feel the need for such an explanation, inasmuch as the socialist revolution was relegated by them to the Hereafter. It is hardly surprising that they took it . . . for a piece of Bolshevik insolence, when along the road of history they did meet up with the revolution. From the viewpoint of this flat and bare historical gradualism, nothing seemed so monstrous as the idea that the Russian revolution, upon attaining victory, could place the proletariat in power; that the victorious proletariat, even if it so desired, would be unable to keep the revolution within the framework of bourgeois democracy. Despite the fact that this historical prognosis was reached almost a decade and a half before the 1917 October Revolution, the Mensheviks, sincerely in their fashion, considered the conquest of political power by the proletariat to be an accident and an "adventure." No less sincerely did they consider the Soviet regime to be a product of the backwardness and barbarousness of Russian conditions. The mechanism of bourgeois democracy was held by these egotistic ideologists of the semi-enlightened Babbitts to be the highest expression of human civilization. They counterposed the Constituent Assembly to the Soviets approximately in the manner that an automobile may be counterposed to a peasant cart.

However, the further course of events continued to unfold contrariwise to the "common-sense" and socially indispensable prejudices of an average middle-class vulgarian. First of all, despite the existence of the Constituent Assembly with all its democratic boons implicit in Weimar[18] there arose in Germany a party which is becoming stronger and stronger and which immediately siphoned off the most heroic elements among the proletariat—a party on whose banner is inscribed: "All Power to the Soviets." No one takes note of the creative labors of the Scheidemannist Constituent Assembly, no one in the world is interested in it. The entire attention not only of the German people but of all mankind is fixed on the gigantic struggle between the ruling clique of the Constituent Assembly and the revolutionary proletariat, a struggle which immediately proved to be outside the framework of legalized Constituent "democracy."

In Hungary and Bavaria this process has already gone beyond that. In these countries, in place of formal democracy, this belated imprint of yesterday which is being converted into a brake upon the tomorrow of revolution, has appeared a truly genuine democracy in the form of the rule of the victorious proletariat.

But while the march of events proceeds not at all in accordance with the itinerary of house-broken gradualists, who long pretended to be Marxists not only in public but also in private, this very march of revolutionary developments demands an explanation. The fact is that the revolution began and led to the victory of the proletariat in the most backward major country of Europe—Russia.

Hungary is unquestionably the more backward half of the former Austro-Hungarian monarchy, which as a whole, in the sense of capitalist and even cultural-political development, stood between Russia and Germany. Bavaria where, following Hungary, Soviet power has been established, represents with respect to capitalist development not the advanced but, on the contrary, a backward section of Germany. Thus the proletarian revolution after starting in the most backward country of Europe, keeps mounting upwards, rung by rung, toward countries more highly developed economically.

What is the explanation for this "incongruity"?

The oldest capitalist country in Europe and the world is—England. Meanwhile England, especially during the last half-century, has been from the standpoint of the proletarian revolution the most conservative country. The consistent social-reformists, *i.e.*, those who try to make both ends meet, hence drew all the conclusions they needed, asserting that it was precisely England that indicated to other countries the possible paths of political development and that in the future the entire European proletariat would renounce the program of the social revolution. For the Marxists, however, the "incongruity" between England's capitalist development and her Socialist movement, as conditioned by a temporary combination of historical forces, did not contain anything disheartening. It was England's early entry onto the path of capitalist development and world robbery that created a privileged position not only for her bourgeoisie but also for a section of her working class. England's insular position spared her the direct burden of maintaining militarism on land. Her mighty naval militarism, although requiring huge expenditures, rested nevertheless on numerically small cadres of hirelings and did not require a transition to universal military service.

The British bourgeoisie skillfully utilized these conditions in order to separate the top labor layer from the bottom strata, creating an aristocracy of "skilled" labor and instilling into it a trade union caste spirit. Flexible despite all its conservatism, the parliamentary machinery of Great Britain, the incessant rivalry between two historical parties—the Liberals and the Tories—a rivalry which at times assumed rather tense form although remaining quite hollow in content, invariably created when the need arose an artificial political safety-valve for the discontent of the working masses. This was supplemented by the fiendish dexterity of the ruling bourgeois clique in the business of spiritually crippling and bribing, quite "exquisitely" at times, the leaders of the working class. Thus thanks to England's early capitalist development her bourgeoisie disposed of resources that enabled them systematically to counteract the proletarian revolution. Within the proletariat itself, or more correctly, within its upper layer, the same conditions gave shape to the most extreme conservative tendencies which manifested themselves in the course of decades prior to the World War. . . . While Marxism teaches that class relations arise in the process of production and that these relations correspond to a certain level of productive forces; while Marxism further teaches that all forms of ideology and, first and foremost, politics correspond to class relations, this does not at all mean that between politics, class groupings and production there exist simple mechanical relations, calculable by the four rules of arithmetic. On the contrary, the reciprocal relations are extremely complex. It is possible to interpret dialectically the course of a country's development, including its revolutionary development, only by proceeding from the action, reaction and interaction of all the material and superstructural factors, national and world-wide alike, and not through superficial juxtapositions, or through formal analogies.

England accomplished her bourgeois revolution in the 17th century; France—at the end of the 18th century. France was for a long time the most advanced, the most "cultured" country on the European continent. The French social-patriots still sincerely believed even at the beginning of this war that the entire fate of mankind rotated around Paris. But once again, just because of her early bourgeois civilization, France developed powerful conservative tendencies within her capitalism. The slow organic growth of capitalism did not mechanically destroy French handicrafts, but pulled them along, simply relegating them to different positions, assigning them a more and more subordinate role. The revolution, by selling the feudal estates at auction to the peasantry, created the French village, extremely viable, tenacious, stubborn and petty-bourgeois. The Great French Revolution of the 18th century, bourgeois both in its most extreme objectives as well as results, was at the same time profoundly national—in the sense that it rallied round itself the majority of the nation and, first and foremost, all of its creative classes. For a century and a quarter this revolution established the bond of common remembrances and traditions between a considerable section of the French working class and the left elements of bourgeois democracy. Juarès[19] was the greatest and last representative of this conservative ideological bond. Under these conditions France's political atmosphere couldn't fail to infect broad layers of the French proletariat, especially the semi-handicraftsmen with petty-bourgeois illusions. Conversely, it was precisely the rich revolutionary past that gave the French proletariat an inclination to settle scores with the bourgeoisie on the barricades. The character of the class struggle, lacking clarity in theory, but extremely tense in practice, kept the French bourgeoisie constantly on guard and compelled it to go over early to the export of finance capital. While on the one hand seducing the popular masses, including the workers, by a dramatic display of anti-dynastic, anti-clerical, republican, radical and other tendencies, the French bourgeoisie, on the other hand, availed itself of the advantages accruing from its primogeniture and from its position of world usurer in order to check the growth of new and revolutionizing forms of industrialism within France herself. An analysis of the economic and political conditions of French evolution, and furthermore not only on a national but an international scale, can alone provide an explanation of why the French proletariat, split up after the heroic eruption of the Paris Commune into groups and sects, anarchist on the one wing, and "possibilist"[20] on the other, proved incapable of engaging in open revolutionary class action, of struggling directly for state power.

For Germany the period of vigorous capitalist flowering began after the victorious wars[21] of 1864–1866–1871. The soil of national unity, drenched by the golden flood of French billions, became the bed of a glittering reign of boundless speculation, but also that of an unprecedented technical development. In contrast to the French proletariat, the working class of Germany grew at an extraordinary rate and expended most of its energies on gathering, fusing, organizing its own ranks. In its irresistible upsurge the working class of Germany got great satisfaction from adding up its automatically growing forces in the reports of parliamentary elections or in the statements of trade union treasuries. The victorious competition of Germany on the world market created conditions equally favorable for the growth of the trade unions as well as for the unquestionable improvement in the living standard of a section of the working class. In these circumstances the German Social Democracy became a living—and later on ever more moribund—incarnation of organizational fetishism. With its roots deeply intertwined in the national state and national industry, and in the process of adaptation to the entire complexity and entanglement of German social-political relations, which are a combination of modern capitalism and medieval barbarism, the German Social Democracy along with the trade unions under its leadership became in the end the most counter-revolutionary force in the political evolution of Europe. The danger of such a degeneration of the German Social Democracy had long ago been pointed out by Marxists, although we must admit that no one had foreseen how catastrophic would be the character of this process in the end. Only by throwing the dead weight of the old party off its back has the advanced German proletariat now been able to enter the road of open struggle for political power.

As regards the development of Austria-Hungary, it is impossible from the viewpoint of interest to us to say anything which would not likewise apply in a clearer form to the development of Russia. The belated development of Russian capitalism immediately imparted to it an extremely concentrated character. When in the 'forties of the last century Knopf[22] established English textile factories in the central Moscow area, and when the Belgians, the French and the Americans transplanted to the virginal Ukrainian and Novorussian steppes the huge metallurgical enterprises constructed in accordance with the latest word in European and American technology, they did not consult textbooks to learn whether they should wait until Russian handicraft developed into manufacture, while manufacture in its turn brought us to the large-scale factory.

On this soil, *i.e.*, on the soil of poorly digested economic textbooks, there once arose the famous but essentially puerile controversy[23] over whether Russian capitalism was "natural" or "artificial" in character. If one were to vulgarize Marx and look upon English capitalism not as the historical starting-moment of capitalist development but rather as the all-imperative stereotype, then Russian capitalism would appear as an artificial formation, implanted from without. But if we analyze capitalism in the spirit of Marx's genuine teachings, that is, as an economic process which first evolved a typical national form and which then outgrew this national framework and evolved world ties; and which in order to bring the backward countries under its sway sees no need of returning to the tools and usages of its infant days, but employs instead the last word in technology, the last word in capitalist exploitation and political blackmail—if we analyze capitalism in this spirit, then the development of Russian capitalism with all its peculiarities will appear wholly "natural," as an indispensable, component part of the world capitalist process.

This applies not alone to Russia. The railways which have cut across Australia were not the "natural" outgrowth of the living conditions either of the Australian aborigines or of the first generations of malefactors who were, beginning with the epoch of the French revolution, shipped off to Australia by the magnanimous English metropolises. The capitalist development of Australia is natural only from the standpoint of the historical process taken on a world scale. On a different scale, on a national, provincial scale it is, generally speaking, impossible to analyze a single one of the major social manifestations of our epoch.

Just because the Russian large-scale industry violated the "natural" order of succession of national economic development, by taking a gigantic economic leap over transitional epochs, it thereby prepared not only the possibility but the inevitability of the proletarian leap over the epoch of bourgeois democracy.

The ideologist of democracy, Jaurès, pictured democracy as the nation's supreme tribunal, rising above the warring classes. However, inasmuch as the warring classes—the capitalist bourgeoisie and the proletariat—not only constitute the formal poles within the nation but are also its chief and decisive elements, what remain as the supreme tribunal, or more correctly the court of arbitration, are only the intermediate elements—the petty bourgeoisie, crowned with the democratic intelligentsia. In France, with her centuries-long history of handicrafts and of handicraft urban culture, with her struggles of city communes and, later, her revolutionary battles of bourgeois democracy, and, finally, with her conservatism of a petty-bourgeois variety, democratic ideology has until recently still rested on a certain historical soil. An ardent defender of the interests of the proletariat, and profoundly devoted to socialism, Jaurès, as the tribune of a democratic nation, came out against imperialism. Imperialism, however, has demonstrated quite convincingly that it is mightier than "the democratic nation" whose political will imperialism is so easily able to falsify by means of the parliamentary mechanism. In July 1914, the imperialist oligarchy, on its way to war, strode over the tribune's corpse; while in March 1919, through the "supreme tribunal" of the democratic nation, it officially exonerated the murderer of Jaurès, thereby dealing a mortal blow to the last remaining democratic illusions of the French working class. . . .

In Russia these illusions from the outset did not have any kind of support beneath them. With the ponderous sluggishness of its meager development our country didn't have time to create an urban handicraft culture. The citizenry of a provincial town like Okurov[24] is equipped for pogroms which once so greatly alarmed Gorki; but it is, without a doubt, unequipped for an independent democratic role. Just because England's development had occurred "according to Marx," the development of Russia according to this same Marx had to proceed in an entirely different way. Nurtured under the high pressure of foreign finance capital and aided by foreign technology, Russian capitalism in the course of a few decades gave form to a million-headed working class, which cut like a sharp wedge into the milieu of All-Russian political barbarism. Without the massive traditions of the past behind it, the Russian workers, in contrast to the Western European proletariat, took on not only traits of cultural backwardness and ignorance—which the semi-literate, indigenous, urban citizens never wearied of pointing out—but also traits of mobility, initiative, and receptivity to the most extreme conclusions deriving from their class position. If Russia's economic backwardness conditioned the spasmodic, "catastrophic" development of capitalism, which immediately acquired the most concentrated character in Europe, then the same universal backwardness of the country under the spasmodic, "catastrophic" development of the Russian proletariat permitted the latter to become—of course only for a segment of a certain historical period—the most irreconcilable, the most self-sacrificing bearer of the idea of social revolution in Europe and throughout the world.

II

Capitalist production in its "natural" evolution is constantly expanding reproduction. Technology keeps rising, the amount of material boons keeps growing, the mass of the population becomes proletarianized. Expanded capitalist production deepens capitalist contradictions. The proletariat grows numerically, constitutes an ever-larger proportion of the country's population, becomes organized and educated, and thus forms an ever-growing power. But this does not at all mean to say that its class enemy—the bourgeoisie—remains at a standstill. On the contrary, expanded capitalist production presupposes a simultaneous growth of the economic and political might of the big bourgeoisie. It not only accumulates colossal riches but also concentrates in its hands the state apparatus of administration, which it subordinates to its aims. With an ever-perfected art it accomplishes its aims through ruthless cruelty alternating with democratic opportunism. Imperialist capitalism is able to utilize more proficiently the forms of democracy in proportion as the economic dependence of petty-bourgeois layers of the population upon big capital becomes more cruel and insurmountable. From this economic dependence the bourgeoisie is able, by means of universal suffrage, to derive—political dependence.

A mechanical conception of the social revolution reduces the historical process to an uninterrupted numerical growth and a steadily mounting organizational strength of the proletariat until, comprising "the overwhelming majority of the population," the proletariat without a battle, or virtually without a fight, takes into its own hands the machinery of bourgeois economy and the state, like a fruit ripe for plucking. In reality, however, the growth of the proletariat's productive role parallels the growth of the bourgeoisie's might. As the proletariat becomes organizationally fused and politically educated the bourgeoisie is in its turn impelled to perfect its apparatus of rule and to arouse against the proletariat ever-newer layers of the population, including the so-called new third estate, *i.e.,* the professional intellectuals who play a most prominent role in the mechanics of capitalist economy. Both enemies gain in strength simultaneously.

The more powerful a country is capitalistically—all other conditions being equal—the greater is the inertia of "peaceful" class relations; all the more powerful must be the impulse necessary to drive both of the hostile classes—the proletariat and the bourgeoisie—out of the state of relative equilibrium and to transform the class struggle into open civil war. Once it has flared, the civil war—all other conditions being equal—will be the more bitter and stubborn, the higher the country's attained level of capitalist development; the stronger and more organized both of the enemies are; the greater the amount of material and ideological resources at the disposal of both.

The conceptions of proletarian revolution which prevailed in the Second International did not in reality transgress the framework of self-sufficient national capitalism. England, Germany, France, Russia were regarded as independent worlds moving in one and the same orbit towards socialism, and located along the different stages of this path. The hour of the coming of socialism strikes when capitalism attains its utmost limits of maturity and thereby the bourgeoisie is compelled to surrender its place to the proletariat, as the builder of socialism. This nationally-limited conception of capitalist development provides the theoretical and psychological grounds of social-patriotism: "Socialists" of each country deem themselves duty-bound to defend the national state as the natural and self-sufficient foundation of socialist development.

But this conception is false to the core and profoundly reactionary. By becoming world-wide, capitalist development thereby snapped those threads which in the past epoch bound the fate of the social revolution with the fate of one or another more highly developed capitalist country. The closer capitalism knit together the countries of the whole world into a single complex organism, all the more inexorably did social revolution, not only in the sense of its common destiny but also in the sense of its place and time of origin, fall into dependence upon the development of imperialism as a world factor, and primarily in dependence upon those military conflicts which imperialism must inevitably provoke and which, in their turn, must shake the equilibrium of the capitalist system to its roots.

The great imperialist war is that frightful instrument by means of which history has disrupted the "organic," "evolutionary," "peaceful" character of capitalist development. Growing out of capitalist development as a whole, and at the same time appearing before the national consciousness of each individual capitalist country as an external factor, imperialism acts as if to discount the difference in levels attained by the development of the respective capitalist countries. At one and the same time, they were all drawn into the imperialist war* their productive foundations, their class relations were shaken simultaneously. Given

---

* Here are some theses one might propose for a Kautskyan dissertation: "Russia intervened prematurely in the imperialist war. She ought to have remained on the sidelines and devoted her energies to developing her productive forces on the basis of national capitalism. This would have provided an opportunity for the social relations to mature for the social revolution. The proletariat might have arrived to power within the framework of democracy." And so on and so forth.

At the beginning of the revolution Kautsky served as a Commissioner under Hohenzollern's Minister for Foreign Affairs. It is too bad that Kautsky did not serve as a Commissioner under the Lord God Jehovah when the latter was pre-determining the paths of capitalist development.—L.T.

this condition the first countries to be driven out of the state of unstable capitalist equilibrium were those whose internal social energy was weakest, *i.e.*, precisely those countries youngest in terms of capitalist development.

Here an analogy virtually imposes itself—the analogy between the inception of imperialist war and the inception of civil war. Two years before the great world slaughter, the Balkan war erupted. Basically, the selfsame forces and tendencies operated in the Balkans as throughout the rest of Europe. These forces were inexorably leading capitalist mankind to a bloody catastrophe. But in the great imperialist countries there likewise operated a mighty inertia of resistance both in domestic as well as foreign relations. Imperialism found it easier to push the Balkans into war precisely because on this peninsula there are smaller weaker states, with a much lower level of capitalist and cultural development—and consequently with less of the inertia of "peaceful" development.

The Balkan war—which arose as a consequence of subterranean earthquakes, not of Balkan but of European imperialism, as the direct forerunner of the world conflict—attained, however, an independent significance for a certain period. Its course and its immediate outcome were conditioned by the resources and forces available on the Balkan peninsula. Hence the comparatively brief duration of the Balkan war. A few months sufficed to measure the national capitalist forces on the poverty-stricken peninsula. With an earlier start the Balkan war found an easier solution. The World War started later precisely because each of the belligerents kept glancing fearfully down into the abyss toward which it was being dragged by unbridled class interests. Germany's extraordinarily augmented power, counterposed to the ancient power of Great Britain, constituted, as is well known, the historical mainspring of the war but this same power long kept the enemies from an open break. When the war did break out, however, the power of both camps conditioned the prolonged and bitter character of the conflict.

The imperialist war, in its turn, pushed the proletariat along the path of civil war. And here we observe an analogous order: Countries with a younger capitalist culture are the first to enter the path of civil war inasmuch as the unstable equilibrium of class forces is most easily disrupted precisely in these countries.

Such are the general reasons for a phenomenon which seems inexplicable at first sight, namely, that in contradistinction to the direction of capitalist development from West to East, the proletarian revolution unfolds from East to West. But since we are dealing with a most complex process, it is quite in the nature of things that upon these indicated basic causes there arise countless secondary causes, some of which tend to reinforce and aggravate the action of the chief factors while others tend to weaken this action.

In the development of Russian capitalism the leading role was played by European finance and industrial capital, particularly and especially that of—France.[25] I have already underscored that the French bourgeoisie in developing its usurious imperialism was guided not only by economic but also by political considerations. Fearful of the growth of the French proletariat in size and power, the French bourgeoisie preferred to export its capital and to reap profits from Russian industrial enterprises; the task of curbing the Russian workers was therewith unloaded on the Russian Czar. In this way the economic might of the French bourgeoisie also rested directly on the labor of the Russian proletariat. This created a certain positive force in favor of the French bourgeoisie in its co-relations with the French proletariat and, conversely, this same fact engendered a certain incremental social force advantageous to the Russian proletariat in its relations with the Russian (but not the world) bourgeoisie. What has just been said applies essentially to all old capitalist countries exporting capital. The social might of the English bourgeoisie rests on the exploitation not only of the English proletariat but also of the colonial toiling masses. Not only does this make the bourgeoisie richer and socially stronger, but this also secures it the possibility of a much wider arena for political maneuvers, both through rather far-reaching concessions to its native proletariat as well as through exerting pressure on it by means of the colonies (import of raw materials and labor forces, transfer of industrial enterprises into the colonies, formation of colonial troops, etc., etc.).

In view of the foregoing reciprocal relations, our October Revolution was an uprising not only against the Russian bourgeoisie but also against English and French capitalism; and this, furthermore, not only in a general historical sense—as the beginning of the European revolution—but in the most direct and immediate sense. In expropriating the capitalists and refusing to pay Czarist state debts, the Russian proletariat thereby dealt the cruelest blow to the social power of the European bourgeoisie. This alone suffices to explain why the counter-revolutionary intervention of the Entente imperialists was inevitable. On the other hand, this same intervention was rendered possible only because the Russian proletariat found itself placed by history in a position which compelled the Russian workers to accomplish their revolution before it could be accomplished by their older and much stronger European brothers. Hence flow those supreme difficulties which the Russian proletariat is compelled to overcome upon taking power.

The Social-Democratic philistines have sought to conclude from this, that there was no need of going out into the streets in October. Unquestionably it would have been far more "economical" for us to have begun our revolution after the English, the French and the German revolutions. But, in the first place, history does not at all offer a free choice in this connection to the revolutionary class and nobody has yet proved that the Russian proletariat is assured a revolution "economical" in character. Second, the very question of revolutionary "economy" of forces has to be reviewed not on a national but on a world scale. Precisely because of the entire preceding development, the task of initiating the revolution, as we have already seen, was not placed on an old proletariat with mighty political and trade union organizations, with massive traditions of parliamentarianism and trade unionism, but upon the young proletariat of a backward country. History took the line of least resistance. The revolutionary epoch burst in through the most weakly barricaded door. Those extraordinary and truly superhuman difficulties which thereupon fell upon the Russian proletariat have prepared, have hastened and have to a certain degree made easier the revolutionary work that lies still ahead for the Western European proletariat.

In our analysis there is not an atom of "messianism." The revolutionary "primogeniture" of the Russian proletariat is only temporary. The mightier the opportunist conservatism among the summits of the German, French or English proletariat, all the more grandiose will be the power generated for their revolutionary onslaught by the proletariat of these countries, a power which the proletariat is already generating today in Germany. The dictatorship of the Russian working class will be able to finally intrench itself and to develop into a genuine, all-sided socialist construction only from the hour when the European working class frees us from the economic yoke and especially the military yoke of the European bourgeoisie, and, having overthrown the latter, comes to our assistance with its organization and its technology. Concurrently, the leading revolutionary role will pass over to the working class with the greater economic and organizational power. If today the center of the Third International lies in Moscow—and of this we are profoundly convinced—then on the morrow this center will shift westward: to Berlin, to Paris, to London. However joyously the Russian proletariat has greeted the representatives of the world working class within the Kremlin walls, it will with an even greater joy send its representatives to the Second Congress of the Communist International in one of the Western European capitals. For a World Communist Congress in Berlin or Paris would signify the complete triumph of the proletarian revolution in Europe and consequently throughout the world.

FIRST PUBLISHED IN *IZVESTIA*,
NOS. 90 AND 92,
APRIL 29–MAY 1, 1919

8. French Socialism on the eve of revolution

The internal situation of France is filled with deepest contradictions. These contradictions sometimes even seem somewhat enigmatic. We receive news far too scant to be able to make out all the zigzags of France's internal development. In recent weeks, the radio brought us tidings of strikes, demonstrations, ferments, tidings of the rising revolutionary surf. At the same time the latest radiograms inform us that imperialist reaction has scored a complete victory in the parliamentary elections.[26] At first glance, what a glaring contradiction! And yet this contradiction is best explained by the theory of Communism (Marxism) and most strikingly corroborates the correctness of this theory.

Parliamentarianism is an instrument of bourgeois rule. Parliamentarianism becomes all the more obsolete the further we move into the epoch of the proletarian revolution. To the extent that the French labor movement assumes the form of the first stages of civil war, to that extent the means and implements of parliamentarianism become more and more openly the patrimony of capitalist cliques, their apparatus of class self-defense.

The victory of Clemenceaunian reaction in the elections is not a refutation of the proximity of the proletarian revolution in France but, on the contrary, its clearest confirmation. At the same time these mutually supplementary contrasts—the growth of reaction in parliament and the growth of insurrection in the streets—are incontrovertible proof that in France, in the land of the so-called "democratic republic," the rule of the proletariat will not be realized in life through the mechanism of bourgeois democracy, but in the form of open class dictatorship, all the more ruthless, the more frantic the resistance of the imperialist bourgeoisie.

To what extent is revolutionary France[*] prepared politically and organizationally for the proletarian dictatorship?

It is necessary to begin by recognizing the enormous difficulties which must be overcome in this connection. France has traditionally been the country of socialist and anarchist sects, engaged in internecine warfare on the soil of the labor movement. The unity of the Socialist Party was gained and secured after cruelest fratricidal struggle only a few years prior to the imperialist war. Both the right and the left wings equally cherished this unity. Meanwhile, it was revealed in the experience of war that the French party as well as the French syndicates (trade unions) have been utterly corroded by conciliationism, chauvinism and

---

* I use for all later reference the packet, just received, of the revolutionary-syndicalist weekly *La Vie Ouvrière*, June to September 1919. This paper is edited by our French friends Monatte[27] and Rosmer[28] who haven't for a moment furled their banner in this epoch of the greatest disintegration and renegacy among the self-styled "leaders."—L.T.

all other reactionary petty-bourgeois prejudices extant in this wide world.

The French proletariat has a glorious revolutionary past. Nature and history have endowed it with a superb warlike temperament. But at the same time it has known far too many defeats, disillusionments, perfidies and betrayals. Prior to the war the unity of the Socialist Party and the trade union syndicalist organization was its last great hope.

The blasting of this hope had a harmful effect upon the consciousness of the advanced workers, and the proletarian movement of France was plunged into protracted paralysis. And today when new and still politically inexperienced masses are pressing against the buttresses of bourgeois society, the incongruity between the old organization and the objective tasks of the movement is becoming disclosed with full force. Hence flows not only the probability but also the inevitability of powerful mass movements unfolding sooner than the new organization will be prepared to lead them.

Quite obvious is the urgency of creating in advance organizational ramparts throughout the districts—organizational points of support with the requisite independence, not bound by the discipline of the old political or trade union organizations, and capable of promptly taking their place at the head of the movement. Our French comrades are wholly occupied with just this. If the revolutionary groupings proved too weak at the outset to give the movement genuine leadership, at a subsequent stage, after the first revolutionary surge, they will quickly gain forces, grow stronger and become consolidated in the course of the struggle itself.

So far as one can judge from afar this twofold task—building the organization virtually anew while at the same time assuming the leadership of a swiftly unfolding mass movement—presents the main difficulty in carrying on revolutionary work in France at present.

"Strikes," says the courageous revolutionary syndicalist, Monatte, "are flaring up on all sides." But its inner bankruptcy "does not permit the General Confederation of Labor (CGT) to lead them." A new apparatus is necessary. It is impossible, however, to postpone the movement until the necessary leading organization is created. On the other hand, these spontaneous strikes, which tend to become transformed into decisive revolutionary events, cannot lead to victory without a genuine revolutionary organization, one that doesn't tell the workers lies, doesn't deceive them, doesn't hide from them nor throw sand into their eyes, doesn't betray them in the cloakrooms of parliamentarianism or of economic conciliationism but leads them unswervingly to the end. Such an organization must still be created.

> Where are we heading? From dissatisfaction to more dissatisfaction, from strike to strike, from semi-economic, semi-political strikes to strikes purely political in character. We are heading directly for the overthrow of the bourgeoisie, that is, revolution. The dissatisfied masses are taking long strides along this path.

So writes *La Vie Ouvrière*, the newspaper of Monatte and Rosmer.

The revolutionary representatives of the French proletariat jointly with the central Communist core (both Socialist as well as syndicalist in origin), who although small numerically are equipped with a clear and conscious knowledge of the aims of the movement, have as their task to firmly integrate all those new leaders who come to the forefront during strikes, demonstrations and, generally, all other manifestations of the genuine mass movement. The task consists, without fearing difficulties, in assuming right now the leadership of this spontaneous movement and in consolidating on this soil one's own organization as an apparatus of the direct uprising of the proletariat.

This presupposes, in its turn, a complete break with the discipline of those organizations which are counter-revolutionary in essence, that is, in relation to the basic tasks of the movement, and which are represented by the parties of Renaudel-Longuet, and the trade unions of Jouhaux-Merrheim.

While the response of the working masses was very meager on July 21 when the strike[29] was called to protest the Entente's intervention in Russian affairs, the blame for it must not be placed on the workers. In the last few years the workers in general and the French workers in particular have been deceived more sedulously, with more fiendish ingenuity, and with more tragic consequences than ever before in history. The majority of those leaders, who used memorized phrases in order to summon the workers to struggle against capitalism, openly put on the livery of imperialism in the autumn of 1914. The official syndical and party organizations, with which the advanced workers had become accustomed to associate the idea of emancipation, became the instruments of capitalism. This fact created not only incredible organizational difficulties for the working class but also became the source of a profound ideological catastrophe, from which the difficulties in recovering are in proportion to the great role played by the old organization in the life of the advanced proletarian layers.

The working class is now heroically striving to regain its feet after the fall, to shake off the effects of the blow. Hence the unprecedented influx into the syndicates. But at the same time a working class, disarmed ideologically and confused politically, is hammering out with difficulty a new orientation for itself. And this work is not facilitated but, on the contrary, impeded in the extreme if the revolutionary leaders remain too long in a transitional position, if they do not appear before the masses with the necessary independence and resoluteness, but remain instead submerged against the main background of the old party and syndicate organizations.

Whatever may be the motivation for preserving the unity of the old organization, it must remain incomprehensible to the revolutionary masses why those who summon them to revolution continue to sit at the same table with individuals who have deceived them, and especially those individuals who so brazenly and shamefully betrayed them during the war. The revolutionary mass dearly values its own unity in struggle, but it is doubtful whether it will easily understand the unity of the revolutionary fighters with the clique of Jouhaux[30]-Merrheim[31] and Renaudel[32]-Longuet.[33]

Under the conditions of the present epoch the slogan of preserving unity flows from the psychology of the official organization: leaders, chairmen, secretaries, parliamentarians, editors and, generally, apparatus functionaries of the old syndical and parliamentary workers' democracy who feel the ground slipping under their feet. The proletariat, however, has today the choice either of disintegrating completely, becoming atomized and bringing forth at the top privileged retainers of triumphant imperialism or of fusing its ranks to rise up against capitalism. The working class needs its unity of revolutionary struggle, the unity of class uprising, whereas the unity of outlived organizations keeps becoming more and more of a barrier along the road to the unity of the proletarian revolutionary uprising. The masses thrown off balance by the war today need more than ever before clarity in ideas, precision in slogans, a road that is straight and leaders who do not waver. Yet the tactic based on preserving the unity of old organizations yields a caricature parliamentarianism within the workers' organizations under the old administration—it is as if they are "ministerial cabinets," with an opposition, with established statutory regulations, official inquiries, votes of confidence, and so forth and so on. By establishing ties with conciliationists through a unified organization, the Communist opposition thereby places itself on fundamental questions in dependence on the will of the conciliationist majority and squanders its energy in adapting itself to syndical and party "parliamentarianism." Petty items and incidents of an internal organizational struggle thus acquire a disproportionate importance at the expense of the basic questions of the revolutionary mass movement.

Caricature "parliamentarianism" within the workers' organizations leads to further consequences. Secretaries and chairmen, Socialist-Ministers, journalists and deputies level charges against the opposition, accusing it of seeking to seize their easy-chairs and portfolios. The opposition excuses itself and not infrequently becomes signatory to declarations of "esteem" for the leading figures of the opposing side, painstakingly underscoring that the opposition conducts a struggle against "principles" and not against "personalities." This leads, in its turn, to the intrenchment of the conciliators in the posts they occupy.

La Vie Ouvrière of September 24 states that the vote of confidence at the Metal Workers Convention was not intended to underwrite the policy of the conciliationist administration but to express personal confidence in and personal sympathy for the secretaries. In other words, it was a vote of middle-class sentimentality, and not that of courageous class policy. Comrade Carron convincingly demonstrates in his article that those who so voted, and especially the masses back of them, are in spirit wholly with the partisans of the Third International. If they nonetheless voted confidence in the leadership, it was solely because their minds are being lulled by false arguments to the effect that one must struggle against ideas and not against personalities. After all, by their vote of confidence in Merrheim they continued in a responsible post a man who fobs off the ideas of opportunism, conciliationism and subservience to capitalism.

At the convention of Postal and Telegraph Workers the conciliationist policy of the administration was approved by 197 votes against 23, with 7 abstentions. A member of the administration, the internationalist Victor Roux, writes that a large number of convention delegates simply felt personal sympathy toward the union's secretary, the conciliationist Borderes, whose moral worth is allegedly beyond dispute. "I personally acknowledge," says the author, "that he has rendered great services to the organization, in difficult times. . . ." And so on and so forth. (*La Vie Ouvrière*, September 15, 1919.)

Jouhaux, Renaudel, Longuet, Merrheim and the like, irrespective of the "services" they rendered in the past, deport themselves today as an integral part of the bourgeois system and are in reality its most important prop. The whole gist of their activity makes it to their interest to exaggerate before the proletariat any and all concessions of the bourgeoisie, for these after all are the fruits of their class diplomacy. While criticizing capitalism, they paint it up, and their final conclusion, after all their oratorical exercises, comes down to the need of adapting oneself, *i.e.,* submitting to the rule of capitalism.

The chief crime of the summits of reigning syndicalism is correctly seen by Alfred Rosmer to lie in this, that the syndical leaders "have replaced the direct action of the working class by solicitation of favors from the government." This counter-revolutionary tactic, however, cannot be changed by "solicitation" of the social-imperialists of the trade union and political movement. While Jouhaux, Renaudel, Merrheim and Longuet are busy convincing the capitalists and the bourgeois deputies that it is necessary to make concessions to the working class, the genuine representatives of the proletariat cannot waste their time convincing Renaudel and Longuet of the need for revolutionary struggle. In order to throw the capitalist and bourgeois deputies off their necks the working class must throw the Renaudels and the Longuets out of its organizations.

The struggle against them must be conducted not as a family squabble or an academic discussion, but in a way corresponding to the gravity of the question, so that the abyss which separates us from the social-imperialists looms before the consciousness of the masses in all its profundity.

Our task consists in utilizing to the very end the appalling lessons of the imperialist war. Into the consciousness of the masses we must inculcate the experiences of the last period and make them understand that it is impossible for them to continue to exist any longer within the framework of capitalism. We must bring to the highest revolutionary pitch the awakening hatred of the masses toward capitalism, toward the capitalists, toward the capitalist state and its organs. We must make hateful in the eyes of the masses not alone the capitalists but also all those who defend capitalism, those who try to camouflage its pestilential sores, those who seek to mitigate its crimes.

After the unsuccessful demonstration of June 21, Monatte wrote:

> The masses will henceforth know that it is no longer possible to vacillate and delude oneself with false hopes; and that it is necessary to mercilessly purge the personnel of the syndicates. (*La Vie Ouvrière*, June 25, 1919.)

In politics the struggle against false principles inescapably implies a struggle against those individuals who personify these principles. To regenerate the labor movement means to drive out of its ranks all those who have dishonored themselves by betrayal and treachery, all those who have undermined among the working masses their faith in revolutionary slogans, *i.e.*, their faith in their own strength. Indulgence, sentimentality and softness in questions of this kind are paid for at the price of the blood-interests of the proletariat. The awakening masses demand that things be said out loud, that things be called by their real names, that there be no indefinite half-tones but clear and precise demarcations in politics, that the traitors be boycotted and hounded, that their places be taken by revolutionists devoted body and soul to the cause.

Comrade Louisa Saumoneau* paints the following pic-

---

* Comrade Saumoneau is conducting a tireless agitation for the ideas of the Third International; together with Comrade Loriot[34] she stands at the head of the Communists of Socialist Party and not syndicalist origin. There are close ties between Communists-Syndicalists and the Communists-Socialists. Loriot and Saumoneau collaborate on the weekly *La Vie Ouvrière*.—L.T.

ture of the struggle during recent elections to spread the influence of the ideas of the Third International:

> Propaganda which must be conducted among the masses both inside and outside the organizations can always most easily be carried on by us at big public meetings during elections. . . . The resistance to the revolutionary International gets its main support among the old cadres who have so poorly piloted our party's ship during wartime. Our young and ardent comrades who are full of revolutionary zeal must exert themselves and their will power, in order to acquire certain practical habits and attainments indispensable for a well functioning organization. This knowledge is quite easily assimilated, and yet under the present conditions of struggle it serves as a cover for all types of nonentities and serves to render the fatal influence of desiccated living corpses in our organizations. The forces of youth must everywhere inspire the revolutionary class which has risen to fight for the cause of the Third International; they must become intrenched everywhere and must, even if it is necessary to throw them out head first, replace all those who are weighted down with four years' renunciation of the socialist way of life . . .

These words show quite clearly a complete understanding of the necessity, in fighting against reactionary ideas, to throw out head first all those individuals who incarnate stagnation and death in the revolutionary movement.

The bankrupt "leaders" of socialism and syndicalism, yesterday's revolutionists of the phrase, today's docile capitulators, place the blame for their renegacy not upon themselves, but upon—the proletariat.

At the Lyons Convention, Bidégarrey, secretary of the Railway Workers Federation, blamed the working masses for everything that had occurred. "To be sure, the trade unions have grown in numbers. But among the organized, there are far too few syndicalists [*i.e.*, conscious revolutionists]. People are concerned solely with their own immediate interests."

"In every human being," philosophizes Bidégarrey, "there is a little swine, lying dormant."

Rouger, delegate from Limoges, similarly blames the proletariat for everything. The proletariat is at fault. "The masses are not sufficiently enlightened. They join the unions only for the sake of getting an increase in wages."

Merrheim, secretary of the Metal Workers Union, boasts on the speakers' stand about his "tranquil conscience." He, you see, went to Zimmerwald on a supernumerary syndical junket. It was, so to speak, a tiny pacifist pilgrimage, undertaken for the absolution of one's conscience. He, Merrheim, fought. But he couldn't awaken the masses. "No, it was not I who betrayed the working class, but it was the working class that betrayed me." These are his literal words!

The syndicalist Dumoulin,[35] an "honest" renegade of the Merrheim type—a Zimmerwaldist at the outbreak of war but today a worthy comrade-in-arms of General Secretary Jouhaux—declared at the Tours Convention of the Teachers Union that France was not ready for revolution, the masses have not yet "matured." Not content with this, Dumoulin fell upon the internationalist teachers blaming them for . . . the backwardness of the proletariat—as if the education of the toiling masses has its source in the miserable bourgeois school for proletarian children and not in the mighty school of life under the influence of the patrons (the employers), the government, the church, the bourgeois press, the parliamentarians and "poor shepherds" of syndicalism.

The renegades, the cowards and skeptics who have reached complete degradation, keep endlessly repeating the phrase: "The masses have not matured." What conclusion follows from this? Only one: the renunciation of socialism, and, moreover, not temporary but complete renunciation. For if the masses, who have gone through the long preparatory school of political and trade union struggle and who then passed through the four years' school of slaughter, have not matured for revolution, then when and how will they ever mature? Do Merrheim and the others think perhaps that victorious Clemenceau will create within the walls of the capitalist state a network of academies for the socialist education of the masses? If capitalism reproduces from one generation to the next the chains of wage slavery, then the proletariat in its deepest layers carries over darkness and ignorance from generation to generation. If the proletarian masses could attain a high mental and spiritual development under capitalism, then capitalism wouldn't be so bad after all and there would be no need of social revolution. The proletariat must have a revolution precisely because capitalism keeps it in mental and spiritual bondage. Under the leadership of the advanced layer the immature masses will reach maturity during the revolution. Without the revolution they will fall into prostration and society as a whole will decay.

Millions of new workers are streaming into the trade unions. In England the great flood tide has doubled the union membership, which at the present has reached the figure of 5,200,000. In France the number of union members has grown from 400,000 on the eve of the war to 2,000,000. What changes does this numerical growth of the organized workers introduce into the policy of syndicalism?

"The workers join the trade unions solely for the sake of immediate material gains," reply the conciliators. This theory is false from beginning to end. The great influx of workers into the trade unions is elicited not by petty, day-to-day questions, but by the colossal fact of the World War. The working masses, not only the top layers but the lowest depths as well, are roused and alarmed by the greatest historical upheaval. Each individual proletarian has sensed to a never equaled degree his helplessness in the face of the mighty imperialist machine. The urge to establish ties, the urge to unification and consolidation of forces has manifested itself with unprecedented power. Hence flows the surge of millions of workers into the trade unions or into the Soviets of Deputies, *i.e.*, into such organizations as do not demand political preparation but represent the most general and most direct expression of the proletarian class struggle.

Having lost faith in the proletarian masses, the reformists of the Merrheim-Longuet stripe must seek for points of support among the "enlightened" and "humanitarian" representatives of the bourgeoisie. And, as a matter of fact, the political insignificance of these people finds its most annihilating expression in their attitude of reverential rapture before "the great democrat" Woodrow Wilson. People who deem themselves the representatives of the working class have shown themselves capable of seriously believing that American capitalism could place at the head of its state a man with whom the European working class could go marching hand in hand. These gentlemen have apparently heard nothing of America's real reasons for intervening in the war, nor of Wall Street's unconscionable machinations, nor of the role of Wilson whom the super-capitalists of the United States have entrusted with raising the slogans of philistine pacifism in order to cover up their bloody extortions. Or was it perhaps their assumption that Wilson could gainsay the capitalists and realize his program in life against the will of the billionaires? Or did they perhaps reckon that Wilson could with his syllables of priestly exhortation compel Clemenceau and Lloyd George to get busy liberating the small and weak peoples and establishing universal peace?

Not so very long ago, that is, after the sobering school of the Versailles "peace" negotiations, Merrheim launched an attack at the Lyons Conference against the syndicalist Lepetit who permitted himself—oh, horror of horrors!—to refer disrespectfully to Mr. Wilson. "No one has the right," Merrheim proclaimed, "to insult Wilson at a syndicalist convention." What price is the tranquillity of Merrheim's conscience? If his groveling is not paid for by American dollars—and we readily grant that such is not the case—it nevertheless remains the selfsame base groveling of a self-effacing flunkey before the "democrat" made mighty by the grace of the dollar. One must indeed reach the last stage of spiritual degradation to be capable of pinning the hopes of the working class upon the bourgeoisie's "men of probity." "Leaders" who are capable of such politics can have nothing in common with the revolutionary proletariat. They must be mercilessly thrown out. "People who have perpetrated all this," said Monatte at the Lyons Convention of the syndicalists, "are unworthy of remaining the interpreters of the ideas of the French labor movement."

The French parliamentary elections will constitute a sharp line of demarcation in the political development of

France. These elections mean that the intermediate political groupings have been thrust aside. Through the parliament the bourgeoisie has handed the power over to the financial oligarchy, and the latter has entrusted the generals with conquering the country for it; having fulfilled their bloody work, the generals, in conjunction with the stockbrokers, utilized the parliamentary apparatus in order to mobilize all the exploiters and vampires, all those who covet and yearn for booty, all those who have become frightened by the revolutionary awakening of the masses.

The parliament is becoming the political general staff of the counter-revolution. The revolution is coming out into the streets and is seeking to create its own extra-parliamentary general staff.

The elimination within the country of intermediate, middle groupings (the Radicals and the Radical-Socialists) leads inevitably to the selfsame thing within the labor movement. Longuet and Merrheim have subsisted on their hopes in the "enlightened" reformist forces of bourgeois society. The bankruptcy of the latter condemns the Longuet-Merrheim tendency to death, for with the disappearance of an object, its shadow likewise disappears.

The countless shadings from Renaudel to Loriot, from Jouhaux to Monatte, will drop out of circulation within the briefest interval. Two fundamental groupings will remain: Clemenceau and his followers, on the one hand; the revolutionary Communists on the other.

There cannot even be talk of any longer preserving unity, even if only a formal one, in the party and syndicalist organizations.

The proletarian revolution must and will create its own central political staff from among the united Socialists and syndicalists of the revolutionary Communist tendency.

Discouraged and left completely at sea by the Russian

and German revolutions, Kautsky pinned all his hopes upon France and England where humanitarianism, accoutred in the vestments of democracy, would be bound to conquer.

In reality we see that in these countries, among the summits of bourgeois society, power is conquered by reaction of the most monstrous sort, reaction reeling through fumes of chauvinism, fangs bared and eyes shot with blood. And to meet it, the proletariat is arising, ready to exact ruthless vengeance for all its past defeats, degradations, and tortures. The combat will be not for quarter but to the death. Victory will be with the working class. The proletarian dictatorship will sweep away the garbage heap of bourgeois democracy and clear the road for the Communist system of society.

NOVEMBER 20, 1919

9. Jean Longuet

Dear friend:

A fortunate accident and Jean Longuet's courteousness, which has become proverbial, provided me with a stenographic text of a speech delivered on September 18 [1919] by this Socialist Deputy in the French Chamber of Deputies as it was last constituted. This speech is entitled, "Against Imperialist Peace—For Revolutionary Russia!" For half an hour I was plunged by Longuet's pamphlet into the French parliamentary atmosphere in the epoch of the bourgeois republic's decline, and it led me to recall the refreshing contempt with which Marx[36] used to refer to the artificial atmosphere of parliamentarianism.

In order immediately to placate his opponents, Jean Longuet begins by reminding his "colleagues" that never, never did he lose his sense of proportion nor his courtesy before the assembled body. He associates himself entirely and wholeheartedly "with those correct considerations which were upheld here by our colleague Viviani[37] with his wonderful eloquence." When Longuet tries to set to work with his lancet of criticism, the most brazen swashbucklers of imperialism instantly try to gag him by shouts of Alsace-Lorraine.[38] Ah, but urbanity is the outstanding trait of Jean Longuet! Out of considerations of urbanity he seeks first of all to find a common ground with his opponents. Alsace-Lorraine! Why didn't he, Longuet, just say that he himself finds a number of fortunate paragraphs in the peace treaty? "An insinuation has just now been made here concerning Alsace-Lorraine. We're all in accord on this score." And Jean Longuet hides instantly in his vest pocket his critical lancet, which bears a remarkable resemblance to a nail-file.

In his criticism of the peace treaty Longuet proceeds from the same concept of the nation as the one proffered by none other than Renan,[39] that reactionary Jesuit without a God. From Renan who serves to assure a common ground with the nationalist parliament, Longuet passes on to the liberationist principle of the self-determination of nations, which had been "advanced by the Russian revolution and embraced by President Wilson."

"It is precisely this principle, Monsieurs, yes, this noble high principle of Renan, Lenin and Wilson" that Jean Longuet would like to see embodied in the [Versailles] peace treaty. However, "in a certain number of cases (these are the actual words: *in a certain number of cases*) the principle of self-determination of nations remained unrealized in the peace treaty." This circumstance makes Longuet sad.

The courteous orator is heckled; he is called an advocate of Germany. Jean Longuet energetically defends himself against the charge that he is a defender of Germany, that is, a defender of a crushed and an oppressed country, as against France, in the person of her ruling executioners. "My friends in Germany," exclaims Longuet "were those who rose up against the Kaiser, those who suffered years of imprisonment, and some of whom gave their lives for a cause which we are defending." Just what "cause" is referred to here—whether it concerns "the restoration of the right trampled upon in 1871" or the destruction of the bourgeois system—Longuet omits to say. The corpses of Liebknecht and Luxemburg are used by him to fend off the attacks of French imperialists. If during their lifetimes these heroes of German Communism were a constant reproach to all the Longuets, who were shareholders in the imperialist bloc, containing the Russian Czar in one of its wings, then after their deaths they serve most conveniently for gulling the French workers with one's claim of their alleged friendship and for tossing their heroic martyrdom as a bone to propitiate the enraged watchdogs of French imperialism.

And immediately following this operation Jean Longuet addresses himself to "the eloquent speech of our friend Vandervelde."[40] I count: exactly three lines in the text separate the reference to the martyred memory of Liebknecht and Luxemburg from the reference to "our friend Vandervelde." Where life itself has dug an abyss, leaving between Liebknecht and Vandervelde nothing save the contempt of a revolutionist toward a traitor, there the courteous Longuet with a single gesture of friendship puts his arms around both the hero and the renegade. Nor is this all. In order to legitimize his respect for Liebknecht—in the parliamentary sense of the word—Longuet calls as witness His Majesty's Minister Vandervelde who recognized—and who should know this better than Vandervelde?—that two people had saved the honor of German Socialism: Liebknecht and Bernstein. But Liebknecht, after all, considered Bernstein a paltry sycophant of capitalism. But Bernstein, after all, considered Liebknecht a madman and a criminal. What of it? On the footboards of expiring parliamentarianism, in the artificial atmosphere of falsehood and conventionality, courteous Jean Longuet effortlessly couples Liebknecht with Vandervelde and with Bernstein just as he had a while earlier effected a merger between Renan, Lenin and Wilson.

But the parliamentary lieutenants of imperialism are in no haste to take their stand upon a common ground, which Longuet has fertilized with his eloquence. No, they refuse to yield an inch of their position. Whatever may have been Vandervelde's testimonials to Liebknecht and Bernstein, the Belgian Socialists did, after all, vote for the peace treaty. "Tell us, Monsieur Longuet, whether the Belgian Socialists voted for the peace treaty? Yes or no? (Hear! Hear!)" Jean Longuet himself is preparing, in order to belatedly repair his Socialist reputation, to vote against the treaty, whose appearance he had prepared by his entire previous conduct. For this reason he simply does not answer this yes-or-no question. Did your Belgian "friends" vote *for* the infamous, ignoble Versailles Treaty, so utterly permeated with cruelty, greed and baseness? Yes or no? Jean Longuet keeps silent. So long as a fact is not mentioned from a parliamentary tribunal, it is virtually nonexistent. Jean Longuet is not obliged to cite the ignoble actions of his "eloquent friend Vandervelde," so long as he is able to quote from Vandervelde's stylized speeches.

And so . . . Vandervelde! Belgium! Violation of Neutrality! "We all stand united here." We all brand this violation of a small country's independence. True, the Germans issued their protests somewhat belatedly. Alas, such is the march of history. "Only slowly, only gradually," with melancholy, Longuet explains, "does the consciousness of a raped and a deceived people awaken. Wasn't that the case in our own country 47 years ago after the Empire?" Just at that moment the vigilant lieutenants of capitalism prick up their ears lest Longuet say: "Don't our own people suffer your rule up to the present day? Aren't our people deceived, scorned and oppressed by you? Isn't it converted by you into an international hangman? Was there ever an epoch, was there ever a people which was constrained by the will and the violence of its government to play a more ignominious, criminal and hangman's role than is now being played by the enslaved people of France?" At just that moment our most courteous Jean Longuet by merely turning a phrase unloaded 47 years from the shoulders of the French people in order to unmask the criminal clique of oppressors, deceiving and trampling upon the people, not among Clemenceau's government of victory but rather among the government of Napoleon III,[41] long ago overthrown and since far surpassed in vileness.

And here again the deputy's hands wield a harmless little lancet. "You are supporting Noske and his 1,200,000 soldiers, who may on the morrow provide the cadres for a great army against us." An amazing charge! Why shouldn't the representatives of the Bourse (the French stock market) support Noske who is the German watchman of the Bourse? They are united in the league of hate against the revolutionary proletariat. But this question, the only one that is real, doesn't exist for Longuet. He dangles before his colleagues the threat that Noske's army will move "against us." Against whom? Noske[42] strangles Rosa Luxemburg, Karl Liebknecht and their party. "Against us"—against the French Communists? No, against the Third Republic, against the joint state enterprise of Clemenceau-Barthou[43]–Briand[44]-Longuet.

And again, Alsace-Lorraine. Again, "we are all united on this score." Of course, it is sad that no plebiscite was held. All the more so since "we" had absolutely nothing to fear from a plebiscite. Incidentally, the coming elections will take the place of a plebiscite. And in the meantime, Millerand[45] will have had the opportunity of carrying out the necessary patriotic, purgative and educational work in Alsace-Lorraine in order thus to effect by means of a future "plebiscite" a complete reconciliation between Longuet's courteous and legalistic conscience and the stark reality of the Foch[46]-Clemenceau policy. Longuet pleads for only one thing—that the work of purgation be done with a sense of proportion in order not to "abate the profound sympathies of Alsace-Lorraine towards France." A small dose of humanitarianism for Millerand—and everything will be for the best in this best of all possible worlds.

French capitalism has seized the Saar coal basin. Here has been no "restoration of violated laws"; here, not a single case-hardened reporter has been able to discover any "profound sympathies." This is theft committed in broad daylight. Longuet is very hurt. Longuet is very sad. Apart from the humanistic side of the matter, "the coal of the Saar basin, we are told by the specialists, is not of the best quality." Was it really impossible—chides Longuet—to obtain the coal "we" need from crucified Germany, from the Ruhr basin, coal of a far better quality, and without incurring parliamentary difficulties in connection with national self-determination? The honorable deputy is, as we see, not bereft of practical sense.

Jean Longuet is, of course, an internationalist. He admits it himself. And who should know better? But what is internationalism? "We never understood it in the sense of the degradation of the fatherland; and our own fatherland is beautiful enough to have no need of counterposing itself to the interests of any other nation. (Chorus of friends: Hear! Hear!)"

This beautiful fatherland, which happens to be at the

disposal of Foch-Clemenceau, is in no case hindered by Longuet's internationalism from utilizing the superior coal of the Ruhr. The sole requirement is: the observance of those forms of parliamentary symmetry which, you will notice, evokes the approbation of all our friends.

Jean Longuet passes on to England. If in appraising the politics of his own country he advanced the authority of Renan, then Longuet likewise appears on the arena of Great Britain's policy in highly respectable company. Inasmuch as it is necessary to mention Ireland, "wouldn't it be permissible to recall the great statesmen of England: Gladstone[47] and Campbell-Bannerman?[48] Should England grant freedom to Ireland, nothing would stand in the way of the unification of these countries in a federation." Having assured Ireland's welfare through the method of the great Gladstone, Longuet runs up against new difficulties: France herself possesses more than one Ireland. Longuet mentions Tunis. "Allow me to remind you, Monsieurs, that for the sake of France this country has borne the most honorable and greatest sacrifices in the course of the war. Out of 55,000 warriors given France by Tunisia, about 45,000 have been killed or wounded—these are official figures. And we have the right to say that this nation . . . by her sacrifices has conquered for herself the right to a larger share of justice and a greater freedom. (Chorus of friends: Hear! Hear!)" The poor, unfortunate Arabs of Tunisia, whom the French bourgeoisie flung into the fiery cauldron of war, this black cannon fodder, fell—without a flicker of ideas—at the Marne and the Somme,[49] perishing along with the imported Spanish horses and American steers. And this revolting smear, one of the vilest in the whole vile picture of the world shambles is depicted by Jean Longuet as a supreme and honorable sacrifice which ought to be crowned with the gift of freedom. After the feeble and idle chatter about internationalism and self-determination, the right of the Tunisian Arabs to a shred of freedom is treated as if it were a tip to be thrown to its slaves by the sated and magnanimous Bourse, at the request of one of its parliamentarian brokers. Where then are the limits of parliamentary degradation?

But now we come to Russia. And here Jean Longuet, with a tactfulness that distinguishes him, begins by bowing low before none other than Clemenceau. "Haven't all of us here unanimously applauded Clemenceau when he read from the tribunal of this Chamber the clause relating to the abrogation of the infamous Brest-Litovsk Treaty?" On recalling the Brest-Litovsk peace, Jean Longuet loses all self-control. "The Brest-Litovsk peace is the monument to the bestiality and ignominy of Prussian militarism." Longuet hurls thunder and lightning. The reason is rather simple: Parliamentary bolts of lightning against the Brest-Litovsk peace which has long ago been swept away by the revolution provides a very favorable and happy background for the deputy's delicate critical operations on the peace of Versailles.

Jean Longuet favors peace with Soviet Russia. But, naturally, not in any compromising sense. No, Longuet has sure knowledge of a good road to this peace. It is the road of none other than Wilson who has sent his plenipotentiary Bullitt[50] to Soviet Russia. The meaning and content of Bullitt's mission are sufficiently well known today. His conditions represented a harsher version of the Brest-Litovsk clauses of Kuehlmann[51] and Czernin.[52] Included were both the dismemberment of Russia and cruel pillage of her economy. But . . . let us choose a different topic for discussion. Wilson is, as everybody knows, in favor of the self-determination of nations, and as for Bullitt. . . . "I consider Mr. Bullitt to be one of the most forthright, one of the most honest, well-intentioned men whom I have had the good fortune to meet." What a consolation it is to learn from Longuet that the American stock market still disposes of men of probity while in the French parliament there are still to be found deputies who know the true worth of American virtue.

Having paid the tribute of gratitude to Clemenceau and Bullitt for their kindness to Russia, Longuet does not refuse to address a few words of encouragement to the Republic of the Soviets. "No one will believe," says he, "that the Soviet regime could have maintained itself for two years unless it had the backing of the broadest masses of the Russian people. It could not have built an army of 1,200,000 soldiers, led by the best officers of old Russia, and fighting with the ardor of the volunteers of 1793."

This point in Longuet's speech is the apogee. Recalling the armies of the Convention,[53] he becomes submerged in national tradition, uses it as a cover for all the class contradictions, embraces Clemenceau in heroic recollections, and at the same time provides a historical formula to effect indirectly the legal adoption of the Soviet State and the Soviet Army.

Such is Longuet. Such is official French Socialism. Such is the parliamentarianism of the Third Republic in its most "democratic" aspect. Conventionalities and phrases, senility and evasiveness, courteous falsehoods, arguments and tricks of a shyster lawyer who, however, seriously takes the planks of the speakers' stand for the arena of history. Today, when class is openly pitted against class, when historical ideas appear armed to the teeth and all litigation is settled by cold steel, "Socialists" of the Longuet type are an outrageous mockery of our epoch. We have just seen him as he is: he kowtows to the Right; bends curtsies to the Left; pays homage to the great Gladstone who deceived Ireland; kneels before his (physical) grandfather, Marx, who despised and hated the hypocrite Gladstone; lauds the Czarist favorite Viviani, the first Minister President of the imperialist war; combines Renan with the Russian Revolution, Wilson with Lenin and Vandervelde with Liebknecht; slips under the "rights of nations" a foundation consisting of Ruhr coal and Tunisian skeletons; and in performing all these incredible wonders, compared with which swallowing fire is child's play, Longuet remains true to himself as the courteous incarnation of official Socialism and the crown of French parliamentarianism.

Dear friend! It is high time to put an end to this protracted misunderstanding. The French working class is faced with problems far too great, with tasks far too important and far too sharply posed to tolerate any longer a combination of contemptible Longuetism with the great reality of the proletarian struggle for power. We need above all clarity and truth. Every worker must clearly understand just who are his friends and enemies; he must clearly know where his reliable comrades-in-arms are and where the base traitor is to be found. Liebknecht and Luxemburg are with us, while Longuet and Vandervelde must be mercilessly thrown into that filthy bourgeois heap from which they seek so vainly to crawl to the socialist road. Our epoch demands ideas and words of full weight as the prerequisites for fully-weighted deeds. We have no need any longer for the obsolete decorations of parliamentarianism, its chiaroscuro, its optical illusions. The proletariat of France needs the clean, brave air of the proletarian streets; it needs clarity of thought in its brain, a firm will in its heart and—a rifle in its hands.

A definitive settlement with Longuetism is the unpostponable demand of political hygiene. And while I have reacted to Longuet's speech with an emotion for which there is no appropriate label in the courteous lexicon of parliamentarianism, here at the close of my letter I am able to think with joy of the superb cleansing job which the ardent French proletariat will accomplish throughout the utterly bespattered edifice of the bourgeois republic, when it finally proceeds to the solution of its last historical task.

DECEMBER 18, 1919.
MOSCOW

10. On the coming congress of the Comintern

A. THE CONDITIONS FOR ENTERING THE THIRD INTERNATIONAL

I

Social-patriots and their bourgeois inspirers are calling attention to the fact that the leaders of the Third International (or "Moscow," or "the Bolsheviks") confront other parties with dictatorial demands pertaining to expulsion of members, changes in tactic, etc., in the guise of conditions for entering the Third International.

Socialists of the Center (Kautskyites, Longuetists) repeat these accusations in a somewhat weaker and diluted form; they seek to cut to the quick the national feelings of the workers in various countries by arousing their suspicions that someone is trying to dictate to them "from outside."

As a matter of fact, these accusations and insinuations give expression to either a malicious bourgeois distortion or a silly petty-bourgeois misconception of the very essence of the Communist International, which is not a simple arithmetical sum of all the labor and socialist associations existing in various countries, but represents a unified, independent, international organization, pursuing definite and precisely formulated aims through definitive revolutionary means.

By joining the ranks of the Third International, an organization of a given country not only becomes subordinate to the common, vigilant and exacting leadership, but itself acquires the right to actively participate in the leadership of all other sections of the Communist International.

Adherence to the International is not a matter of fulfilling international etiquette but of undertaking revolutionary fighting tasks. For this reason it cannot in any case be based on omissions, misunderstandings or ambiguities. The Communist International contemptuously rejects all those conventionalities which used to entangle relations within the Second International from top to bottom; and which had as their mainstay this, that the leaders of each national party pretended not to notice the opportunist, chauvinist declarations and actions of the leaders of other national parties, with the expectation that the latter would repay in the same coin. The reciprocal relations among the national "Socialist" parties were only a shabby counterpart of the relations among the bourgeois diplomats in the era of armed peace. Precisely for this reason, no sooner had the capitalist generals thrust capitalist diplomacy aside, than the conditional diplomatic falsehood of the "fraternal" parties of the Second International was supplanted by the naked militarism of its leaders.

The Third International is the organization of revolutionary action of the international proletariat. Those elements who declare their readiness to join the Third International but who at the same time object to conditions imposed upon them from "outside," thereby demonstrate their utter worthlessness and insolvency from the standpoint of the Third International's principles and methods of action. An international organization of struggle for the proletarian dictatorship can be created only on one condition, namely, that the ranks of the Communist International are made accessible only to those collective bodies which are permeated with a genuine spirit of proletarian revolt against bourgeois rule; and which therefore are themselves interested in seeing to it that in their own midst as well as among other collaborating political and trade union bodies there is no room left not only for turncoats and traitors, but also for spineless skeptics, eternally vacillating elements, sowers of panic and of ideological confusion. This cannot be attained without a constant and stubborn purging from our ranks of false ideas, false methods of action, and their bearers.

This is exactly the object of those conditions which the Third International has presented and will continue to present to every organization entering its ranks.

Let us repeat, the Communist International is not an arithmetical sum of national workers' parties. It is the Communist Party of the international proletariat. The German Communists have the right and the obligation to raise pointblank the question: on what grounds is Turati[54] a member of their party? In reviewing the question of the entry of the Independent German Social Democrats and of the French Socialist Party into the Third International, the Russian Communists have the right and the obligation to pose such conditions as would, from their viewpoint, secure our international party against dilution and disintegration. Every organization entering the ranks of the Communist International acquires in its turn the right and the opportunity to actively influence the theory and practice of Russian Bolsheviks, German Spartacists, etc., etc.

II

In its comprehensive address to the Independent Party of Germany, the Executive Committee of the Communist International (ECCI) establishes an identity in principle between the German Independents and the French Longuetists. This is unquestionably correct. But, at present, since the question of the French Socialist Party arises more practically, it is necessary, side by side with the basic features of similarity, to establish the dissimilarities as well.

The fact that the French Socialist Party has, as a whole, manifested an inclination toward the Third International is sufficient by itself to arouse perfectly natural fears from the outset. These fears can only be enhanced if one juxtaposes more concretely the situation of Socialism in France with that in Germany.

The old German Social Democracy is now split into three parts: (1) The openly chauvinist, governmental, Social Democracy of Ebert-Scheidemann; (2) the "Independent" Party, whose official leaders try to remain within the framework of a parliamentary opposition at the time when the masses are straining toward an open uprising against bourgeois society; and (3) the Communist Party, an integral part of the Third International.

In reviewing the question of admitting the Independent Party into the Third International, we establish, first of all, the foregoing discrepancy between the line of the official leaders and the aspirations of the masses. This discrepancy is the fulcrum for our lever. As touches Scheidemann's Social Democracy, which with the formation of a pure bourgeois government is today going over into semi-opposition, it is impossible for even the question of admitting this party into the Third International to arise among us, nor is there a possibility of any kind of negotiations with them. Meanwhile, the French Socialist Party is by no means equivalent as an organization to the German Independent Party as the latter is now constituted, since there has been no split whatever in the French Socialist Party, and the French Eberts, Scheidemanns and Noskes retain all their responsible posts.

During the war the conduct of the leaders of the French Socialist Party was not an iota superior to the conduct of the most stereotyped German social-traitors. In both cases, class betrayal touched the selfsame depths. As regards the outward forms it assumed, it was even noisier and more obscene in the French party than in Scheidemann's camp. But while the German Independent Social Democracy has under the pressure of the masses broken with its Scheidemanns—Messrs. Thomas,[55] Renaudel, Varenne,[56] Sembat[57] and the rest continue to remain as heretofore in the ranks of the French Socialist Party.

Most important, however, is the prevailing actual, practical attitude of the leaders of the official French Socialist Party toward the question of the revolutionary struggle for the seizure of power. Led by the Longuetists, the Socialist Party is not only failing to prepare for this struggle through all the measures, open and secret alike, of agitation and organization, but is instead, in the persons of its representatives, instilling into the masses the idea that the present times of economic disorder and ruin are unfavorable to the rule of the working class. In other words, led by the Longuetists, the French Socialist Party imposes passive and dilatory tactics upon the working masses, and instills in them the fiction that the bourgeoisie is capable, in the epoch of imperialist catastrophes, of leading the country out of the condition of economic chaos and poverty, and thereby preparing "favorable" conditions for the dictatorship of the proletariat. Needless to say, should the bourgeoisie succeed in accomplishing what it cannot in any case accomplish, *i.e.,* regenerate France and Europe economically, then the French Socialist Party would have even less reasons, possibilities and interest than it has today to summon the proletariat for the revolutionary overthrow of bourgeois rule.

In other words, on the fundamental question the French Socialist Party, led by the Longuetists, is playing a counter-revolutionary role.

True, in contrast to Scheidemann's party, the French Socialist Party has left the ranks of the Second International. But if one takes into account that this departure was effected without harming the unity with Renaudel, Thomas and all the other servants of the imperialist war, then it becomes absolutely clear that for a considerable section of the representatives of official French Socialism this parting from the Second International has nothing in common with a renunciation of the latter's methods, but is instead a mere maneuver with the object of further deceiving the toiling masses.

During the war, the French Socialist Party opposed itself so vehemently to Scheidemann's Kaiser-Socialism that nowadays not only Longuet, Mistral,[58] Pressemane[59] and other adherents of the Center but also Renaudel, Thomas, and Varenne find it extremely awkward to remain within the purlieus of the Second International, and rub elbows with Ebert, Scheidemann and Noske as closest co-thinkers. Thus the exodus from Huysmans'[60] kitchen was dictated to official French Socialism by the primacy of its patriotic position. True, everything was done to invest this patriotic refusal of immediate collaboration with Noske and Scheidemann with the guise of a gesture dictated by internationalism as well. But the phraseology of the Strasbourg resolution can neither erase nor even mitigate the significance of the fact that the French Communists are not in the ranks of the Strasbourg party majority while it does include all the notorious chauvinists.

The Independent Party of Germany, opposed as an organization to the patriotic Social Democracy, is compelled to conduct an open ideological and political struggle against the latter in the press and at public meetings; and thereby despite the super-opportunist character of its newspapers and leaders it is aiding in the revolutionization of the working masses. In France, on the contrary, we observe in the recent period a growing rapprochement between the former majority and the former Longuetist minority; and the disappearance of any serious ideological, political and organizational struggle between them.

Under these conditions the question of admitting the French Socialist Party into the Third International presents even more difficulties and dangers than the entry of the German Independent Social Democracy.

III

Before the French Socialist Party, insofar as it is nowadays raising practically the question of entering the Third International, we must pose completely clear and precise questions, based upon the foregoing considerations. Only forthright and precise answers, confirmed by the "party," *i.e.*, by the action of its corresponding section, can give a real content to the question of the entry of the French

Socialists and their party into the International Communist Organization.

These questions are approximately as follows:

1. Do you recognize as heretofore that it is the duty of a socialist party to advocate national defense with regard to the bourgeois state? Do you consider it permissible to support the French bourgeois republic directly or indirectly in those military clashes with other states which might arise? Do you consider it permissible to vote for war credits either at the present time or in the event of a new world war? Do you reject categorically the treacherous slogan of national defense? Yes or no?

2. Do you consider it permissible for Socialists to participate in a bourgeois government either in peace time or in war? Do you consider it permissible for a Socialist fraction in parliament to support a bourgeois government directly or indirectly? Do you consider it possible to any longer tolerate in the ranks of your party scoundrels who sell their political services to the capitalist government, or to capitalist organizations and the capitalist press, either in the capacity of responsible agents for the thievish League of Nations (Albert Thomas), or as editors of the bourgeois press (A. Varenne), or as attorneys and parliamentary defenders of capitalist interests (Paul Boncour[61]), etc., etc.? Yes or no?

3. In view of the thievish and predatory violence done by French imperialism to a number of weak peoples, especially the backward colonial peoples of Africa and Asia, do you consider it your duty to conduct an irreconcilable struggle against the French bourgeoisie, against its parliament and its army in questions of world spoliation? Do you assume the obligation of supporting, by all available means, this struggle wherever it arises, and—above all—in the form of an open uprising of the oppressed colonial peoples against French imperialism? Yes or no?

4. Do you consider it necessary to immediately launch a systematic and ruthless struggle against official French syndicalism which has entirely oriented itself toward economic conciliationism, class collaboration, patriotism, etc., and which is systematically replacing the struggle for revolutionary expropriation of the capitalists through the proletarian dictatorship by a program of nationalizing railways and mines under the capitalist state? Do you consider it the duty of the Socialist Party—hand in hand with Loriot, Monatte, Rosmer, and others—to initiate an energetic campaign among the working masses in favor of purging the French trade union movement of Jouhaux, Dumoulin, Merrheim and other betrayers of the working class? Yes or no?

5. Do you believe it possible to tolerate in the ranks of the Socialist Party disseminators of passivity who paralyze and drain the revolutionary will of the workers by instilling in them the idea that the "present moment" is unfavorable for their dictatorship? Or, on the contrary, do you consider it your duty to unmask before the working masses that piece of deception according to which the "present moment," as interpreted by agents of the bourgeoisie, always remains suitable only for the rule of the bourgeoisie? This was so on the day before yesterday—because Europe was then living through a period of mighty industrial boom, which tended to decrease the number of those dissatisfied; it was so yesterday—because the issue was that of national defense; it is so today—because it is necessary to heal the wounds suffered through the heroic feats of national defense; and it will be so on the morrow—because the restorationist work of the bourgeoisie will lead to the provocation of a new war, and together with it will also arise the duty of national defense. Do you consider it the duty of the Socialist Party immediately to undertake a genuine ideological and organizational preparation for a revolu-

tionary assault against bourgeois society, with the object of winning state power as quickly as possible? Yes or no?

B. GROUPINGS WITHIN THE FRENCH LABOR MOVEMENT AND THE TASKS OF FRENCH COMMUNISM

I

In the pre-war years, the French Socialist Party furnished in its leading summits the most complete and finished expression of all the negative aspects of the Second International: a constant inclination toward class-collaboration (nationalism, participation in the bourgeois press, votes for the budget and votes of confidence in bourgeois ministries, etc., etc.); an attitude of contempt or indifference toward socialist theory, that is, toward the fundamental social-revolutionary task of the proletariat; superstitious worship[62] of the idols of bourgeois democracy (Republic, Parliament, Universal Suffrage, Responsible Ministry, etc., etc.); internationalism purely decorative in character, accompanied by extreme national narrow-mindedness, middle-class patriotism and, not infrequently, crudest chauvinism.

II

Revolutionary French syndicalism was the clearest form of protest against these aspects of the Socialist Party. Inasmuch as the practice of parliamentary reformism and patriotism was clothed in tatters of pseudo-Marxist theory, syndicalism sought to reinforce its opposition to parliamentary reformism by means of anarchist theory, adapted to the methods and forms of the trade union movement.

The struggle against parliamentary reformism became transformed into a struggle not only against parliamentarianism but also against "politics" in general, into a bald renunciation of the state as such. The syndicates (trade unions) were proclaimed as the sole legitimate and genuine revolutionary form of the labor movement. Counterposed to parliamentary representation and to the behind-the-scenes replacement of the working class was the direct action of the working masses, and therewith the leading role was assigned to a formless, initiating minority, as the organ of this direct action.

This brief characterization of syndicalism attests to the fact that syndicalism tried to give expression to the demands of the impending revolutionary epoch. But its fundamental theoretical errors (the errors of anarchism) militated against the creation of a stable, ideologically-fused revolutionary core, capable of counterposing itself in action to the patriotic and reformist tendencies. The social-patriotic fall of French Socialism paralleled the fall of the Socialist Party. While on the [Socialist] party's extreme left flank the insurrectionary banner against social-patriotism was raised by a small group headed by Loriot, the same role, on the extreme Left Wing of [the movement for] socialism, fell in the beginning to the lot of a small group, the group of Monatte-Rosmer: the necessary ideological and organizational ties were soon established between these two groups.

III

We have already indicated that the formless and spineless Longuetist party majority has tended to fuse with the Renaudelist minority.

As for the so-called syndicalist minority, which at the last syndicalist Convention of Lyons obtained on certain questions the support of one-third of the total number of delegates, it still represents an extremely formless tendency in which revolutionary Communists stand shoulder to shoulder with anarchists who still haven't broken with their old prejudices, and with the "Longuetists" (conciliationists) of French syndicalism. Within this minority there still exists very strong anarchist superstitions against the conquest of state power, and moreover, in many cases, behind such superstitions there lurks a plain and simple fear of revolutionary initiative, along with an absence of will to action. From the milieu of this syndicalist minority came the idea of a general strike as the means of realizing in life the nationalization of railways. Advanced jointly with the reformists as a slogan of conciliation with bourgeois classes, the program of nationalization is essentially being counterposed as an all-national task to the pure class program, *i.e.*, the revolutionary expropriation of the railways and of other capital by the working class. But the conciliationist-opportunist character of the slogan, superimposed upon the general strike, acts precisely to paralyze the revolutionary ardor of the proletariat; introduces uncertainty and waverings amid the workers and compels them to retreat irresolutely when it comes to applying, in the name of purely reformist, radical-bourgeois aims, so extreme a measure as the general strike which demands the greatest sacrifices of the proletariat.

Only by clearly and precisely formulating the revolutionary tasks can the Communists introduce the necessary clarity among the syndicalist minority, cleanse it of prejudices and of accidental fellow-travelers; and—what is most important—provide the revolutionary proletarian masses with a precise program of action.

IV

Purely intellectual groupings like *Clarté*[63] are highly symptomatic of a pre-revolutionary epoch, when the small and best section of bourgeois intelligentsia, sensing the approach of a profoundly revolutionary crisis, edges away from the utterly rotted ruling classes and seeks a new ideological orientation for itself. Organically inclined toward individualism and toward separating out as isolated groupings on the basis of personal sympathies and views, elements of this type are, by their very nature as intellectuals, capable neither of elaborating nor—all the less so—of applying a definitive system of revolutionary ideas; and they therefore reduce their work to an abstract and purely idealistic propaganda, painted up to resemble Communism and diluted with a purely humanitarian bias. Sincerely sympathetic to the proletarian Communist movement, elements of this type, however, tend not infrequently to swerve away from the proletariat at the most critical moment when the weapon of criticism is replaced by the criticism of weapons—only in order once again to resume their sympathies for the proletariat when the latter, gaining the opportunity, takes the power in its hands and is thus enabled to unfold its cultural creativeness. The task of revolutionary Communism lies in explaining to the advanced workers the purely symptomatic significance of groupings of this sort; and in criticizing their idealistic passivity and limitedness. The advanced workers can in no case group themselves into a chorus for the intellectual prima donnas—they must create an independent organization, which carries on its work independently of the ebb and flow of sympathies of even the best section of bourgeois intellectuals.

V

Side by side with a fundamental review of the theory and practice of French parliamentary socialism, what is needed today in France is a thoroughgoing review of the theory and practice of French syndicalism, lest its obsolete prejudices muddle up the development of the revolutionary Communist movement.

a) It is quite self-evident that a continued "denial" of politics and of the state by French syndicalism would constitute a capitulation to bourgeois politics and to the capitalist state. It is not enough to deny the state—it is necessary to conquer the state in order to surmount it. The struggle for the conquest of the state apparatus is—revolutionary politics. To renounce it is to renounce the fundamental tasks of the revolutionary class.

b) The initiating minority, to whom syndicalist theory assigns the leadership, actually placing it above the mass trade union organizations of the proletariat, cannot remain formless. But if this initiating minority of the working class is correctly organized; if it is bound by internal discipline, corresponding to the implacable demands of the revolutionary epoch; if it is armed with the correct doctrine, the scientifically constructed doctrine of the proletarian revolution—then we shall obtain nothing other than the Communist Party, standing above the syndicates as well as above all other forms of the labor movement, fructifying them ideologically and directing all their work.

c) The syndicates, in which workers are grouped according to industry, cannot become the organs of the revolutionary rule of the proletariat. For such an apparatus the initiating minority (the Communist Party) can use only the Soviets, which embrace the workers in all the districts, the workers of all branches of industry, the workers in all trades; and which for this very reason advance to the fore the fundamental and the most general, *i.e.*, social-revolutionary interests of the proletariat.

VI

Hence flows the iron necessity of creating the French Communist Party which must wholly absorb both the existing revolutionary wing of the Socialist Party as well as the revolutionary detachment of French syndicalism. The party must create its own apparatus, absolutely independent, rigidly centralized, and separate and apart from both the present Socialist Party as well as the CGT and the local syndicates.

The current position of the French Communists, who constitute, on the one hand, an internal opposition within the CGT, and on the other, an internal opposition within the Socialist Party, seems to convert French Communism into a non-independent factor, into a sort of negative supplement to the existing basic organs (the party and the syndicates); and deprives it of the necessary fighting power, of direct ties with the masses and of its authority of leadership.

French Communism must emerge at all costs from this preparatory stage.

The way out is: to undertake immediately the building of the centralized Communist Party and, above all, to establish immediately in the chief centers of the labor movement daily newspapers which—in contrast to the existing dailies—will not be organs of internal organizational criticism and abstract propaganda, but organs of direct revolutionary agitation for, and political leadership of the struggle of the proletarian masses.

The creation of the combat Communist Party of France is at the present time a life-and-death question for the revolutionary movement of the French proletariat.

JULY 22, 1920

III

The Second World Congress

Editor's note

The Second World Congress took place from July 17 to August 7, 1920. The Congress opened its sessions in Petrograd where Lenin delivered his report on the world situation and the tasks of the Communist International. Subsequent sessions were held in Moscow from July 23 to August 6.

Despite the Allied blockade, delegates came to the Congress from Europe, America, Africa, Asia and Australia. In all, 37 countries were represented by 218 delegates of whom 169 had decisive votes and 49 consultative votes. The major reports on the Congress agenda were: Zinoviev's report on the role of the Communist Party in the proletarian revolution (July 23); Lenin's report on the national and colonial questions (July 26); Zinoviev's report on the conditions of admission to the CI (July 29); Bukharin's report on parliamentarianism (August 2); Radek's report on the trade union movement (August 3); Zinoviev's report on the conditions for the organization of Soviets (August 5); and Trotsky's report on the Manifesto at the concluding session of August 7. Among the important discussions was that of August 6 devoted to the question of the entry of Communists into the British Labor Party. The Congress concluded its work by electing the Executive Committee.

The Russian Bolshevik Party was represented by a large delegation consisting of Lenin, Trotsky, Zinoviev, Radek, Bukharin, Dzerzhinsky, Rykov, Ryazanov, Tomsky, Krupskaya, Pokrovsky, Rudzutak, and others. (Stalin was so unimportant at the time that he was not included in the delegation.)

11. Speech on Comrade Zinoviev's report on the role of the party[1]

Comrades! It may seem fairly strange that three-quarters of a century after the appearance of the *Communist Manifesto,* discussion should arise at an International Communist Congress over whether a party is necessary or not. Comrade Levi[2] has underscored just this aspect of the discussion, pointing out that for the great majority of the Western European and American workers this question was settled long ago, and that in his opinion a discussion of this question will hardly help raise the prestige of the Communist International. For my part I proceed from the assumption that there is a rather sharp contradiction between the march of historical events and the opinion expressed here with such Marxist magnanimity to the effect that the broad masses of workers are already excellently aware of the necessity of the party. It is self-evident that if we were dealing here with Messrs. Scheidemann, Kautsky or their English co-thinkers, it would, of course, be unnecessary to convince these gentlemen that a party is indispensable to the working class. They have created a party for the working class and handed it over into the service of bourgeois and capitalist society.

But if what we have in mind is the proletarian party, then it is observable that in various countries this party is passing through different stages of its development. In Germany, the classic land of the old Social Democracy, we observe a titanic working class, on a high cultural level, advancing uninterruptedly in its struggle, dragging in its wake sizable remnants of old traditions. We see, on the other hand, that precisely those parties which pretend to speak in the name of the majority of the working class, the parties of the Second International, which express the moods of a section of the working class, compel us to pose the question whether the party is necessary or not. Just because I know that the party is indispensable, and am very well aware of the value of the party, and just because I see Scheidemann on the one side and, on the other, American or Spanish or French syndicalists who not only wish to fight against the bourgeoisie but who, unlike Scheidemann, really want to tear its head off—for this reason I say that I prefer to discuss with these Spanish, American and French comrades in order to prove to them that the party is indispensable for the fulfillment of the historical mission which is placed upon them—the destruction of the bourgeoisie. I will try to prove this to them in a comradely way, on the basis of my own experience, and not by counterposing to them Scheidemann's long years of experience and saying that for the majority this question has already been settled. Comrades, we see how great the influence of anti-parliamentary tendencies still is in the old countries of parliamentarianism and democracy, for example France, England, and so on. In France I had the opportunity of personally observing, at the beginning of the war, that the first audacious voices against the war—at the very moment when the Germans stood at the gates of Paris—were raised in the ranks of a small group of French syndicalists. These were the voices of my friends—Monatte, Rosmer and others. At that time it was impossible for us to pose the question of forming the Communist Party: such elements were far too few. But I felt myself a comrade among comrades in the company of Comrades Monatte, Rosmer and others with an anarchistic past.

But what was there in common between me and a Renaudel who excellently understands the need of the party; or an Albert Thomas and other gentlemen whom I do not even want to call "comrades" so as not to violate the rules of decency?

Comrades, the French syndicalists are conducting revolutionary work within the syndicates. When I discuss today, for example, with Comrade Rosmer, we have a common ground. The French syndicalists, in defiance of the traditions of democracy and its deceptions, have said: "We do not want any parties, we stand for proletarian syndicates and for the revolutionary minority within them which applies direct action." What the French syndicalists understood by this minority—was not clear even to themselves. It was a portent of the future development, which, despite their prejudices and illusions, has not hindered these same syndicalist comrades from playing a revolutionary role in France, and from producing that small minority which has come to our International Congress.

What does this minority mean to our friends? It is the chosen section of the French working class, a section with a clear program and organization of its own, an organization where they discuss all questions, and not alone discuss but also decide, and where they are bound by a certain discipline. However, proceeding from the experience of the proletarian struggle against the bourgeoisie, proceeding from its own experience and the experience of other countries, French syndicalism will be compelled to create the Communist Party.

Comrade Pestaña[3] says: "I don't want to touch this question—I am a syndicalist and I don't want to talk politics, still less do I want to talk about the party." This is extremely interesting. He does not want to talk about the Communist Party so as not to insult the revolution. This means that the criticism of the Communist Party and of its necessity appears to him within the framework of the Russian Revolution as an insult to the revolution. That's how it is. It was the same in Hungary.

Comrade Pestaña, who is an influential Spanish syndicalist, came to visit us because there are among us comrades who to one degree or another take their stand on the soil of syndicalism; there are also among us comrades who are, so to speak, parliamentarians, and others who are neither parliamentarians nor syndicalists but who stand for mass action, and so on. But what do we offer him? We offer him an International Communist Party, that is, the unification of the advanced elements of the working class who come together with their experience, share it with the others, criticize one another, adopt decisions, and so on. When Comrade Pestaña returns to Spain with these decisions his comrades will want to know: "What did you bring back from Moscow?" He will then present them with the theses and ask them to vote the resolution up or down; and those Spanish syndicalists, who unite on the basis of the proposed theses, will form nothing else but the Spanish Communist Party.

Today we have received a proposal from the Polish government to conclude peace. Who decides such questions? We have the Council of People's Commissars but it too must be subject to certain control. Whose control? The control of the working class as a formless, chaotic mass? No. The Central Committee of the party is convened in order to discuss the proposal and to decide whether it ought to be answered. And when we have to conduct war, organize new divisions and find the best elements for them—where do we turn? We turn to the party. To the Central Committee. And it issues directives to every local committee pertaining to the assignment of Communists to the front. The same thing applies to the agrarian question, the question of supplies, and all other questions. Who will decide these questions in Spain? The Spanish Communist Party—and I am confident that Comrade Pestaña will be one of the founders of this party.

Comrade Serrati[4]—to whom it is, of course, unnecessary to prove the need of a party, for he is himself the leader of a large party—asks us ironically: "Just what do we understand by a middle peasant and a semi-proletarian? and isn't it opportunism for us to make them various concessions?" But what is opportunism, Comrades? In our country the power is in the hands of the working class, which is under the leadership of the Communist Party and which follows the lead of the party that represents it. But in our country there exists not only the advanced working class, but also various backward and non-party elements who work part of the year in the village and the other part in the factory; there exist various layers of the peasantry. All this has not been created by our party; we inherited it from the feudal and capitalist past. The working class is in power and it says: "Now I can't change all this today or on the morrow; I must make a concession here to backward and barbaric relations."

Opportunism manifests itself whenever those who represent the toiling class make such concessions to the ruling class as facilitate the latter's remaining in power. Kautsky reproaches us because our party is seemingly making the greatest concessions to the peasantry. The working class, in power, must hasten the evolutionary process of the greatest part of the peasantry, helping it to pass over from a feudal mode of thinking to Communism; and must make concessions to the backward elements. Thus I think that the question for which a solution has been found that appears opportunist to Comrade Serrati is not at all a question that lowers the dignity of the Communist Party of Russia. But even if such were the case, even if we had committed this or that mistake, it would only mean that we are operating in a very complex situation and are compelled to maneuver. Power is in our hands but just the same we had to retreat before German imperialism at Brest-Litovsk and, later, before English imperialism. And, in this particular instance, we are maneuvering between the various layers of the peasantry—some we attract to us, others we repel, while a third layer is crushed by us with an iron hand. This is the maneuvering of the revolutionary class which is in power and which is capable of committing mistakes, but these mistakes enter into the party's inventory—an inventory of the party which concentrates the entire experience accumulated by the working class. That is how we conceive of our party. That is how we conceive of our International.

12. Manifesto of the Second World Congress

I
INTERNATIONAL RELATIONS AFTER VERSAILLES

The bourgeoisie throughout the world sorrowfully recalls its yesteryears. All of its mainstays in foreign and domestic relations have been either overthrown or shaken. "Tomorrow" looms like a black threat over the exploiters' world. The imperialist war has completely destroyed the old system of alliances and mutual guarantees which lay at the bottom of the world balance of power and armed peace. The Versailles Treaty has created no new balance of power in place of the old.

First *Russia,* and then *Austria-Hungary* and *Germany* were eliminated as factors from the world arena. The mightiest countries which had occupied first places in the system of world seizures found themselves transformed into objects of plunder and dismemberment. Before the victory-flushed imperialism of the Entente there opened up new and vast horizons of colonial exploitation, beginning immediately beyond the Rhine, embracing all of Central and Eastern Europe and extending far to the Pacific Ocean. Are either the Congo or Syria,[5] Egypt or Mexico in any way comparable to the steppes, forests and mountains of Russia and the skilled labor power of Germany? The new colonial program of the conquerors is self-determined: the workers' republic in Russia is to be overthrown, Russian raw material is to be plundered, and the German worker coerced into processing it with the aid of German coal, while the armed German entrepreneur acts as overseer—thus assuring a flow of finished products and, with them, profits to the victors. The program of "organizing Europe," advanced by German imperialism at the moment of its greatest military successes, has been inherited by—the victorious Entente. When the rulers of the Entente place the defeated bandits of the German Empire in the defendant's dock, the latter will truly be judged by a "court of peers"—their peers in crime.

But the victors' camp likewise contains a number of those who have themselves been vanquished.

Intoxicated by chauvinist fumes of a victory which she won for others, bourgeois France considers herself the commandress of Europe. In reality, never before has *France* and the very foundations of her existence been so slavishly dependent upon the more powerful states—England and North America—as she is today. For Belgium, France prescribes a specific economic and military program, transforming her weaker ally into an enslaved province, but in relation to England, France herself plays the role of Belgium, only on a somewhat larger scale.

From time to time the English imperialists allow the French usurers to exercise their arbitrary rule within specified limits on the continent. In this way they skillfully divert from themselves, and unload on France, the sharpest indignation of the toilers of Europe and of England herself. The power of ruined and blood-drained France is illusory, almost burlesque in character; sooner or later this will penetrate even into the brains of French social-patriots.

The specific weight of *Italy* in world affairs has dropped even lower. Without coal, without grain, without raw materials, with her internal equilibrium completely disrupted by the war, bourgeois Italy is incapable, though not from lack of ill will, of fully realizing in life her right to plunder and violate even those colonial nooks and corners allotted her by England.

Japan, torn within her feudal shell by capitalist contradictions, stands on the verge of the profoundest revolutionary crisis which is even now, despite a favorable international situation, paralyzing her flight into the imperialist skies.

And so, there remain only two genuine world powers: *Great Britain* and the *United States*.

English imperialism has rid itself of the Asiatic rivalry of Czarism and of the terrible German competition. British naval might has reached its zenith. Great Britain encircles continents with a chain of subject peoples. Having laid violent hands upon Finland, Esthonia and Latvia, she is depriving Sweden and Norway of their last vestiges of independence and is transforming the Baltic Sea into one of Britain's bays. She faces no opposition in the North Sea. By means of the Cape Colony, Egypt, India, Persia, Afghanistan, she has transformed the Indian Ocean into a British sea. Ruling the oceans, England controls the continents. Her role as a world power is delimited only by the American Dollar Republic and by—the Russian Soviet Republic.

The World War has completely dislodged the United States from its continental conservatism ("isolationism").

The program of an ascending national capitalism—"America for the Americans" (the Monroe Doctrine[6])—has been supplanted by the program of imperialism: "The Whole World for the Americans." After exploiting the war commercially-industrially and through stock market speculation; after coining European blood into neutral profits, America went on to intervene in the war, played the decisive role in bringing about Germany's debacle, and has poked its fingers into all the questions of European and world politics.

Under the "League of Nations" flag, the United States made an attempt to extend to the other side of the ocean its experience with a federated unification of large, multi-national masses—an attempt to chain to its chariot of gold, the peoples of Europe and other parts of the world, and bring them under Washington's rule. In essence the League of Nations was intended to be a world monopoly corporation, "Yankee and Co."

The President of the United States, the great prophet of platitudes, has descended from Mount Sinai in order to conquer Europe, "14 Points" in hand. Stockbrokers, cabinet members and businessmen never deceived themselves for a moment about the meaning of this new revelation. But by way of compensation the European "Socialists," with doses of Kautskyan brew, have attained a condition of religious ecstasy and accompanied Wilson's sacred ark, dancing like King David.

When the time came to pass to practical questions, it became clear to the American prophet that despite the dollar's excellent foreign exchange rate, the first place on all sea lanes, which connect and divide the nations, continued as heretofore to belong to Great Britain, for she possesses a more powerful navy, longer transoceanic cables and a far older experience in world pillage. Moreover, on his travels Wilson encountered the Soviet Republic and Communism. The offended American Messiah renounced the League of Nations, which England had converted into one of her diplomatic chancelleries, and turned his back upon Europe.

It would, however, be childish to assume that American imperialism, beaten back by England during its first offensive, will withdraw into the shell of the Monroe Doctrine. No, by continuing to subordinate the Western Hemisphere to itself more and more violently, by transforming the countries of Central and South America into its colonies, the United States, through its two ruling parties—the Democrats and the Republicans—is preparing to create, as a counterweight to the English League of Nations, a league of its own, *i.e.*, a league with North America as the center of the world system. To begin the job properly, the United States intends during the next three to five years to make its navy more powerful than England's. Therewith imperialist England is confronted with the question: "To be or not to be?" The ferocious rivalry of these two giants in the field of naval construction is accompanied by a no less ferocious struggle over oil.

France—who had reckoned on playing the role of arbiter between England and the United States, but found herself drawn instead into the British orbit as a second-class satellite—discerns in the League of Nations an intolerable yoke and is seeking a way out by inflaming the antagonisms between England and the United States.

These are the most powerful forces working toward and preparing a new world conflict.

The program of liberation of small nations, advanced during the war, has led to the complete ruination and enslavement of the Balkan peoples, victors and vanquished alike, and to the Balkanization of a large part of Europe.

Their imperialist interests have impelled the conquerors onto the road of carving out isolated, small national states from the territories of the defeated great powers. There is not even a semblance here of the so-called national principle: imperialism consists of overcoming national frameworks, even those of the major states. The new and tiny bourgeois states are only by-products of imperialism. In order to obtain temporary points of support imperialism creates a chain of small states, some openly oppressed, others officially protected while really remaining vassal states—Austria, Hungary, Poland, Yugoslavia, Bohemia,[7] Finland, Esthonia, Latvia, Lithuania, Armenia, Georgia, and so on. Dominating over them with the aid of banks, railways, and coal monopolies, imperialism condemns them to intolerable economic and national hardships, to endless friction and bloody collisions.

What a savage irony of history is there in the facts that the restoration of Poland—which was part of the program of revolutionary democracy and which led to the first manifestations of the international proletariat—has been achieved by imperialism with the object of counteracting the revolution; and that "democratic" Poland, whose warrior-pioneers died on all of Europe's barricades, is today playing the role of a foul and bloody tool in the thievish hands of Anglo-French gangsters—against the first workers' republic in the world!

Alongside Poland stands "democratic" Czechoslovakia, selling herself to French capitalism, supplying White Guard detachments against Soviet Russia and Soviet Hungary.

The heroic attempt of the Hungarian proletariat to break out of Central Europe's state and economic chaos onto the road of a Soviet Federation—the only road of salvation—was strangled by the combined forces of capitalist reaction at a time when the proletariat of the strongest states of Europe, deceived by its parties, proved incapable as yet of fulfilling its duty both toward Socialist Hungary and toward itself.

The Soviet government in Budapest was overthrown with the collaboration of the social-traitors who, in their turn, after maintaining themselves in power for three and a half days, were cast aside by the unbridled counter-revolutionary scum whose bloody crimes surpassed those of Kolchak, Denikin,[8] Wrangel[9] and other agents of the Entente. But even though temporarily crushed, Soviet Hungary[10] is like a beacon light to all the toilers of Central Europe.

The Turkish people refuse to submit to the ignominious peace terms concocted for them by London despots. In order to enforce these terms, England has armed and incited Greece against Turkey.[11] Thus the Balkan peninsula and Asia Minor, Turks and Greeks alike, are condemned to utter devastation and mutual destruction.

In the struggle between the Entente and Turkey, *Armenia* has played the same programmatic role as Belgium did in the struggle against Germany; as Serbia in the struggle against Austria-Hungary. After the creation of Armenia—lacking any frontiers and without any possibility of remaining alive—Wilson spurned the Armenian mandate proffered him by the League of Nations: Armenia's soil abounds neither in oil nor platinum. "Emancipated" Armenia is more defenseless today than ever before.

Virtually each one of the newly created "national" states has an *irredenta* of its own, *i.e.*, its own internal national ulcer.

At the same time, the national struggle within the dominions of the victor countries has reached the peak of intensity. The English bourgeoisie, which seeks to be guardian over the peoples in the four corners of the world, is incapable of solving the Irish question under its very nose.

Even more grave is the national question in the colonies. Egypt, India, Persia are convulsed by insurrections. From the advanced proletarians of Europe and America the colonial toilers are acquiring the slogan: Soviet Federation.

Official, governmental, national, civilized, bourgeois Europe—as it has issued from the war and the Versailles Peace—resembles an insane asylum. Artificially split-up little states, whose economy is choking to death within their borders, snarl at one another, and wage wars over harbors, provinces and insignificant towns. They seek the protection of larger states, whose antagonisms are likewise increasing day by day. Italy stands hostilely opposed to France and is inclined to support Germany against France, the moment Germany is able to raise her head again. France is eaten by envy of England and in order to collect her dividends is ready to set Europe on fire again from all its four corners. England, with the help of France, keeps Europe in a condition of chaotic impotence, thus untying her own hands for world operations aimed against the United States. The United States allows Japan to become mired in Eastern Siberia in order meanwhile to secure by the year 1925 its naval preponderance over Great Britain—provided, that is, Britain doesn't decide to measure forces before then.

In harmony with this picture of world relations Marshal Foch, military oracle of the French bourgeoisie, has issued a warning that the next war will begin where the last one left off, namely, with airplanes and tanks, with automatic arms and machine guns instead of hand weapons, with grenades instead of bayonets.

Workers and peasants of Europe, America, Asia, Africa and Australia! You have suffered ten million dead, twenty million wounded and crippled. Today you at least know what you have gained at this price!

II
THE ECONOMIC SITUATION

Meanwhile the impoverishment of mankind proceeds apace.

Through its mechanisms the war has destroyed those world economic ties whose development once constituted one of the most important conquests of capitalism. Since the year 1914 England, France and Italy have been cut off from Central Europe and the Near East; since the year 1917—from Russia.

A few war years destroyed what it took a whole number of generations to create; human labor, expended even to this end, was reduced to a minimum. Throughout these years wherever it was necessary to process existing supplies of raw material into the shape of finished goods, labor was employed primarily to produce the means and tools of destruction.

In those basic branches of economy where mankind enters directly into a struggle against nature's niggardliness and inertia, in extracting fuel and raw materials from the bowels of the earth, production has steadily waned. The victory of the Entente and the Versailles Peace have not halted the process of economic ruination and decay, but have only altered its paths and forms. The blockade of Soviet Russia and the artificial incitement of civil war on her fertile borderlands have caused and continue to cause incalculable harm to the welfare of all mankind. With a minimum of technical aid, Russia, thanks to her Soviet forms of economy, could supply Europe—and the Communist International attests to this before the entire world—with double and triple the quantity of foodstuffs and raw materials that Czarist Russia used to supply. Instead of this, Anglo-French imperialism has compelled the Toilers' Republic to devote all its forces to self-defense. In order to deprive the Russian workers of fuel, England has kept her clutches on Baku, whence she has been able to export for her own use only an insignificant portion of the oil output. The rich Donetz coal basin has been periodically laid waste by White Guard bands of the Entente. French engineers and sappers have labored not little over the destruction of Russian bridges and railways. Japan is right now pillaging and devastating Eastern Siberia.

German technology and the high productivity of German labor, these most important factors in the regeneration of world economy, are being even more paralyzed after the Versailles Peace than was the case in wartime. The Entente is faced with an insolvable contradiction. In order to exact payment, one must provide the possibility of work. In order to make work possible one must make it possible to live. And giving crushed, dismembered, exhausted Germany the possibility to live means—to make it possible for her to resist. Fear of Germany's revenge dictates the policy of Foch: a policy of ever tightening the military vise to prevent Germany's regeneration.

Everywhere there is scarcity; everywhere there is need. Not only Germany's trade balance but also that of France and England is decidedly on the deficit side. The French national debt has grown to 300 billion francs, of which, according to the reactionary French Senator Gaudin de Villaine, two-thirds accrues from embezzlements, thefts and general chaos.

The work of restoring the war-ruined areas accomplished in France is a mere drop in this ocean of devastation. Lack of fuel, lack of raw materials and lack of labor forces create insurmountable obstacles.

France needs gold; she needs coal. With his finger pointed at the countless graves of the war cemeteries, the French bourgeois demands his dividends. Germany must pay! After all, Marshal Foch still has enough black-skinned regiments to occupy German cities. Russia must pay! To inoculate the Russian people with this idea, the French government is expending for the devastation of Russia billions originally collected for the regeneration of France.

The international financial agreement, intended to lighten France's tax burden through a more or less complete annulment of war debts, has not been reached: the United States shows no signs whatever of a desire to make Europe a gift of ten billion dollars.

The issuance of paper money assumes ever greater proportions. While in Soviet Russia the growth of paper money and its depreciation, side by side with the simultaneous development of state-ized economy, its planned distribution of necessities and its ever-expanding payment of wages in kind, signify only one of the results of the withering away of commodity-money economy; in capitalist countries the growing mass of paper money signifies the deepening of economic chaos and an inevitable crash.

The conferences of the Entente travel from one locality to the next; they seek inspiration in all of Europe's vacation resorts. All hands are outstretched, demanding reimbursement in proportion to the number of men killed in the war. This traveling Stock Exchange of Death, which every two weeks decides anew whether France is to receive 50 or 55 percent of German indemnities, which Germany cannot possibly pay, is the crowning achievement of the oft-proclaimed "organization of Europe."

Capitalism has degenerated in the course of the war.

The systematic extraction of surplus value from the process of production—the foundation of profit economy—seems far too boresome an occupation to Messrs. Bourgeois who have become accustomed to double and decuple their capital within a couple of days by means of speculation, and on the basis of international robbery.

The bourgeois has shed certain prejudices which used to hamper him, and has acquired certain habits which he did not formerly possess. The war has inured him to subjecting a whole number of countries to a hunger-blockade, to bombarding from the air and setting fire to cities and villages, expediently spreading the bacilli of cholera, carrying dynamite in diplomatic pouches, counterfeiting his opponent's currency; he has become accustomed to bribery, espionage and smuggling on a hitherto unequaled scale. The usages of war have been taken over, after the conclusion of peace, as the usages of commerce. The chief commercial operations are fused nowadays with the functions of the state, which steps to the fore as a world robber gang equipped with all the implements of violence.

The narrower the world's productive basis, all the more savage and more wasteful the methods of appropriation [of surplus value].

Rob! This is the last word of capitalist policy that has come to supplant the policies of free trade and protectionism. The raid of the Rumanian gangsters upon Hungary, whence they carried off locomotives and finger-rings, is a fitting symbol of the economic philosophy of Lloyd George and Millerand.

In its domestic economic policy the bourgeoisie scurries to and fro between the program of more extensive nationalization, regulations and controls on the one hand, and, on the other, protests against the state intervention which had grown so during the war. The French parliament is busy trying to square the circle, namely, creating a "unified command" for the republic's railroad network without doing damage to the private capitalist interests of the railway corporations. At the same time, the capitalist press of France is conducting a vicious campaign against *"étatism"** which tends to hamper private initiative. The American railways, disorganized by the state during the war, have fallen into an even worse condition with the removal of state control. Meanwhile, the Republican Party has adopted a plank in its platform, promising to keep economic life free from arbitrary government intervention.

That old watchdog of capitalism, Samuel Gompers,[12] head of the American Federation of Labor, is conducting a campaign against the nationalization of railroads which is being advocated in America, in France and other countries as a panacea by the simpletons and charlatans of reformism. As a matter of fact, the sporadic violent intrusions of the state into the economy only serves to compete with the pernicious activity of speculators in increasing the chaos of capitalist economy during its epoch of decline. A transfer of the principal branches of industry and transport from the hands of individual trusts into the hands of the "nation," *i.e.*, the bourgeois state, that is, into the hands of the most powerful and predatory capitalist trust, signifies not the elimination of the evil but only its amplification.

The fall of prices and the rise of the rate of exchange are merely superficial and temporary phenomena, occurring against the background of unchecked ruination. The fluctuation of prices does not alter the basic facts: *viz.*, the

---

* *Etatism*—a word coined in France at the start of state intervention. To convey the meaning in English it is likewise necessary to coin a word in the same way, *i.e.*, state-ization, state-ize.—*Trans.*

shortage of raw materials and the decline in the productivity of labor.

After undergoing the frightful hardships of war, the laboring masses are incapable of working with the same intensity under the same conditions. The destruction within a few hours of values it had taken years to create, the obscene dance of the billions engaged in by the financial clique which keeps rising higher and higher on heaps of bones and ruins—these object lessons of history are hardly helpful in maintaining within the working class the automatic discipline inherent in wage labor. Bourgeois economists and publicists speak of a "wave of laziness," which, according to them, is sweeping over Europe and undermining its economic future. The administrators seek to mend matters by granting privileges to the topmost layers of the working class. In vain! In order to revive and further develop its productivity of labor it is necessary to give the working class the assurance that every blow of its hammer will tend to improve its own welfare and raise its level of education, without again subjecting it to the danger of mutual extermination. It can receive this assurance only from the social revolution.

The rising cost of living is the mightiest factor of revolutionary ferment in all countries. The bourgeoisie of France, Italy, Germany and other states is endeavoring by means of relief payments to ameliorate the destitution caused by high prices, and to check the growth of the strike movement. To recompense the agricultural classes for a part of their expenditure of labor power, the state, already deeply in debt, engages in shady speculation; it steals from itself in order to defer the hour of settlement. Even if certain categories of workers now enjoy higher living standards than they did before the war, this fact does not in any way tally with the actual economic condition of capitalist countries. These ephemeral results are obtained by borrowing fraudulently from the future, which, when it finally arrives, will bring with it catastrophic destitution and calamities.

But what about the United States? "America is the hope of humanity!" Through the lips of Millerand, the French bourgeois repeats this phrase of Turgot[13] in the hope of having his own debts remitted, although he himself never remits anyone's debt. But the United States is incapable of leading Europe out of its economic blind alley. During the last six years, American reserves of raw material have been depleted. The adaptation of American capitalism to the exigencies of the World War has resulted in a narrowing of its industrial foundation. European immigration has stopped. A wave of emigration has deprived American industry of many hundreds of thousands of Germans, Italians, Poles, Serbs, Czechs, who were drawn to Europe either by war mobilization or by the mirages of a newly acquired fatherland. Shortages of raw material and labor forces hang over the trans-Atlantic republic and are engendering a profound economic crisis; and as a result, the American proletariat is entering upon a new revolutionary phase of struggle. America is becoming rapidly Europeanized.

Nor have the neutral countries escaped the consequences of war and blockade; like liquid in connected vessels, the economy of interconnected capitalist states, both large and small, both belligerents and neutrals, both victors and vanquished, is tending toward one and the same level—that of poverty, starvation and extinction.

Switzerland lives from hand to mouth and every unexpected event threatens to disrupt her equilibrium. In Scandinavia the abundant influx of gold does not solve the food problem; coal must be obtained from England in dribbles, begging hat in hand. Despite the famine in Europe the fishing industry is living through an unprecedented crisis in Norway. Spain, from where France has pumped men, horses and foodstuffs, is unable to emerge from a grave food scarcity which brings in its train stormy strikes and street demonstrations of the starving masses.

The bourgeoisie firmly relies upon the countryside. Bourgeois economists assert that the welfare of the peasantry has improved extraordinarily. This is an illusion. It is true that the peasants who bring their produce to the market have prospered more or less in all countries during the war. They sold their products at high prices and used cheap money to pay off debts contracted when money was dear. For them this is an obvious advantage. But their economy has become disorganized and depleted during the war. They are in need of manufactured goods, but prices for these have risen in proportion to the declining value of money. The demands of the state budget have become so monstrous that they threaten to devour the peasant with all his land and products. Thus after a period of temporary improvement, the condition of the small peasantry is becoming more and more intolerable. Their dissatisfaction with the outcome of the war will continually increase; and in the guise of the regular army, the peasantry has not a few unpleasant surprises in store for the bourgeoisie.

The economic restoration of Europe, about which its statesmen talk so much, is a lie. Europe is being ruined and the whole world along with it.

On capitalist foundations there is no salvation. The policy of imperialism does not lead to the abolition of want but to its aggravation owing to the predatory waste of existing reserves.

The question of fuel and raw material is an international question which can be solved only on the basis of a planned, collectivist, socialist production.

It is necessary to cancel the state debts. It is necessary to emancipate labor and its products from the monstrous tribute extorted by the world plutocracy. It is necessary to overthrow this plutocracy. It is necessary to remove the barriers which tend to atomize world economy. The Supreme Economic Council of the Entente imperialists must be replaced by the Supreme Economic Soviet of the world proletariat, to effect the centralized exploitation of all the economic resources of mankind.

It is necessary to destroy imperialism in order to give mankind an opportunity to live.

III
THE BOURGEOIS REGIME AFTER THE WAR

The entire energy of the propertied classes is concentrated upon two questions: to maintain themselves in power in the international struggle and to prevent the proletariat from becoming the master of the country. In conformity with this, the former political groupings of the bourgeoisie have lost their power. Not only in Russia, where the banner of the Cadet Party[14] became at the decisive stage of struggle the banner of all the property owners against the workers' and peasants' revolution, but even in countries with an older and deeper-rooted political culture, the former programs which used to separate diverse layers of the bourgeoisie have disappeared, almost without a trace, prior to the open outbreak of the proletarian revolution.

Lloyd George steps forward as the spokesman for the amalgamation of the Tories, Unionists[15] and Liberals for a joint struggle against the approaching rule of labor. This hoary demagogue singles out the saintly church as the central power station whose current equally feeds all the parties of the propertied classes.

In France the epoch of anti-clericalism, so noisy only a brief while ago, seems like a sepulchral ghost. The Radicals, Royalists and Catholics are now constituted in a bloc of "national law and order" against the proletariat that is lifting its head. Ready to extend its hand to every reactionary force, the French government supports the Black-Hundred gangster Wrangel and reestablishes diplomatic relations with the Vatican.

Giolitti,[16] confirmed champion of neutrality and Germanophile, has taken the helm of the Italian government as the joint leader of interventionists, neutralists, clericals and Mazziniists.[17] He is ready to tack and veer on the subordinate questions of domestic and foreign policy in order all the more ruthlessly to repel the offensive of the revolutionary proletarians of city and country. Giolitti's government rightfully considers itself the last serious stake of the Italian bourgeoisie.

The policy of all the German governments and government parties since Hohenzollern's downfall has been to find in concert with the Entente ruling classes a common ground of hatred of Bolshevism, that is, of the proletarian revolution.

While the Anglo-French Shylock is tightening more and more savagely the noose around the neck of the German people, the German bourgeoisie, regardless of party affiliations, entreats its enemy to loosen the noose just enough to enable it to strangle the vanguard of the German proletariat with its own hands. This is the gist of the periodic conferences and agreements on disarmament and the delivery of war material.

In America the line of demarcation between the Republicans and the Democrats has been completely erased. These two powerful political organizations of the exploiters, adapted to the hitherto narrow circle of American relations, revealed their total hollowness the instant the American bourgeoisie entered the arena of world plunder.

Never before have the intrigues of individual leaders and cliques—in the opposition and in the Ministries alike—been marked by such open cynicism as now. But at the same time all of the leaders, cliques and parties of the world bourgeoisie are building a united front against the revolutionary proletariat.

Whilst the Social-Democratic blockheads persist in counterposing the "peaceable" road of democracy to the violent road of dictatorship, the last vestiges of democracy are being trampled underfoot and destroyed in every state throughout the world.

Since the war, during which the federal electoral bodies played the part of impotent but noisy patriotic stooges for their respective ruling imperialist cliques, the parliaments have fallen into a state of complete prostration. All the important issues are now decided outside the parliaments. Nothing is changed in this respect by the window-dressing display of enlarged parliamentary prerogatives, so solemnly proclaimed by the imperialist mountebanks of Italy and other countries. The real masters of the situation and the rulers of state destiny are—Lord Rothschild and Lord Weir,[18] Morgan and Rockefeller, Schneider and Loucheur,[19] Hugo Stinnes and Felix Deutsch,[20] Rizello and Agnelli[21]—these gold-, coal-, oil-, and metal-kings—who operate behind the scenes and who send their second-rank lieutenants into parliaments—to carry out their instructions.

The French parliament—more discredited than any other by its rhetoric of falsehood, cynicism and prostitution, and whose chief amusement lies in the procedure of thrice reading the most insignificant legislative acts—this parliament suddenly learns that the four billions appropriated by it for the restoration of the devastated regions of France had been expended by Clemenceau for entirely different purposes, in particular for the further devastation of Russian regions.

The overwhelming majority of members of the supposedly all-powerful English parliament are scarcely more informed concerning the actual intentions of Lloyd George and Lord Curzon[22] with regard to Soviet Russia, or even France, than are the withered old women in the villages of Bengal.

In the United States, Congress is a docile or disgruntled chorus for the President, who is himself a creature of the electoral machine, which is in its turn the political apparatus of the trusts—more so since the war than ever before.

Germany's belated parliamentarianism, an abortion of the bourgeois revolution, which is itself an abortion of history, suffers in its infancy from every disease peculiar to curs in their senility. "The-most-democratic-in-the-world" Reichstag of Ebert's republic is impotent, not only before the Marshal's baton of Foch but even before the stock market manipulations of its own Stinneses, let alone the military plots of its officer clique. German parliamentary democracy is nothing but a void between two dictatorships.

The very composition of the bourgeoisie has undergone profound modifications in the course of the war. Against the background of universal impoverishment throughout the world, the concentration of capital has made a sudden and colossal leap forward. Firms hitherto standing in the shadows have stepped to the forefront. Solidity, stability, tendency toward "reasonable" compromises, observance of a certain decorum both in exploitation and in the utilization of its fruits—all this has been washed away by the torrents of the imperialist flood.

To the foreground have stepped the newly rich: war contractors, shoddy profiteers, upstarts, international adventurers, smugglers, refugees from justice bedecked with diamonds, every species of unbridled scum greedy for luxury and capable of any bestiality against the proletarian revolution from which they can expect nothing but the hangman's noose.

The existing system stands before the masses in all its nakedness as the rule of plutocracy. In America, in France, in England, indulgence in postwar luxury has assumed a maniacal character. Paris, jammed with international patriotic parasites, resembles, as admitted by *Le Temps*,[23] Babylon on the eve of its destruction.

Politics, courts, the press, the arts and the church fall in line with this bourgeoisie. All restraint has been thrown to the winds. Wilson, Clemenceau, Millerand, Lloyd George and Churchill[24] do not shrink from the most brazen deceit and the biggest lie and when caught red-handed they calmly go on to new criminal feats. The classical rules of political duplicity as expounded by old Machiavelli[25] become innocent aphorisms of a provincial simpleton in comparison with those principles which guide bourgeois statesmen today. The law courts, which formerly concealed their bourgeois essence under democratic finery, have now openly become the organs of class brutality and counter-revolutionary provocation. The judges of the Third Republic have, without blinking an eye, acquitted the murderer of Jaurès. The courts of Germany, which has proclaimed itself a socialist republic, give encouragement to the murderers of Karl Liebknecht, Rosa Luxemburg and many other martyrs of the proletariat. The juridical tribunals of bourgeois democracies have become the organs for the solemn legalization of all the crimes of the White Terror.

The bourgeois press has openly engraved the stamp of bribery, like a trade mark, on its forehead. The leading newspapers of the world bourgeoisie are monstrous factories of falsehood, libel and spiritual poison.

The moods of the bourgeoisie fluctuate as nervously as the prices on its market. In the initial months following the termination of the war, the international bourgeoisie, especially the French, was shaken by chills and fever from the fear of oncoming Communism. It gauged the degree of its imminent peril by the enormity of the bloody crimes it had committed. But it has been able to withstand the first onslaught. The Socialist parties and the trade unions of the Second International, bound by chains of common guilt to the bourgeoisie, have rendered it their final service by absorbing the first wrathful blow of the toilers. At the price of the complete collapse of the Second International the bourgeoisie has bought a respite. The counter-revolutionary elections to parliament engineered by Clemenceau, a few months of unstable equilibrium, and the failure of the May strike—these sufficed to imbue the French bourgeoisie with confidence in the security of its regime. Its class arrogance has risen to the same heights today as did its fears of yesterday.

Threats have become the bourgeoisie's sole means of persuasion. The bourgeoisie has no faith in words, it demands deeds: arrests, dispersals (of demonstrations), confiscations, firing squads. Striving to impress the bourgeoisie, bourgeois ministers and parliamentarians pose as men of steel. Lloyd George drily counsels the German ministers to shoot their own Communards, following the example of France in 1871. Any third-rank functionary can bank on tumultuous plaudits in the Chamber of Deputies so long as he concludes his inane report with a few threats addressed to the workers.

While the official state apparatus is being more and more openly transformed into an organization for the sanguinary suppression of the toilers, alongside it, and under its auspices and at its disposal, various private counter-revolutionary organizations are being formed—for breaking strikes by force, for acts of provocation, for staging frame-up trials, wrecking revolutionary organizations, raiding and seizing Communist institutions, organizing pogroms and incendiarism, assassinating revolutionary leaders and other similar measures devoted to the defense of private property and democracy.

Younger sons of landlords and of the big bourgeoisie, petty bourgeois who have lost their bearings, and all other declassed elements, among whom the bourgeois-noble émigrés from Soviet Russia occupy the most prominent place, form an inexhaustible reservoir for the guerrilla detachments of the counter-revolution. At their head stands the corps of officers who have gone through the school of the imperialist slaughter.

Some 20,000 professional officers of the Hohenzollern army have formed themselves—especially after the Kapp-Luettwitz putsch[26]—into a strong counter-revolutionary nucleus which the German democracy is powerless to dissolve, and which can be crushed only by the sledgehammer of the proletarian dictatorship. This centralized organization of the old regime terrorists is supplemented by the White Guard guerrilla detachments organized on the Junker estates.

In the United States organizations like the "National Security League," the "Loyal American League" and other "Knights of Liberty" constitute the storm troops of capitalism, at the extreme wings of which operate the ordinary murder gangs in the person of private detective agencies.

In France the *Ligue Civique* represents a socially-select organization of strikebreakers, while the reformist Confederation of Labor has been outlawed.

The officers' Maffia of White Hungary, which exists clandestinely alongside of the government of counter-revolutionary hangmen supported by England, has given the world proletariat a sample of that civilization and humanitarianism which Wilson and Lloyd George advocate as against the Soviet power and revolutionary violence.

The "democratic" governments of Finland and Georgia, Latvia and Esthonia, are striving might and main to emulate this Hungarian model of perfection.

In Barcelona there is an underground gang of assassins, operating under police orders. And so it goes, and so it is everywhere.

Even in a defeated and ruined country like Bulgaria, the officers, left without jobs, are uniting into secret societies, biding the first opportunity to demonstrate their patriotism upon the backs and bones of Bulgarian workers.

The program of smoothing over contradictions, the program of class collaboration, parliamentary reforms, gradual socialization and national unity appears like a grim joke in the face of the bourgeois regime as it has emerged from the World War.

The bourgeoisie has entirely abandoned the idea of reconciling the proletariat by means of reform. It corrupts an insignificant labor aristocracy with a few sops and keeps the great masses in subjection by blood and iron.

There is not a single serious issue today which is decided by ballot. Of democracy nothing remains save memories in the skulls of reformists. The entire state organization is reverting more and more to its primordial form, *i.e.*, detachments of armed men. Instead of counting ballots, the bourgeoisie is busy counting up bayonets, machine guns and cannons which will be at its disposal at the moment when the question of power and property forms is posed pointblank for decision.

There is room for neither collaboration nor mediation. To save ourselves we must overthrow the bourgeoisie. This can be achieved only by the rising of the proletariat.

IV
SOVIET RUSSIA

Amidst the unbridled elements, in the maelstrom of chauvinism, avarice and destruction, only the principle of Communism has revealed a great power for life and creativeness. In spite of the fact that in the course of historical development Soviet power has for the first time been established in the most backward and ruined country of Europe, surrounded by a host of mightiest enemies—despite all this, the Soviet power has not only maintained itself in the struggle against such unprecedented odds but it has also demonstrated in action the vast potentialities inherent in Communism. The development and consolidation of the Soviet power in Russia is the most momentous historical fact since the foundation of the Communist International.

In the eyes of class society the creation of an army has usually been regarded as the supreme test of economic and state construction. The strength or weakness of an army is taken as an index of the strength or weakness of economy and the state.

The Soviet power has created a mighty armed force while under fire. The Red Army has demonstrated its unquestionable superiority not alone in the struggle against old bourgeois-monarchist Russia, which imperialism is endeavoring to reestablish by the aid of the White Armies of Kolchak, Denikin, Yudenich,[27] Wrangel, *et al.*, but also in the struggle against the national armies of those "democracies" which world imperialism is implanting for its own benefit (Finland, Esthonia, Latvia, Poland).

In the sphere of economy the Soviet Republic has performed a great miracle by virtue of the single fact that it has succeeded in maintaining itself during the first three trying and most difficult years. It remains inviolate and continues to develop because it has torn the instruments of exploitation out of the hands of the bourgeoisie and has transformed them into the means of planned economy.

Amid the roar of battle along her illimitable fronts, Soviet Russia has not let slip a single opportunity for economic and cultural construction. In the interval between the crushing defeat of Denikin and the murderous assault of Poland, the Soviet power undertook an extensive organization of labor conscription, inaugurated a more precise registration and application of the forces and means of production, attracted sections of the army to the accomplishment of industrial tasks, and above all, began to restore its system of transportation.

Only the monopoly by the socialist state of the necessities of life, coincident with a ruthless struggle against speculation, has saved the Russian cities from starvation and made it possible to supply the Red Army with food. Only the unification by the state of scattered factories, plants, privately-owned railroads and ships has assured the possibility of production and transport.

The concentration of industry and transport in the hands of the state leads, through standardization, to the socialization of technology itself. Only upon the principles of socialism is it possible to fix the minimum number of types of locomotives, freight cars and steamships to be manufactured and repaired, and to carry on and periodically standardize mass production of machinery and machine parts, thus securing incalculable advantages from the crucial standpoint of raising the productivity of labor. Economic progress, the scientific organization of industry, the introduction of the Taylor system—divested of its capitalist-sweatshop features—no longer face any obstacles in Soviet Russia, save for those interposed from abroad by imperialist violence.

At the time when national interests, clashing with imperialist encroachments, are a constant source of incessant conflicts, uprisings and wars throughout the world, socialist Russia has shown how painlessly the workers' state is able to reconcile national requirements with those of economic life, by purging the former of chauvinism and by emancipating the latter from imperialism. Socialism strives to bring about a union of all regions, all provinces and all nationalities by means of a unified economic plan. Economic centralism, freed from the exploitation of one class by another, and of one nation by another and, hence, equally beneficial to all alike, can be instituted without in any way infringing upon the real freedom of national development.

The example of Soviet Russia is enabling the peoples of Central Europe, of the southeastern Balkans, of the British dominions, all the oppressed nations and tribes, the Egyptians and the Turks, the Indians and the Persians, the Irish and the Bulgarians to convince themselves of this, that the fraternal collaboration of all the national units of mankind is realizable in life only through a Federation of Soviet Republics.

The revolution has made Russia into the first proletarian state. For the three years of its existence its boundaries have undergone constant change. They have shrunk under the external military pressure of world imperialism. They expanded whenever this pressure relaxed. The struggle for Soviet Russia has become merged with the struggle against world capitalism. The question of Soviet Russia has become the touchstone by which all the organizations of the working class are tested. The German Social Democracy committed its second greatest treachery—greatest in point of infamy since the betrayal of August 4, 1914—when in obtaining control of the government it sought the protection of Western imperialism instead of seeking an alliance with the revolution in the East. A Soviet Germany united with Soviet Russia would have represented a force exceeding from the very start all the capitalist states put together!

The Communist International has proclaimed the cause of Soviet Russia as its own. The world proletariat will not sheathe its sword until Soviet Russia is incorporated as a link in the World Federation of Soviet Republics.

V
THE PROLETARIAN REVOLUTION AND THE COMMUNIST INTERNATIONAL

Civil war is on the order of the day throughout the world. Its banner is the Soviet Power.

Capitalism has proletarianized immense masses of mankind. Imperialism has thrown these masses out of balance and started them on the revolutionary road. The very concept of the term "masses" has undergone a change in recent years. Those elements which used to be regarded as the masses in the era of parliamentarianism and trade unionism have now become converted into a labor aristocracy. Millions and tens of millions of those who formerly lived beyond the pale of political life are being transformed today into the revolutionary masses. The war has roused everybody. It has awakened the political interest of the most backward layers; it aroused in them illusions and hopes and it has deceived them. The craft division of labor with its caste spirit, the relative stability of the living standards among the upper proletarian strata, the dumb and apathetic hopelessness among the thickest lower layers, in short, the social foundations of the old forms of the labor movement have receded beyond recall into the past. New millions have been drawn into the struggle.

Women who have lost their husbands and fathers and have been compelled to take their places in labor's ranks are streaming into the movement. The working youth, which has grown up amid the thunder and lightning of the World War, hails the revolution as its native element.

In different countries the struggle is passing through different stages. But it is the final struggle. Not infrequently the waves of the movement flow into obsolete organizational forms, lending them temporary vitality. Here and there on the surface of the flood old labels and half-obliterated slogans float. Human minds are still filled with much confusion, many shadows, prejudices and illusions. But the movement as a whole is of a profoundly revolutionary character. It is all-embracing and irresistible. It spreads, strengthens and purifies itself; and it is eliminating all the old rubbish. It will not halt before it brings about the rule of the world proletariat.

The basic form of this movement is the strike. Its simplest and most potent cause lies in the rising prices of primary necessities. Not infrequently the strike arises out of isolated local conflicts. It arises as an expression of the masses' impatience with the parliamentary Socialist mish-mash.

It originates in the feeling of solidarity with the oppressed of all countries, including one's own. It combines economic and political slogans. In it are not infrequently combined fragments of reformism with slogans of the program of social revolution. It dies down, ceases, only in order again to resurrect itself, shaking the foundations of production, keeping the state apparatus under constant strain, and driving the bourgeoisie into all the greater frenzy because it utilizes every pretext to send its greetings to Soviet Russia. The premonitions of the exploiters are not unfounded, for this chaotic strike is in reality the social-revolutionary roll call and the mobilization of the international proletariat.

The profound interdependence between one country and another, which has been so catastrophically revealed during the war, invests with particular significance those branches of labor which serve to connect the various countries, and puts the railroad workers and transport workers in general into a most prominent position. The transport proletarians have had occasion to display some of their power in the boycott of White Hungary and White Poland. The strike and the boycott, methods resorted to by the working class at the dawn of its trade union struggles, *i.e.,* even before it began utilizing parliamentarianism, are today assuming unprecedented proportions, acquiring a new and menacing significance, similar to an artillery preparation before the final attack.

The ever-growing helplessness of an individual before the blind interplay of historic events has driven into the unions not only new strata of working men and women but also white-collar workers, functionaries and petty-bourgeois intellectuals. Prior to the time when the proletarian revolution will of necessity lead to the creation of Soviets, which will immediately assume ascendancy over all of the old labor organizations, the toilers are streaming into the traditional trade unions, tolerating for the time being their old forms, their official programs, their ruling aristocracy, but introducing into these organizations an ever-increasing and unprecedented revolutionary pressure of the many-millioned masses.

The lowliest of the lowly—the rural proletarians, the agricultural laborers—are raising their heads. In Italy, Germany and other countries we observe a magnificent growth of the revolutionary movement among the agricultural workers and their fraternal rapprochement with the urban proletariat.

The poorest layers among the peasantry are changing their attitude toward socialism. Whereas the intrigues have remained fruitless which the parliamentary reformists sought to base upon the muzhik's proprietary prejudices, the genuine revolutionary movement of the proletariat and its implacable struggle against the oppressors have given birth to glimmers of hope in the hearts of the most backward and most benighted and ruined peasant-proprietor.

The ocean of human privation and ignorance is bottomless. Every social layer that rises to the surface leaves beneath it another layer just about to rise. But the vanguard doesn't have to wait for the ponderous rear to come up before engaging in battle. The work of awakening, uplifting and educating its most backward layers will be accomplished by the working class only after it is in power.

The toilers of the colonial and semi-colonial countries have awakened. In the boundless areas of India, Egypt, Persia, over which the gigantic octopus of English imperialism sprawls—in this uncharted human ocean vast internal forces are constantly at work, upheaving huge waves that cause tremors in the City's stocks and hearts.

In the movements of colonial peoples, the social element blends in diverse forms with the national element, but both of them are directed against imperialism. The road from the first stumbling baby steps to the mature forms of struggle is being traversed by the colonies and backward countries in general through a forced march, under the pressure of modern imperialism and under the leadership of the revolutionary proletariat.

The fruitful rapprochement of the Mohammedan and non-Mohammedan peoples who are kept shackled under British and foreign domination, the purging of the movement internally by doing away with the influence of the clergy and of chauvinist reaction, the simultaneous struggle against foreign oppressors and their native confederates—the feudal lords, the priests and the usurers—all this is transforming the growing army of the colonial insurrection into a great historical force, into a mighty reserve for the world proletariat.

The pariahs are rising. Their awakened minds avidly gravitate to Soviet Russia, to the barricade battles in the streets of German cities, to the growing strike struggles in Great Britain, to the Communist International.

The Socialist who aids directly or indirectly in perpetuating the privileged position of one nation at the expense of another, who accommodates himself to colonial slavery, who draws a line of distinction between races and colors in the matter of human rights, who helps the bourgeoisie of the metropolis to maintain its rule over the colonies instead of aiding the armed uprising of the colonies; the British Socialist who fails to support by all possible means the uprisings in Ireland, Egypt and India against the London plutocracy—such a Socialist deserves to be branded with infamy, if not with a bullet, but in no case merits either a mandate or the confidence of the proletariat.

Yet, the proletariat is being thwarted in its international revolutionary actions not so much by the half-destroyed barbed-wire entanglements that remain set up between the countries since the war, as it is by the egotism, conservatism, stupidity and treachery of the old party and trade union organizations which have climbed upon its back during the preceding epoch.

The leaders of the old trade unions use every means to counteract the revolutionary struggle of the working masses and to paralyze it; or, if they cannot do it otherwise, they take charge of strikes in order all the more surely to nullify them by underhand machinations.

The historical treachery perpetrated by the international Social Democracy is unequaled in the annals of the struggle against oppression. It had its most terrible consequences in Germany. The defeat of German imperialism was at the same time the defeat of the capitalist system of economy. Save for the proletariat there was no other class that could pretend to state power. The success of the socialist overturn was amply assured by the development of technology and by the numerical strength and the high cultural level of the working class. But the German Social Democracy blocked the road along which this task could be accomplished. By means of intricate maneuvers in which cunning vied with stupidity, it was able to divert the energy of the proletariat from its natural and necessary task—the conquest of power.

For a number of decades the Social Democracy had labored to gain the confidence of the proletarian masses only in order to place—when the critical moment came and when the existence of bourgeois society was at stake—its entire authority in the service of the exploiters.

The treachery of liberalism and the collapse of bourgeois democracy are insignificant episodes in comparison with the monstrous betrayal of the toiling classes by the Socialist parties. Even the part played by the Church, the central powerhouse of conservatism, as Lloyd George has defined it, is dimmed beside the anti-socialist role of the Second International.

The Social Democracy justified its betrayal of the revolution during the war by the slogan, *National Defense*. Its counter-revolutionary policy following the conclusion of peace it cloaks with the slogan, *Democracy*. *National defense* and *democracy*—here are the solemn formulas of the capitulation of the proletariat to the will of the bourgeoisie!

But the depths of the fall are far from plumbed by this. In pursuance of its policy of defending the capitalist system, the Social Democracy is compelled, on the heels of the bourgeoisie, to openly trample underfoot both "national defense" and "democracy." Scheidemann and Ebert are licking the hands of French imperialism, whose help they seek against the Soviet revolution. Noske has become the personification of the White Terror of the bourgeois counter-revolution.

Albert Thomas becomes a hired clerk of the League of Nations, that filthy agency of imperialism. Vandervelde, the eloquent incarnation of the superficiality of the Second International which he used to head, becomes the Royal Minister, the confederate of Delacrois[28]—member of the Clerical Party, defender of the Belgian Catholic priests and advocate of capitalist atrocities against the Negroes in the Congo.

Henderson,[29] who apes the great men of the bourgeoisie, who appears on the scene now as His Majesty's Minister and then again as a member of the Labor opposition to His Royal Highness; Tom Shaw[30] who demands of the Soviet government documentary proof that there are crooks, thieves and perjurers in the London government—who are all these gentlemen if not the sworn enemies of the working class?

Renner and Seitz,[31] Niemetz[32] and Tuzar, Troelstra and Branting,[33] Dasczinski and Chkheidze[34]—each of them translates the shameful collapse of the Second International into the language of his respective petty-government chicanery.

Finally Karl Kautsky, ex-Marxist and ex-theoretician of the Second International, has become the sniveling privy counsellor for the yellow press of the world.

Under the pressure of the masses the more pliant elements of the old Socialism have changed their appearance and coloring, without changing in essence; they break away or are preparing to break away from the Second International, and meanwhile invariably shrink, as usual, from every genuine mass and revolutionary action and even from every serious preparation for action.

In order to characterize and at the same time brand the actors in this masquerade it suffices to point out that the Polish Socialist Party, led by Dasczinski and patronized by Pilsudski,[35] this party of petty-bourgeois cynicism and chauvinist fanaticism, has announced its break with the Second International.

The leading parliamentary élite of the French Socialist Party, which is now casting its votes against the budget and against the Versailles Treaty, remains in essence one of the mainstays of the bourgeois republic. These gestures of opposition go only so far as is necessary to regain, from time to time, the semi-confidence of the most conservative layers of the proletariat.

So far as the fundamental questions of the class struggle are concerned, French parliamentary Socialism continues as heretofore to disintegrate the will of the proletariat by instilling into the workers the idea that the present moment is not propitious for the conquest of power, because France is too ruined, just as the situation was equally unpropitious yesterday because of the war; while on the eve of the war it was the industrial boom that interfered, and still earlier it was the industrial crisis. Alongside of parliamentary Socialism—and not a whit above it—there is the garrulous and mendacious syndicalism of the firm of Jouhaux & Bros.

The creation of a strong, firmly welded and disciplined Communist Party in France is a life-and-death question for the French proletariat.

In the strikes and uprisings a new generation of workers is being educated and tempered in Germany. They are getting their experience at the price of victims whose number grows in proportion with the length of time during which the Independent Socialist Party continues to remain under the influence of conservative Social Democrats and routinists who keep sighing for the Social Democracy of Bebel's[36] days, who do not understand the character of the present revolutionary epoch, who flinch from civil war and revolutionary terror, who doddle along at the tail end of events and who live in the expectation of a miracle which is to relieve them of their incapacity. In the heat of battle, the party of Rosa Luxemburg and Karl Liebknecht is teaching the German workers to find the correct road.

Routinism among the summits of the labor movement in England is so ingrained that they have yet even to feel the need of rearming themselves: the leaders of the British Labor Party are stubbornly bent upon remaining within the framework of the Second International.

At a time when the march of events during recent years has undermined the stability of economic life in conservative England and has made her toiling masses most receptive to a revolutionary program—at such a time, the official machinery of the bourgeois nation: the Royal House of Windsor, the House of Lords, the House of Commons, the Church, the trade unions, the Labor Party, George V, the Archbishop of Canterbury and Henderson—remains intact as a mighty automatic brake upon progress. Only the Communist Party—a party free from routine and sectarianism, and closely bound up with the mass organizations—will be able to counterpose the proletarian rank and file to this official aristocracy.

In Italy where the bourgeoisie itself openly admits that the keys to the country's future destiny are in the hands of the Socialist Party, the policy pursued by the Right Wing headed by Turati is to divert the proletarian revolution, which is developing powerfully, into the channel of parliamentary reforms. At the present moment this internal sabotage represents the greatest menace.

Proletarians of Italy, remember the fate of Hungary, which has entered the annals of history as a terrible warning to the proletariat that in the struggle for power as well as after the conquest of power, it must stand firm on its own feet, sweeping aside all elements of indecision and hesitation and dealing mercilessly with all attempts at treachery!

The upheavals caused by the war, which has brought a profound economic crisis in its wake, have ushered in a new chapter in the labor movement of the United States as well as in the other countries of the Western Hemisphere. The liquidation of the Wilsonian bombast and falsehood is at the same time the liquidation of that American Socialism which was a mixture of pacifist illusions and high-pressure salesmanship and which served as a domesticated supplement from the left to the trade unionism of Gompers and Co. The integration of the revolutionary proletarian parties and organizations of the American continent—from Alaska to Cape Horn—into a firmly welded American Section of the Communist International, which will stand up against the mighty enemy, U.S. imperialism—this is the task which must and will be accomplished in the struggle against all the forces which the Dollar will mobilize in its own defense.

The governmental and semi-governmental Socialists of various countries have no lack of pretexts on which to ground the charge that the Communists by their intransigent tactics provoke the counter-revolution into action, and help it mobilize its forces. This political accusation is nothing but a belated parody of the hoary plaints of liberalism. The latter always maintained that the independent struggle of the proletariat is driving the rich into the camp of reaction. This is incontestable. If the working class refrained from encroaching upon the foundations of capitalist rule, the bourgeoisie would have no need of repressive measures. The very concept of counter-revolution would have never arisen if revolutions were not known to history. That the uprisings of the proletariat inevitably entail the organization of the bourgeoisie for self-defense and counter-attack, simply means that the revolution is the struggle between two irreconcilable classes which can end only with the final victory of one of them.

Communism rejects with contempt the policy which consists in keeping the masses inert, in intimidating them with the bludgeon of counter-revolution.

To the disintegration and chaos of the capitalist world, whose death agony threatens to destroy all human culture, the Communist International counterposes the united struggle of the world proletariat for the abolition of private ownership of the means of production and for the reconstruction of national and world economy on the basis of a single economic plan, instituted and realized in life by a society of producers, a society of solidarity.

Rallying millions of toilers in all parts of the world round the banner of the dictatorship of the proletariat and the Soviet form of government, the Communist International purifies, builds up and organizes its own ranks in the fire of the struggle.

The Communist International is the party of the revolutionary education of the world proletariat. It rejects all those organizations and groups which openly or covertly stupefy, demoralize and weaken the proletariat, exhorting it to kneel before the fetishes which are a facade for the dictatorship of the bourgeoisie: legalism, democracy, national defense, etc.

Neither can the Communist International admit into its ranks those organizations which, after inscribing the dictatorship of the proletariat in their program, continue to conduct a policy which obviously relies upon a peaceful solution of the historical crisis. Mere recognition of the Soviet system settles nothing. The Soviet form of organization does not possess any miraculous powers. Revolutionary power lies within the proletariat itself. It is necessary for the proletariat to rise for the conquest of power—then and only then does the Soviet organization reveal its qualities as the irreplaceable instrument in the hands of the proletariat.

The Communist International demands the expulsion from the ranks of the labor movement of all those leaders who are directly or indirectly implicated in political collaboration with the bourgeoisie. We need leaders who have no other attitude toward bourgeois society than that of mortal hatred, who organize the proletariat for an irreconcilable struggle and who are ready to lead an insurgent army into the battle, who are not going to stop half-way, whatever happens, and who will not shrink from resorting to ruthless measures against all those who may try to stop them by force.

The Communist International is the world party of proletarian uprising and proletarian dictatorship. It has no aims and tasks separate and apart from those of the working class itself. The pretensions of tiny sects, each of which wants to save the working class in its own manner, are alien and hostile to the spirit of the Communist International. It does not possess any panaceas or magic formulas but bases itself on the past and present international experience of the working class; it purges that experience of all blunders and deviations; it generalizes the conquests made and recognizes and adopts only such revolutionary formulas as are the formulas of mass action.

The trade union organization, the economic and political strike, the boycott, the parliamentary and municipal elections, the parliamentary tribunal, legal and illegal agitation, auxiliary bases in the army, the cooperative, the barricade—none of the forms of organization or of struggle created by the labor movement as it evolves is rejected by the Communist International, nor is any one of them singled out and sanctified as a panacea.

The Soviet system is not an abstract principle opposed by Communists to the principle of parliamentarianism. The Soviet system is a class apparatus which is destined to do away with parliamentarianism and to take its place during the struggle and as a result of the struggle. Waging a merciless struggle against reformism in the trade unions and against parliamentary cretinism and careerism, the Communist International at the same time condemns all sectarian summonses to leave the ranks of the multimillioned trade union organizations or to turn one's back upon parliamentary and municipal institutions. The Communists do not separate themselves from the masses who are being deceived and betrayed by the reformists and the patriots, but engage the latter in an irreconcilable struggle within the mass organizations and institutions established by bourgeois society, in order to overthrow them the more surely and the more quickly.

Whereas under the aegis of the Second International the methods of class organization and of class struggle which were almost exclusively of a legal character have turned out to be, in the last analysis, subject to the control and direction of the bourgeoisie, who use its reformist agency as a bridle on the revolutionary class, the Communist International, on the other hand, tears this bridle out of the hands of the bourgeoisie, conquers all the methods and organizations of the labor movement, unites all of them under its revolutionary leadership and through them puts before the proletariat one single goal, namely, the conquest of power for the abolition of the bourgeois state and for the establishment of a Communist society.

In all his work whether as leader of a revolutionary strike, or as organizer of underground groups, or as secretary of a trade union, or as agitator at mass meetings, whether as deputy, cooperative worker or barricade fighter, the Communist always remains true to himself as a disciplined member of the Communist Party, a zealous fighter, a mortal enemy of capitalist society, its economic foundation, its state forms, its democratic lies, its religion and its morality. He is a self-sacrificing soldier of the proletarian revolution and an indefatigable herald of the new society.

Working men and women! On this earth there is only

one banner which is worth fighting and dying for. It is the banner of the *Communist International!*

The Second World Congress of the Communist International
(*Signed*)[37]

RUSSIA: N. Lenin; G. Zinoviev; N. Bukharin; L. Trotsky.
GERMANY: P. Levi; E. Meyer; J. Walcher; R. Wolfstein.
AUSTRIA: K. Steinhardt; K. Tomann; Stroemer.
FRANCE: A. Rosmer; J. Sadoul; H. Guilbeaux.
ENGLAND: T. Quelch; W. Gallacher; S. Pankhurst; MacLaine.
AMERICA (U.S.A.): Flynn; A. Fraina; Williams; J. Reed.
ITALY: D.M. Serrati; N. Bombacci; Graziadei; A. Bordiga.
NORWAY: J. Fries; Schefflo; A. Madsen.
SWEDEN: K. Dahlstroem; Samuelson; Winberg.
DENMARK: O. Joergenson; M. Nilsen.
HOLLAND: Wynkoop; Janson; Van Leueven.
BELGIUM: Van Overstraaten.
SPAIN: Pestaña.
SWITZERLAND: Herzog; Humbert-Droz.
HUNGARY: Rakoszy; A. Rudnyansky; Varga.
GALICIA: Levitzky.
POLAND: J. Markhlevsky.
LATVIA: Stuchka; Krastyn.
LITHUANIA: Mitskevich-Kapsukas.
CZECHOSLOVAKIA: Vanek; Gula; Zapototsky.
ESTHONIA: R. Wakmann; G. Poegelmann.
FINLAND: J. Rakhia; Letonmyaki; K. Manner.
BULGARIA: Kabakchiev; Maximov; Chablin.
YUGOSLAVIA: Milkich.
GEORGIA: M. Tsakhaya.
ARMENIA: Nazarityan.
TURKEY: Nikhad.
PERSIA: Sultan-Saade.

INDIA: Acharia; Sheffik; M.N. Roy.
CHINA: Laou Siu-chau.
KOREA: Pak Djinshoun; Kin-Tulin.
MEXICO: R. Allen; F. Seaman.
DUTCH EAST INDIES: Maring.

IV

From the Second to the Third World Congress

Editor's note

The interval from the Second to the Third Congress covered approximately 10 months from August 7, 1920 to June 22, 1921. In Soviet Russia it marked the concluding period of the Civil War, the definitive victory of the Red Army and the beginnings of the transition to a peacetime economy.

In March 1921, the Kronstadt mutiny occurred. After its liquidation the first steps were taken toward the New Economic Policy (NEP). The first trade agreements were made by the Soviet government with England (March 16, 1921) and with Germany (May 8, 1921).

In Europe the working class suffered a major defeat in Italy where the revolutionary movement reached its zenith in the seizure of factories, mills, and estates by the workers in the autumn of 1920 only to be betrayed by the treacherous SP leadership. Another defeat followed in Germany as a consequence of the March (1921) adventure, or the "March action."

Despite the economic crisis which erupted in the capitalist world, the first signs of a temporary capitalist stabilization became manifest, necessitating an abrupt change of tactics by the Comintern on the world arena.

13. On the policy of the KAPD[1]

Speech delivered at the session of the ECCI, November 24, 1920

A programmatic speech, as Comrade Zinoviev has remarked, cannot be delivered extemporaneously; I shall have to confine myself to critical remarks pertaining to the programmatic speech made here by Comrade Gorter[2] for the edification of the Communist International. But first, a few preliminary remarks.

Comrade Gorter didn't simply express the views of his own particular tendency—he excoriated and lectured us, poor orphans of Eastern Europe, purportedly in the name of Western Europe. Unfortunately I haven't seen Comrade Gorter's mandate and so I can't tell whether he was really delegated by Western Europe to give us his edifying lecture. But insofar as I am able to judge, Comrade Gorter's speech is nothing but a repetition of those criticisms and denunciations and formulations which have been offered us more than once in counterpoise to the programmatic and tactical principles of the Third International which are, as everybody knows, elaborated not solely by us—

Oriental Socialists—but jointly with our numerous and ever-growing Western European friends and co-thinkers. Conversely, we can't possibly forget that Comrade Gorter is the spokesman of a very small and scarcely influential group in the labor movement of Western Europe. In order to eliminate any possible misunderstanding, it is necessary to establish this at the outset.

Had I wanted to emulate Comrade Gorter in undertaking an evaluation of revolutionary political views along cultural-national lines, I might have begun by saying that Comrade Gorter reasons not so much after the Western European manner as after the manner of—the Dutch. He speaks not in the name of France or Germany or England with their rich experience of proletarian struggles, but primarily in the name of a section of a small Dutch party which possesses certain virtues of its own but which has thus far been deprived of an opportunity of functioning at the head of great masses in the capacity of a guiding revolutionary force. It partakes more of the nature of a propaganda group than of a combat party. This group contains workers whom we esteem very highly but who are hardly implicated in the sin which Comrade Gorter has so haughtily charged against Comrade Zinoviev (in connection with the latter's speech at the Party Convention in Halle)—namely, the sin of "chasing after the masses." A party which in the course of several decades[3] has gained 2,000 members cannot really be accused of chasing after the masses, at any rate, not of chasing them successfully. But according to Comrade Gorter himself, it appears that among these 2,000 Dutch Communists whom Comrade Gorter educated and together with whom he received his own education, no unanimity was reached when it came to an appraisal of the most important events: during the war one section accused the other of supporting the Entente. Holland is a wonderful country but it is not yet the arena of those mighty revolutionary battles for which and through which the ideas of the Communist International are taking shape.

Comrade Gorter has accused us of being Russian, much too Russian. Of course, no human being is so gifted as to be able to leap over his own head. But we still think that his approach to the question is much too geographic; and that this tends to bring him politically into much too close a proximity with opportunists and yellow Socialists, especially when he says to us: "If the Chinese tried to prescribe methods and forms of struggle to the Russians, you would probably tell them that their proposals smack too much of China and cannot be deemed obligatory by you." Here Comrade Gorter falls into extreme national narrow-mindedness, even if from an opposite direction. From our standpoint world economy is viewed as an organic unity on whose ground the world proletarian revolution evolves; and the Communist International takes its orientation from the entire world economic complex, analyzing it by means of the scientific methods of Marxism and utilizing all the experiences of past struggles. This does not, of course, exclude but rather presupposes that the development of each country has its own peculiar features, that specific situations have their peculiarities, and so on. But in order to correctly evaluate these peculiarities, it is necessary to approach them in their international context. Comrade Gorter fails to do this and this is the source of his cruel blunders.

Thus his assertion, that the proletariat remains isolated in England whereas in Russia it is leading the peasant masses behind it, is a generalization naked in point of form, one-sided, and therefore false. The English proletariat is far from being isolated, for after all England is a world state. English industry and the position of English capitalism depend wholly upon the colonies and, in consequence, the struggle of the English proletariat likewise depends on the struggle of the colonial popular masses. The tasks which the English proletariat sets itself in its struggle against English capitalism must likewise take their orientation in harmony with the interests and moods of the Indian peasantry. English proletarians cannot attain their final victory until the peoples of India rise and until the English proletariat provides this uprising with a goal and a program; and in India victory is out of the question without the aid and the leadership of the English proletariat. Here you have the revolutionary collaboration between the proletariat and the peasantry within the confines of the British Empire.

We Russians find ourselves—in terms both of sociology and geography—on the border-line between those countries which possess colonies and those which are themselves colonies. We are a colony in the sense that our largest factories in Petrograd, in Moscow and in the South were obtained by us ready-made from the hands of European and American finance capital which formerly drew off the profits. That a Russian industrial capitalist was merely a third-rate agent of world finance capitalism—this fact tended immediately to invest the struggle of the Russian worker with an international revolutionary character. Russian workers had before their eyes: on the one hand, the combined money-bags of Russia, France, Belgium, etc.; and on the other—the backward peasant masses, entangled in semi-feudal agricultural relations. At one and the same time we thus had in our country both London and India. This, despite all our backwardness, brought us flush up against European and world tasks in their most developed historical forms.

Our understanding of questions of revolutionary struggle, however, was not gained by us on our national soil alone. After all, virtually from the time we first learned to think, we were handed Marx's teachings which are permeated with the entire experience of the world proletarian struggle in modern times; and with the aid of the Marxist method we analyzed the conditions under which our own struggle occurred. If only partially to atone for our Russian ossification, allow me to recall that many of us participated for a number of years in the Western European labor movement. The leaders of the Russian Communist Party have in their majority lived and fought in Germany, Austria, France, England, America, working there shoulder to shoulder with the best proletarian fighters. In analyzing our Russian conditions and in connecting them up with the march of the world revolution we were not aided by any indigenous Russian theory, but by the theory of Marxism and by the fact that entire generations of Russian revolutionary fighters had occasion to go to the revolutionary school of Western Europe. With your permission I shall only add this, that when Marx and Engels formulated the *Communist Manifesto* they also happened to belong to the industrially most backward country in Europe at the time. But armed with a method of which they were the creators, they based themselves, in evaluating German conditions, upon an analysis of the experiences of the French revolutions and of English capitalism.

Let me repeat: when Comrade Gorter says that in contrast to Russia the Western proletariat will remain in an entirely isolated position, he here touches upon an indubitable difference between the position of the Russian peasantry and that of Western Europe. But concurrently, he ignores another fact, not of a lesser but greater importance, namely, the international character both of the revolution itself and of world ties. He approaches things from an English insular standpoint, forgetting about Asia and about Africa, overlooking the connection between the proletarian revolution in the Occident and the national-agrarian revolutions in the Orient. This is the Achilles' heel of Comrade Gorter.

He holds an extremely confused position on the question of craft and industrial unions. Sometimes it seems that the question, so far as he is concerned, touches only a change of organizational forms. But in reality it goes much deeper than that. Comrade Gorter's entire speech is shot through and through with fear of the masses. The essence of his views is such as to make him a pessimist. He has no faith in the proletarian revolution. It is not for nothing that he speaks so arrogantly of the Third International's chasing after the masses. Of the social revolution Comrade Gorter speaks like an artist-soloist, like a lyricist, but he lacks confidence in the material base of the revolution—the working class. His point of view is individualistic and aristocratic in the extreme. But revolutionary aristocratism always goes hand in hand with pessimism. Comrade Gorter says that we Orientals are unaware of the degree to which the working class has become "bourgeoisified"; and that for this reason, the greater the masses we embrace, the greater is the danger we face. Here is the genuine keynote of his speech: he doesn't believe in the revolutionary spirit of the working class. He doesn't see the great masses of the proletariat beneath the crust of a privileged and bureaucratized aristocracy.

What does Comrade Gorter propose? What does he want? Propaganda! This is the gist of his entire method. Revolution, says Comrade Gorter, is contingent neither upon privations nor economic conditions, but upon mass consciousness; while mass consciousness is, in turn, shaped by propaganda. Propaganda is here taken in a purely idealistic manner, very much akin to the concept of the eighteenth century school of enlightenment and rationalism.[4] If the revolution is not contingent upon the living conditions of the masses, or much less so upon these conditions than upon propaganda, then why haven't you made the revolution in Holland? What you now want to do amounts essentially to replacing the dynamic development of the International by methods of individual recruitment of workers through propaganda. You want some sort of simon-pure International of the elect and select, but precisely your own Dutch experience should have prompted you to realize that such an approach leads to the eruption of sharpest divergences of opinion within the most select organization.

As a result of his idealistic point of view Comrade Gorter staggers from one contradiction to another. He begins with propaganda as the all-encompassing means of educating the masses and later arrives at the assertion that the revolution is accomplished by "deeds and not words." He needs this for his fight against parliamentarianism. By no means unilluminating is the fact that Comrade Gorter was compelled to deliver a ninety-minute speech in order to prove that revolutions are not accomplished by speeches but by actions. Previously he had informed us that the masses can be prepared for actions by propaganda, *i.e.*, again, mind you, by speeches. But the whole gist of the matter is this, that Comrade Gorter wants a select group of agitators, propagandists and writers, who remain undefiled by such vulgar activities as parliamentary elections, or by participation in the life of trade unions, but who through impeccable speeches and articles keep on "educating" the masses until they become capable of accomplishing the Communist revolution. This approach, I repeat, is utterly permeated with individualism.

Absolutely false and anti-revolutionary at bottom is Comrade Gorter's assertion that the Western European working class has become bourgeoisified as a whole. If such were the case, it would be tantamount to a death sentence for all our expectations and hopes. To engage in a struggle against the capitalist colossus which has succeeded in bourgeoisifying the proletariat when one's entire equipment consists of propaganda by a select handful—that is a hopeless utopia. In reality, it is only the labor aristocracy, although rather large numerically, that has become bourgeoisified, and not the working class as a whole.

Let us take the trade unions. Before the war they numbered two to three millions in Germany and in England; approximately 300,000 in France and so on. Today they embrace some eight to nine millions in Germany and England and more than two millions in France, and so on. How can we seek to exercise influence over the masses separate and apart from these powerful organizations into which, thanks to the upheavals of war, fresh millions have been drawn? Comrade Gorter points out that many more workers remain outside the framework of the unions than are contained within them. In general, this is quite correct. But just how does Comrade Gorter hope to reach these most backward layers who even under the influence of the greatest war convulsions failed to join the organized economic struggle of the working class? Or does he perhaps think that only the bourgeoisified proletarians streamed into the unions, whereas the pure ones refused to cross the threshold of the unions? This would be the height of innocence! In addition to hundreds of thousands of privileged and corrupted workers, the unions have been entered by millions of the most militant and class-conscious elements, separate and apart from whom we can never find the road to the most backward, oppressed and ignorant layers of the proletariat. The creation of Communist nuclei within the trade unions signifies that our party is rooting itself in the most active, the most class-conscious and, therefore, the most easily accessible—to us—section of the working class. Whoever fails to understand this; whoever fails to see the proletarian masses within the trade unions on account of the crust of the labor bureaucracy and the privileged layer; whoever wants to engage in actions by going over the heads of the unions—whoever does this, incurs the risk of remaining a prophet in the wilderness.

Comrade Gorter looks upon trade unions and parliamentarianism as supra-historical categories, as magnitudes that are given once and for all. And since the utilization of the trade unions and of parliamentarianism by the Social Democracy failed to lead to revolution, therefore Comrade Gorter proposes that we turn our backs upon the trade unions and parliamentarianism, not noticing that he thereby is, at the given moment, turning his own back upon the working class itself.

As a matter of fact, the Social Democracy—from whom we broke by breaking with the Second International—marked a certain epoch in the development of the working class. This was not the epoch of revolution but the epoch of reform. Future historians, comparing the bourgeoisie's course of evolution with that of the proletariat, may say that the working class, too, had a reformation of its own.

What was the gist of the bourgeois Reformation? At the dawn of its independent historical action, the bourgeoisie did not immediately set itself the task of conquering power but sought instead to secure for itself, within the framework of feudal society, living conditions most comfortable and best suited to its needs. It proceeded to enlarge the framework of the feudal state, to alter its forms and to transform it into a bureaucratic monarchy. It transfigured religion, personalizing the latter, that is, adapting religion to bourgeois conformities. In these tendencies we find expressed the relative historical weakness of the bourgeoisie. After securing these positions for itself, the bourgeoisie went on to the struggle for power. Social Democracy proved incapable of translating Marxism into social-revolutionary action. The role of the Social Democracy dwindled to an attempt to utilize bourgeois society and the bourgeois state in the interests of the working masses. The goal of the conquest of power, although formally set forth, exercised virtually no effect upon the actual practice. Activities were not directed toward the revolutionary utilization of parliamentarianism but toward adapting the working class to bourgeois democracy. This adaptation of a proletariat not yet fully conscious of its own strength to the social, state and ideological forms of bourgeois society was apparently a historically inevitable process, but it was just that and nothing more, that is, a historical process delimited by the given conditions of a given epoch. This epoch of proletarian reformation gave birth to a special apparatus of a labor bureaucracy with special mental habits of its own, with its own routine, pinch-penny ideas, chameleon-like capacity for adaptation, and predisposition to myopia. Comrade Gorter identifies this bureaucratic apparatus with the proletarian masses upon whose backs this apparatus has climbed. Hence flow his idealistic illusions. His thinking is not materialistic, non-historical. He understands the reciprocal relations neither between the class and the temporary historical apparatuses, nor between the past epoch and the present. Comrade Gorter proclaims that the trade unions are bankrupt; that the Social Democracy is bankrupt; that

Communism is bankrupt and the working class is bourgeoisified. According to him we must begin anew and start off with—the head, *i.e.,* with select groups, who separate and apart from the old forms of organization will carry unadulterated truth to the proletariat, scrub it clean of all bourgeois prejudices and, finally, spruce it up for the proletarian revolution. As I have already said, idealistic arrogance of this type is the obverse side of profoundest skepticism.

And today, in relation to the epoch in which we live and particularly in relation to the German revolution, Comrade Gorter retains intact all the peculiarities of his anti-materialistic, anti-dialectical, anti-historical thinking. In Germany the revolution has endured for two years. We observe in it shifts of certain groupings, moods, methods, and so on. These shifts follow an inner logic of their own which can and must be foreseen and which we, on the basis of our analysis and experience, did foresee and did forecast. Meanwhile, Comrade Gorter lacks the least ground for an attempt either to prove or even to claim that the viewpoint he represents is making systematic and planful headway in Germany and is increasing its influence by becoming enriched with the experiences of the revolution.

Comrade Gorter refers with supreme contempt to the split in the ranks of the Independent German Social Democracy. For him this is an episode amongst opportunist and petty-bourgeois babblers, unworthy of his notice. But this only corroborates how completely superficial his viewpoint is. For, back in its formative days and prior to its formal foundation, the Communist International foresaw, in the person of its theoreticians, both the inevitable growth of the Independent Party as well as its subsequent degeneration and split. For us this split is no hollow episode but a highly significant phase in the revolutionary development of the German proletariat. We forecast it at the beginning of the revolution. We had our attention fixed on it. We prepared it side by side with the German Communists. Now we have attained it. The creation of a unified Communist Party in Germany is not a hollow episode but a historical event of the greatest importance. Leaving everything else aside for the moment, this fact has once again demonstrated the correctness of our historical prognosis and of our tactics. In making his formal propagandistic, rationalistic speeches, Comrade Gorter should have thought ten times before pronouncing an anathema against that tendency which is growing up together with the revolution, which is able to foresee its own tomorrow and the day after tomorrow, which is setting itself clear goals and knows how to achieve them. But let us return to parliamentarianism.

Comrade Gorter tells us: "You Orientals are inexperienced in questions of bourgeois-democratic politics and culture; you haven't got a clear and full picture of what parliament and parliamentarianism signify to the labor movement." And for the sake of enlightening us, even if only partially, Comrade Gorter explains to us the corrupting influence of parliamentary reformism. Now, if the limited intelligence of Orientals is generally incapable of orientation upon these questions, it is a waste of time even to discuss with us. But I am very much afraid that what is being uttered through the lips of Comrade Gorter is not at all the latest word of Western European revolutionary thought, but only one side of it: conservative narrow-mindedness. Naturally, the *Communist Manifesto* seemed in its day, and even seems today to many French and British "Socialists," to be a product of German cultural and political backwardness. No, the argument from the terrestrial meridian doesn't carry sufficient weight. Although we are now engaged in a discussion at the meridian of Moscow, we nevertheless consider ourselves to be participants in the world experiences of the working class; we know—and our knowledge comes not from books alone—about the epoch of the struggle between reformism and Marxism in the world labor movement; we have closely and critically followed Social-Democratic parliamentarianism in a whole number of countries and we have a sufficiently clear picture of its place in the development of the working class.

The hearts of workers—according to Comrade Gorter—are far too filled with a slavish worship of parliamentarianism. This is true. But one ought to add that in the hearts of certain ideologists this slavish worship is supplemented by a mystical fear of parliamentarianism. Comrade Gorter thinks that if he keeps a kilometer away from the buildings of parliament that thereby the workers' slavish worship of parliamentarianism will be weakened or destroyed. Such a tactic rests on idealistic superstitions and not upon realities. The Communist point of view approaches parliamentarianism in its connection with all other political relations, without turning parliamentarianism into a fetish either in a positive or negative sense. The parliament is the instrumentality whereby the masses are politically deceived and benumbed, whereby prejudices are spread and illusions of political democracy maintained, and so on and so forth. No one disputes all this. But does the parliament stand secluded by itself in this respect? Isn't petty-bourgeois poison being spread by the columns of the daily newspapers, and, first and foremost, by the Social-Democratic dailies? And oughtn't we perhaps on this account refrain from utilizing the press as an instrument of extending Communist influence among the masses?

Or does the mere fact that Comrade Gorter's group turns its back upon the parliament suffice to discredit parliamentarianism? Were this the case it would signify that the idea of the Communist revolution, as represented by Comrade Gorter's group, is cherished by the masses above everything else. But in that case the proletariat would naturally disperse the parliament without much ado and take power into its own hands. But such is not the case. Comrade Gorter himself, far from denying, on the contrary grotesquely exaggerates the masses' respect and slavish worship of parliamentarianism. Yet what conclusion does he draw? That it is necessary to preserve the "purity" of his own group, *i.e.,* sect. In the final analysis Comrade Gorter's arguments against parliamentarianism can be leveled against all forms and methods of the proletarian class struggle, inasmuch as all of these forms and methods have been deeply infected with opportunism, reformism and nationalism. Warring against the utilization of trade unions and parliamentarianism, Comrade Gorter ignores the difference between the Third International and the Second International, the difference between Communism and Social Democracy; and, what is most important, he fails to grasp the difference between two specific historic epochs and two specific world situations.

Comrade Gorter admits, incidentally, that prior to the revolution Liebknecht's parliamentary speeches were of great significance. But, says he, once the revolution starts, parliamentarianism loses all meaning. Unfortunately Comrade Gorter does not explain to us just what revolution he is talking about. Liebknecht made his speeches in the Reichstag on the eve of the bourgeois revolution. Today in Germany both the bourgeois government and the country are heading for the proletarian revolution.

In France the bourgeois revolution took place long

ago, but the proletarian revolution has still not arrived and there is no guarantee that it will arrive tomorrow, or next week or even next year. Comrade Gorter admits, as we all heard, that the utilization of parliamentarianism is admissible and advantageous prior to the revolution. Splendid! But after all, Germany as well as France as well as England—alas!—all civilized countries of the world in general haven't yet entered the proletarian revolution. We are living through an epoch preparatory to the revolution. If in the period prior to the revolution Liebknecht's parliamentary speeches could possess a revolutionary significance, why does Comrade Gorter reject parliamentarianism for the current preparatory epoch? Or is he overlooking the difference between the bourgeois and proletarian revolution in Germany? Has he failed to notice an interval of two years between them, an interval which may even last much longer? Comrade Gorter obviously suffers here from an incompleteness of thought, which results in contradictions. Apparently he reckons that since Germany has entered "in general" into a period of revolution, therefore it is necessary to reject parliamentarianism "in general." But if so, then what about France? Only idealistic prejudices could prompt us to renounce the parliamentary tribunal which we can and must utilize precisely in order to dispel the superstitions of parliamentarianism and bourgeois democracy among the workers.

It is entirely possible that each parliamentary utterance of Liebknecht had a much larger audience in pre-revolutionary Germany than it might have found today. I readily admit that in general parliamentary speeches, even the most revolutionary ones, cannot in an epoch of impending revolution exert the same influence as they did or could exert several years ago, in the hour of militarism's supreme domination. It is not at all our contention that parliamentarianism always and everywhere has one and the same significance. On the contrary, parliamentarianism and its place in the struggle of the proletariat must invariably be evaluated from the standpoint of the concrete conditions of time and place. But precisely for this reason, a wholesale denial of parliamentarianism is sheer superstition. In the long run, as like two peas in a pod, so such a denial resembles a virtuous man's dread of walking the streets lest his virtue be subjected to temptation. If you are a revolutionist and a Communist, working under the genuine leadership and control of a centralized proletarian party, then you are able to function in a trade union, or at the front, or on a newspaper, or on the barricade, or in the parliament; and you will always be true to yourself, true to what you must be—not a parliamentarian, nor a newspaper hack, nor a trade unionist, but a revolutionary Communist who utilizes all paths, means and methods for the sake of the social revolution.

Finally we come to Comrade Gorter's last chapter, "The Masses and the Leaders." On this question his idealism and formalism are no less clearly expressed than on all other questions. "Don't chase after the great masses," Comrade Gorter lectures us. "It is better to have a smaller number, but of good comrades."

In this form, the prescription is worthless. In the first place, the example of Holland, and elsewhere as well, shows us that an organization with a small and strictly vacuum-packed membership is not at all safeguarded from ideological vacillations, but, on the contrary, is more subject to them, inasmuch as organizations of the sectarian type cannot possess the necessary stability. Second—and this is most important—it is impermissible to forget that our goal is nothing short of the revolution. But only a mass organization can lead the revolution.

Gorter's struggle against the "leader cult" is of a purely idealistic, almost verbalistic character; and, furthermore, he stumbles into contradictions at every step. He says that we don't need leaders, that the center of gravity must be shifted over to the masses. But on the other hand he also warns us: don't chase after the masses! The bond between the party and the class is fixed—according to Gorter—through a purely pedagogic interrelation between a small propaganda society and the proletariat infected with bourgeoisification. But it is precisely in organizations of this sort, organizations where the fear of the masses reigns, where there is no confidence in the masses, where members are recruited individually through propaganda, where activities are conducted not on the basis of the class struggle but on the basis of idealistic enlightenment—it is precisely within such organizations that the leaders are bound to play a disproportionate role. I don't have to adduce examples. Comrade Gorter can bethink himself of not a few. (Shouts: The German Communist Party!) The history of the German Communist Party is much too recent. It has as yet led far too few masses behind it to enable anyone to adequately determine on the basis of actual experience the interrelationship between the masses and the leaders. Only now, only after the split in the Independent Socialist Party, which has taken place thanks to the work of the Communist Party (and despite its unquestionable isolated mistakes on which you harp so much), only now is a new epoch beginning in the life of the German proletariat and of German Communism. The education of the masses and the selection of the leaders, the development of the self-action of the masses and the establishment of a corresponding control over the leaders—all these are mutually connected and mutually conditioned phenomena and processes. I don't know of any prescription by means of which it would be possible to artificially transfer the center of gravity from the leaders to the masses. Gorter points to propaganda by the select. Let us grant this for a moment. However, until this propaganda has seized hold of the masses, and has raised them, the center of gravity will obviously remain with those who conduct this propaganda, *i.e.*, the initiators or the leaders. Time after time in the struggle against leaders, we find expressed in a demagogic form the struggle against ideas and methods, represented by certain leaders. If these ideas and methods are correct, then the influence of these particular leaders amounts to the influence of correct methods and correct ideas; whereas those individuals who are incapable of conquering the masses invariably step to the fore as spokesmen for the masses. Generally speaking, the relationship between the leaders and the masses is conditioned by the cultural and political level of the working class; and it is contingent upon the extent of revolutionary traditions and habits of mass action, as well as upon how large a layer of the proletariat has gone through the school of class organization and Marxist education. The problem of "leaders and masses" has no independent existence. By extending the scope of its ideological influence, by penetrating into all the fields of proletarian life and struggle, by drawing ever-broader labor masses into active struggle under the banner of the revolution—the Communist Party thereby extends and deepens the self-action of the working masses; and without in any way depreciating the role of the leaders, but, on the contrary, raising it to heights unprecedented in history. This entire process, however, tends to bind up this role ever more closely with the self-action of the masses and subordinates the leaders to the organized and conscious control of the masses.

Comrade Gorter says that it is impossible to start the revolution until the leaders have raised the intellectual level of the working class to the point where the latter completely grasps its historical task. This is simon-pure idealism! The situation is depicted as if the starting moment of the revolution actually depended solely upon the degree of the proletariat's enlightenment and not upon a whole series of other factors—both domestic and international, both economic and political, and, in particular, the effect of privations upon the most disinherited toiling masses. For the privations of the masses remain—with Comrade Gorter's permission—the most important mainspring of the proletarian revolution. It may very well be that with the further worsening of Europe's economic position, the revolution may erupt in Holland at a moment when the Dutch Communist Party still represents only a group, few in numbers. Plunged into the revolutionary maelstrom, the Dutch workers will not pause to inquire whether they oughtn't wait until the Communist Party succeeds in training them to the point where they are able to participate in events most consciously and planfully. It is quite probable that England will enter the epoch of proletarian revolution with a Communist Party still comparatively small. One can do nothing about it, because the propaganda of Communist ideas is not the sole factor in history. The only conclusion that flows from this is: that the working class of England—if through the criss-crossing of major historical causes it finds itself in the near future already drawn into an unfolding proletarian revolution—will have to create, expand and consolidate its mass party in the very course of the struggle for power and in the period immediately following the conquest of power; while, during the initial phase of the revolution, the numerically small Communist Party will—without tearing itself away from the mainstream of the movement, and by taking into account the existing organizational level of the proletariat and its degree of class-consciousness—seek to introduce the maximum of Communist consciousness into the actually unfolding revolution.

But let us return to Germany. When the epoch of revolution began, the German proletariat found itself without a combat party organization at its head. The working class was compelled to build its genuine revolutionary party in the very course of open struggle. Hence—the extremely protracted character of this struggle, and its toll of great sacrifices. What do we observe in Germany? A whole series of offensives followed by retreats, of uprisings followed by defeats; transitions from attack to defense, and throughout: critical self-analysis, self-purification, splits, reevaluations of leaders and of methods, new splits and new unifications.

In this crucible of struggle, and on the anvil of revolutionary experiences never before equaled, a genuine Communist Party is being forged. A contemptuous attitude toward this process as if it were a tussle among "leaders" or a family squabble among opportunists etc.—such an attitude is proof of extreme nearsightedness, not to say blindness. When you see how the German working class permitted its "leaders"—the Scheidemanns, Eberts and others—to enslave it for the glory of imperialism; and how, later, the great masses broke with their imperialist leaders and, seeking a new orientation, created temporary conditions favorable for the growing influence of the Kautskys and the Hilferdings;[5] and how, still later, the best and most militant section among these masses created the Communist Party, numerically small at the outset, but calmly and correctly banking upon the continuing process of the revolutionization of the proletarian masses; and when, moreover, you see the differentiation within the Independent Party and the *de facto* split between the opportunist leaders, between the democracy of labor and the revolutionary masses who are pulling along with them the best section of the leadership—when you appraise this process in its full scope not from a pedant's standpoint, but from the standpoint of a revolutionist who thinks materialistically, then you must say to yourself: Here within the framework of a unified Communist Party a new groundwork is being laid in a new situation for the genuine development of the revolutionary party of the proletariat. If Comrade Gorter can't see this, one can only feel sorry for him. If the organization which he represents here, the KAPD (Communist Workers Party of Germany)—and which no doubt contains many splendid worker-revolutionists—if this numerically small organization fears to join the United Communist Party[6] which is not being created through superficial recruiting campaigns but in the birth pangs of the revolution and after a protracted profound struggle, after splits and purifications—if such is the case, then this fear simply means that the leaders of the KAPD still play an inordinate role within this organization; and that they keep infecting the workers under their leadership with the same mistrust of the proletarian masses as permeated Comrade Gorter's entire speech.

FIRST PUBLISHED IN THE
COMMUNIST INTERNATIONAL,
NO. 17, 1921

14. Speech delivered at the Second World Conference of Communist Women

Comrades! We are now convening—your Conference of Communist Women and the current Congress of the Communist International—we are now convening and carrying on our work at a moment which does not seem to have that definitiveness, that clarity and those graphic fundamental features which appeared, at first sight, as the distinguishing traits of the First World Congress when it met directly following the war. Our enemies and our opponents are even saying that we have been completely and utterly mistaken in our calculations. We Communists had supposed and hoped, so say our opponents, that the world proletarian revolution would break out either during the war or immediately afterwards. But now the third year since the war is already ending, and while during this interval many revolutionary movements have taken place, it is only within one country, namely, in our own economically, politically and culturally backward Russia, that the revolutionary movement has led to the dictatorship of the proletariat—a dictatorship which has been able to maintain itself to the present day and which I hope will continue to maintain itself for a long time to come. In other countries the revolutionary movements have led only to the replacement of the Hohenzollern and Habsburg regimes by bourgeois regimes, in the form of bourgeois republics. Finally, in a whole number of countries the movement ebbed away in strikes, demonstrations and isolated uprisings which were crushed. In general, the mainstays of the capitalist regime have been preserved throughout the whole world, with the sole exception of Russia.

From this our enemies have drawn the conclusion that since capitalism hasn't collapsed as a result of the World War in the course of the first two to three postwar years when the balance sheets were being drawn, it follows that the world proletariat has demonstrated its incapacity, while, conversely, world capitalism has demonstrated its capacity and power to retain its positions, to reestablish its equilibrium.

And at this very moment the International is discussing the question: Will the period immediately ahead, the next few years, entail the reestablishment of capitalist rule on new and higher foundations? or will it entail a mounting assault by the proletariat upon capitalism, an assault which will bring about the dictatorship of the working class? This is the fundamental question for the world proletariat and, consequently, also for its women's section. Of course, comrades, I can't even attempt here to give a complete answer to this question. The time at my disposal is too brief. I shall attempt to do this, as assigned by the ECCI, at the Congress. But one thing, I believe, is completely clear to us, to Communists, to Marxists. We know that history and its movement are determined by objective causes but we also know that history is accomplished by human beings and through human beings. The revolution is accomplished through the working class. Essentially history thus poses the question before us in the following way: Capitalism prepared the World War; the World War erupted and destroyed millions of lives and billions of dollars' worth of national wealth. It has shaken everything. And here on this half-ruined foundation, two basic classes are locked in struggle—the bourgeoisie and the proletariat. The bourgeoisie seeks to restore capitalist equilibrium and its class rule; the proletariat seeks to overthrow the rule of the bourgeoisie.

It is impossible to settle this matter with pencil in hand, like adding up a list of groceries. It is impossible to say: History has taken a turn toward the reestablishment of capitalism. It is only possible to say that if the lessons of the entire preceding development—the lessons of the war, the lessons of the Russian Revolution, the lessons of the semi-revolutions in Germany, Austria and elsewhere—if these lessons go for nought, if the working class once again agrees to keep its neck within the capitalist yoke, then, perhaps, the bourgeoisie will be able to restore its equilibrium, by destroying the civilization of Western Europe and by transferring the center of world development to America, to Japan, to Asia. Entire generations would have to be destroyed in order to create this new equilibrium. To this end the diplomats, the military men, the strategists, the economists, the brokers of the bourgeoisie are now directing all their efforts. They know that while history has its profound causes, it is nonetheless made through human beings, through their organizations and through their parties; and, consequently, our Congress and your Women's Conference have gathered here precisely in order to introduce into this unsettled historical situation the certainty of the consciousness and the will of the revolutionary class. This is the gist of the moment through which we are living and herein is the gist of its tasks as well.

We can say that the assumption of power no longer appears so simple a matter as it did to many of us two or three years ago. On the world scale this business of conquering power is extremely difficult and complicated. One must be aware that within the proletariat itself there are diverse layers, diverse levels of historical development and even diverse temporary interests. All this inevitably makes itself felt in its own due time. Layer after proletarian layer is drawn into the revolutionary struggle, passes through its own school, burns its fingers, retreats to the rear. They are followed by another layer, in whose wake comes still another and all of them are not drawn in simultaneously but at different periods; they pass through the kindergarten, the first, the second, and other grades of revolutionary development. And to combine all this into a unity—ah, this is a colossally difficult task! The example of Germany has already shown us this. There, in Central Germany, that section of the proletariat which prior to the war was the most backward and the most devoted to the Hohenzollerns, that section has today become the most revolutionary and dynamic.

The same thing happened in our country when the most backward proletarian section—the Ural proletariat—owing to a whole number of causes became at a certain moment the most revolutionary. They underwent a major inner crisis. And on the other hand, turning back to Germany, let us take for example the advanced workers of Berlin and Saxony who entered upon the road of the revolution early, and immediately succeeded in burning their fingers; not only did they fail to take power, but they suffered a defeat and have therefore since then become much more cautious. At the same time the workers' movement in Central Germany, a very revolutionary movement which began with such great enthusiasm—this movement failed to coincide with the movement of those workers who were much more highly developed, but who were more cautious and, in some ways, more conservative. From this example alone you can already see, comrades, how difficult it is to combine the disparate manifestations among workers of different trades and on different levels of development and culture. In the progress of the world labor movement, women proletarians play a colossal role. I say this not because I am addressing a women's conference but because sheer numbers indicate what an important part the woman worker plays in the mechanism of the capitalist world—in France, in Germany, in America, in Japan, in every capitalist country. . . . Statistics inform me that in Japan there are many more women than men workers; and consequently, if the data at my disposal is credible, in the labor movement of Japan they, the proletarian women, are destined to play the decisive role and to occupy the decisive place. And generally speaking, in the world labor movement the woman worker stands closest precisely to the section of the proletariat represented by the miners of Central Germany to whom I have just referred; that is, that section of labor which is the most backward, the most oppressed, the lowliest of the lowly. And just because of this, in the years of the colossal world revolution this section of the proletariat can and must become the most active, the most revolutionary, and the most initiative section of the working class.

Naturally, mere energy, mere readiness to attack are not enough. But at the same time history is filled with instances such as these: that during a more or less protracted epoch prior to the revolution, within the male section of the working class, especially among its more privileged layers, there accumulates excessive caution, excessive conservatism, too much opportunism and over-much adaptivity. And the reaction to their own backwardness and degradation which is evinced by women, that reaction, I repeat, can play a colossal role in the revolutionary movement as a whole. There is added reason to believe that we have at present come up against a kink in history, a temporary stoppage. Three years after the imperialist war capitalism remains in existence. This is a fact. This stoppage shows how slowly the object lessons of events and facts make their impress upon human minds, upon the psychology of the masses. Consciousness lags tardily behind the objective events. We see this before our very eyes. Nevertheless the logic of history will cut its way through to the consciousness of the woman toiler both in the capitalist world and in the Asiatic East. And once again it will be the task of our Congress not only to reaffirm anew but also to formulate factually and precisely that the awakening of the toiling masses in the East is today an integral part of the world revolution, just as much so as the rising of the proletarians in the West. And the reason for it is this: If English capitalism, the most powerful capitalism in weakened Europe, has succeeded in maintaining itself, it is precisely because it rests not alone on the scarcely revolutionary English workers, but also upon the inertia of the toiling masses of the East.

In general and on the whole, despite the fact that events are unfolding much more slowly than we had expected and wished, we can say that we have grown stronger in the interval since the First World Congress. True enough, we have shed certain illusions, but by way of compensation we have taken note of our mistakes and have learned a few things; and in place of illusions we have acquired a clearer perception. We have grown up; our organizations have become stronger. Nor have our enemies wasted this interval. All this goes to show that the struggle will be fierce and hard. This struggle sums up the significance of the work of your conference. Henceforth woman will be to a far lesser degree than ever in the past a "sister of mercy," in the political sense of the term, that is. She will become a far more direct participant on the main revolutionary battlefront. And that is why from the bottom of my heart, even if somewhat tardily, I hail your Women's World Conference and cry out together with you: *Long Live the World Proletariat! Long Live the Women Proletarians of the World!*

JULY 15, 1921

15. Letter to Comrade Monatte

My dear friend, I take this opportunity to send my warmest regards and to express my personal views on the state of affairs in French syndicalism—views that are, I trust, in complete harmony with the guiding line of the Third International as a whole.

I shall not hide from you that our joy in following the constant successes of revolutionary syndicalism is tinged with deepest concern over the future development of ideas and relations within the French labor movement. Today the revolutionary syndicalists of all tendencies still remain an opposition and are being held together precisely by their oppositional status. Tomorrow, the instant that you conquer the General Confederation of Labor[7]—and we don't doubt that this day is nigh—you will come up against the fundamental questions of the revolutionary struggle. And precisely here we enter the zone of our grave worries.

The official program of revolutionary syndicalism is

the Charter of Amiens.[8] In order to immediately express my thought as sharply as possible, let me say flatly—*every reference to the Charter of Amiens is not an answer but an evasion.* To every thinking Communist it is perfectly clear that pre-war French syndicalism represented a profoundly significant and important revolutionary tendency. The Charter of Amiens was an extremely precious document of the proletarian movement. But this document is historically restricted. Since its adoption a World War has taken place, Soviet Russia has been founded, a mighty revolutionary wave has passed over all of Europe, the Third International has grown and developed. The old syndicalists and the old Social Democrats have split into two and even three hostile camps. New questions of gigantic proportions have risen before us as practical questions on the order of the day. No answer to these questions is contained in the Amiens Charter. In the columns of *La Vie Ouvrière* I am able to glean no answers to the fundamental problems of the revolutionary struggle. Can it possibly be that our task today, in the year 1921, lies in returning to the positions of 1906 and in bringing about the "revival" *(réconstruction)* of pre-war syndicalism? Such a position greatly resembles, in principle, the position of those political "revivalists" *(réconstructeurs)* who are dreaming of a return to "pure" socialism, as it existed prior to its fall into sin during the war. Such a position is amorphous; it is conservative and it threatens to become reactionary.

Just how do you envisage the leadership of the syndicalist movement, from the moment you obtain the majority of the General Confederation of Labor? The ranks of the syndicates embrace party Communists, revolutionary syndicalists, anarchists, Socialists and broad non-party masses. Naturally, every issue involving revolutionary action must in the last analysis be brought before the entire syndicalist apparatus, embracing hundreds of thousands and millions of workers. But who will sum up the revolutionary experience, analyze it, draw all the necessary conclusions from it, formulate the specific proposals, slogans and methods of struggle, and transmit them to the broad masses? Who will lead? Are you perhaps of the opinion that this work can be carried out through the circle of *La Vie Ouvrière?* If such be the case, then one can state with certainty that alongside you other circles will arise to challenge your right to leadership under the banner of revolutionary syndicalism. And besides—what about the large contingent of Communists in the syndicates? What will be the relations between them and your group? The leading organs of one syndicate may be dominated by party Communists, while in the organs of another syndicate, revolutionary non-party syndicalists may predominate. The proposals and slogans of the *La Vie Ouvrière* group may diverge from the proposals and slogans of the Communist organization. This danger is profoundly real, it may become fatal, and because of it our victory in the syndicalist movement may be followed within a few months by the return of Jouhaux, Dumoulin and Merrheim to power.

I am well acquainted with bias against "parties" and against "politics" prevalent among French workers who have passed through the anarchist school. I completely agree that no single sharp blow can possibly break these moods, which were wholly justified in the past but which are extremely dangerous for the future. With regard to this question I can fully understand a *gradual* transition from the old state of disarrangement to the complete fusion of revolutionary syndicalists and Communists within a single party. But one must clearly and firmly set himself this goal. If centrist tendencies still obtain within the party the syndicalist opposition likewise has them within it. More education and further ideological purification are necessary among both of them. At issue is not at all the question of subordinating the syndicates to the party, but the question of uniting the revolutionary Communists and revolutionary syndicalists within the framework of a single party; and of all the members of this unified party carrying on harmonious centralized activity within the syndicates, which remain throughout autonomous and independent of the party organizationally. At issue is this, that the genuine vanguard of the French proletariat be welded together for the sake of its fundamental historical task—the conquest of power—and that under this banner it carry out its line within the syndicates, these basic and decisive organizations of the working class as a whole.

There is a certain psychological obstacle blocking a man's crossing the party's threshold after he has spent many years in revolutionary struggle outside the party. But to yield to this is to shy away from an outward form while causing the greatest damage to the inner essence. For it is my contention that your entire past activity was nothing else but preparation for the creation of the Communist Party of the proletarian revolution. Pre-war revolutionary syndicalism was a Communist Party in embryo. To return to the embryo would be a monstrous retrogression. Conversely, active participation in the building of a genuine Communist Party means the continuation and development of the best traditions of French syndicalism.

In these years each of us has had occasion to renounce one part of his already obsolete past in order to preserve, develop and assure victory to that other part of his past which did meet the test of events. An inner revolution of this type does not come easily. But only at this price, and at this price alone, can one acquire the right to really participate in the revolution of the working class.

Dear friend! I consider that the present moment will decide for a long time to come the destiny of French syndicalism, and, consequently, of the French revolution. In this decision you hold an important place. You would deal a cruel blow to the cause which numbers you among its best workers, were you today, when the choice must be definitely made, to turn your back upon the Communist Party. I have no doubt that this will not happen.

I warmly shake your hand and remain devotedly yours.

JULY 13, 1921

16. Letter to Comrades Cachin[9] and Frossard[10]

Dear friends,

Through this personal letter I shall attempt to dispel any possible misconceptions or misunderstandings which might have arisen owing to the extremely poor connections between Paris and Moscow. Since the revolutionary events in Germany, in March of this year, the German bourgeois press has kept reiterating that the March movement was provoked by orders from Moscow, because of our internal difficulties. This has caused me and, I believe, other comrades to fear lest these rumors arouse alarm among other Communist parties of Europe. Let us hope that the Third World Congress has served to dispel all doubts and fears in this connection. The fears themselves insofar as they arose here and there (perhaps even in France) could be sustained only by lack of adequate information. It is absolutely self-evident that even if we held the standpoint of serving only the interests of the Russian Soviet Republic and not those of the European revolution, even in that case we would have to say that real assistance could not be rendered us by partial uprisings, and all the less so, artificially provoked ones, but only by the revolutionary victory of the European proletariat. The interests of Russia are therefore served by only those movements, those uprisings, which flow from the internal development of the European proletariat. In and of itself this excludes the possibility of Moscow's issuing any kind of adventuristic "orders." But Moscow does not at all hold a "Muscovite" point of view. For us the Russian Soviet Republic constitutes only the point of departure for the European and world revolution. The interests of the latter are for us decisive in every major question. I trust that the Third World Congress has left no room for doubt on this score.

Insofar as one can judge from afar, the political preparation for the revolution in France is proceeding splendidly and systematically. An epoch of Kerenskyism is clearly approaching in your country; the regime of the Radical-Socialist Bloc is the first confused rebound from the war epoch. French Kerenskyism—which combines the irritation and despair of the petty bourgeois with the egotism of the peasant who doesn't want to pay for the dishes broken by the war and with the conservatism of the more privileged worker who hopes to retain the position created by the war, etc., etc.—French Kerenskyism will signify an extreme shakiness of the state apparatus. Between the imperialist clique and their candidates for the role of Gallifet[11] on the one hand, and the growing proletarian revolution on the other, there will be temporarily injected as a buffer the impotent bloc of the Radicals and the Socialists—Caillaux,[12] Longuet and Company. This will be an excellent prologue to the proletarian revolution. Should the expiring National Bloc succeed in passing its law against the Communists, one would have to thank fate for such a gift. Police and administrative persecutions, arrests and raids, will prove an extremely useful school for French Communism on the eve of its entry into the phase of decisive events. Through the columns of *l'Humanité* we are following with great interest and attention how energetically you are conducting the campaign against the Briand-Barthou Act. Should you defeat this enterprise, the party's authority will be greatly enhanced. Should this law be enacted, you will likewise stand to gain by it.

To the extent that *l'Humanité* reflects the line of the leading party circles, it shows clearly that this line is becoming increasingly radical and resolute. Unfortunately it is difficult to judge from *l'Humanité* what the mood is among the broadest working-class circles. Thus *l'Humanité* carries virtually no letters from workers, no correspondence from factories and plants, nor other material which directly reflects the day-to-day life of the masses. It is of utmost importance to French and world Communism alike to get a far clearer picture of just what circles of the proletariat read *l'Humanité* and just what it is that they read in the paper. A well established network of worker-collaborators and worker-correspondents can become at a certain moment the apparatus of the revolutionary uprising and will transmit to the masses the slogans and directives of their paper, investing the spontaneous movement with that unity which was so often lacking during revolutions in the past. The revolutionary newspaper cannot hang suspended over the masses; it must sink many roots into the masses.

The question of the party's relation to the working class is primarily the question of the *party's relation to the syndicates*. Insofar as one can judge from afar, this is today the most acute and most disturbing question in the French labor movement. The *La Vie Ouvrière* group represents a precious section of the French labor movement, if only because it has coalesced a rather considerable number of trustworthy, devoted and tested workers. But if this group continues—as I don't believe it will—to uphold its isolation and its shut-in character, it will incur the danger of becoming transformed into a sect and turning into a brake upon the future development of the syndicates and of the party. By its present formless policy toward the syndicates—in the spirit of Verdier's article—the party is helping to conserve the weak sides of *La Vie Ouvrière* while retarding the development of its strong sides. The party must set itself the task of *conquering the syndicates from within*. It is not a question either of depriving the syndicates of their autonomy or of subordinating them to the party (this is nonsense!); it is a question of the Communists becoming the best trade unionists within the syndicates, of their conquering the confidence of the masses, and their gaining the decisive role within the syndicates. It is self-understood that within the syndicates the Communists act as disciplined party members who carry out the basic party directives. At all costs, the Central Committee of the party must have within it several worker-Communists who play a prominent part in the syndicalist movement. It is indispensable that the Communists who work in the syndical movement should meet periodically and discuss the methods of their work under the leadership of members of the party's Central Committee.

Naturally, we must maintain the friendliest relations with the non-party revolutionary syndicalists, but we must at the same time create right now within the syndicates our own party nuclei, which can later join in the mixed nuclei with anarcho-syndicalists. Only if the Communist cells in the syndicates are firmly welded and disciplined will we be able to recruit growing numbers of disjointed anarcho-syndicalist elements, by convincing them through experience how indispensable are the discipline and the centralized unity of a guiding line, *i.e.,* the *party.*

If we simply slur over our differences with the syndicalists and the anarchists, these differences can later break catastrophically over our heads at the decisive moment.

I ask you to accept with good grace the fact that I express my views so freely about the situation in France with which you are more familiar than I am. I am impelled to do so on the one side by the fresh experience of the Russian Revolution; and on the other by my deep interest in the questions of the French labor movement. Together with other comrades I share in the disappointment that you were not present at the Congress. Isn't it possible that both of you, or each one separately, might be able to come to Moscow prior to the next Congress of the French Party? Unquestionably, your meeting with the new Executive Committee of the Comintern would prove of great value to both sides, serving to eliminate the possibility of all sorts of misunderstandings and to still further strengthen the organizational and ideological bonds between us.

I shake your hands and salute you heartily.

JULY 14, 1921

17. On 'l'Humanité,' the central organ of the French Party

Dear comrade,[13]

In accordance with your expressed desire, I shall formulate in greater detail my views concerning *l'Humanité*.

1) Parliamentary reports occupy a very important place in the French Communist newspaper. Not because we consider—like the reformists—participation in parliament to be either the basic or supremely important method of working-class struggle; but precisely because we must—while assigning to parliament and parliamentarianism that place which is actually occupied by them in modern society—work to dispel both the prejudices of parliamentary reformism as well as the anti-parliamentary superstitions of anarchism. Through parliamentary reports our aim is to show the workers the real role of parliament and of the parties represented there. However, in my opinion, this department is at bottom incorrectly organized in *l'Humanité*. The debates are treated in a light journalistic vein, with quips, jokes, sly hints, etc. No mention is ever made of

the party to which this or that orator belongs, nor is it pointed out just what class or sectional interests he happens to represent; the class character of the espoused ideas is never laid bare; neither speeches nor proposals are ever reduced to their essentials but everything is slurred over in catching up superficial contradictions, and in making puns, jokes, etc. I have no doubt that out of 100 workers whom you might approach at factory gates and to whom you might read a parliamentary report from *l'Humanité*, 99 would understand nothing and learn nothing, while the hundredth one might perhaps understand something but he, too, could learn nothing. In a workers' newspaper it is impermissible to write about the parliament and its internal struggles in the style of journalists discussing among themselves in a cloakroom in parliament.

In this field, clarity, precision and a popular style are particularly indispensable. I don't at all mean to say that one should give dry summaries of the debates, interspersed with commentaries on the orators and their parties. On the contrary, the reports must be written in a lively agitational manner. But this means that the writer must have his audience clearly in mind, and must set himself the task of laying bare before his audience the class essence of parliamentary activities and machinations. Sometimes a couple of words out of a whole speech suffice to characterize not alone the orator but his party as well. It is necessary constantly to repeat, underscore and hammer away, and then to repeat and to underscore all over again, instead of fluttering journalistically over the surface of parliamentary discussions.

2) *L'Humanité*'s attitude toward the Dissidents[14] is far too vague and at times utterly false: A split is a very serious matter, and once we recognize that a split is inevitable, then it is necessary to make its full meaning comprehen-

sible to the masses. It is necessary to mercilessly expose the policy of the Dissidents. It is necessary to make their leaders and their press ludicrous and hateful in the eyes of the masses. In this way the broad party mass attains a far greater political distinctness and clarity. In the April 17 (1921) issue of *l'Humanité* Comrade Launat takes a position toward the Dissidents that is absolutely incorrect. He expresses the hope for an early publication of the text of Paul Boncour's bill in order that it may be possible to corroborate whether the differences are really as irreconcilable as Blum[15] claims. This entire article, together with some others on the same subject, is written in a spirit as if we were engaged not in an irreconcilable political struggle with the Longuetists, but simply in a comradely discussion. This is false to the core. Naturally, we must tear away from the Longuetists the section of workers who follow them. But we shall attain this only through a merciless campaign against Longuetism in all of its manifestations.

3) I read Comrade Frossard's article in the May 5 issue: *"Sang Froid et Discipline"* (Composure and Discipline). The article is in the main quite correct, insofar as it tells what to do and how to do it. But it is inadequate, because it doesn't give vent to the feeling of protest prevalent among the best elements of the working class. The newspaper's tone is not firm and energetic enough. The paper failed to supplement the parliamentary fraction, whose public speeches were exceedingly feeble and even wrong in principle. I can't say so definitively, but in all likelihood protests could have been made in such a form as would not have committed the party to any decisive actions. There were no indications of this in *l'Humanité*.

4) The issue for April 3 contains a leading article: "Christianity and Socialism." This article is in glaring contradiction with Marxism, for it seeks to justify socialism by

platitudes from the Bible. The author cites the example of Soviet Russia where the church is tolerated and puts forth the demand that the French Communist Party emulate the Soviet Republic in this respect. But this is a monstrous confusion of concepts. The Soviet Republic is a state, constrained to tolerate prejudices and their organized expression—the church—in its midst. The Communist Party is a voluntary association of co-thinkers and cannot tolerate in its ranks propaganda of Christian Socialism, nor make the pages of its central organ available to such propaganda, all the less so in the guise of leading articles. The party can reconcile itself to the fact that individual members, especially workers and peasants, remain as yet not free from religious prejudices, but the party as a party, in the person of its leading organs, is duty-bound to conduct genuine educational activity. In any case, we cannot permit mystic-intellectuals to exploit the party as an auditorium for their religious ravings. At the decisive moment elements of this type will nine times out of ten espouse their fifty percent Christian self and become a brake upon revolutionary action.

5) The Luxembourg comrades have complained about the party's apathy in connection with the military brutalities perpetrated by the French government upon the workers of Luxembourg. On this subject I was able to find in *l'Humanité* one solitary article by Comrade Victor Méric.[16] Unquestionably, it is possible and necessary to conduct far more agitation around precisely such issues.

6) Colonial questions are treated in the pages of *l'Humanité* in much too weak a tone. Yet its attitude toward colonial slavery is a genuine test for the revolutionary spirit of a proletarian party. The leading article in the May 20 issue dealing with the alleged conspiracy in Indo-China is written in a democratic and not Communist spirit. We must

utilize every opportunity to implant in the minds of workers that the colonies have the right to rise up against and separate from the metropolises. In every instance we are obliged to underscore that it is the duty of the working class to support the colonies in their uprisings against the metropolises. Not alone in England but in France as well, the social revolution implies not only the uprising of the proletariat but also the uprising of the colonial peoples against the metropolises. Any vagueness in this connection becomes a source of and a cover for chauvinism.

7) In a number of articles and particularly among the commentaries there is a careless handling of concepts: fatherland, republic, love for one's country, etc., etc. Precision in terminology and a firmly sustained class character of political phraseology are more important in France than anywhere else.

8) I shall refrain from citing numerous instances of extreme vagueness and outright indecision in *l'Humanité*'s line with regard to syndicalism. A number of articles directly violate the fundamental principles of Marxism and Communism. Communists write articles which are directed wholly against the party line. Syndicalist resolutions are published without any commentaries. To be sure, the columns of *l'Humanité* should be opened up at present for a discussion on the trade union question, with the opposing side given an opportunity to express itself. But in every case the editorial board must make its voice heard, otherwise the reader becomes hopelessly disoriented and confused. A discussion on this question especially in France must inescapably partake of the nature of pandemonium. This can give rise to the greatest disorder, if the editorial board vacillates. On the other hand, if the editorial board steers a firm course, the masses will choose the principled, correct and firmly sustained Communist

line, and reject the confusion, equivocation and contradictoriness of all other lines.

9) *L'Humanité* readily publishes photographs of German and English ministers, including German Social Democrats and others. In my opinion it would be desirable to carry instead pictures of Communists. It is necessary to bring the Communist parties closer to one another, in personal respects as well.

10) In conclusion I take the opportunity to express again my admiration for the work of your wonderful cartoonist, Gassier.[17]

With comradely greetings.

JULY 23, 1921. MOSCOW

V

The Third World Congress

Editor's note

The Third Congress of the Comintern convened in Moscow from June 22 to July 12, 1921. The Congress began its sessions with 509 delegates representing 48 countries; 291 had decisive votes; 218 were consultative. Toward the close the number of delegates increased to 603.

Twenty-four full plenary sessions were held. The agenda was as follows: (1) Report of the ECCI (reporter: Zinoviev); (2) The World Economic Crisis and the New Tasks of the CI (reporter: Trotsky); (3) The German Communist Workers Party (KAPD); and the Italian Question; (4) The Tactics of the CI (reporter: Radek); (5) The Trade Union Question: a) The Red Trade Union International; b) The Struggle Against the Amsterdam International (reporters: Zinoviev, Heckert); (6) The Tactics of the Communist Party of Russia (reporter: Lenin); (7) The Youth Movement; (8) The Women's Movement (reporter: Clara Zetkin); (9) Communist Work in the Cooperatives; (10) The Organizational Structure of the Communist Parties and the Methods and Content of Their Work; (11) The Organizational Structure of the Comintern; (12) The Eastern Question; (13) Election of the ECCI.

The Russian Bolshevik Party was represented by 72 delegates, among them: Lenin, Trotsky, Zinoviev, Kamenev, Radek, Bukharin, Rykov and others.

The "Left Communists" were very strongly represented and at one time even appeared to have a majority at the Congress. Lenin demonstratively announced that at this Congress he was with the "Right Wing." The line of Lenin and Trotsky finally carried the day.

18. The Red Army to the General Staff of the Revolution

June 13, 1921, Moscow

Warriors of the Red Army!

For the third time the World Congress of the Communist International convenes in Moscow.

It is a great joy and honor for the workers, peasants and Red soldiers of Russia to greet within the walls of the Red capital the best representatives of the world working class.

Red warriors! For three and a half years you have defended the first Toilers' Republic in the world against the uninterrupted predatory attempts and attacks of the brigands and oppressors of all countries. On the Volga and the Obi, on the Northern Dvina and the Neva, on the Berezina and the Dnieper, on the Don and the Kuban, you have fought and died under the banner of the International. You have shed your blood in defending Soviet Russia—the fortress of the world proletariat. At the same time you have defended the heart of Soviet Russia—Red Moscow. You have assured to the representatives of the world working class the opportunity to come together under your protection in order to elaborate the further ways and methods of waging the struggle against capitalist coercion—in the name of the fraternity, liberty and happiness of all oppressed mankind.

On June 17, in the name of the entire Red Army, the Moscow garrison will solemnly greet our dear guests, our brothers in struggle. Revolutionary fighters—Red soldiers, commanders, commissars! Let us join in a fervent cheer for the Communist International!

L. Trotsky,
PEOPLE'S COMMISSAR OF WAR
AND NAVAL AFFAIRS.

FIRST PUBLISHED IN
IZVESTIA, ISSUE NO. 128,
JUNE 14, 1921

19. Report on the world economic crisis and the new tasks of the Communist International

Second Session, June 23, 1921

1917–1921

With the imperialist war we entered the epoch of revolution, that is, the epoch when the very mainstays of capitalist equilibrium are shaking and collapsing. Capitalist equilibrium is an extremely complex phenomenon. Capitalism produces this equilibrium, disrupts it, restores it anew in order to disrupt it anew, concurrently extending the limits of its domination. In the economic sphere these constant disruptions and restorations of the equilibrium take the shape of crises and booms. In the sphere of inter-class relations the disruption of equilibrium assumes the form of strikes, lockouts, revolutionary struggle. In the sphere of inter-state relations the disruption of equilibrium means war or—in a weaker form—tariff war, economic war, or blockade. Capitalism thus possesses a dynamic equilibrium, one which is always in the process of either disruption or restoration. But at the same time this equilibrium has a great power of resistance, the best proof of which is the fact that the capitalist world has not toppled to this day.

The last imperialist war was an event which we rightfully appraised as a colossal blow, unequaled in history, to the equilibrium of the capitalist world. Out of the war has actually risen the epoch of the greatest mass movements and revolutionary battles. Russia, the weakest link in the capitalist chain, was the first to lose her equilibrium and the first to enter the road of revolution in 1917—in the month of February. Our February Revolution had great repercussions among the working masses of England. 1917 in England was the year of the greatest strike struggles through which the English proletariat succeeded in checking the war-produced process of declining living conditions among the toiling masses. In October 1917 the working class of Russia took power. Strike struggles extended throughout the entire capitalist world, beginning with the neutral countries. In the autumn of 1918 Japan passed through a zone of tumultuous "rice" disorders, which according to some figures involved upwards of 25 percent of the population and which were met with cruel repressions on the part of the Mikado's government. In January 1918, mass strikes took place in Germany. Toward the end of 1918, following the collapse of German militarism, revolutions took place in Germany and Austria-Hungary. The revolutionary movement keeps expanding. The most critical year for capitalism—at any rate for European capitalism—arrives: the year 1919. In March 1919 a Soviet Republic is formed in Hungary. In January and March 1919 fierce battles between the revolutionary workers and the bourgeois republic break out in Germany. In France there is tension in the atmosphere during the period of demobilization, but the illusions of victory and the hopes for its golden fruits still remain too strong; the struggle does not even begin to approximate here the proportions it assumes in the conquered countries. In the United States toward the end of 1919 the strikes acquire a mighty sweep, embracing the railway workers, the miners, the steel workers, etc. Wilson's government unleashes wild repressions against the working class.

In the spring of 1920 in Germany an attempt to install counter-revolution through the Kapp putsch mobilizes and drives the working class to struggle. The intense but formless movement of the German workers is again mercilessly crushed by Ebert's republic, which they had saved. In France the political situation reaches the pitch of intensity in May of last year during the proclamation of the general strike which, incidentally, proved to be far from general and which was poorly prepared and betrayed by the opportunist leaders who did not want the strike but didn't dare admit it. . . . In August the Red Army's advance on Warsaw—likewise a part of the international revolutionary struggle—meets with failure. In September the Italian workers, taking seriously the verbalistic-revolutionary agitation of the Socialist Party, seize plants and factories, but are shamefully betrayed by the party, suffer defeat all along the line, and are then subjected to a ruthless counter-offensive by the unified reaction. In December the revolutionary mass strike unfolds in Czechoslovakia. Finally, at the beginning of the current year, revolutionary battles with their toll of mass victims erupt in Central Germany; England witnesses the resumption of the stubborn miners' strike, which hasn't ended to this very day; and a general strike breaks out in Norway.

When in the initial postwar period we observed the unfolding revolutionary movement, it might have seemed to many of us—and with ample historical justification—that this ever-growing and ever-strengthening movement must terminate directly in the conquest of power by the working class. But now almost three years have already elapsed since the war. Throughout the world, with the single exception of Russia, power continues to remain in the hands of the bourgeoisie. In the interim the capitalist world did not, of course, remain standing still. It has been undergoing change. Europe and the entire world have lived through a period of postwar demobilization, an extremely acute and dangerous period for the bourgeoisie—the demobilization of people and the demobilization of things, *i.e.*, industry—the period of wild postwar commercial boom followed by a crisis which has yet to terminate. And now we are confronted in its full scope by the question: Does development actually proceed even now in the direction of revolution? Or is it necessary to recognize that capitalism has succeeded in coping with the difficulties arising from the war? And if it has not already restored, is it either restoring or close to restoring capitalist equilibrium upon new postwar foundations?

The bourgeoisie gains appeasement

If, before analyzing this question from its main economic aspects, we approach it purely politically, we shall have to set down a whole number of symptoms, facts and statements which attest to this, that the bourgeoisie has become stronger and more stable as the class in power, or at all events feels that way. In 1919 the European bourgeoisie was in a state of extreme confusion. Those were the days of panic, the days of a truly insane fear of Bolshevism, which then loomed as an extremely misty and therefore all the more terrifying apparition and which used to be portrayed on Parisian posters as a killer clenching a knife in his teeth, etc., etc. As a matter of fact, incarnated in this specter of Bolshevism with a knife was the European bourgeoisie's fear of retribution for its war crimes. The bourgeoisie at any rate was aware how little the results of the war corresponded with the promises it had made. It knew the exact cost in lives and wealth. It feared an accounting. The year 1919 was, without doubt, the most critical year for the bourgeoisie. In 1920 and 1921 we observe a gradual influx of self-assurance among the bourgeoisie and along with this an undeniable consolidation of its state apparatus, which immediately following the war was actually on the verge of disintegration in various countries, for example, Italy. The bourgeoisie's recovery of its self-assurance took on especially graphic forms in Italy after the cowardly treachery of the Socialist Party in September. The bourgeoisie had imagined itself to be confronted with horrible bandits and assassins; it found instead—cowards.

Owing to an illness which removed me from active work in the last period, I have had an opportunity to read many foreign newspapers and I have accumulated a whole file of clippings that graphically characterize the shift in the bourgeoisie's mood and its new appraisal of the world political situation. All the evidence points to one thing: the bourgeoisie's self-assurance is undeniably firmer today than in 1919, or even 1920.

With your permission I shall adduce a few very instructive citations.

The *Neue Zuercher Zeitung,* a rather sober Swiss bourgeois conservative newspaper, which has been following with great interest and considerable perspicacity the political developments in Germany, France and Italy, stated the following in connection with the March action in Germany:

> Germany of 1921 bears no resemblance to Germany of 1918. Governmental consciousness has become so

strong that Communist methods meet with opposition among almost all the layers of the population, although the number of Communists, who during the revolutionary days comprised a small and resolute handful, has since grown inordinately.

On April 28, when both camps were preparing for May Day, the Paris newspaper, *Le Temps,* wrote:

> It suffices to survey the road traversed since last year in order to become completely reassured: Last year's May Day was set as the beginning of a general strike which was in its turn to usher in the first phase of the revolution. Today, absolute confidence prevails in the nation's effort to surmount all the crises consequent upon the war.

The selfsame *Neue Zuercher Zeitung* wrote in April of this year concerning the situation in Italy as follows:

> *The year 1919:* the bourgeois parties, verging on complete collapse, in a state of hopeless division and suicidal resignation are in full retreat before the energetic onslaught of well-disciplined Red forces; *the year 1921:* the bourgeois cohorts firmly coalesced and imbued with faith in victory enter into battle with the Bolsheviks, who are completely dispirited and hardly dare stir. And this thanks to the fascists.

My next illustration comes from an entirely different source, namely, a quotation from a resolution of our sister Communist Party of Poland.

If I am not mistaken, this party held a conference in April where a decision was adopted to participate in the forthcoming parliamentary elections. The motivation for this decision reads as follows:

> After the turn in the winter of 1918 when the struggle began to favor the bourgeoisie which had by then succeeded in setting its state apparatus in order; after the Workers' Soviets had been crushed by the government, with the cooperation of the PPS (the Polish Socialist Party)—after this, the party is obliged to utilize the electoral struggle and the rostrum of the Sejm.

There cannot of course be any talk here to the effect that the Polish Communist Party intends to change its principled position. It is simply evaluating the current situation as different from that of 1919.

The objective situation of the Social-Democratic parties in relation to the state and to the bourgeois parties has likewise correspondingly altered. Social Democrats are everywhere being pushed out of the government. If they are again drawn into the government, it is only temporarily and owing to outside pressure, as was the case in Germany. The Independent Party [of Germany] has made a complete turn to the right, likewise under the direct or indirect influence of the new situation, whose meaning it tends greatly to exaggerate. The Independents of all countries and the Social Democrats of all countries, who seemed to differ so much a year or a year and a half ago, have been brought closer together today, with the cooperation of Amsterdam.[1]

Thus the enhancement of the bourgeoisie's self-assurance as a class is absolutely undeniable; and equally undeniable is the actual consolidation of the police-state apparatus after the war. But in and of itself this fact—important though it is—does not by far settle the question; and, in any case, our enemies are overhasty in trying to draw from it the conclusion that our program is bankrupt. We had, of course, hoped that the bourgeoisie would be overthrown in 1919. But, of course, we were not sure of it; nor did we build and rest our program of action upon this date. When Herr Otto Bauer[2] and other theoreticians of the Second and Two-and-a-Half Internationals say that our predictions have been proved bankrupt, one might think that involved here were predictions concerning some astronomical event. It is as if we have been mistaken in our mathematical calculations that a solar eclipse would occur on such and such a day, and were consequently proved to be poor astronomers. But that is not at all how the matter stands in reality. We had not predicted a solar eclipse, *i.e.,* an event beyond our will and entirely independent of our actions. Involved is a historical event which can and will occur with our participation. When we spoke of the revolution resulting from the World War, it meant that we were and are striving to utilize the consequences of the World War in order to speed the revolution in every way possible. That the revolution hasn't taken place to this very day throughout the world, or at least in Europe, does not at all signify "the bankruptcy of the Communist International," for the program of the Comintern is not based on astronomical data. Every Communist who has to any measure thought out his ideas understands this. But inasmuch as the revolution has not come hot on the tracks of war, it is absolutely self-evident that the bourgeoisie has utilized the breathing space afforded it, if not to surmount and eliminate the most frightful and terrible consequences of the war, then at least to camouflage them, patch them up, etc., etc. Has it succeeded in accomplishing this? In part, yes. To what extent? It is here that we touch the essence of the question which involves the restoration of capitalist equilibrium.

Has world equilibrium been restored?

What is the meaning of capitalist equilibrium concerning which international Menshevism speaks nowadays with such complete assurance? For their part, the Social Democrats provide no analysis of this concept of equilibrium. They neither separate out its component parts or give any clear exposition. The equilibrium of capitalism contains a great many factors, events and facts—some basic, others secondary, and still others tertiary. Capitalism is a world phenomenon. Capitalism has succeeded in embracing the entire terrestrial globe; and this manifested itself most acutely during the war and during the blockade when one country, bereft of a market, was producing surpluses, while another, in need of commodities, lacked access to them. And today this interdependence of the dismembered world market manifests itself here and everywhere. Capitalism, at the stage attained before the war, is based on a world division of labor and a world exchange of products. America has to produce a certain quantity of grain for Europe. France has to produce a certain quantity of luxury goods for America. Germany has to produce a certain quantity of cheap consumer goods for France. This division of labor is in its turn not something constant, something given once and for all. It takes shape historically; it is constantly disrupted by crises and competition—let alone tariff wars. And it is restored over and over again only to be again and again disrupted. But world economy on the whole rests on a lesser or greater division among the respective countries of the production of corresponding necessities. Now it is this world division of labor that has been severed at its roots by the war. Has it been restored or no? This is one aspect of the question.

In each country agriculture supplies industry with prime necessities for the workers and with goods for productive use (raw materials), whereas industry supplies the village with household goods, consumer goods and the means of agricultural production. Here, too, certain reciprocal relations become established. Finally, within industry itself there is the production of the means of production and the production of the means of consumption, and between these two main branches of industry a certain interrelationship is established, which undergoes constant disruption in order to be regenerated over and over again on new foundations. The war has drastically disrupted all these interrelations and proportions if only by virtue of this single fact, that during the war Europe's industry and to a large measure also that of America and Japan produced not consumer goods and the means of production so much as the means of destruction. To the extent that consumer goods continued to be produced, they were utilized not so much by the workers who produce as by those who destroy—the soldiers of imperialist armies. Now, has this disrupted harmonious relationship between city and country, between the various branches of industry within each country—has this been restored or no?

Next follows the class equilibrium which rests upon the economic equilibrium. In the pre-war period a state of so-called armed truce prevailed in international relations. But not alone there, for between the bourgeoisie and the proletariat we also had by and large a reign of armed truce, maintained by a system of collective wage agreements concluded between the centralized unions and the ever more centralized industrial capital. This equilibrium has likewise been wholly disrupted by the war—and it was this that led to the colossal strike movement throughout the world. The relative class equilibrium of bourgeois society without which production is unthinkable—has this been restored or no? And if it has, upon what foundation?

Class equilibrium is closely bound up with political equilibrium. During the war and even prior to the war the bourgeoisie kept its mechanism in balance—although this escaped our notice at the time—through the medium of the Social Democrats, the social-patriots, who were the bourgeoisie's most important agency and who kept the working class within the bounds of bourgeois equilibrium. Only thanks to this was the bourgeoisie enabled to venture into the war. Has it restored anew the equilibrium of its political system today? And to what extent have the Social Democrats preserved or squandered their influence over the masses and how much longer can they play their part as guardians of the bourgeoisie?

Next in order is the question of the international equilibrium, *i.e.,* the world co-existence of capitalist states separate and apart from which the restoration of capitalist economy is, of course, impossible. Has equilibrium in this sphere been reached or no?

One must evaluate all these varied aspects of the question before it is possible to answer whether the world situation remains revolutionary, or whether they are correct who consider our revolutionary perspectives to be utopian.

An analysis of each aspect of this question must be illustrated by a great many facts and figures which are difficult to report to a large gathering and which are hard to remember. I shall therefore try to give only the basic data required for an orientation on this question.

Europe's economic decline—in figures

Has a new world division of labor been established? Of decisive importance in this sphere is the fact that the center of gravity of capitalist economy and bourgeois power has shifted from Europe to America. This is a fundamental fact which every comrade must firmly and clearly bear in mind in order to understand the events now unfolding before us and those which will unfold in the course of the next few years. Prior to the war Europe was the heart of the capitalist world, it was the globe's chief market place, its main factory and its main bank. The European industrialist—first the English and next the German; the European merchant—primarily the English; the European usurer—first the English and next the French—these were the actual directors of world economy and, therefore, of all world politics as well. Today this is no longer the case. Europe has been hurled back.

Let us try to fix in figures, even if these are extremely approximate, the shift of the economic center of gravity and the proportions of Europe's economic decline.

I shall begin with the simplest and most elementary facts, with the world production of material values. First, let us take agriculture. If we compare the 1920 crop with the average crop for the last five pre-war years, we shall find that it is almost 20 million double-quintals [4,408,800 tons] below the average. Moreover, in the belligerent European countries the crop is 37 percent below the pre-war average; in the neutral countries it remains at its previous levels, while in the trans-Atlantic countries it is 21 percent above. Russia is not included in this calculation. Before the war Russia used to supply the world market with about 100 million double-quintals on the average. The world market was poorer this year by some 120 million double-quintals. In spite of this, however, on American farms one can to this day find great quantities of grain which remain unsold because of the decline in prices on the world market.

If we turn to cattle-raising, we get almost an identical picture. World production of cattle remains virtually in the same condition as before the war. Cattle-raising among the belligerent European countries has been considerably reduced. The neutral countries have retained their pre-war levels, while the trans-Atlantic countries have greatly raised theirs. But now we find that meat prices on the Chicago meat market—the most important in the world—are today below the pre-war prices. Despite the war and its casualties, the population of the belligerent countries is today greater than before the war. There are 80 million individuals more. The quantity of grain in the market has been reduced by 120 million double-quintals. Meat and grain products are actually available, but remain scarce—for lack of money. This means that the world has become poorer and hungrier. This is the first fact, bare and simple.

If we analyze the world's coal consumption, we shall find almost the same picture, but in even bolder outline. The total world consumption of coal in 1920 amounted to 97 percent of the total consumed in 1913; consequently, it has dropped. In comparison with the pre-war period, Europe produced 18 percent less, while North America stepped up her output 13 percent. The same thing applies to cotton. The sum total of all products has declined. Europe has gone down. America has gone up.

Before the war, the national wealth, that is, the aggregate possessions of all the citizens and states participating in the last war was estimated at approximately 2,400 billion gold marks. The annual income of all these countries, that is, the quantity of products produced by them in a year, was estimated at 340 billion gold marks. How much did the war expend and destroy? In the neighborhood of 1,200 billion gold marks, *i.e.*, not less than one-half of what all the belligerent countries had accumulated in the course of their entire existence. Naturally, the war expenditures were in the first place covered by levies on current revenue. But if we assume that in each country the national income during the war dropped even by one-third because of the huge diversion of labor, it follows that it then amounted to 225 billion gold marks; and if we further assume that all the non-military expenditures swallowed 55 percent, it follows that war expenditures could be covered out of current national revenues to the sum of not more than 100 billion gold marks a year. For the four war years this comes to 400 billion gold marks. Which means that the deficit of 800 billion had to be made up by dipping into the basic capital of the belligerent nations, primarily by failing to replenish their productive apparatus. It therefore follows that after the war the total wealth of the belligerent countries amounted not to 2,400 billion gold marks, but only to 1,600 billion, *i.e.*, one-third less.

However, not all of the belligerent countries became impoverished at the same rate. On the contrary, there are among the belligerents—as we shall presently see—countries that have grown richer, namely, the United States and Japan. This means that the European countries which participated in the war have lost more than a third of their national wealth, and some of them—Germany, Austria-Hungary, Russia, the Balkans—considerably more than half.

Capitalism as an economic system is, you know, full of contradictions. During the war years these contradictions have reached monstrous proportions. To obtain the resources required for war, the state resorted primarily to two measures: first, issuance of paper money; second, flotation of loans. Thus an ever-increasing amount of the so-called "valuable paper" (securities) entered into circulation, as the means whereby the state pumped real material values out of the country in order to destroy them in the war. The greater the sums expended by the state, *i.e.*, the more real values it destroyed, the larger the amount of pseudo-wealth, of fictitious values accumulated in the country. State-loan paper has piled up mountain-high. Superficially it might seem that a country had grown extremely rich, but in reality the ground was being cut under the economic foundation, shaking it apart, bringing it to the verge of collapse. State debts have climbed to approximately 1,000 billion gold marks, which adds up to 62 percent of the present national wealth of the belligerent countries. Before the war, the world total of paper and credit money approximated 28 billion gold marks, today the amount is between 220 and 280 billion, *i.e.,* ten times as much. And this, of course, does not include Russia, for we are discussing only the capitalist world. All this applies primarily, if not exclusively, to European countries, mainly continental Europe and particularly Central Europe. On the whole, as Europe kept growing poorer and poorer—as she has to this very day—she became and is still becoming incased in ever-thicker layers of paper values, or what is known as fictitious capital. This fictitious capital—paper currency, treasury notes, war bonds, bank notes, and so on—represent either mementos of deceased capital or expectations of capital yet to come. But at the present time they are in no way commensurate to genuine existing capital. However, they function as capital and as money and this tends to give an incredibly distorted picture of society and modern economy as a whole. The poorer this economy becomes, all the richer is the image reflected by this mirror of fictitious capital. At the same time, the creation of this fictitious capital signifies, as we shall see, that the classes share in different ways in the distribution of the gradually constricting national income and wealth. National income, too, has become constricted, but not to the same extent as the national wealth. The explanation for this is quite simple: The candle of capitalist economy was being burned at both ends. In order to finance the war and the postwar state economy, they drained not only the national income but the basic funds of national wealth as well.

When a government issues a loan for productive purposes, say, for the Suez Canal, behind the particular government bonds there is a corresponding real value. The Suez Canal supplies passageway for ships, collects tolls, provides revenue and, in general, participates in economic life. But when a government floats war loans, the values mobilized by means of these loans are subjected to destruction, and in the process additional values are obliterated. Meanwhile, the war bonds remain in the citizens' pockets and portfolios. The state owes hundreds of billions. These hundreds of billions exist as paper wealth in the pockets of those who made loans to the government. But where are the real billions? They no longer exist. They have been burned. They have been destroyed. What can the owner of these securities hope for? If he happens to be a Frenchman, he hopes that France will be able to wring billions out of German hides, and pay him.

In many respects the havoc among the mainstays and the productive apparatuses of the capitalist nations has been more far-reaching than can be established by means of statistics. This is most clearly to be seen in housing. All the energies of capitalism had been directed—because of the frenzied war and postwar profits—toward the production of new items for personal or military use. But the restoration of the basic productive apparatus was neglected more and more. This applies wholly to urban housing. Old houses were poorly repaired while new ones were erected in insignificant numbers. Hence the terrible housing shortage throughout the capitalist world. Owing to the current crisis the destruction of the productive apparatus may not be so noticeable today because the major capitalist countries are utilizing not more than one-half or one-third of their productive capacities. But in the sphere of housing, owing to the constant increase of population, the disorganization of the economic apparatus manifests itself with full force. America, England, Germany, France need hundreds of thousands and even millions of apartments. But the necessary work cannot be undertaken in the face of the insurmountable obstacles arising from the universal impoverishment. Capitalist Europe must and will tighten its belt, reduce the scope of its operations and drop to a lower level for many years to come.

As I have said, within the framework of Europe's universal impoverishment, different countries have become impoverished at different rates. Let us take Germany as the country that has suffered the most among the major capitalist powers. I shall adduce key figures which characterize Germany's economic position as it was before the war and as it is today. These figures are not very exact. A statistical computation of national wealth and national income is a very difficult thing under capitalist anarchy. A real audit of revenue and property will be possible only under socialism, an audit in terms of units of human labor, and taken naturally under a socialist society with a well organized and well functioning mechanism, from which we are still very, very far removed. But even inexact figures are of service to us inasmuch as they enable us to roughly approximate the changes that have occurred in the economic position of Germany and other countries during the past 6 or 7 years.

On the eve of war Germany's national wealth was estimated at 225 billion gold marks, while the highest pre-war national income was 40 billion. Prior to the war Germany was, as you know, growing rich very swiftly. In

1896 her income was 22 billion. Within 18 years (from 1896 to 1913) it had increased by 18 billion, that is, at an average rate of a billion a year. These 18 years generally marked a period of great capitalist prosperity throughout the world, and especially in Germany. Today her national wealth is estimated at 100 billion marks, while her national income is 16 billion, *i.e.,* 40 percent of the prewar level. True enough, Germany has lost a part of her territory, but the main losses are bound up with the war expenditures and the postwar rape of Germany. According to the calculations of the German economist Richard Calwer[3] commodity production in 1907 is equivalent to the labor productivity of 11.3 million workers. Working conditions have since then undergone a drastic change. There has been a reduction in working time, the intensity of labor has dropped, and so forth and so on. He therefore arrives at the conclusion that Germany's labor force expressed in 1907 units amounts to 4.8 million, *i.e.,* not more than 42 percent.

In analyzing agriculture Calwer gets the same result.

Calwer's calculations thus completely corroborate the figures cited by me. Meanwhile Germany's national debt has grown to 250 billion marks, *i.e.,* it is two and a half times greater than Germany's national wealth today. In addition, reparations to the sum of 132 billion marks have been imposed on Germany. Were the English and the French to demand full and immediate payment of these sums—they would have to put in their pockets all of Germany, beginning with Stinnes' mines and ending with President Ebert's cuff-links. Germany's emission of paper currency amounts today to 81 billion marks. Of these not more than 5 billion are secured by gold. Consequently, the German mark is worth 6–7 pfennigs today.

True, following the war Germany scored great successes

on the world market, exporting her commodities at very cheap prices. While this cheapness meant big profits for the German merchants and exporters, for the German population as a whole it spelled in the final analysis ruin, since cheap prices on the world market were contingent upon low wages and malnutrition for the workers, state subsidies for grain, and rent regulations—which in their turn were accompanied by a complete stoppage of housebuilding, minimum of repairs, etc., etc. Thus with every German product dumped on the world market a certain part of Germany's national wealth is carried away for which she receives no equivalent in exchange.

In order to "revive" German economy it is necessary to stabilize her currency, *i.e.*, it is necessary to halt the emission of more paper money and to reduce the quantity already in circulation. And to do that, it is necessary to renounce debt payments, *i.e.*, declare state bankruptcy.[*]

But this measure in and of itself implies a dire disruption of the equilibrium, for it involves a transfer of property from the present holders to other hands and it must therefore provoke a fierce class struggle over the new dis-

---

[*] The inevitability of Germany's state bankruptcy is conceded even by so conservative an economist as Calwer who in his rather interesting pamphlet on state bankruptcy comes to the following conclusion:

"This end-result, pregnant with dire consequences in currency and fiscal policy, will unquestionably come in a violent manner, inasmuch as under the existing economic state of the country, a gradual return to normal conditions of the money market and state finances is absolutely inconceivable. The violent culmination of the entire development is, in the last analysis, nothing else but actual state bankruptcy thereby finally disclosing the long standing insolvency of the state."

A great many books are being generally published today in Germany which deal with state bankruptcy from the standpoint of philosophy, morality, jurisprudence, etc. Be it moral or immoral, these gentlemen will have to declare state bankruptcy.—*L.T.*

tribution of the national income. Meanwhile Germany grows poorer and keeps declining.

Let us next take a victor country—France.

France, according to the ballyhoo in her bourgeois newspapers, is a country whose wounds are healing. It is undeniable that in certain fields France has achieved some successes during the postwar period. But to exaggerate them is to commit a very great blunder. It is very difficult to adduce statistics relating to French economy because much more is kept hidden there than in other countries. This is done both by the French bourgeoisie and by the French government. It must be said that more lying is done by the French capitalist press than by any other, and this probably includes the field of economic statistics.

I shall now cite some figures which the French bourgeois economists are boastfully using in an attempt to prove that capitalist economy has been restored. Let us take the sphere of agriculture. Before the war France used to produce annually 86 million quintals of wheat (a quintal is 100 kilograms, a little over 220 pounds); oats—52 million; potatoes—132 million. In 1919 her wheat crop was 50 million, and the last crop (1920)—63 million. In 1919, potatoes—77 million, and the last year—103 million.

Now let us take cattle-raising. In 1913 there were approximately 15 million head of horned cattle, but today—12.8. Horses in 1913 numbered 7 million, today—4.6. Sheep in 1913 numbered 16 million, today—9. Pigs were 7 million, today—4. A sharp decrease.

Let us take coal, a very important product and a key factor in industry. In 1913 France mined 41 million tons of coal; in 1919—22 million; in 1920—25. And if we include Alsace-Lorraine and the Saar Basin,[4] then the 1919 output will come to 35.6 million tons of coal. We have here an increase. But this increase still leaves coal production far below its pre-war level. But how have these rather modest successes been achieved? In agriculture they have been achieved primarily through the stubborn and diligent labor of the French peasant. But in the purely capitalist sphere these successes were achieved primarily by looting Germany, by taking away her cows, seed, machinery, locomotives, gold and especially coal.

From the general economic standpoint there is nothing positive here, for instead of creating new values there was primarily a transposition of old values. Moreover it ought to be added that Germany's losses were 1½ to 2 times as great as France's gains.

We thus discovered that having stripped Germany of her key metallurgical and coal areas, France has nevertheless far from reached her pre-war levels. Let us now take France's foreign trade. Trade balances are highly symptomatic of world economic equilibrium, *i.e.,* of the existing state of exchange among the various countries. A capitalist country considers itself to be in a good position if it exports more than it imports. The difference is paid off in gold. Such a balance is called favorable. When a country is compelled to import more than it exports, the balance is unfavorable, and such a country must add a part of its gold reserve to its exports. The gold reserve begins melting away and the ground is gradually cut under the country's monetary and credit system. If we take France during the last two years—1919 and 1920, that is, during the French bourgeoisie's two years' work of "reconstruction"—we shall find that in 1919 the trade balance was unfavorable to the tune of 24 billion francs, while in 1920 the deficit amounted to 13 billion. Before the war, the French bourgeois never saw such figures, not even in his wildest dreams. In two years the trade deficit totals 27 billions. True enough, for the first quarter of the current year France managed to keep her trade balance without a deficit, that is, her exports equaled her imports. Certain bourgeois economists started beating the drums in this connection: France was, mind you, restoring her trade balance. But the leading organ of the French bourgeoisie *Le Temps* had the following to say on this score on May 18:

> You are mistaken, we didn't have to pay out gold during these three months only because we imported very little raw material. But that simply means that in the latter part of the year we shall export few products which we manufacture from foreign raw materials in general and American raw materials in particular. Consequently, while we have managed to keep a favorable trade balance during these three months, in the next period the trade deficit will inescapably begin to grow.

And so the trade balance has not been improved through either the revival of economy or an increase in exports, but through a decrease in raw material imports, *i.e.*, at the cost of lowering tomorrow's productivity.

Before the war the amount of paper currency in circulation was less than 6 billion francs; today—more than 38 billion. As touches the purchasing power of the franc, it is pointed out by the same newspaper that toward the end of March, when the crisis was already raging throughout the world, American prices were 23 percent above pre-war, *i.e.*, less than one-quarter higher, whereas French prices had gone up 260 percent, that is, more than three and a half times the pre-war levels. This means that the purchasing power of the franc has depreciated several times over. Now let us take up the French budget. It falls into two sections: normal expenditures and emergency funds. The normal budget comes to 23 billion francs—a sum unknown in pre-war times! How are these huge sums allocated? 15 billion are to cover interest on the debt; 5 billion—to maintain the army. A total of 20 billion. That's all the French government proposed to wring from the taxpayers. In reality they succeeded in wringing out some 17.5 billion. The "normal" government income is, therefore, hardly sufficient to cover even the interest on the debt and the upkeep of the army. But in addition there are emergency expenses to be met: more than 5 billion for the army of occupation, and 23 billion for all sorts of war compensation and work of restoration. These expenses are debited to Germany. But it is quite self-evident that as time goes on Germany is less and less able to pay them. Meanwhile, however, the French government subsists either by floating new loans or by issuing additional paper currency. A prominent French financial journalist, Léon Chavenon, the director of *l'Information,* the foremost economic periodical in France, is in favor of continuing the issuance of paper money. He declares: "Apart from this, the only other way out is through open bankruptcy." This means that the only alternative is: either a masked bankruptcy through further emissions of paper money, or an open declaration of bankruptcy. That is how matters stand with France, a victor country which occupies a favorable position in ruined Europe in the sense that she could and can restore her equilibrium at Germany's expense. The situation in Italy and Belgium is at all events not superior to that of France.

Let us pass now to Great Britain, the richest and most powerful country in Europe. During the war we grew accustomed to saying that England was getting rich from the war, that the British bourgeoisie had plunged Europe into war and was feathering its nest. This was true, but only within certain limits. England made profits in the initial period of the war but began to suffer losses in the second period. The impoverishment of Europe, especially of Central Europe, acted to disrupt trade relations between England and the rest of the continent. In the last analysis this had to hurt and did hurt England's industry and finances. Moreover, England herself was compelled to shoulder enormous war expenditures. Today England is in a state of decline, and this decline is becoming more and more precipitous. This fact may be illustrated by industrial and commercial indices which I shall presently cite, but the fact itself is incontestable and is corroborated by a whole series of public and wholly official declarations by the most eminent English bankers and industrialists. During the months of March, April and May, the respective English publications carried the annual reports of corporations, banks, and so on. These authoritative gatherings, where the leaders of the various enterprises make their reports, assessing the general state of affairs in the country or in their own particular branch of industry, provide exceptionally instructive material. I have gathered a whole file of such reports. All of them bear out one and the same thing: England's national income, *i.e.*, the aggregate income of all her citizens and the state, has dropped considerably below the pre-war total.

England is poorer. The productivity of labor has fallen. Her world trade for 1920 has, in comparison to the last pre-war year, declined by at least one-third, and in some of the most important branches, even more. Especially sudden is the change undergone by the coal industry which used to be the main branch of English economy, or more precisely, the root and trunk on which England's entire world economic system rested. For the coal monopoly was the root of the power, vigor and prosperity of all other branches of English industry. Not a trace of this monopoly remains today. Here are the basic factual data on the state of English economy. In 1913 England's coal industry supplied 287 million tons of coal; in 1920—233 million tons, *i.e.,* 20 percent less. In 1913, the production of iron amounted to 10.4 million tons; in 1920—a little more than 8 million tons, *i.e.,* again 20 percent less. The export of coal in 1913 amounted to 73 million tons; in 1920—all told only 25 million tons, *i.e.,* one-third of the pre-war total. But during the current year, 1921, the slump in the coal industry and coal exports took on absolutely abnormal proportions. In January the coal output was 19 million tons (*i.e.,* below the 1920 monthly average); in February—17; in March—16. And then the general strike erupted and the coal output verged on zero. For the first five months of 1921 the exports are 6 times below what they were for the same period in 1913. Expressed in prices England's entire export for May of this year is three times below that of May of last year. As of August 1, 1914 England's national debt was 700 million pounds sterling; on June 4 of this year—7,709 million pounds, *i.e.,* an elevenfold increase. The budget has swelled threefold.

If you thumb through the reports of the directories of banks and industrial enterprises for March and April you will find that England's national income has declined one-third or one-quarter as against the pre-war period. That is how matters stand in England, the richest country in Europe, a country which suffered the least from military operations and gained the most from the war in its initial period.

The most graphic proof of the decline of English economic life lies in the fact that the English pound sterling is no longer a pound sterling; that is, it is no longer equivalent to the set of figures which once exercised their sway everywhere and which are still imprinted on it. Today it is only 76 percent of what it pretends to be. As against the incumbent sovereign of the money market—the U.S.

Dollar—the pound has lost 24 percent of its nominal magnitude. What could better characterize the instability of our epoch than the fact that the most stable, absolute and incontestable thing in the whole world—the English sovereign (in English this word signifies both "pound sterling" and "ruler")—has lost its former position and has become transfigured into a relative magnitude! Considering that nowadays in Germany the sphere of philosophy has become activated over relativity—and I refer here to Einstein's philosophy[5]—one ought perhaps to interpret German philosophy as an act of revenge against English economics, inasmuch as the English pound sterling has after all become—relative. Incidentally, it has ever been the custom in Germany to reply to economic poverty by exacting revenge in the field of philosophy.

The data we have cited adequately characterizes the situation throughout Europe. Among the belligerent countries we find Austria at one pole, as the country that has suffered the most (if we leave out Russia), and at the other pole—England. Between them are located Germany, Italy, Belgium, France. The Balkan countries are completely ruined and have been thrown back into the economic and cultural conditions of barbarism. So far as the neutral countries are concerned, in the first period they undoubtedly profited by the war; however, since they cannot play an independent economic role but must live in the interstices among the big countries and are economically dependent upon the latter, it follows that the decline of the major European countries has produced the greatest economic difficulties among the neutral countries who have likewise sunk today far below the levels attained in the first period of the war.

Thus Europe's income as a whole, that is, the quantity of material values produced by all the European populations, has fallen at least by one-third as compared to prewar times. But far more decisive, as I have stated before, is the slump in the basic apparatus of economy. The peasant was unable to obtain synthetic fertilizers, agricultural implements and machines; the mine owner, spurred on by high coal prices, did not bother to renovate the equipment in the mines; the stock of locomotives became worn out, the railways remained by and large in a state of disrepair, and so forth and so on. All this has acted upon the main fabric of economy to render it weaker, frailer, less reliable. How to measure and compute all this? Capitalist statistics fall far short of this. Such an inventory, that is, an inventory in terms of values of the productive condition not of an isolated enterprise but of entire countries and the whole of Europe, would undoubtedly show that the war and postwar regimes alike survived and continue to survive at the expense of Europe's basic productive capital. This means, for example, that Germany instead of allotting 50,000 workers to recondition the pits, consigns 50,000 workers more to mine the coal which must go to France. France, on the other hand, in an attempt to reduce her trade deficit seeks to export the greatest possible volume of goods abroad and does not recondition her equipment to the necessary extent, either. And this applies to all European countries, for Europe as a whole shows a deficit, *i.e.*, an unfavorable trade balance. The debilitation of Europe's economic foundations will manifest itself on the morrow even more acutely than it has yesterday or today. History's great mole is burrowing its tunnels ever deeper beneath the very foundations of Europe's economy.

America's economic flowering

We get an entirely different picture when we step into the Western Hemisphere. America has passed through a development of a diametrically opposite character. She has meanwhile enriched herself at a dizzy pace. In the war she participated chiefly as a quartermaster. True, she had to bear expenses herself consequent to the conduct of the war but these expenditures were insignificant as against not merely her war profits but also all the advantages opened up by the war for America's economic development. The United States not only obtained in the person of warring Europe a virtually unlimited buyer who bought anything and everything, and at higher prices besides; but for a number of years was relieved of her chief competitors in the world market—Germany and England, whose main occupation was the war. Till the very eve of the war the bulk of American exports, that is, two-thirds, consisted of agricultural products and raw materials. During the war U.S. exports grew uninterruptedly and even feverishly. Suffice it to point out that American exports climbed to a total 2½ times greater than the highest prewar one, and that in 6 years (from the beginning of 1915 to the end of 1920) exports exceeded imports by 18 billion dollars. Furthermore the exports have altered drastically in their nature. Today the United States exports 60 percent manufactured goods and only 40 percent agricultural produce, meat products, raw materials (cotton, etc.).

To sketch the main outlines of the present role of the United States in world economy I shall cite the following key figures. Within the boundaries of the United States live 6 percent of the world's population; 7 percent of the earth's surface falls to the share of the United States. Of the world's annual gold production the United States supplies 20 percent; the United States' share of the world's shipping tonnage is 30 percent, whereas before the war it had not more than 5 percent. Of the world's iron and coal the United States produces 40 percent; tin—40 percent; silver—40 percent; zinc—50 percent; coal—45 percent; aluminum—60 percent; the same proportion of copper and cotton; oil from 66 to 70 percent; corn—75 percent; automobiles—85 percent. Throughout the whole world there are today a little less than 10 million automobiles. Of these America's share is 8,500,000, while the rest of the world has 1,400,000. There is one automobile to every twelve Americans. Today the center of gravity of world economy is no longer to be found in Europe, but in the United States. Europe has slumped and continues to drop lower and lower. The United States has all the while experienced an unprecedented growth, whose key data are as follows:

The number of horses has increased from 20 to 22 million. Cattle—from 62 to 68 million. This doesn't, of course, amount to a great deal. But if we take the coal output, we find that in 1913 it amounted to 517 million tons; in 1920—580 million, *i.e.,* a rather appreciable increase. Oil production rose from 248 million barrels in 1913 to 442 million in 1920. Here we already have a large increase. Cotton and iron have remained virtually at pre-war levels; but in sea-going ships, we find a huge increase. In 1913 the ships built for the merchant marine had a freight-carrying capacity of 276,000 tons, while in 1919—4,075,000 tons; and in 1920—2,746,000 tons. This stepped-up shipbuilding has enabled the United States to catch up with the leading great power in this sphere—England. While before the war Great Britain possessed more than half of the world tonnage, and the United States only 5 percent, today the interrelationship has sharply altered. England now has not more than 35 percent while the United States possesses 30 percent of the world tonnage. Thus the United States is challenging England's domination of the seven seas.

The United States has completely taken over the domination of the coal market, which England once had. No less important is America's crushing superiority in the sphere of oil whose role in industrial and military affairs grows apace. But the same change has occurred not only in the sphere of industry and world trade but also in the money market. England was the pre-war world's chief usurer, next came France. The whole world was in debt to them, including America. Today, however, the only country that owes no one but to whom everybody else is in debt is—the United States. Europe, *i.e.*, European governments, cities and enterprises, owe the United States 18 billion gold dollars. But this is only the beginning. Each passing day sees this debt increased by $10 million, because of failure to pay the accruing interest and through the extension of new American credits. In tune with this, as I have already remarked, the Dollar has become the "Sovereign" of the world financial market. Hitherto, in presenting its references, the Dollar would say: My name is the Dollar and I represent approximately one-fifth of a pound sterling. So far as the latter was concerned, it needed no references; it came and went as the Pound Sterling, and that's all there was to it. Things have now changed drastically. Nowadays the pound sterling travels with a passport, like all of the other monetary units; and this passport states that the pound sterling is actually not a pound sterling at all but just so many dollars (nearly one-fourth below the figure given in old pre-war financial handbooks).

Almost one-half of the world's gold reserve, on which the entire monetary system rests, is now concentrated in the United States. Almost one-half of the world reserve!

Such is the postwar position of the United States. How was it brought into being? It grew out of Europe's war market which was unlimited and which bought at any price. In the English colonies, in Asia, in Africa, and in South America, too, there were no competitors to be met, they had almost completely disappeared, and the United States had free play for its fullest development. We thus had, in the space of seven years, a complete reversal in the sphere of world division of labor. For four-odd years Europe became converted into a sheet of fire fed not only by Europe's income but also by her basic capital, while the American bourgeoisie warmed its hands at the flames. America's productive capacity has grown extraordinarily but her market has vanished because Europe is impoverished and can no longer buy American goods. It is as if Europe had first done everything in her power to help America climb to the topmost rung and then pulled the ladder out.

The other countries—the crisis

Japan has likewise used the war epoch to advantage and her capitalism has achieved great successes which, of course, are in no way commensurate to the development of the United States. Certain branches of Japanese industry blossomed at hothouse tempos. However, while in the absence of competitors Japan proved capable of swiftly expanding individual branches of her industry, today when many of these competitors have returned she has not always been able to retain positions already conquered. The total number of Japanese working men and women (in Japan woman labor is employed on an extremely large scale) runs to 2,370,000, of whom 270,000 (some 12 percent) are organized in trade unions.

In the colonial and semi-colonial countries, in the East Indies, in China, capitalism has scored great conquests during the last seven years. Before the war Asia yielded 56 million tons of coal. In 1920 her yield was 76 million tons, *i.e.*, 36 percent more.

Today the entire world is living through a cruel crisis which began last spring in Japan and America, *i.e.,* precisely in those countries which were on the upgrade and not in decline during the recent period.

The *Economist,* the most authoritative English economic periodical, tells a rather curious story of how the crisis started. It is a very interesting episode. The American worker, mind you, began rolling in wealth and started buying silk shirts, the manufacture of which is a most important branch of the Japanese textile industry. The Japanese silk industry expanded rapidly in a brief space of time, but since the workers' purchasing capacity is all in all very limited and took a sudden drop the instant that American industry began its reconversion upon the signing of the peace, the Japanese silk industry fell immediately into the throes of a sharp crisis, which was then transmitted to other branches of industry, pounced upon America and then leaped across the ocean, and today the crisis in the entire world has plumbed depths unprecedented in the history of capitalism. Thus it all started with a trifle—a little silk shirt—and ended up in something big: prices plummeted downward and at a mad pace factories began to close down, workers were thrown out into the streets. In America there are now not less than five million and, according to some, six million unemployed.

In the history of the crisis, the silk shirt episode plays approximately the same part as a flap of a bird's wings that brings down the avalanche. The avalanche was obviously about to descend anyway. But this episode is likewise of interest because it illustrates an undeniable improvement in living standards, at least among certain categories of American workers, in recent years. Of the 8.5 million automobiles a rather considerable number is owned by skilled American workers; but today and especially in the next period American workers will not have the means for automobiles and silk shirts.

Well, there is a crisis in Europe and a crisis—in America. But these crises are of a different order. Europe is poorer, while America wallows in wealth. America's productive apparatus remains in comparatively good condition. Her factories are first class. Equipment and supplies are at hand. True, the quality of goods has deteriorated in wartime, the railways have been worn out, since the main concern of the capitalists was to deliver merchandise to the eastern ports. But, on the whole, America has not only preserved her economic apparatus but also expanded it.

Europe's purchasing capacity has shrunk. She has nothing to offer in exchange for American goods. The world's economic center of gravity has sharply shifted to America, and partly to Japan. While Europe is suffering from anemia, the United States suffers no less today from plethora.

This abnormal incongruity between the conditions of European and American economies—an incongruity ruinous to both sides—finds its most graphic expression in the sphere of sea transport. In this sphere as in so many others, the dominant position before the war belonged to England. She held in her hands about 50 percent of the world tonnage. Seeking to gain domination in every field, the United States has built up its merchant fleet as its trade expanded in wartime. U.S. tonnage has been raised from three or four million to 15 million tons, and is today almost on par with England.

In recent years, the world tonnage has increased in absolute figures by approximately one-fifth. Yet industry and world trade have fallen. There is little or nothing to export. Europe's anemia and America's plethora act equally to paralyze the functioning of the Atlantic transport system.

Before I go on to deal with the nub of the question as

to whether or not this picture will subsequently undergo change in the sense that an equilibrium will be restored, allow me to add a brief comment. Capitalist statisticians and economists may, after all, say that Russia's economy hasn't been improved during this period either. Comrade Lenin will make the report on Russia's economic situation. The few words I wish to say on this subject are in an entirely different connection. The U.S. Secretary of State, Mr. Hughes,[6] wrote in a letter to the famous Mr. Gompers, who is also notorious in some ways, that it was senseless to reestablish economic relations with Russia inasmuch as she represents nothing but a gigantic vacuum at the present time. The impoverishment and decline of Russian economy cannot possibly be blamed, in Mr. Hughes' opinion, upon the blockade and the Civil War; because, in the first place, those branches of industry have suffered which used to stand on their own feet before the war, and secondly, because far fewer people were mobilized for the Civil War than for the World War. Now, this last argument—if Mr. Hughes will indulge me—is just a little too clever because everyone knows that the World War has played a role in the decline of Russian economy. But apart from this, the argument is equally fallacious in other respects, because during the great imperialist war the Czarist government kept the key skilled labor forces in the factories. It didn't need them for the conduct of the war as we did. It had its nobility, its cadre of highly trained officers. Our military apparatus, in the most difficult days, consisted first and foremost of skilled workers whom we were, in general, compelled to mobilize forthwith. Today when we are already in the midst of demobilization, I can let out the secret that at the time when we fought on 24 fronts our army numbered 5,300,000 men and of these not less than 750,000 were skilled workers.

And this means that the economy had incurred the direst and most unbearable of losses. Conversely Mr. Hughes completely forgets that capitalist Russia was an integral sector of the world capitalist economic system, and took part in the world market's process of circulation. We are now suffering from the shortage of the most insignificant and minor items which our country did not produce before the war, and whose production couldn't possibly be organized in the midst of blockade and civil war. The comrades in charge of our industry have cited several instances of this sort. For example, we need drills, gauges, calipers and other measuring instruments; we need steel cables and belts for the coal mines. These articles were never manufactured in our country. The Donetz coal industry suffers incredibly from the lack of steel cables. The whole world knows that metal screens, so essential in the paper industry, were always imported by us from Germany and England and never produced in our country. Similarly in need are those branches of our industry which before the war stood on their own feet. But it is self-evident (and very easy to prove) that no other system, under the given conditions following the first imperialist war, following the complete collapse of the Czarist army and capitalist economy—no other system except the Soviet system could have waged a new war for three years, could have supplied and equipped an army without perishing in the process. By all this, it is understood, I do not at all mean to deny that we committed great blunders in this sphere.

Boom and crisis

Bourgeois and reformist economists who have an ideological interest in embellishing the plight of capitalism say: In and of itself the current crisis proves nothing whatever; on the contrary, it is a normal phenomenon. Following the war we witnessed an industrial boom, and now—a crisis; it follows that capitalism is alive and thriving.

As a matter of fact, capitalism does live by crises and booms, just as a human being lives by inhaling and exhaling. First there is a boom in industry, then a stoppage, next a crisis, followed by a stoppage in the crisis, then an improvement, another boom, another stoppage and so on.

Crisis and boom blend with all the transitional phases to constitute a cycle or one of the great circles of industrial development. Each cycle lasts from 8 to 9 or 10 to 11 years. By force of its internal contradictions capitalism thus develops not along a straight line but in a zigzag manner, through ups and downs. This is what provides the ground for the following claim of the apologists of capitalism, namely: Since we observe after the war a succession of boom and crisis it follows that all things are working together for the best in this best of all capitalist worlds. It is otherwise in reality. The fact that capitalism continues to oscillate cyclically after the war merely signifies that capitalism is not yet dead, that we are not dealing with a corpse. So long as capitalism is not overthrown by the proletarian revolution, it will continue to live in cycles, swinging up and down. Crises and booms were inherent in capitalism at its very birth; they will accompany it to its grave. But to determine capitalism's age and its general condition—to establish whether it is still developing or whether it has matured or whether it is in decline—one must diagnose the character of the cycles. In much the same manner the state of the human organism can be diagnosed by whether the breathing is regular or spasmodic, deep or superficial, and so on.

The gist of the matter, comrades, may be depicted as follows: Let us take the development of capitalism—the growth of coal production, textiles, pig iron, steel, foreign trade, etc.—and draw a curve delineating this development. If in the deflexions of this curve we have expressed the true course of economic development, we shall find that this curve does not *swing upwards* in an unbroken arc but in zigzags, looping up and down—up and down in correspondence with the respective booms and crises. Thus the curve of economic development is a composite of two movements: a primary movement which expresses the general upward rise of capitalism, and a secondary movement which consists of the constant periodic oscillations corresponding to the various industrial cycles.

In January of this year the London *Times* published a table covering a period of 138 years—from the war of the 13 American colonies for independence to our own day. In this interval there have been 16 cycles, *i.e.*, 16 crises and 16 phases of prosperity. Each cycle covers approximately 8⅔, almost 9 years. Let me call your attention to the zigzags which depict the movements. At a certain point the *Times'* table shows a rise. It begins with the sum of 2 pounds sterling, or 25 gold marks per Englishman. The population has in this interim increased approximately fourfold, foreign trade to an even larger extent, so the per capita figure climbs to 30.5 pounds: and by 1920, expressed in money but not in real values it already equals 65 pounds per person. In the production of iron we observe a similar development. We see that at the early part of 1851 the demand for iron came to 4.5 kilos per capita. This figure rises to 46 kilos by 1913. Then follows a movement in reverse. This is the general balance sheet, this is the generic result of 138 years of development. If we analyze the curve of development more closely, we shall find that it falls into five segments, five different and distinct periods. From 1781 to 1851 the development is very slow; there is scarcely any movement observable. We find that in the course of 70 years foreign trade rises only from 2 to 5 pounds sterling per capita. After the revolution of 1848 which acted to extend the framework of the European market, there comes a breaking point. From 1851 to 1873 the curve of development rises steeply. In 22 years foreign trade climbs from 5 to 21 pounds sterling, while the quantity of iron rises in the same period from 4.5 to 13 kilograms per capita. Then from 1873 on there follows an epoch of depression. From 1873 till approximately 1894 we notice stagnation in English trade (even if we take into account the interest on capital invested in foreign enterprises); there is a drop from 21 to 17.4 pounds sterling—in the course of 22 years. Then comes another boom, lasting till the year 1913—foreign trade rises from 17 to 30 pounds. Then, finally, with the year 1914, the fifth period begins—the period of the destruction of capitalist economy.

How are the cyclical fluctuations blended with the primary movement of the capitalist curve of development? Very simply. In periods of rapid capitalist development the crises are brief and superficial in character, while the booms are long-lasting and far-reaching. In periods of capitalist decline, the crises are of a prolonged character while the booms are fleeting, superficial and speculative. In periods of stagnation the fluctuations occur upon one and the same level.

This means nothing else but that it is necessary to determine the general condition of the capitalist organism by the specific way in which it breathes, and the rate at which its pulse beats.

The postwar boom

Immediately following the war, an indeterminate economic situation arose. But by the spring of 1919 a boom set in; stock markets became active—prices bounded upward like a column of mercury plunged into boiling water, speculation swirled in seething whirlpools. And industry? In Central, Eastern and Southern Europe the slump continued, as attested by the statistics we have just cited. In France there was a certain improvement, primarily due to the looting of Germany. In England—partly stagnation, partly slump, with the sole exception of the commercial fleet whose tonnage has risen proportionately to the decline in actual trade. Thus on the whole the boom in Europe assumed a semi-fictitious and speculative character; and it does not signify progress, but a further decline of economy.

In the United States, following the war, industry slowed down its war production and began reconversion to a peacetime basis. There was a noticeable upswing in the petroleum, automobile and shipbuilding industries.

Year	Oil in millions of barrels	Automobiles in units	Shipbuilding in thousand tons
1918	356	1,153,000	3,033
1919	378	1,974,000	4,075
1920	442	2,350,000	2,746

In his valuable pamphlet, Comrade Varga quite correctly says:

> The fact that the postwar boom was speculative in character is most clearly revealed by the example of Germany. At the time when prices had septupled in the course of 18 months, Germany's industry kept retrogressing. . . . Her economic conjuncture was the conjuncture of liquidation sales: the remainders of the existing commodity reserves on the domestic market were dumped abroad at fabulously cheap prices.

Prices rose to their highest levels in Germany, where industry slumped lower and lower. Prices rose the least in the United States where industry continues to rise. France and England stand in between Germany and the United States.

How explain these facts and the boom itself? In the first place, by economic causes: after the war international connections were resumed, even though in an extremely abridged form, and there was a universal demand for every type of merchandise. Secondly, by political-financial causes: the European governments were in mortal fear of the crisis that had to follow the war and they resorted to any and all measures to sustain during the period of demobilization the artificial boom created by the war. The governments continued to put in circulation great quantities of paper currency, floated new loans, regulated profits, wages and bread prices, thus subsidizing the earnings of demobilized workers by dipping into the basic national funds, and thus creating an artificial economic revival in the country. Thus, throughout this interval, fictitious capital continued to distend, especially in those countries where industry continued to slump.

The fictitious postwar boom had, however, great political consequences. There is some justification for saying that it saved the bourgeoisie. Had the demobilized workers from the very beginning run up against unemployment, against living standards lower even than those before the war, it might have led to consequences fatal to the bourgeoisie. In this connection an English professor, Edwin Cannan, wrote in the *Manchester Guardian*'s New Year's review that "the impatience of men returning from the battlefields is a very dangerous thing." And he goes on quite correctly to explain the favorable transition through the gravest postwar period—the year 1919—by the fact that the government and the bourgeoisie had through their joint efforts postponed and delayed the crisis, by creating an artificial prosperity through the further destruction of Europe's basic capital. Says Cannan: "Had the same economic situation obtained in January 1919 as in 1921, chaos might have descended upon Western Europe." The violent fever of the war was prolonged for another year and a half, and the crisis erupted only after the demobilized masses of workers and peasants had already been more or less pigeonholed in their little cells.

The current crisis

Having coped with the demobilization and having withstood the first onslaught of the working masses, the bourgeoisie emerged from its state of confusion, alarm and even panic, and regained its self-confidence. It became subject to the hallucination that an epoch had finally arrived of the greatest prosperity, the end of which would never come. Eminent English political and financial figures proposed to float an international loan of two billion pounds for the work of reconstruction. It seemed as if a shower of gold would drench Europe, creating universal welfare. In this way Europe's devastation, the ruination of her cities and villages were transmuted into riches by fantastic loan figures, which actually were in themselves only poverty's gigantic shadow. Reality, however, quickly shook the bourgeoisie out of its dream world. I have already described how the crisis began in Japan (in March) and in the United States (in April), and then leaped over to England, France, Italy; and by the latter part of the year had spread throughout the world. My entire previous presentation makes it quite self-evident that we are not dealing with mere fluctuations in the course of a recurrent industrial cycle, but with a period of retribution for the havoc and waste of the entire war and postwar epoch.

In 1913 the net import of all the states totaled 65 to 70 billion gold marks. Of this sum Russia purchased 2.5 billion; Austria-Hungary—3 billion; the Balkans—1 billion; Germany—11 billion gold marks. Central and Eastern Europe's share thus came to a little more than one-fourth of the world's total imports. At the present time all these countries import less than one-fifth of their previous amount. This last figure alone sufficiently characterizes Europe's current purchasing capacity.

Europe has declined, her productive apparatus has considerably shriveled since before the war. The economic center of gravity has shifted to America, not through gradual evolution, but through America's exploitation of Europe's war market and Europe's exclusion from world trade.

Thereby America obtained the opportunity to experience a short-lived period of the greatest flowering. However, this phenomenon is an unrepeatable one, because Europe by her retrogression created an absolutely artificial market for America which cannot be replaced by any other today. Having fulfilled this role, Europe has since completely lost its capacity to repeat anything like it. Before the war the European market used to absorb more than half, almost 60 percent of all the exports of American industry; in the course of the war Europe became even more important for America, inasmuch as Europe's imports almost trebled those of the pre-war days. But out of the war Europe emerged as a greatly impoverished continent and is completely deprived of the possibility of obtaining goods from America for lack of equivalents in the shape of gold or other goods. The explanation for the crisis which started in Japan and America is to be found in just this circumstance. After a brief and highly favorable conjuncture of almost two years' duration, there has arrived a completely genuine crisis, whose meaning for Europe is as follows: "You're poor, you must cut your coat according to your cloth; you're no longer in a position to import the goods you need from America." For America this selfsame crisis means the following: "You've enriched yourself because you were placed in a position to siphon off Europe's wealth. This lasted four or five or six years, as long as the war continued. But now an end has come to this affluent state of affairs." Some countries are completely ruined, their productive apparatus must be rebuilt anew. Within each people the division of labor must be resumed. French and German economies still continue to function mechanically owing to the impetus prior to and during the war. Germany, however, must fall back in order to introduce concord and order into her economic apparatus; and just as it was necessary to organize the economy during the war in order to mitigate the privations resulting from it, just so Germany must continue the selfsame policy today, unless the revolution intervenes. Should developments proceed along present lines, it will be necessary to introduce organization into the country's economic life and to establish, first and foremost, the necessary proportion between the means of production and the means of consumption. In other words, the necessary and correct reciprocal relation will be created through the medium of new wars and all sorts of palliative measures, unless the revolution erupts. The very same thing applies to France and to Europe as a whole so long as this period of regression in economic life continues, a period in which the capitalist countries tend to sink to the level of those that have suffered the most and have become the poorest. During this leveling-out process America will have to forget about maintaining her greatest and most important markets on their former scale. And this means that the foregoing crisis is not a transitory normal crisis for America but the beginning of a prolonged epoch of depression. Let us refer back to our table in which the various periods are delineated: first, the epoch of stagnation, which lasted 70 years, followed by the epoch of boom from 1851 to 1873. These 22 years of turbulent expansion were marked by two crises and two favorable conjunctural periods, and therewith these favorable conjunctures were genuinely such, while the crises were of very weak character. Next, from 1873 up to the middle of 1890, stagnation sets in again, or at any rate the development slows down exceedingly. Then, there is unprecedented expansion once again. All this is a process of adaptation, a process of leveling out. Whenever capitalism in any one country runs up against a saturation of this or that market, it is compelled to seek other markets. Major historical events—economic crises, revolutions, and so on—will determine whether we observe stagnation, booms or regressions in such periods. These are the main features of capitalist development.

At the given moment capitalism has entered a period of prolonged and profound depression. Strictly speaking, this epoch should have set in—insofar as one can prophesy about the past—as far back as 1913 when the world market as a result of 20 years of turbulent development had already become inadequate for the development of German, English and North American capitalism. These giants of capitalist development took it fully into account. They said to themselves: In order to avoid this depression which will linger for many years, we shall create an acute war crisis, destroy our rival and gain unchallenged domination over the world market that has become too constricted. But the war lasted far too long, provoking not only an acute crisis but a protracted one; it destroyed completely Europe's capitalist economic apparatus, thereby facilitating America's feverish development. But after exhausting Europe, the war led in the long run to a great crisis in America, too. Once again we are witnessing that selfsame depression which they had sought to escape, but which has been intensified many-fold owing to Europe's impoverishment.

And so, what are the immediate economic perspectives?

It is quite obvious that America will have to suffer curtailment since the European war market is gone beyond recall. On the other hand, Europe will likewise have to level herself out in accordance with the most backward, *i.e.,* the most ruined areas and branches of industry. This will mean an economic leveling out in reverse, and, consequently, a prolonged crisis: in some branches of economy and some countries—stagnation; in others—a weak development. Cyclical fluctuations will continue to take place but, in general, the curve of capitalist development will slope not upwards but downwards.

Crisis, boom and revolution

The reciprocal relation between boom and crisis in economy and the development of revolution is of great interest to us not only from the point of theory but above all practically. Many of you will recall that Marx and Engels wrote in 1851—when the boom was at its peak—that it was necessary at that time to recognize that the Revolution of 1848 had terminated, or, at any rate, had been interrupted until the next crisis. Engels wrote that while the crisis of 1847 was the mother of revolution,[7] the boom of 1849–51 was the mother of triumphant counter-revolution. It would, however, be very one-sided and utterly false to interpret these judgments in the sense that a crisis invariably engenders revolutionary action while a boom, on the contrary, pacifies the working class. The Revolution of 1848 was not born out of the crisis. The latter merely provided the last impetus. Essentially the revolution grew out of the contradictions between the needs of capitalist development and the fetters of the semi-feudal social and state system. The irresolute and half-way Revolution of 1848 did, however, sweep away the remnants of the regime of guilds and serfdom and thereby extended the framework of capitalist development. Under these conditions and these conditions alone, the boom of 1851 marked the beginning of an entire epoch of capitalist prosperity which lasted till 1873.

In citing Engels it is very dangerous to overlook these basic facts. For it was precisely after 1850, when Marx and Engels made their observations, that there set in not a normal or regular situation, but an era of capitalist *Sturm und Drang* (storm and stress) for which the soil had been cleared by the Revolution of 1848. This is of decisive importance here. This storm-and-stress era, during which prosperity and the favorable conjuncture were very strong, while the crisis was merely superficial and short-lived—it was precisely this period that ended with revolution. At issue here is not whether an improvement in the conjuncture is possible, but whether the fluctuations of the conjuncture are proceeding along an ascending or descending curve. This is the most important aspect of the whole question.

Can we expect the same effects to follow the economic upswing of 1919–20? Under no circumstances. The extension of the framework of capitalist development was not even involved here. Does this mean that a new commercial-industrial upswing is excluded in the future, and even in the more or less near future? Not at all! I have already said that so long as capitalism remains alive it continues to inhale and exhale. But in the epoch which we have entered—the epoch of retribution for the drain and destruction of wartime, the epoch of leveling out *in reverse*—upswings can be only of a superficial and primarily speculatory character, while the crises become more and more prolonged and deeper-going.

Historical development has not led to the victorious proletarian dictatorship in Central and Western Europe. But it is the most brazen and at the same time the most stupid lie to attempt to conclude from this, as do the reformists, that the economic equilibrium of the capitalist world has been surreptitiously restored. This is not claimed even by the crassest reactionaries, who are really capable of thinking, for example, Professor Hoetzch. In his review of the year this professor says in effect that the year 1920 did not bring victory to the revolution, but neither did it restore capitalist world economy. It is only an unstable and extremely temporary equilibrium. Mr. Chavenon says: "In France we now see only the possibility of the further ruination of capitalist economy by state finances, currency inflation and open bankruptcy." I have already tried to show you what this means. I have depicted the acutest crisis which the capitalist world has ever experienced. Three or four weeks ago in the capitalist press, gusts of an approaching improvement could be felt, the approach of an epoch of prosperity. But it is already obvious that this spring breeze was premature. A certain improvement has taken place in the financial situation, *i.e.*, it is no longer as grave as before. In the markets prices have fallen, but this by no means implies a revival of trade. The stock markets are at a standstill, while in production the regression still continues. American metallurgy is operating now only at one-third capacity. In England the last blast furnaces have been shut down. This shows that the curtailment of production continues.

This movement in reverse will not, of course, continue interminably at one and the same tempo. This is absolutely excluded. There must come a breathing spell for the capitalist organism. But from the fact that it will inhale a little fresh air and that a certain improvement will come about, it is still too early to conclude prosperity. A new phase will set in, when they will try to eliminate the contradiction between the basic poverty and the overproduction of fictitious wealth. After which the paroxysms of the economic organism will continue. All this gives us, as has been said, a picture of profound economic depression.

On the basis of this economic depression the bourgeoisie will be compelled to exert stronger and stronger pressure upon the working class. This is already to be seen in the cutting of wages which has started in the full-blooded capitalist countries: in America and in England, and then throughout all of Europe. This leads to great struggles over wages. Our task is to extend these struggles, by basing ourselves on a clear understanding of the economic situation. This is quite obvious. It might be asked whether the great struggles over wages, a classic example of which is the miners' strike in England, will lead automatically to the world revolution, to the final civil war and the struggle for the conquest of political power. However, it is not Marxist to pose the question in such a way. We have no automatic guarantees of development. But when the crisis is replaced by a transitory favorable conjuncture, what will this signify for our development? Many comrades say that if an improvement takes place in this epoch it would be fatal for our revolution. No, under no circumstances. In general, there is no automatic dependence of the proletarian revolutionary movement upon a crisis. There is only a dialectical interaction. It is essential to understand this.

Let us look at the relations in Russia. The 1905 revolution was defeated. The workers bore great sacrifices. In 1906 and 1907 the last revolutionary flare-ups occurred and by the autumn of 1907 a great world crisis broke out. The signal for it was given by Wall Street's Black Friday. Throughout 1907 and 1908 and 1909 the most terrible crisis reigned in Russia too. It killed the movement completely, because the workers had suffered so greatly during the struggle that this depression could act only to dishearten them. There were many disputes among us over what would lead to the revolution: a crisis or a favorable conjuncture?

At that time many of us defended the viewpoint that the Russian revolutionary movement could be regenerated only by a favorable economic conjuncture. And that is what took place. In 1910, 1911 and 1912, there was an improvement in our economic situation and a favorable conjuncture which acted to reassemble the demoralized and devitalized workers who had lost their courage. They realized again how important they were in production; and they passed over to an offensive, first in the economic field and later in the political field as well. On the eve of the war the working class had become so consolidated, thanks to this period of prosperity, that it was able to pass to a direct assault. And should we today, in the period of the greatest exhaustion of the working class resulting from the crisis and the continual struggle, fail to gain victory, which is possible, then a change in the conjuncture and a rise in living standards would not have a harmful effect upon the revolution, but would be on the contrary highly propitious. Such a change could prove harmful only in the event that the favorable conjuncture marked the beginning of a long epoch of prosperity. But a long period of prosperity would signify that an expansion of the market had been attained, which is absolutely excluded. For after all, capitalist economy already embraces the terrestrial globe. Europe's impoverishment and America's sumptuous renascence on the huge war market corroborate the conclusion that this prosperity cannot be restored through the capitalist development of China, Siberia, South America and other countries, where American capitalism is of course seeking and creating outlet markets but on a scale in no way commensurate to Europe. It follows that we are on the eve of a period of depression; and this is incontestable.

With such a perspective, a mitigation of the crisis would not signify a mortal blow to the revolution but would only enable the working class to gain a breathing spell during which it could undertake to reorganize its ranks in order subsequently to pass over to attack on a firmer basis. This is one of the possibilities. The content of the other possibility is this: that the crisis may turn from acute into chronic, become intensified and endure for many years. All this is not excluded. The possibility remains open in such a situation that the working class would gather its last forces and, having learned from experience, conquer state power in the most important capitalist countries. The only thing excluded is the automatic restoration of capitalist equilibrium on a new foundation and a capitalist upswing in the next few years. This is absolutely impossible under the conditions of modern economic stagnation.

Here we approach the question of social equilibrium. After all, it is frequently said—and this is the guiding thought not only of a Cunow[8] but also of Hilferding—that capitalism is being automatically restored on a new foundation. Faith in automatic evolution is the most important and the most characteristic trait of opportunism.

If we grant—and let us grant it for the moment—that the working class fails to rise in revolutionary struggle, but allows the bourgeoisie the opportunity to rule the world's destiny for a long number of years, say, two or three decades, then assuredly some sort of new equilibrium will be established. Europe will be thrown violently into reverse gear. Millions of European workers will die from unemployment and malnutrition. The United States will be compelled to reorient itself on the world market, reconvert its industry, *and suffer curtailment for a considerable period.* Afterwards, after a new world division of labor is thus established in agony for 15 or 20 or 25 years, a new epoch of capitalist upswing might perhaps ensue.

But this entire conception is exceedingly abstract and one-sided. Matters are pictured here as if the proletariat had ceased to struggle. *Meanwhile, there cannot even be talk of this if only for the reason that the class contradictions have become aggravated in the extreme precisely during the recent years.*

Herein is the nub of the schematic exposition of restored equilibrium which Herr Heinrich Cunow and others see in their daydreams. Each measure to which capitalism is constrained in order to make a step forward in restoring equilibrium, each and all of this immediately acquires a decisive significance for the social equilibrium, tends more and more to undermine it, and ever more powerfully impels the working class to struggle. The first task in achieving equilibrium is to set the productive apparatus in order, but to do so it is indispensable to accumulate capital. But to make accumulation possible it is necessary to raise the productivity of labor. How? Through an augmented and intensified exploitation of the working class, inasmuch as the decline in the productivity of labor power during these three postwar years is a widely known fact. To reestablish world economy on capitalist foundations, it is indispensable to dispose again of a world equivalent—the gold standard. Without it capitalist economy cannot exist, inasmuch as there cannot be any production while prices dance their dance of death, increasing 100 percent in the course of a single month as happens in Germany, contingent upon the fluctuations of German currency. A capitalist is not interested in production. For he is being lured from afar by speculation, which tempts him by much greater profits than can be gained from slowly developing industry. What does the stabilization of currency signify? For France and Germany it signifies a declaration of state bankruptcy. But to declare a state insolvent is to incur a vast shift of property relations within the nation. And those states which have declared themselves insolvent have become the arena for a new struggle over the distribution of the new national wealth, which is a giant step toward the sharpening of the class struggle. At the same time all this signifies a renunciation of social and political equilibrium, *i.e.*, a revolutionary flux. However, the declaration of state bankruptcy does not make it possible immediately to pass to the restoration of equilibrium. This must likewise be followed by the lengthening of the working week, the repeal of the 8-hour day, and more intensive exploitation. Therewith it, of course, becomes necessary to overcome the resistance of the working class. In short, speaking theoretically and abstractly, the restoration of capitalist equilibrium is possible. But it does not take place in a social and political vacuum—it can take place only through the classes. Every step, no matter how tiny, toward the restoration of equilibrium in economic life is a blow to the unstable social equilibrium upon which the Messrs.

Capitalists still continue to maintain themselves. And this is the most important thing.

The aggravation of social contradictions

Economic development is thus not an automatic process. The issue is not restricted solely to the productive foundations of society. Upon these foundations there live and work human beings and the development occurs through these human beings. What, then, has taken place in the field of relations between human beings, or, more precisely, between classes? We have seen that Germany and other European countries too have been thrown back 20 or 30 years in terms of their economic level. Have they perhaps been simultaneously thrown back in social terms, in the class sense? Not at all. The classes of Germany, the number of workers and their concentration, the concentration of capital and its organizational form—all this had taken shape prior to the war, and in particular as a result of the last two decades of prosperity (1894–1913). And later on, all this became still more aggravated: during the war—with the aid of the state intervention; after the war—through the fever of speculation and the growing concentration of capital. We thus have two processes of development. National wealth and national income keep falling, *but the development of classes continues therewith not to regress but to progress.* More and more people are becoming proletarianized, capital is being concentrated in fewer and fewer hands, banks keep merging, industrial enterprises become concentrated in trusts. As a result, the class struggle inevitably becomes sharper on the basis of a declining national income. Herein is the whole gist of the matter. The more restricted becomes the material foundation under their feet, the more fiercely must classes and groups fight for their share of this national income. We must not lose sight of this circumstance for a single moment. While Europe has been thrown back 30 years with regard to her national wealth this does not at all mean that she has grown thirty years younger. No, in the class sense, she has become thirty years older.

The peasantry

During the first period of the war it was said and written that the peasantry throughout Europe was profiting by the war. And indeed the state was in critical need of bread and meat for the army. For all this, insane prices which kept soaring were paid, and the peasants stuffed their pockets with paper money. With this paper money which kept depreciating, the peasants paid debts which they had previously contracted when currency was at par. Of course this was a very profitable operation for them.

Bourgeois economists reckoned that the prosperity of peasant economy would secure the stability of capitalism after the war. But they miscalculated. The peasants paid off their mortgages but husbandry nowise consists solely of paying off debts to bankers. It consists of cultivating the soil, fertilizing it, acquiring inventory and good seeds, making technological improvements, and so on. This was either not done at all, or it cost wild sums of money. Moreover, there was a scarcity of labor, agriculture declined and the peasants, after the initial semi-fictitious boom, began to face ruin. This process is to be observed in its various stages throughout Europe. But it has also manifested itself very acutely in America. There was extreme suffering among the American, Canadian, Australian and South American farmers when it was revealed that ruined Europe was no longer able to buy their grain. The price of grain dropped. Among farmers there is ferment and dissatisfaction throughout the world. *The peasantry thus ceases to be one of the mainstays of law and order. Before the working class opens up the possibility of attracting to its side in the struggle at least a section of the peasantry (the lowest ranks), of neutralizing another section (the middle peasants), and of isolating and paralyzing the tops (the kulaks, the well-to-do farmers).*

The new middle estate

The reformists pinned great hopes upon the so-called middle estate. Engineers, technicians, doctors, lawyers, bookkeepers, accountants, functionaries, civilians and government employes alike, and so on—all these constitute a semi-conservative stratum which stands between capital and labor and which must, in the opinion of reformists, reconcile both sides, while directing and at the same time supporting democratic regimes. This class has suffered even more than the working class during the war and after, that is, its living standards have deteriorated to an even greater degree than the living standards of the working class. The main reason for this is the decline in the purchasing power of money, the depreciation of paper currency. In all European countries this has given rise to sharp discontent among the lowest and even middle ranks of functionaries and the technological intelligentsia. In Italy, for example, the functionaries are engaged in a bitter strike at this very hour. Of course, functionaries in government or civil employ, bank clerks, etc., etc., have not become a proletarian class, but they have shed their former conservative character. They do not prop up the state so much as shake and convulse its apparatus by their dissatisfaction and protests.

The discontent of the bourgeois intelligentsia is further aggravated by its intimate ties with the commercial-industrial petty and middle bourgeoisie. The latter feel themselves slighted, cheated of their rightful share. The cartel-ized bourgeoisie continues to wallow in wealth, notwithstanding the country's ruination. It arrogates to itself an ever-increasing portion of the declining national income. The uncartel-ized bourgeoisie and the new middle estate are sinking both absolutely and relatively. As regards the proletariat, it is quite probable that despite the deterioration of its living standards, its common share in the declining national income is greater today than before the war. Cartel capital seeks to slash the worker's share by driving it down to pre-war levels. The worker, however, takes as his starting point not the statistical charts but his reduced living standards and strives to increase his share of the national income. *And so, the peasants are disgruntled by the decline of the economy; the intelligentsia is growing poorer and sinking; the petty and middle bourgeoisie are ruined and discontented. The class struggle is sharpening.*

International relations

International relations of course play an enormous role in the life of the capitalist world. The latter had this brought home to it all too clearly during the World War. And at the present time when we pose the question of whether it is possible or impossible for capitalism to restore its world equilibrium, we must take note of the international conditions under which this work of reconstruction is being done. It is not hard to ascertain that the international relations have become far more strained, far less compatible with the "peaceful" evolution of capitalism than was the case prior to the war.

Why did the war occur? Because the productive forces found themselves too constricted within the frameworks of the most powerful capitalist states. The inner urge of imperialist capitalism was to eradicate the state boundaries and to seize the entire terrestrial globe, abolishing tariffs and other barriers which restrict the development of the productive forces. Herein are the economic foundations of imperialism and the root causes of the war. What were the results? Europe is now richer in boundaries and tariff walls than ever before. A whole galaxy of tiny states has been formed. The territories of the former Austro-Hungarian empire are now criss-crossed by a dozen tariff lines. The Englishman Keynes[9] has called Europe a madhouse, and indeed from the standpoint of economic development this entire particularism of tiny states with their shut-inness, their tariff systems and so on, represent a monstrous anachronism, an insane implantation of medievalism into the twentieth century. While the Balkan peninsula is being barbarianized, Europe is becoming Balkanized.

The relations between Germany and France militate as heretofore against the possibility of any kind of European equilibrium. France is compelled to loot and rape Germany in order to maintain her own class equilibrium, which is not commensurate to the depleted foundation of French economy. Germany will not and cannot remain the object of this pillage. At the present time, true enough, an agreement has been reached. Germany has pledged to pay annually 2 billion gold marks, plus 26 percent of her exports. This transaction represents a victory for England's policy, which aims to hinder the occupation of the Ruhr by France. At the present time the bulk of European iron ore is in the hands of France; the bulk of coal—in Germany's hands. The cardinal condition for the regeneration of European economy is the productive combination of French ore with German coal, but such a combination, unconditionally essential for economic development, happens to be mortally dangerous to English capitalism. All the efforts of London are for this reason directed to prevent either a warlike or peaceable combination of French ore with German coal. But this leads to a still greater aggravation of the antagonism between England and France.

France has temporarily accepted the compromise, all the more so since her disorganized productive apparatus is incapable of digesting even the coal with which Germany is now forcibly compelled to supply her. But this does not at all mean that the question of the Ruhr has been definitively settled. The very first infraction by Germany of her reparation obligations will inevitably raise once again the question of the Ruhr's fate.

The growth of France's influence in Europe, and partly in the world as well, during the past year is due not to the strengthening of France but to the patent progressive weakening of England.

Great Britain has conquered Germany. This was the chief issue settled by the last war. And in essence the war was not a world war but a European war, even though the struggle between the two mightiest European states—England and Germany—was resolved with the participation of the forces and resources of the entire world. England has conquered Germany. But today, England is much weaker in the world market, and generally in the world situation, than she was before the war. The United States has grown at England's expense much more than England has at the expense of Germany.

America is battering England down, first of all by the more rationalized and more progressive character of its industry. The productivity of an American worker is 150 percent above the productivity of an English worker. In other words, two American workers produce, thanks to a more perfectly equipped industry, as much as five English workers. This fact alone, established by English statistical researches, testifies that England is doomed in a struggle with America; and this alone suffices to push England toward a war with America, so long as the English fleet preserves its preponderance on the oceans.

American coal is crowding out English coal throughout the world and even in Europe. Yet, England's world trade has been based primarily on her export of coal. In addition, oil is now of decisive significance for industry and defense; oil not only runs automobiles, tractors, submarines, airplanes, but is greatly superior to coal even for the big ocean liners. Up to 70 percent of the world's oil is produced within the boundaries of the United States. Consequently, in the event of war all this oil would be in the hands of Washington. In addition America holds in her hands Mexican oil, which supplies up to 12 percent of the world output. True, Americans are accusing England of having cornered, outside the United States borders, up to 90 percent of the world oil sources and of shutting off the Americans from access to them, while American oil fields face exhaustion within the next few years. But all these geological and statistical computations are quite dubious and arbitrary. They are compiled to order so as to justify American pretensions to the oil of Mexico, Mesopotamia, and so on. But were the danger of exhaustion of American oil fields actually to prove real, it would constitute one more reason for speeding up the war between the United States and England.

Europe's indebtedness to America is a touchy question. The debts on the whole amount to $18 billion. The United States always has the opportunity of creating the greatest difficulties in the English money market by presenting its demands for payment. As is well known, England has even proposed that America cancel English debts, promising in turn to cancel Europe's debt to England. Since England owes America much more than the continental countries of the Entente owe her, she stands to profit from such a transaction. America has refused. The capitalist Yankees showed no inclination to finance with their own funds Great Britain's preparations for war with the United States.

The alliance between England and Japan, which is fighting America for preponderance on the Asiatic continent, has likewise aggravated in the extreme the relations between the United States and England.

But most acute in character, in view of all the indicated circumstances, is the question of the navy. Wilson's government, upon running up against England's opposition in world affairs, launched a gigantic program of naval construction. Harding's government has taken this program over from its predecessor and this program is being rushed through at top speed. By 1924 the U.S. Navy will not only be far more powerful than that of England, but also superior to the English and Japanese fleets put together, if not in tonnage, then in firing power.

What does this mean from the English point of view? It means that by 1924 England must either accept the challenge and try to destroy the military, naval and economic might of the United States by taking advantage of her present superiority, or she must passively become converted into a power of the second or third order, surrendering once and for all domination of the oceans and seas to the United States. Thus the last slaughter of the peoples, which "settled" in its own way the European question, has for this very reason raised in all its scope the world question, namely: Will England or the United States rule the world? The preparations for the new world war are proceeding full speed ahead. The expenditures for the army and the navy have grown extraordinarily as compared with pre-war times. The English military budget has increased threefold, the American—three and a half times.

The contradictions between England and America are being transformed into a process of automatic proliferation, an automatic approach closer and closer to tomorrow's sanguinary conflict. Here we actually are dealing with automatism.

On January 1, 1914, that is, at the moment when the "armed peace" was under its greatest strain, there were approximately 7 million soldiers with bayonets throughout the world. At the beginning of the current year there were about 18 million soldiers with bayonets. The bulk of these armies weighs down, of course, upon exhausted Europe.

Consequently, militarism has grown. All this is one of the most important obstacles in the way of economic progress. One of the main causes of the war was the intolerable burden of armed peace upon the European economy. A horrible end was preferable to horror without end. But it turned out that this is no end at all, that horror *after* the end is even more horrible than it was before the horrible end, that is, before the last war.

The grave crisis, arising from the constriction of the world market, acts to aggravate extremely the struggle between the capitalist states, depriving world relations of any kind of stability. Not only Europe but the whole world is being turned into a madhouse! Under these conditions there is hardly any necessity to speak of the restoration of capitalist equilibrium.

The working class after the war

From the standpoint of the revolution, in general and on the whole, all this creates for the working class a very favorable and at the same time an extremely complex situation. After all, what lies ahead of us is not a chaotic, spontaneous assault, the first stage of which we observed in Europe in 1918–19. It seemed to us (and there was some historical justification for it) that in the period when the bourgeoisie was disorganized this assault could mount in ever-rising waves, that in this process the consciousness of the leading layers of the working class would become clarified, and that in this way the proletariat would attain state power in the course of one or two years. There was this historical possibility. But it did not materialize. History has—with the assistance of the bourgeoisie's bad or good will, its cunning, its experience, its organization and its instinct for power—granted the bourgeoisie a fairly prolonged breathing space. No miracles have taken place. What has been destroyed, or burned, or ruined, has not come to life again; but the bourgeoisie did prove itself capable of orientation in a pauperized milieu; it restored its state apparatus and knew how to utilize the weakness of the working class. From the standpoint of revolutionary perspectives, the situation has become more complicated, but still remains favorable. It is perhaps with greater assurance that we can say today that on the whole the situation is fully revolutionary. But the revolution is not so docile, nor so domesticated as to be led on a leash, as we once imagined. The revolution has its own fluctuations, its own crises and its own favorable conjunctures.

Immediately after the war, the bourgeoisie was in a state of highest confusion and alarm—the workers, especially those returning from the army, were in a peremptory mood. But the working class as a whole was disoriented, uncertain of just what forms life would take after the war, unsure of what and how to demand, dubious of what road to take. . . . The movement, as we saw at the beginning of this report, assumed an extremely stormy character, but the working class lacked a firm leadership.

On the other hand, the bourgeoisie was ready to make very great concessions. It kept up the financial and economic war regime (loans, emission of paper currency, grain monopoly, relief for the unemployed working masses, etc., etc.). In other words, the ruling bourgeoisie continued to disorganize the economic foundation and to disrupt more and more the productive and financial equilibrium in order to bolster up the equilibrium between the classes during the most critical period. Up to now it has more or less succeeded in accomplishing this.

At the present time the bourgeoisie is proceeding to solve the question of restoring the economic equilibrium. Involved here are not temporary concessions or sops to the working class but measures of a fundamental character. The disorganized productive apparatus must be restored. Currency must be stabilized, for the world market is unthinkable without a universal world equivalent, and, therefore, equally unthinkable without a universal equivalent is a "balanced" national industry, tied up with the world market.

To restore the productive apparatus is to curtail work on consumer goods and to step up work on the means of production. It is necessary to augment accumulation, *i.e.*, to raise the intensity of labor and slash wages.

To stabilize the currency it is necessary, apart from refusing to pay intolerable debts, to improve the trade balance, *i.e.*, import less and export more. And to this end it is necessary to consume less and produce more, *i.e.*, once again slash wages and raise the intensity of labor.

Every step toward the restoration of capitalist economy is bound up with boosting the norm of exploitation and will therefore unfailingly provoke resistance on the part of the working class. In other words, every effort by the bourgeoisie to restore the equilibrium in production or in distribution or in state finances must inescapably disrupt the unstable equilibrium between the classes. Whereas during the two postwar years, the bourgeoisie was guided in its economic policy primarily by the desire to propitiate the proletariat, even at the cost of further economic ruination, at the present time, in the epoch of unprecedented crisis, the bourgeoisie has begun mending the economic situation by steadily increasing the pressure on the working class.

England provides us with a most graphic illustration of how this pressure engenders resistance. And the resistance of the working class acts to disrupt economic stability and to transform all speeches anent the restoration of equilibrium into so many empty sounds.

The struggle of the proletariat for power has been unquestionably protracted. We did not get an overwhelming onslaught, we did not see a picture of wave mounting upon wave, rolling onward incessantly until the capitalist system was swept away in the final surge.

In this struggle we observed both ups and downs, both offense and defense. Class maneuvering was far from always skillful on our part. The reason for it is twofold: In the first place, the weakness of the Communist parties, which arose only after the war, which lacked the necessary experience and the necessary apparatus, which were without sufficient influence and—what is the most important—didn't know how to pay sufficient attention to the working masses. In this sphere we have in any case taken a big step forward during the recent years. The Communist parties have grown stronger and have developed. The second reason for the protracted and uneven character of the struggle lies in the heterogeneous composition of the working class itself, as it emerged from the war.

Least shaken by the war are the labor bureaucracy, the

trade union and party bureaucracy and the parliamentarians. Capitalist states in all countries have shown utmost attention to and solicitude for this superstructure, understanding excellently that without it the working class could not possibly have been kept in submission through the years of bloodletting. The labor bureaucracy received all sorts of privileges and emerged from the war with the same habits of bovine conservatism with which it had entered the war, but somewhat more discredited and more intimately bound up with the respective capitalist states. Skilled workers of the oldest generation, inured to their trade union and party organizations, especially in Germany, have by and large remained to this very day the main support of the labor bureaucracy, but their inertia is by no means absolute. Those workers who have passed through the school of war—and they are the pith of the working class—have introduced a new psychology among the proletariat, new habits and new attitudes to the questions of struggle, to the questions of life and death. They are ready to solve questions by means of force, but they have firmly assimilated from the war that a successful application of force presupposes correct tactics and strategy. These elements will march into battle but what they want is a firm leadership and a serious preparation. Many backward categories of workers, including women workers whose number has grown prodigiously during the war, have now become, as a consequence of an abrupt turn in their consciousness, the most militant, though not always the most class-conscious section of the working class. Finally, at the extreme left wing we see the working-class youth, who have grown up during the war amid the roar of battles and revolutionary paroxysms and who are destined to fill a great place in the coming struggle.

All these extraordinarily augmented proletarian masses—

the old workers and the worker-recruits, the workers who remained in the rear and the workers who spent several years under fire—this entire multimillion-headed mass is passing through the school of revolution not in the same way and not at the same time.

This was brought home to us again in the instance of the March events in Germany, where the workers of Central Germany, the most backward elements before the war, were eager to rush into battle in March without pausing to consider what were the chances for success whereas the Berlin workers and those of Saxony in the course of revolutionary battles gained some experience and became more cautious. It is undeniable that the general course of the postwar struggle and especially the current offensive of capitalism are fusing together all the layers of the working class with the sole exception of its privileged aristocracy. The Communist parties are getting more and more opportunities for establishing a genuine working-class united front.

Immediate perspectives and tasks

The revolution has three sources which are interconnected. The revolution's first source is the decline of Europe. Class equilibrium in Europe was maintained first of all by England's dominant position on the world market. Today this dominant position of Europe has been completely lost, and irretrievably so. Hence the inevitability of powerful revolutionary paroxysms which can terminate either in the victory of the proletariat or in Europe's complete downfall.

The second source of the revolutionary struggle is in the severe spasms of the entire economic organism of the United States: an unprecedented boom, elicited by the European war, and next—a cruel crisis engendered by the drawn-out consequences of this war. The revolutionary movement of the American proletariat can under these conditions acquire the same tempo, unequaled in history, as the economic development of the United States in recent years.

The third source of revolutionary struggle is the industrialization of the colonies, above all, India. The basis for the liberationist struggle of the colonies is constituted by the peasant masses. But the peasants in their struggle need leadership. Such a leadership used to be provided by the native bourgeoisie. The latter's struggle against foreign imperialist domination cannot, however, be either consistent or energetic inasmuch as the native bourgeoisie itself is intimately bound up with foreign capital and represents to a large measure an agency of foreign capital. Only the rise of a native proletariat strong enough numerically and capable of struggle can provide a real axis for the revolution. In comparison to the country's entire population, the size of the Indian proletariat is, of course, numerically small, but those who have grasped the meaning of the revolution's development in Russia will never fail to take into account that the proletariat's revolutionary role in the Oriental countries will far exceed its actual numerical strength. This applies not only to purely colonial countries, like India, or semi-colonial countries like China, but also to Japan where capitalist oppression blends with a feudal-caste, bureaucratic absolutism.

Thus both the world situation and the future perspectives are profoundly revolutionary in character.

When the bourgeoisie resorted after the war to throwing sops to the working class, the conciliators obsequiously converted these sops into reforms (the 8-hour day, unemployment insurance, and so on); and discovered—amid the ruins—the era of reformism. Today the bourgeoisie has passed over to a counter-offensive all along the line, and even the London *Times*—a super-capitalist daily—refers with alarm to capitalist "Bolsheviks." The current epoch is the epoch of counter-reformism. The English pacifist Norman Angell has called the war a miscalculation. The experience of the last war has shown that the calculation, from the bookkeeping standpoint, was indeed a false one. After the war it might have seemed that the triumph of pacifism was about to arrive and that the League of Nations was its manifestation. Today we see that the calculation of pacifism was a miscalculation. Never before has capitalist mankind engaged in such frenzied preparation for a new war as at the present time. Democracy is being stripped of its illusions even in the eyes of the most conservative layers of the working class. Not so long ago democracy used to be counterposed only to the dictatorship of the proletariat with its terror, its *Cheka,* and so forth and so on. Nowadays democracy is being ever more counterposed to any and all forms of the class struggle. Lloyd George has advised the coal miners to solicit Parliament with their grievances and has branded their strike as an act of violence upon the will of the nation.

Under the Hohenzollern regime the German workers found a certain stability and well-defined limits. The workers knew on the whole what could be done and what was forbidden. In Ebert's republic a worker-striker always incurs the risk of having his throat cut in the streets or in a police station, without further ado. Ebertian "democracy" offers the German workers as little as do high wages in terms of completely depreciated currency.

The task of the Communist parties lies in encompassing the existing situation as a whole, and intervening actively in the struggle of the proletariat in order to conquer the majority of the working class on the basis of this struggle.

Should the situation in this or that country become extremely exacerbated, we must pose the basic question pointblank and we must join battle in whatever condition the events catch us.

However, if the march of events proceeds more evenly and smoothly, then we must utilize all the possibilities in order *to gain the majority of the working class prior to the decisive events.*

We do not as yet have the majority of the working class throughout the world; but a much larger section of the proletariat is with us today than a year or two ago. After we have actually analyzed the existing situation, which is one of the important tasks of our Congress; after we have reviewed the situation in each given country, we must say to ourselves: The struggle will perhaps be long and we shall not advance at so feverish a pace as we should like to. The struggle will be very harsh and will exact many sacrifices. We have become stronger through accumulated experience. We shall know how to maneuver in this struggle. We shall know how to graph for our tactics not only an ideal mathematical line, but also the sinuosities in a shifting situation, amidst which the revolutionary line must cut its way. We shall understand how to maneuver actively amid the decomposition of the capitalist class; we shall be able to mobilize the forces of the workers for the social revolution. I believe that our successes as well as our failures have demonstrated that the difference between us and the Independent Social Democrats does not consist in our having said that we would make the revolution in the year 1919 while they kept maintaining that the revolution would come much later. No, that's not where the difference lies. The difference lies in this, that the Social Democracy and the Independent Social Democrats support the bourgeoisie against the revolution under any and all circumstances. Whereas we were and are ready to utilize every situation, no matter what changes it may undergo, for the revolutionary offensive and for the conquest of political power. [Long, enthusiastic applause.]

In today's defensive economic struggles unfolding on the basis of the crisis, the Communists must participate most actively in all the trade unions, in all the strikes and demonstrations, and in all kinds of movements, always maintaining their inner ties unbroken in their work, and always stepping to the forefront as the most resolute and best disciplined wing of the working class. Depending upon the course of the crisis and the shifts in the political situation, the defensive economic struggle may become extended, embracing ever-newer layers among the working class, among the population and among the army of the unemployed; and on becoming transformed at a certain stage into a revolutionary offensive struggle, it may be crowned with victory. It is precisely to this end that our efforts must be directed.

But what if in place of the crisis an improvement should come in the world economic conjuncture? What then? Would this signify that the revolutionary struggle is checked for an indefinite period?

From my entire report, comrades, it follows that a new upswing, which can be neither prolonged nor profound, can by no means act as a check upon the revolutionary development. The industrial boom of 1849–51 dealt a blow to the revolution only because the Revolution of 1848 had expanded the framework of capitalist development. As touches the events of 1914–21, they have acted not to expand but to contract in the extreme the framework of the world market, and therefore the curve of capitalist development as a whole will much sooner slope downwards in the next period. In these conditions a temporary boom can only strengthen the class self-assurance of the workers and fuse their ranks not only in the factories but also in struggles and it can provide the impulse not only for their economic counter-offensive but also for their revolutionary struggle for power.

The situation is becoming more and more favorable for us but it is also growing extremely complex. Victory will not come to us automatically. The ground under the enemy's feet is undermined, but our enemy remains strong, our enemy keenly discerns our weak spots, veers and maneuvers, always being guided by icy calculation. We—the entire Communist International—have a great deal to learn from the experience of our battles during these three years, and especially from the experience of our mistakes and our failures. Civil war demands political, tactical and strategical maneuvering; it demands that the peculiarities of each given situation, the strong and the weak sides of the enemy, be taken into account; it demands a combination of enthusiasm with icy calculation; it demands not only the ability to assume the offensive but also the readiness to temporarily retreat in order to preserve one's forces so as to deal all the surer a blow.

Let me repeat, the world situation and the future perspectives remain profoundly revolutionary. This creates the necessary premises for our victory. But full guarantees can be given only by our expert tactics, by our strong organization. To raise the Communist International to a higher level, to make it more expert tactically—that is the basic task of the Third World Congress of the Communist International.

20. Summary speech

Third Session, June 24, 1921

Comrades! The first speaker in the discussion, Comrade Brand,[10] made a very interesting speech on which I shall not dwell since I am in general agreement with it. I merely want to comment on his concluding remark. Now I assume that he didn't fully express himself inasmuch as he was somewhat rushed by the chairman but his statement might lead to some misunderstanding. Comrade Brand said that we will conquer the bourgeoisie not with statistics but by the sword and he tried to underscore this eventuality by the fact that I delivered the report here. Let me state quite candidly that I have had a great deal more to do with the Red Army's statistics than with its sword. [Laughter.] If Comrade Brand and other comrades believe that I participated, so to speak, sword in hand in the battles of the Red Army, they have a too romantic conception about my functions. I have had a great deal more to do with counting up the number of boots, trousers, and— with your permission—drawers, than with wielding the sword. [Loud laughter.] Generally speaking, I believe that there is no contradiction whatever between swords and statistics, and that statistics relating to military equipment play a very big role in war. Napoleon used to say: *"Dieu est toujours avec les gros bataillons"*[11]—"God is always on the side of the heaviest battalions." And statistics, as you know, also takes in the strength of battalions. Comrade Brand will recall that during our advance on Warsaw, we committed some errors in our statistics, failing to calculate exactly the distances and the forces, and not allowing sufficiently for the enemy's power of resistance. In short, a good sharp sword and good statistics relating to swords and everything else connected with swords, go excellently together. [Applause.]

Comrade Seemann[12] has picked up a remark of Comrade Brand's and has repeated it in a much sharper form, declaring that what we need is not to demonstrate the necessity of revolution but to carry it out. This is in part correct, but in a certain sense it is also incorrect. We must prove to the workers what the essence of the revolution is and why it is possible, necessary and inevitable; whereas so far as the bourgeoisie is concerned we must carry it through by force. And I think that Comrade Seemann and others who spoke in the same vein are somewhat mistaken in deeming that the objective analysis of economic development has proved that the revolution is inevitable, as Comrade Sachs or Comrade Seemann put it, at some fixed point of historical development. After all, this is what the Social Democrats of the Second International have likewise always reiterated. This doesn't interest us any more. We must set ourselves a goal and achieve it through a corresponding organization and tactic. Yes, just as it is impermissible to counterpose a sword to statistics, so is it impermissible to counterpose the subjective factors of history—the revolutionary will and the revolutionary consciousness of the working class—to the objective conditions. After all, the opportunists—the Hilferdings and the Kautskys and the Kautskyites—render automatic the process of mental and spiritual development, by introducing into their prodigious historical statistics only the objective factor, the will of the hostile class—which is for us an objective factor. And by virtually excluding the subjective factor, the dynamic revolutionary will of the working class, they thereby falsify Marxism, converting it into sophistry. But there is still another method of organizing the revolution methodologically—a method of revolutionary thinking, whose representatives were to be observed in large numbers on the soil of Russia, that is, the Social Revolutionaries, and especially their Left Wing. They generally scoffed at objective thinking. They scoffed at the analysis of economic and political development and the analysis of the objective, or philosophically speaking, immanent tendencies of this economic and political development; and the S.R.'s counterposed to all this free will and the revolutionary action of a minority. Once we divorce the subjective aspect from the objective, such a philosophy becomes transformed into sheer revolutionary adventurism. And I believe that in the great school of Marxism we have learned to couple the objective with the subjective both dialectically and practically, *i.e.,* we have learned to ground our actions not only on the subjective will of this or that individual but also on our conviction that the working class must follow this subjective will of ours and that the working class's will to action is determined by the objective situation. That is why for our proofs we must utilize economic analysis along with statistics so as to accurately mark off our own road and to march along this road, sword in hand, prepared for decisive action.

Comrade Sachs[13] is of the opinion that the theses are not fitting as a document of the Communist International since they do not treat the decline and progress of European economy critically enough. I shall merely refer you to page 9 of the theses where this is formulated quite definitively. Furthermore Comrade Sachs is of the opinion that precisely the proletariat is the subjective factor of history, whereas the theses have failed to emphasize this subjective standpoint. I think that Comrade Sachs, who differs in his tendencies from most of the speakers who have taken the floor today, has this much in common with them, namely—both he and they haven't read the theses. In thesis 34 we definitely state:

> At bottom, the question of reestablishing capitalism on the foundations outlined above means the following: Will the working class be willing to make under the new and incomparably more difficult conditions (this seems to be subjective enough!) those sacrifices which are indispensable for reinstalling the stable conditions of its own slavery, harsher and crueler than those which reigned before the war?

Then we go on to develop the idea of how necessary accumulation is, intensified accumulation, how necessary is currency stabilization, and so on. And throughout, one and the same thought is expressed. Economic equilibrium is not something abstract or mechanical. It can be reestablished only through the handiwork of classes. But the classes rest on the economic foundation. The bourgeoisie has succeeded in the course of the three postwar years in maintaining an equilibrium. The bourgeoisie still remains at the helm of the state. How? As I have already said, by new issuances of paper currency and thanks to the fact that the bourgeoisie in Italy, France and Germany is dipping into the disrupted state finances in order to supplement wages in the form of lower bread prices and cheaper rents. Every piece of German merchandise dumped on the English market denotes an unpaid part of a German dwelling which is falling into ruin, a part of a German house which cannot be renovated. And so, to restore class equilibrium they are compelled to ruin the economy, and conversely, in seeking to restore the economy they are compelled to disrupt class equilibrium. It is a vicious circle. This is the central idea of the theses. Those who have failed to cull this idea from the theses should, at my request, read them over again carefully.

Comrade Seemann said that Soviet Russia can serve as a safety valve for capitalism and thereby disrupt the development of the world revolution. Well, things are not yet so terrible as to cause European or American capitalism to throw itself at Soviet Russia in seeking salvation from the plight into which capitalism has fallen as a consequence of unemployment at home. The situation is still far from being so terrible, and our country unfortunately is far too ruined to attract foreign capital on a scale capable of becoming a threat to the development of the revolution in America and Europe. This is absolutely excluded.

I come now to the objections of Comrade Pogany.[14] He has found in our theses an inconsistency and a deficiency, and they are on pages 4 and 14. The contradiction, in his opinion, consists of this: We first say that prosperity has tended to weaken and mitigate the revolutionary explosions and then we go on to declare that the artificial prosperity will not retard the revolution but, on the contrary, will in a certain sense aid its development.

Yes, the pseudo-prosperity of the past and the pseudo-prosperity of the future are evaluated quite differently by me. Comrade Pogany finds in this an inconsistency. But there is none here. For my analysis of prosperity is made in its historical context, in the concrete historical setting of the entire world and of the individual states. Comrade Pogany's mode of thinking is at least in this question somewhat automatic and to employ the old terminology, somewhat metaphysical, inasmuch as he thinks that crises like prosperity always call forth one and the same tendencies. This is absolutely false. In the first place, such an interpretation of the theses leads to countless fallacies. He says that the theses want to do two things: first, wait for an Anglo-American war; second, wait for a period of prosperity. But it was not I who introduced, so to speak, prosperity into our tactics; I did not open the doors to prosperity and invite it to come in and change the situation. It is out of the question. What do our theses say? They say that we are living through a profound and acute crisis, which has acted to produce an intensified offensive by the capitalist class against the proletariat. The proletariat is nowadays everywhere on the defensive. Our task is to extend this defensive struggle of the proletariat on the economic plane, to deepen it, to enlighten the consciousness of the embattled proletariat by clearly and precisely formulating the conditions of struggle, to invest it with political forms and to transform it into the struggle for political power. This is our task, and it is self-understandable. Furthermore, I have stated in my report, and together with Comrade Varga I have written it into our theses, that should an improvement in the situation occur within the next two or three months, or half a year from now, then it is axiomatic that this will happen only provided the revolution does not erupt in the meantime.

If it does erupt, then together with Comrade Pogany we shall not, of course, contravene this event, but shall on the contrary participate in it might and main. But let us pose the question: What if this doesn't happen, Comrade Pogany? What if instead of the revolution an improvement occurs in the economic situation? Comrade Varga points in his pamphlet to many symptoms of this improvement; and even were the case such that it would not be possible to speak at present of improvement, then it is nonetheless necessary to establish that the tempo of deterioration is being retarded. This we know for certain. Prices are no longer falling as precipitately as hitherto. The financial market is under much less strain, and here and there one can perceive minor and superficial indications of an improvement in production. To be sure, they are very insignificant. It is quite possible that only a tiny zigzag is involved and that the development will soon move backwards again. But it is also possible that a more serious improvement will ensue. This depends not upon me, nor on Comrade Pogany, nor on the resolutions of the Congress. This is truly an external, automatic occurrence independent of our will. Does it herald the coming of a new epoch of economic development? In no case. Comrade Pogany thinks that should a revival take place within the next three months in the English market, export and production, then one would have to cast away all hope of a direct development of the revolution, the conquest of political power. We don't think so. There is a great difference between the prosperity which came directly after the war, and the prosperity that is in prospect today. After the war the working class was still full of illusions. The working class was still disorganized like the bourgeoisie. A universal disorganization of classes reigned. Only a small minority of the bourgeoisie was clearly aware of its aims, while an equally small minority of the working class—the Communist group—was likewise aware of its aim. The great masses were wavering. Under these conditions it was extremely important whether upon returning from the war the worker would remain unemployed or would receive a fairly decent wage, whether he would get cheap or expensive bread because he matched his demands with his hardships and bloody sacrifices on the field of battle. The bourgeoisie created, through major financial concessions and at the cost of the further dislocation of the economic foundation, conditions which kept the masses in a mood of indecision for two years. Manifestly, entire layers of the workers nevertheless split off, but on the whole the existing regime has remained intact up to the present day. But now unemployment has caused great privations among the masses. The Communist parties which were in process of formation are crystallized; the disillusionment and disenchantment of the masses proceeds with giant strides and we are now conducting the struggle on the basis of the crisis and we shall continue to conduct it on this basis. It is not excluded that in the course of this struggle and this crisis we may come to power in this or that country. But if this struggle does not lead to positive results—to victory—then (and this is stated in the theses) the pseudo-prosperity will in no case act to stupefy the workers. On the contrary, every worker will, at the first signs of prosperity, recall all the disenchantments which he has suffered, all the sacrifices which he has borne and he will demand recompense for all this, including the wage cuts and the crisis. This is grounded historically, economically and psychologically. As regards the bad music, which Comrade Pogany overheard in my speech—to the effect that I am waiting for a new war and prosperity—I am not sure whether my voice is not musical enough, whether Comrade Pogany's ear is insufficiently musical or whether perhaps the acoustics are poor. [Laughter.] In any case there is some sort of discrepancy between my organ of speech and Comrade Pogany's organ of hearing. I propose to no one to wait for a war between America and England. Had I known that this date—the year 1924—would lead anyone into temptation, I would, of course, have renounced this accursed number inasmuch as it plays no role whatever in my conclusions. I adduced it merely for the sake of illustration. I was analyzing the question of economic equilibrium and I asked: How do matters stand in this connection in the international relations between the states? And I said that we had already lived through an armed peace on the eve of 1914, when everybody was preparing for war. But it then entered no one's mind that the tempo would be so rapid and no one felt certain that the conflict would inevitably occur within two or three or four years. This inevitable conflict is not a mathematical point in historical development; it continues to exert influence on the modern groupings of the European states, as well.

Comrade Thalheimer[15] has repeated this selfsame charge that I allegedly seek to keep the revolutionary energy of the proletariat in reserve until the outbreak of war in 1924. This has a rather peculiar ring. Then he said that I orient myself, so to speak, upon the peaceful disintegration of capitalism. He plainly stated that the theses take their orientation from this. Here, too, I shall refer to thesis 34 in which just the opposite is written. It states that so far as the automatic disintegration of capitalism is concerned, it is possible to restore the equilibrium, but that this process takes place precisely through the medium of the class struggle, and that therefore the equilibrium may not be restored.

The indemnity question was likewise analyzed in this connection. We were told that German indemnities must serve as a means of restoring the stability of Entente capitalism. Absolutely correct, but first the indemnities must be paid. And in order to pay them, the German proletariat must produce not only for itself, not only for the profits of its bourgeoisie, for its state, but also for these reparations. This implies an intensified exploitation which in turn implies a sharpening of the class struggle, but by no means the restoration of equilibrium.

The question, which is raised by many comrades abstractly, of just what will lead to revolution: impoverishment or prosperity, is completely false when so formulated. I have already tried to prove this in my report. One Spanish comrade told me in a private conversation that in his country it was precisely the prosperity which came to Spanish industry through the war that produced a revolutionary movement on a large scale, whereas previously stagnation had prevailed. Here we have an example that is not Russian but Spanish—an example from the other side of Europe. Comrades! Neither impoverishment nor prosperity as such can lead to revolution. But the alternation of prosperity and impoverishment, the crises, the uncertainty, the absence of stability—these are the motor factors of revolution.

Why has the labor bureaucracy become so conservative? In most cases it consists of weak creatures who live on a moderate scale, whose existence is nowise marked by luxury; but they have grown accustomed to stable living conditions. They have no fear of unemployment so long as they can keep themselves within the framework of the normal party and trade union life. This tranquil mode of existence has also exerted its influence upon the psychology of a broad layer of workers who are better off.

But today this blessed state, this stability of living conditions, has receded into the past; in place of artificial prosperity has come impoverishment. Prices are steeply rising, wages keep changing in or out of consonance with currency fluctuations. Currency leaps, prices leap, wages leap and then come the ups and downs of feverish fictitious conjunctures and of profound crises. This lack of stability, the uncertainty of what tomorrow will bring in the personal life of every worker, is the most revolutionary factor of the epoch in which we live. And this is quite lucidly stated in the theses. In them we refer to the crisis as such, and also to prosperity. On page 13 we say:

> The instability of living conditions which mirrors the universal instability of national and world economic conditions is today one of the most important factors of revolutionary development.

This applies equally to the period of crisis as well as the periods of prosperity. This also covers the political conditions under which the working class lives. Before the war it had grown accustomed to the Prussian regime. This was, true enough, a frame of iron, yet a wholly reliable one. One knew that this could be done, while that was prohibited. Today this regime of Prussian stability has vanished. Before the war a worker earned 3 marks a day. But these marks had a clear ring, with them one could buy something. Today the worker receives (I don't know exactly) 20 or 30, 40 or 50 marks a day, but he gets little for them. True, there used to be a German Kaiser, but by way of compensation you knew that you wouldn't be killed on the streets if you were out on strike. In the most extreme case you'd be thrown in jail. Today, however, you might get shot while taking a stroll as a free citizen of the republic. This absence of stability drives the most imperturbable worker out of equilibrium. It is a revolutionary motor power. Remarks were made here to the effect that both the theses and I center our attention exclusively on the conflict between England and America, while ignoring all other conflicts. This is completely false. The theses deal clearly and specifically with everything that was said by Koenen[16] concerning the mutual relations between France and Germany. Even the recent capitulation and everything connected with it is treated on page 10. There it is stated:

> Germany's capitulation in May on the question of indemnities signifies a temporary victory for England and is the warranty of the further economic disintegration of Central Europe, without at all excluding the occupation of the Ruhr province by France in the immediate future.

Everything Comrade Koenen said has already been said in principle by the theses. Obviously, we cannot in the question of international politics center all our attention on the looming year of 1924. We must meet with open eyes every eventuality, we must study each day's events and prepare energetically. And I believe that precisely in the sphere of international relations we have before us the greatest perspectives in the sense of attracting the proletariat to our side. Which is the most important thing. To conquer power and supremacy one must first conquer the proletariat. What is the position of the Second and 2½ Internationals on this question? I must call your attention to a minor example; the polemic between the *Vorwaerts* [central organ of the German SP] and the Belgian newspaper *Le Peuple*. I don't know whether this controversy has been adequately utilized in Germany. This polemic between two party organs who belong to one and the same Second International over the most burning and vital question—German reparations—is instructive to the highest degree for every German, Belgian and French worker. At the moment Briand was threatening to occupy the Ruhr province, *Le Peuple,* the Belgian yellow Socialist sheet, asked its German comrades the following questions:

> We have seen, wrote *Le Peuple,* the German workers conduct themselves courageously in the days of the Kapp putsch. Why then are they silent now? Why don't the labor organizations from one end of Germany to the other express their will clearly to prevent the occupation of the Ruhr province and its operation under military control?

This means: Since my government, the Belgian—together with the French—will crush you, the German worker, in case your government is remiss in its payments of fixed indemnities to the French government, it follows that it is your duty, German worker, to make a revolution against your bourgeoisie, and compel it to pay indemnities so that my bourgeoisie be not compelled to crush you. [Laughter.] This smacks of turning revolutionary duty into a football, and kicking it around like clowns in a circus. Your duty is to subordinate your bourgeoisie to mine lest I be compelled to go to war against yours. [Applause.]

In reply to this, the *Vorwaerts* wrote:

> Each one of these questions we return in full to the Belgian labor organizations. After all, it is not our armies that must be kept from advancing.

This is said by the same *Vorwaerts* and the same Social-Democratic leaders who in their day supported the Brest-Litovsk Treaty. One can talk about these creatures before the Belgian and the French and also the German working class only with a dog whip in hand.

Comrades, the revolution flows along three channels and of one of them we were reminded by Comrade Roy. The first great channel of revolutionary development is dying Europe. Europe's social equilibrium, and above all that of England, has always been based on the preponderant position of Great Britain and of Europe throughout the world. This preponderance is forever gone. Fluctuations may take place. But the preponderance of Europe is a thing of the past and so is the preponderance of the European bourgeoisie, and that of the European proletariat as well. This is the first great channel of the revolution.

The second is the feverish development of America. We have here a great and feverish upswing, created by conditions which can never be stabilized, nor repeated, *i.e.*, a great upsurge which must inevitably be followed by a great crisis and a great depression. These ups and downs, these unprecedented ups and downs of a great nation, of a great society, are a mighty revolutionary factor, and the possibility is not at all excluded that the revolutionary development of the United States may proceed at a genuinely American tempo today.

The third channel—the colonies. During the war, when the European countries were cut off from the world market, the colonies developed quite energetically in the capitalist direction. This was of no especially great economic significance for the world market. The Indian, Chinese and Japanese capitalisms do not play in it a decisive or prominent role. But for the revolutionary development of Japan, China and India, the development of capitalism, its already attained level of development, does play a decisive role. In India, a backward proletariat exists. But how great a role the proletariat can play in such a country with its semi-feudal agrarian relations—this you can gather from all of Russia's modern history. The proletariat will play there a role which will be absolutely incommensurate to the stage of capitalist development and even to the numerical strength of the workers; for the peasantry of India or China has no other possibility, no other center of concentration than the young proletariat capable of struggle. And so, the colonial struggle is the third important channel of the revolutionary movement. They must not be counterposed to one another, for the movement flows parallel along these three channels, and they reciprocally influence one another all the time. And it is impossible to tell in advance when the movement will become sharpened in one or another. But, in general, the objective conditions, the automatic elements in history, are working splendidly in our favor. I hope that in life as well as in my speech the subjective factor is not being restrained nor smothered as so many comrades fear but, on the contrary, that the objectively-revolutionary is acting hand in hand with the subjectively-revolutionary, and that both of them together are accomplishing splendid work.

A proposal has been made that the Congress refer the theses back to the Commission. It is, of course, necessary for the Commission to go over the theses again, and revise them in the light of the discussion that has taken place here. But nevertheless I ask the Congress to accept our theses in principle as the basis, before they are sent back to the Commission. [Stormy applause.]

21. Theses of the Third World Congress on the international situation and the tasks of the Comintern

Adopted unanimously at the Sixteenth Session, July 4, 1921

I
THE CRUX OF THE QUESTION

1. The revolutionary movement at the termination of the imperialist war and after this war is marked by an amplitude unequaled in history. In March 1917 Czarism is overthrown. In May 1917 a stormy strike struggle erupts in England. In November 1917 the Russian proletariat conquers state power. In November 1918, the downfall of the German and Austro-Hungarian monarchies. The strike movement sweeps over a number of European countries, constantly gaining in scope and intensity in the course of the succeeding year. In March 1919 the Soviet Republic is installed in Hungary. Toward the close of that year the United States is convulsed by turbulent strikes of steel workers, coal miners and railway men. In Germany, following the January and March battles of 1919, the movement reaches its apogee shortly after the Kapp mutiny in

March 1920. In France the tensest moment in the internal situation occurs in May 1920. In Italy the movement of the industrial and rural proletariat grows incessantly and leads in September 1920 to the seizure of factories, mills, and landlord estates by the workers. In December 1920 proletarian mass strikes take place in Czechoslovakia. In March 1921, the uprising of workers in Central Germany and the coal miners' strike in England.

The movement attains its greatest amplitude and highest intensity in those countries which had been involved in the war, and especially in the defeated countries; but it spreads to the neutral countries as well. In Asia and Africa the movement arouses or reinforces the revolutionary indignation of the multimillioned colonial masses.

This mighty wave, however, does not succeed in overthrowing world capitalism, not even European capitalism.

2. During the year that elapsed between the Second and Third Congress of the Communist International a series of working-class uprisings and battles have resulted in partial defeats (the Red Army offensive against Warsaw in August 1920; the movement of the Italian proletariat in September 1920; the uprising of the German workers in March 1921).

The first period of the revolutionary movement after the war is characterized by the elemental nature of the onslaught, by the considerable formlessness of its methods and aims and by the extreme panic of the ruling classes; and it may be regarded by and large as terminated. The class self-confidence of the bourgeoisie and the outward stability of its state organs have undoubtedly become strengthened. The dread of Communism has abated, if not completely disappeared. The leaders of the bourgeoisie are now even boasting about the might of their state apparatus and have everywhere assumed the offensive against the working masses, on both the economic and the political fronts.

3. In view of this situation the Communist International presents to itself and to the entire working class the following questions: To what extent do these new political interrelations between the bourgeoisie and the proletariat correspond to the more profound interrelationship of forces between these two contending camps? Is it true that the bourgeoisie is about to restore the social equilibrium which had been upset by the war? Are there grounds for assuming that the epoch of political paroxysms and class battles is being superseded by a new and prolonged epoch of restoration and capitalist growth? Doesn't this necessitate a revision of program or tactics on the part of the Communist International?

II
THE WAR, THE SPECULATIVE PROSPERITY, THE CRISIS AND THE COUNTRIES OF EUROPE

4. The two decades preceding the war were the epoch of an exceptionally powerful capitalist ascension. The periods of prosperity were marked by their intensity and long duration, the periods of depression, of crisis, were marked by their brevity. In general, the curve sloped sharply upwards; the capitalist nations were growing rich.

Having tested out the world market through their trusts, cartels and consortiums, the rulers of the world's destiny took into account that this mad growth of capitalism must run up against the limits of the capitalist world market's capacity—the world market which capitalism itself had created. And they tried to find a way out of this situation by a surgical method. The sanguinary crisis of the World War was intended to supersede an indefinitely long period of economic depression, and it all came to one and the same result, namely, the wholesale destruction of productive forces.

The war, however, combined the extremely destructive power of its methods with an unexpectedly lengthy time interval during which these were applied. As a result the war not only caused the economic destruction of "surplus" productive forces, but also weakened, shattered and undermined the fundamental productive apparatus of Europe. At the same time it contributed to the mighty capitalist development of the United States and to the feverish rise of Japan. The center of gravity of world economy has shifted from Europe to America.

5. The period of the cessation of the four years' slaughter, the period of demobilization and of the transition from the state of war to the state of peace, inevitably accompanied by an economic crisis as a result of the exhaustion and chaos caused by the war, was regarded by the bourgeoisie—and with full justification—as its most dangerous period. And actually, during the two postwar years the belligerent countries became the arena of mighty movements of the proletariat.

One of the principal causes enabling the bourgeoisie to nevertheless preserve its ruling position was the economic upswing instead of the seemingly unavoidable crisis which marked the first few months after the war. This upswing lasted approximately one year and a half. Industry absorbed nearly all the demobilized workers. Wages, although they could not as a general rule catch up with the cost of living, nevertheless kept rising sufficiently to create the mirage of economic gains.

It was precisely this *commercial-industrial upswing of 1919–20* which relieved the most acute phase of postwar liquidation, that caused an extraordinary recrudescence of self-confidence among the bourgeoisie and *raised the question of the advent of a new epoch of organic capitalist development.*

Meanwhile the revival of 1919–20 was not at bottom the beginning of the postwar regeneration of capitalist economy, but a mere prolongation of the artificial state of industry and commerce which had been created by the war.

6. The imperialist war erupted in the period when the commercial-industrial crisis, which even at that time had its origin in America (1913), began to loom menacingly over Europe. The normal development of the industrial cycle was cut short by the war, which itself became the most powerful economic factor. The war created virtually unlimited markets for the basic branches of industry, completely secure against competition. This reliable and insatiable customer was ever in want of goods. The production of the means of production was replaced by the production of the means of destruction. Primary necessities were devoured at ever-higher prices by millions of individuals engaged not in production but in destruction. This process meant ruin. But by virtue of the monstrous contradictions of capitalist economy this ruin assumed the guise and form of enrichment. The state floated loan after loan, one issue of paper money followed upon another and the state budgets which used to carry millions began carrying billions. Machines and equipment became worn out and were left unrepaired. The land was poorly cultivated. The capital construction work in the cities and on the systems of communication was discontinued. Meanwhile the number of government bonds, credits and treasury bills and notes kept growing incessantly. Fictitious capital swelled in proportion as productive capital kept being destroyed. The credit system became transformed from a means of circulating commodities into a means of mobilizing national wealth, including that which is

still to be created by future generations, for war purposes.

It was precisely because they feared a crisis which might prove catastrophic that the capitalist state continued after the war to follow the same policy as it did during the war, namely: new currency issues, new loans, regulation of prices of primary necessities, guarantee of profits, subsidies for grain and other forms of government subsidies for salaries and wages, plus military censorship and military dictatorship.

7. At the same time the cessation of hostilities, and the resumption of international relations, limited though it was, brought to the fore the demand for all sorts of commodities, from all parts of the globe. The war left huge stocks of unexpended products. Enormous sums of money were left concentrated in the hands of dealers and speculators who invested them wherever the greatest profits offered at the moment. Hence the feverish commercial boom, accompanied by an unprecedented rise of prices and fantastic dividends, while none of the basic branches of industry anywhere in Europe approached the pre-war level.

8. At the cost of the further organic dislocation of the economic system (growth of fictitious capital, depreciation of currency, speculation instead of economic rehabilitation) the bourgeois governments in league with the banking consortiums and industrial trusts succeeded in postponing the beginning of the economic crisis till the moment when the political crisis consequent upon demobilization and the first squaring of accounts was already allayed. Having thus obtained an important breathing space, the bourgeoisie imagined that the danger of crisis had been averted for an indefinite time. Supreme optimism reigned. It seemed as if the needs of reconstruction had opened up a lasting epoch of prosperity in industry, in commerce and especially in speculation. The year 1920 was the year of shattered hopes.

Manifesting itself first in the field of finances and next in commerce and finally in industry, the crisis began in March 1920 in Japan, in April in the United States (a slight fall of prices had already set in by January); it passed on in April to England, France and Italy; it reached the neutral countries of Europe, manifested itself in a mitigated form in Germany and in the second half of 1920 spread throughout the entire capitalist world.

9. Thus *the crisis of 1920*—and this is the key to the understanding of the world situation!—is not a periodic stage of "normal" industrial cycle but a more profound *reaction consequent to the fictitious prosperity during the war and the next two postwar years, prosperity based on ruination and exhaustion.*

The normal alternation of booms and crises used to occur along the upward curve of industrial development. During the last seven years Europe's productive forces have not been rising but falling abruptly.

The dislocation of the very foundations of economy has still to make itself felt throughout the entire superstructure. To achieve any kind of internal coordination, Europe's economy must in the course of the next few years shrink and shrivel. The curve of development of the productive forces will drop from the present fictitious heights. Therewith the upswings can be only short-lived and of a speculative character to a large measure. The crises will be hard and lasting. The present crisis in Europe is a crisis of underproduction. It is the reaction of impoverishment against the efforts to produce, to trade and to live on the same capitalist scale as formerly.

10. Economically, the strongest country and the one least damaged by the war in Europe is *England*. Nevertheless even with regard to this country one cannot say that capitalist equilibrium has been restored after the war. True, thanks to her world organization and her position as vic-

tor, England has attained certain *commercial and financial* successes after the war: she has improved her trade balance and has raised the exchange rate of the pound and has recorded a fictitious surplus in her budget. But in the sphere of *industry* England has since the war moved backwards not forwards. Both the productivity of labor in England and her national income are far below the pre-war levels. The situation of the basic branch of her industry, the coal industry, is getting worse and worse, pulling down all other branches of her economy. The incessant paroxysms caused by strikes are not the cause but the consequence of the decline of English economy.

11. *France, Belgium, Italy* are irreparably ruined by the war. The attempt to restore the economy of France at the expense of Germany is savage looting, coupled with diplomatic blackmail; and it is being accomplished through the further ruination of Germany (coal, machinery, cattle, gold), without, however, bringing salvation to France. This attempt causes heavy damage to the entire economy of continental Europe. France has gained far less than Germany has lost. Despite the fact that the French peasants have, through superhuman exertions, recovered for agriculture large tracts of the devastated regions; despite the fact that whole branches of industry were greatly developed (chemical industry, war industries) during the war, France is heading for economic ruin. State debts and state expenditures (on militarism) have climbed to insupportable heights. At the close of the last economic upswing, French currency had dropped 60 percent. The revival of French economy is obstructed by the heavy losses in manpower caused by the war, losses which are especially grave owing to the low birth rate in France. The economies of Italy and Belgium are in much the same position.

12. The illusory character of prosperity is most strik-

ingly evidenced by *Germany*. While prices increased sevenfold in a year and a half, the country's production has continued to decline sharply. Germany's seemingly triumphant participation in the postwar world market is being paid for at a double price: the squandering of the nation's basic capital (the destruction of her productive transport and credit systems); and the progressive lowering of the living standards of her working class. The profits gained by German exporters represent pure loss from the social-economic standpoint. Under the guise of exports Germany is being auctioned off at cheap prices. The capitalist masters are securing for themselves an ever-increasing share of the ever-decreasing national wealth. The German workers are becoming the coolies of Europe.

13. As the political pseudo-independence of the *small neutral countries* rests upon the antagonisms between the great powers, just so do they eke out their economic existence in the interstices of the world market, whose essential nature used to be determined before the war by England, Germany, the United States and France. During the war the bourgeoisie of the small neutral European countries made fabulous profits. But the ruination of the belligerent countries of Europe has brought economic disorganization to neutral countries as well. Their debts have increased, their currency exchange has dropped. The crisis deals them blow after blow.

III
THE UNITED STATES, JAPAN, SOVIET RUSSIA AND THE COLONIAL COUNTRIES

14. The development of the *United States* during the war is in a certain sense the diametrical opposite of Eu-

rope's development. The participation of the United States in the war was in the main that of a quartermaster. The United States did not directly experience the destructive effects of war. The indirect destructive effect on its transport, agriculture, etc., was far weaker than in England, let alone France or Germany. On the other hand, the United States fully exploited the fact that European competition had either been eliminated entirely or had become extremely weak; and developed a number of its most important branches of industry (oil, shipbuilding, automobiles, coal) to heights it had never anticipated. Today most of the countries of Europe are dependent on America not only for their oil and grain, but also for their coal.

While prior to the war America's exports consisted chiefly of agricultural products and raw materials (making up more than two-thirds of the total exports), her main export at present consists of manufactured goods (60 percent of her export trade). While America before the war was a debtor country, she is today the world's creditor. Approximately one-half of the world's gold reserve is concentrated in the United States and the gold continues to flow in. The leading role on the world money market has passed from the pound sterling to the dollar.

15. However, American capitalism, too, has lost its equilibrium. America's extraordinary industrial expansion was determined by an exceptional combination of world conditions, namely, the elimination of European competition, and, what is most important, the demands of the European war market. If ruined Europe as a competitor of America is unable to regain her pre-war position on the world market even after the war, then, on the other hand, Europe as a market for America can preserve only an insignificant part of her former importance. Meanwhile United States economy has become an export

economy to an incomparably greater extent than prior to the war. Its productive apparatus, super-developed during the war, cannot be operated at full capacity for lack of outlets. Individual branches of industry are becoming converted into seasonal industries, operating only part of the year. The crisis in the United States constitutes the beginning of a profound and lasting economic disorganization resulting from the European war. This is the result of the fundamental disruption of the world division of labor.

16. *Japan* has also exploited the war to improve her position on the world market. Her development, far more limited in scope than the development of the United States, is of a hothouse character in a number of branches of industry. While Japan's productive forces proved adequate for conquering a market depleted of competitors, they proved inadequate for retaining that market in the struggle with the more powerful capitalist countries. Hence the acute crisis which commenced precisely in Japan.

17. The *transoceanic countries* which export raw materials, including the purely *colonial countries* (South America, Canada, Australia, China, India, Egypt and others), have in their turn utilized the rupture of international ties for the development of their native industries. The world crisis has now spread to these countries as well. The development of national industries in these countries is in its turn becoming a source of new commercial difficulties for England and for Europe as a whole.

18. In the sphere of production, commerce and credit—and moreover not merely in Europe but on a world scale—there is, in consequence, no ground whatever to speak of any restoration of a stable equilibrium after the war.

Europe continues to decline economically, and the destruction of the foundations of European economy is still to make itself felt in the next few years.

The world market is disorganized. Europe needs American products, but has nothing to offer in return. Europe suffers from anemia, America—from plethora. The gold standard has been overthrown. The depreciated currencies of European countries (reaching in some cases 99 percent) presents almost insurmountable obstacles to the world exchange of commodities. The incessant, sharp fluctuations of the rate of exchange have converted capitalist economy into an orgy of speculation. The world market remains without a universal equivalent.

The restoration of the gold standard in Europe cannot be achieved except by an increase in exports and a decrease in imports. But this is just what ruined Europe is in no condition to do. America, in her turn, defends herself against the artificial European exports (dumping) by raising her tariff.

Europe continues to remain a madhouse. Most of the states have passed prohibitive measures relating to the import and export of certain commodities and have multiplied their custom duties. England has introduced prohibitive custom duties. German exports as well as the entire economic life of Germany are at the mercy of a gang of Entente speculators, especially Parisian speculators. The former territories of Austria-Hungary are now crisscrossed by a dozen custom borders. The net of Versailles gets more and more tangled from every side.

The exclusion of Soviet Russia from the world market as a consumer of manufactured goods and as a supplier of raw materials has contributed in a very high degree to the disruption of economic equilibrium.

19. The reappearance of Russia on the world market cannot produce any appreciable changes in it in the period immediately ahead. The capitalist organism of Russia has always been, with regard to the means of pro-

duction, completely dependent on world industry, and this dependence particularly with regard to the Entente countries became still further intensified during the war when Russia's industry was almost completely mobilized for war purposes. The blockade has at a single stroke cut off all these vital ties. It was entirely out of the question for this exhausted and utterly ruined country to organize during the three years of incessant civil war a number of new branches of industry, without which the old branches faced inevitable ruin through the wear and tear of their basic inventory. In addition to this hundreds of thousands of the best proletarian elements, comprising a large number of the most highly skilled workers, had to be drawn into the Red Army. Under these historical conditions, surrounded by the iron ring of blockade, carrying on incessant warfare, suffering from the terrible heritage of ruin—no other regime could have maintained the country's economic life and created a centralized administration. But it is undeniable that the struggle against world imperialism was carried on at the cost of the further deterioration of the productive forces in many of the basic branches of the economy. Only now, with the relaxation of the blockade, and with the establishment of sounder transitional forms in the interrelations between the city and the country, has the Soviet power received the opportunity of exercising a gradual and unwavering centralized direction of the country's economic revival.

IV
THE AGGRAVATION OF SOCIAL CONTRADICTIONS

20. The war which brought about the destruction of productive forces on a scale unequaled in history has not

brought the process of social differentiation to a standstill; on the contrary, the proletarianization of broad intermediate classes including the new middle estate (employes, functionaries, and so on) and the concentration of property in the hands of tiny cliques (trusts, consortiums, and so on) have for the last seven years made monstrous progress in the countries that have suffered the most from the war. The Stinnes question has become the main question of the economic life of Germany.

The soaring of prices on all commodities, coincident with the catastrophic depreciation of currency in all the belligerent European countries, signified in and of itself a redistribution of the national income to the detriment of the working class, the functionaries, the employes, the small *rentiers*, and generally all categories with a more or less fixed income.

Thus while in relation to her material resources Europe has been thrown back for a number of decades, the process of the aggravation of social contradictions has not only not retrogressed or been suspended but has, on the contrary, acquired an exceptional acuteness. This cardinal fact is of itself sufficient to dispel all hopes of a lasting and peaceful development under the forms of democracy: *the progressive differentiation ("Stinnezation") on the one side, and on the other, proletarianization and pauperization on the basis of economic decline, predetermine the intense, convulsive and fierce character of the class struggle.*

In this connection the present crisis is merely continuing the work of the war and of the postwar speculative boom.

21. The rise of prices in agricultural products, while creating an illusion that there has been a general enrichment of the village, has in reality increased the welfare of the rich peasants. The peasants have indeed succeeded in paying off their debts with cheap paper currency, debts

which they had contracted when currency was at par. But husbandry does not consist solely of paying off mortgages.

Despite the enormous increases in land prices, despite the unscrupulous abuse of the monopoly of primary necessities, despite the enrichment of big landowners and village kulaks, the decline of Europe's agriculture remains self-evident. We witness in many places a reversion to more extensive forms of agriculture, the conversion of arable lands into pastures, the slaughter of cattle, three-field farming. This decline was also caused by the scarcity of labor, the depletion of herds, the lack of artificial fertilizers, the dearness of manufactured goods; and in Central and Eastern Europe also by the deliberate curtailment of agricultural production, which came as a reaction to the attempts made by the state to seize control of agricultural products. The large, and partly also the middle peasants, are creating strong political and economic organizations to protect themselves against the burdens of reconstruction; and they are trying to take advantage of the bourgeoisie's difficult position to extort from the state tariff and taxation measures beneficial only to the peasantry as the price of their support against the proletariat. All this hampers capitalist revival. A split arises between the urban and the rural bourgeoisie, which impairs the strength of the bourgeois state.

Coincident with this, large sections of the poor peasantry are becoming proletarianized, the village is becoming a breeding place of discontent, the class-consciousness of the rural proletariat is growing stronger.

On the other hand, the universal impoverishment of Europe, rendering her incapable of purchasing the necessary quantities of American grain, has led to a heavy crisis in farming across the ocean. We are observing the ruination of peasants and small farmers not only in Europe but also in the United States, Canada, Argentina, Australia, South Africa.

22. The position of *government and private employes* has, owing to the fall in the purchasing power of money, worsened as a rule much more sharply than the position of the proletariat. Torn out of their former stable conditions of existence, the middle and lower functionaries are becoming factors of political unrest which undermine the stability of the state apparatus they serve. The "new middle estate" which, according to the reformists, represented the bulwark of conservatism, tends, in the transitional epoch, to become a rather revolutionary factor.

23. Capitalist Europe has completely lost her dominant economic position in the world. Yet her relative class equilibrium had rested wholly on this world rule. All the efforts of European countries (England and partly France) to restore former conditions only tend to intensify the instability and chaos.

24. While in Europe the concentration of property is taking place on the soil of ruin, in the United States the growth of concentration and the growth of class contradiction have reached their peak on the basis of feverish capitalist enrichment. The sharp fluctuations in the conjuncture, resulting from the general instability of the world market, impart to the class struggle on American soil an extremely intense and revolutionary character. The period of upswing unprecedented in the history of capitalism is bound to be followed by an extraordinary upswing of the revolutionary struggle.

25. The emigration of workers and peasants across the ocean has always served as a safety valve to the capitalist regime in Europe, and it invariably increased during the epochs of prolonged depressions or after the defeats of revolutionary movements.

At the present time America and Australia are putting

ever-greater obstacles in the way of émigrés from Europe. The safety valve of emigration has been shut off.

26. The vigorous development of capitalism in the Orient, especially in India and China, has created there new social foundations for the revolutionary struggle. The bourgeoisie of these countries, its capitalist core, has become even more intimately tied to foreign capital and thus constitutes an essential instrument of foreign domination. Its struggle against foreign imperialism—the struggle of a weaker competitor—is by its very nature only halfhearted and semi-fictitious. The development of the native proletariat paralyzes the revolutionary-nationalist tendencies of the colonial bourgeoisie. But concurrently, in the person of the conscious Communist vanguard, the multimillioned peasant masses obtain a genuinely revolutionary leadership.

The combination of military-national oppression of foreign imperialism, of the capitalist exploitation by foreign and native bourgeoisies, and the survivals of feudal bondage are creating favorable conditions in which the young colonial proletariat is bound to develop swiftly and take its place at the head of the vast revolutionary movement of the peasant masses.

The revolutionary peoples' movement in India and in other colonies is today as much an integral part of the world revolution of the toilers as is the uprising of the proletariat in the capitalist countries of the old and the new worlds.

V
INTERNATIONAL RELATIONS

27. The general state of world economy—above all the decline of Europe—predetermines a period of the gravest

economic hardships, convulsions, crises of a general and partial character, and so on. International relations, as they have emerged from the war and from the Versailles Peace, are rendering the situation even more hopeless.

While imperialism was engendered by the needs of the productive forces to eradicate the framework of national states and to convert Europe and the rest of the world into one economic territory, the result of the dog fight between the hostile imperialist powers was to pile up in Central and Eastern Europe a whole number of new boundaries, new custom barriers and new armies. In the state-economic sense, Europe has been thrown back to medievalism.

The soil which has been exhausted and ruined is now being called upon to sustain an army one and a half times as large as that of 1914, that is, in the heyday of "armed peace."

28. The policy of France who today dominates the European continent falls into two parts: first, the blind rage of a usurer ready to strangle his insolvent debtor; and second, the greediness of predatory heavy industry which is—with the aid of the Saar, Ruhr and Upper Silesian coal basins—seeking to create conditions for industrial imperialism to supersede bankrupt financial imperialism.

But these efforts run counter to the interests of England. The latter's task is to keep German coal away from French ore, the coupling of which is one of the most indispensable conditions for the regeneration of Europe.

29. The British Empire is today at the peak of its power. It has retained all its old dominions and has acquired new ones. But it is precisely the present moment that reveals that England's dominant world position stands in contradiction to her actual economic decline. Germany, with her capitalism incomparably more progressive in respect to technology and organization, has been crushed by force of arms.

But in the person of the United States, which economically subjected both Americas, there has now risen a triumphant rival, even more menacing than Germany. Thanks to its superior organization and technology, the productivity of labor in U.S. industry is far above that of England. Within the territories of the United States 65–70 percent of the world's petroleum is being produced, upon which depends the automobile industry, tractor production, the navy and the air fleet. England's age-long monopoly in the coal market has been completely undermined; America has taken first place; her exports to Europe are increasing ominously. In the field of the merchant marine America has almost caught up with England. The United States is no longer content to put up with England's world transoceanic cable monopoly. In the field of industry Great Britain has gone over to the defensive, and under the pretext of combating "unwholesome" German competition is now arming herself with protectionist measures against the United States. Finally, while England's navy, comprising a large number of outdated units, has come to a standstill in its development, the Harding administration has taken over from Wilson's administration the program of naval construction intended to secure the preponderance of the American flag on the high seas within the next two or three years.

The situation is such that either England will be automatically pushed back and, despite her victory over Germany, become a second-rate power or she will be constrained in the near future to stake in mortal combat with the United States her entire power gained in former years.

That is just the reason why England is maintaining her alliance with Japan and is making concessions to France in order to secure the latter's assistance or at least neutrality. The growth of the international role of the latter country—within the confines of the European continent—during the last year has been caused not by a strengthening of France but by the international weakening of England.

Germany's capitulation in May on the question of indemnities signifies, however, a temporary victory for England and is the warranty of the further economic disintegration of Central Europe, without at all excluding the occupation of the Ruhr and Upper Silesian basins by France in the immediate future.

30. The antagonism between Japan and the United States, temporarily veiled by their joint participation in the war against Germany, is today openly developing its tendencies. As a result of the war Japan has come closer to American shores, taking possession of islands in the Pacific which are of great strategical importance.

The crisis of Japanese industry, following its rapid expansion, has again aggravated the problem of emigration: thickly populated and poor in natural resources, Japan is compelled to export either goods or human beings. In either case she collides with the United States: in California, in China, and on the little island of Yap.

More than half of her budget is being spent by Japan on her army and navy. In the struggle between England and America Japan has in store for her the same role on the sea as that played by France on land during the war with Germany. While Japan is today profiting from the antagonism between Great Britain and America, the final struggle between these two titans for world domination will be fought out primarily on Japan's spine.

31. The last great war was—in its origin, its immediate causes and in its principal participants—a European war. The axis of the struggle was the antagonism between England and Germany. The intervention of the United States extended the framework of the struggle, but it did not divert it from its fundamental course. The European conflict

was settled by the resources of the whole world. The war, which in its own way settled the contest between England and Germany and to that extent also the conflict between the United States and Germany, not only failed to solve the question of interrelations between the United States and England but has, for the first time, posed it in its full scope as the basic question of world politics, just as it posed the question of interrelations between the United States and Japan as one of the second order. Thus, the last war was a European prelude to a genuine world war which is to solve the question of who will exercise the rule of *imperialist autocracy*.

32. But this constitutes only one of the axes of world politics. There is yet another axis. The Russian Soviet Federation and the Third International were born as a result of the last war. The combined forces of the world revolution are arrayed wholly against all the imperialist combinations.

Whether the alliance between England and France is going to be maintained or broken is, from the standpoint of the interests of the proletariat and of securing peace, worth just as little as the renewal or the non-renewal of the Anglo-Japanese alliance, as the entry or the non-entry of the United States into the League of Nations. The proletariat can in no case see a guarantee of peace in the transient, predatory and perfidious combination of capitalist powers, whose policy turns to an ever-increasing extent around the antagonism between England and America, fostering that antagonism and preparing a new sanguinary explosion.

The conclusion of peace treaties and trade agreements by certain capitalist countries with Soviet Russia does not at all mean that the world bourgeoisie has renounced the idea of destroying the Soviet Republic. We have here only a change—perhaps a temporary one—of forms and methods of struggle. The Japanese coup in the Far East[17] may perhaps serve as an introduction to a new phase of armed intervention.

It is absolutely self-evident that the more protracted the world proletarian revolutionary movement is in its character, the more inevitably will the bourgeoisie be impelled by the contradictions of the world economic and political situation to engage in another bloody denouement on a world scale. This would signify that the task of "restoring capitalist equilibrium" after the new war would have for its basis conditions of economic havoc and cultural savagery in comparison with which the present state of Europe might be regarded as the height of well-being.

33. Despite the fact that the experience of the last war has furnished fearsome proof that "war is a miscalculation"—a truth which exhausts all of bourgeois and socialist pacifism—the process of economic, political, ideological and technical preparation for a new war is going on at full speed throughout the capitalist world. Humanitarian and anti-revolutionary pacifism has become an auxiliary force of militarism.

The Social Democrats of every variety and the Amsterdam trade unionists, who are trying to instil into the world proletariat the idea that the workers ought to adjust themselves to those economic and international-state norms that have arisen as a result of the war, are thereby rendering the imperialist bourgeoisie irreplaceable services in the matter of preparing a new slaughter which threatens to completely destroy civilization.

VI
THE WORKING CLASS AFTER THE WAR

34. At bottom the question of reestablishing capitalism on the foundations outlined means the following: Will

the working class be willing to make under the new and incomparably more difficult conditions those sacrifices which are indispensable for reinstalling the stable conditions of its own slavery, harsher and crueler than those which reigned before the war?

To restore Europe's economy it is indispensable to restore the productive apparatus destroyed during the war and to create new capital. This would be possible only if the proletariat were willing to work harder and to submit to drastic wage cuts. This is what the capitalists are insisting upon; this is what the treacherous leaders of the Yellow International are urging the proletariat to do, namely, first help restore capitalism and only then fight for the betterment of their own conditions. But the European proletariat is not willing to make these sacrifices. It demands a higher standard of living, which is in direct contradiction to the objective possibilities of the capitalist system. Hence the interminable strikes and uprisings; hence the impossibility of the economic reconstruction of Europe. To stabilize currency means for a number of European states (Germany, France, Italy, Austria, Hungary, Poland, the Balkans, etc.) first of all to throw off the burden of intolerable obligations, *i.e.*, to declare themselves bankrupt. But to do so is to give a powerful impulsion to the struggle of all classes over a new distribution of the national income. To stabilize the currency means to further reduce state expenditures to the detriment of the masses (to forego the regulation of wages and of prices on articles of prime necessity), to shut off the import of cheaper foreign consumer goods and to increase the volume of export by lowering the cost of production, *i.e.*, once again primarily by intensifying the exploitation of labor. Every serious measure tending to restore capitalist equilibrium must by its very nature further impair the already disrupted class equilibrium and lend a new impetus to the revolutionary struggle. The question of whether capitalism can be revived becomes in consequence a question which involves the struggle between living forces: the contending classes and their parties. If, of the two main classes in society—the bourgeoisie and the proletariat—one of them, the latter, renounces the revolutionary struggle, then the former, the bourgeoisie, would undeniably in the final analysis establish a new capitalist equilibrium—one based on material and spiritual degeneration—by means of new crises, new wars, progressive pauperization of entire countries and the steady dying out of millions of toilers.

But the present state of the world proletariat furnishes the least justification for a prognosis of this kind.

35. The elements of stability, of conservatism and of tradition, completely upset in social relations, have lost most of their authority over the consciousness of the toiling masses. While the Social Democracy and the trade unions still continue in most cases to exercise an influence over a considerable section of the proletariat, thanks to the organizational machines they have inherited from the past, this influence is, in its turn, completely bereft of stability. The war has modified in the extreme not only the moods of the proletariat but also the very composition, and these modifications are utterly incompatible with the organizational gradualism of the pre-war days.

Among the summits of the proletariat in most countries the formal ruling position is still held by the labor bureaucracy, whose numbers have greatly swollen, whose ranks remain tightly knit, whose own habits and methods of domination are being constantly elaborated, and who are tied by thousands of threads to the institutions and organs of the capitalist state.

Then comes the section of workers who are more favorably situated in industry, who occupy or look forward to occupying some administrative post and who constitute the most reliable support of the labor bureaucracy.

And next is the older generation of Social Democrats and trade unionists, skilled workers in the main who have become attached to the organizations through decades of struggle and cannot make up their minds to break with them, despite all the sellouts and betrayals. In many industries, however, skilled workers have become intermixed with the unskilled laborers, predominantly women.

There are millions of workers who have directly passed through the school of war, who have become accustomed to handling weapons, and who are now for the most part prepared to turn these weapons against the class enemy—but only provided the indispensable conditions for success obtain, namely, serious preparation and a firm leadership.

Millions of new workers, particularly women workers, drawn into industry during the war, have brought with them into the proletariat not only their petty-bourgeois prejudices but also their impatient aspirations for better conditions of life.

Millions of young working men and women who have grown up amid the tempests of war and revolution are the most receptive to the ideas of Communism and are burning with the desire to act.

Finally, there is the gigantic army of unemployed, for the most part declassed and semi-declassed elements, whose ebbs and flows illustrate most strikingly the process of capitalist economic disintegration and who represent a constant menace to bourgeois "law and order."

All these layers of the proletariat, so diverse in origin and character, have been and are being drawn into the postwar movement neither simultaneously nor homogeneously. Hence the fluctuations, the flows and ebbs, the offensives and retreats in the revolutionary struggle. But the overwhelming majority of the proletarian masses is being rapidly welded together by the shattering of old illusions, by the terrible uncertainty of existence, by the autocratic domination of the trusts, by the bandit methods of the militarized state. This multimillion-headed mass is seeking a firm and lucid leadership, a clear-cut program of action and thus creates the premises for the decisive role which the closely welded and centralized Communist Party is destined to play.

36. The position of the working class has perceptibly worsened during the war. Certain groups of workers have prospered. Families in which several members could hold war jobs in factories succeeded in maintaining and even improving their living standards. But on the whole wages could not keep up with the soaring cost of living.

In Central Europe the proletariat has been doomed to ever-greater privations since the war. In the Allied continental countries the decline of living standards has been less abrupt, until recently. In England, in the last period of the war, the proletariat by means of an energetic struggle had arrested the process of lowering the living standards.

In the United States some layers of the working class have improved their position; others retained their former levels, while still others had their living standards lowered.

The crisis has descended upon the world proletariat with terrific force. Wage cuts have exceeded the fall in prices. The number of unemployed or semi-employed has reached dimensions unprecedented in capitalist history.

The sharp fluctuations in personal living conditions not only produce extremely negative effects on the productivity of labor but also act to exclude the possibility of restoring class equilibrium in the basic sphere—that of production. The instability of living conditions, which mirrors the universal instability of national and world economic conditions, is today one of the most important factors of revolutionary development.

VII
PERSPECTIVES AND TASKS

37. The war was not directly terminated in the proletarian revolution. The bourgeoisie has with some justification recorded this fact as a major victory for itself.

Only petty-bourgeois blockheads can construe the bankruptcy of the program of the Communist International from the fact that the European proletariat did not overthrow the bourgeoisie during the war or immediately after it. That the Communist International bases its policy on the proletarian revolution does not at all mean either dogmatically fixing any definite date for the revolution or issuing any pledges to bring it about mechanically at a set time. The revolution was and remains a struggle of living forces waged upon given historical foundations. The world-wide disruption of capitalist equilibrium by the war creates conditions favorable to the basic force of the revolution, which is the proletariat. All the efforts of the Communist International were and remain directed toward taking full advantage of this situation.

The differences between the Communist International and the Social Democrats of both groups do not arise from our alleged attempt to force the revolution on a fixed date whereas they are opposed to utopianism and putschism; the difference lies in this, that the Social Democrats obstruct the actual development of the revolution by rendering, whether as members of the administration or as members of the opposition, all possible assistance in restoring the equilibrium of the bourgeois state, whereas the Communists are exploiting every means, every method, every possibility for the purpose of overthrowing and abolishing the bourgeois state through the establishment of the dictatorship of the proletariat.

In the course of the two and a half years that have elapsed since the war, the proletariat of various countries has exhibited so much energy, such readiness for struggle, such a spirit of self-sacrifice as would have more than sufficed to bring victory to the revolution, provided there had been at the head of the working class an International Communist Party strong, centralized and ready for action. But during the war and immediately thereafter, by force of historic circumstances, there stood at the head of the European proletariat the organization of the Second International which has become and which remains an invaluable political weapon in the hands of the bourgeoisie.

38. In Germany at the end of 1918 and at the beginning of 1919 the power was actually in the hands of the working class. The Social Democrats—the majority faction, the Independents, and the trade unions alike—used their whole apparatus and all their traditional influence for the purpose of returning this power into the hands of the bourgeoisie.

In Italy the stormy revolutionary movement of the proletariat has for one and a half years kept swirling over the country, and it was only thanks to the petty-bourgeois impotence of the Socialist Party, to the treacherous policy of its parliamentary fraction, to the cowardly opportunism of the trade union organizations, that the bourgeoisie found itself enabled to repair its apparatus, to mobilize its White Guards and to assume the offensive against the proletariat which had thus been temporarily disheartened by the bankruptcy of its old leading organs.

The mighty strike movement in England was shattered again and again during the last year by the ruthless application of military force, which intimidated the trade union leaders. Had these leaders remained faithful to the cause of the working class, the machinery of the trade unions despite all of its defects could have been used for revolutionary battles. The recent crisis of the Triple Alliance[18] furnished the possibility of a revolutionary collision with the bourgeoisie but this was frustrated by the conservatism, cowardice and treachery of the trade union leaders. Were the machinery of the English trade unions to develop today half the amount of energy in the interests of socialism it has been expending in the interests of capitalism, the English proletariat could conquer power with a minimum of sacrifice and could start a systematic reconstruction of the country's economic system.

The same applies in a greater or lesser degree to all other capitalist countries.

39. It is absolutely incontestable that on a world scale the open revolutionary struggle of the proletariat for power is at present passing through a stoppage, a slowing down in tempo. But in the very nature of things, it was impossible to expect that the revolutionary offensive after the war, insofar as it failed to result in an immediate victory, should go on developing uninterruptedly along an upward curve. Political evolution, too, has cycles of its own, its ups and downs. The enemy does not remain passive, but keeps on fighting. If the offensive of the proletariat is not crowned by victory, the bourgeoisie seizes the very first opportunity for a counter-offensive. The loss by the proletariat of some of its easily won positions produces a temporary depression in its ranks. But it remains equally incontestable that in our epoch the curve of capitalist development as a whole is constantly moving—through

temporary upswings—*downwards;* while the curve of the revolution—through all its fluctuations—is constantly moving *upwards*.

Since the restoration of capitalism presupposes a great intensification of exploitation, the annihilation of millions of lives, the degradation of other millions below subsistence levels, and the perpetual insecurity of the proletariat, it follows that the workers will be driven again and again to engage in strikes and to rise in revolt. Under this oppression and pressure, and in the course of these battles, the will of the masses to abolish the capitalist system will grow and become tempered.

40. The fundamental task of the Communist Party in the current crisis is to lead the present defensive struggles of the proletariat, to extend their scope, to deepen them, to unify them, and in harmony with the march of events, *to transform them into decisive political struggles for the ultimate goal.*

But should the tempo of development slacken, and the current commercial-industrial crisis be superseded by a period of prosperity in a greater or lesser number of countries, this would in no case signify the beginning of an "organic" epoch. So long as capitalism exists, cyclical oscillations are inevitable. These will accompany capitalism in its death agony, just as they accompanied it in its youth and maturity. In case the proletariat should be forced to retire under the onslaught of capitalism in the course of the present crisis, it will immediately resume the offensive as soon as any amelioration in the conjuncture sets in. Its economic offensive, which would in that case inevitably be carried on under the slogan of revenge for all the deceptions of the war period and for all the plunder and abuses of the crisis, will tend to turn into an open civil war, just as the present defensive struggle does.

41. Whether the revolutionary movement develops in the next period at a swift or slow tempo, the Communist Party must in either case remain the *party of action*. It stands at the head of the struggling masses; it firmly and clearly formulates its fighting slogans, exposing and sweeping aside all the equivocal slogans of the Social Democracy which are always based on compromise and conciliationism. Whatever the shifts in the course of the struggle, the Communist Party always strives to consolidate organizationally new bases of support, trains the masses in active maneuvering, arms them with new methods and practices, designed for direct and open clashes with the enemy forces. Utilizing every breathing spell in order to assimilate the experience of the preceding phase of the struggle, the Communist Party seeks to deepen and extend the class conflicts, to coordinate them nationally and internationally by unity of goal and unity of practical action, and in this way, at the head of the proletariat, shatter all resistance on the road to its dictatorship and the socialist revolution.

22. Speech on the Italian question at the Third Congress of the Communist International[19]

Ninth Session, June 29, 1921

Comrades, I shall not dwell on the past of the Italian Socialist Party. Enough has already been said on this subject. The key question is the crisis of last September which has produced the present state of affairs. Even a cursory review of the political situation leaves one with the impression and even the conviction that the orientation of the Italian proletariat in the years following the war was purely revolutionary. Everything written in *Avanti*[20] and everything uttered by the spokesmen of the Socialist Party was taken by the masses as a summons to the proletarian revolution. And this propaganda struck a responsive chord in the hearts of the working class, awakened their will and called forth the September events.

Were one to judge the party from the political standpoint, one would have to conclude—for this is the only possible explanation—that the ISP verbally conducted a revolutionary policy, without ever taking into account any of its consequences. Everybody knows that during the September events no other organization so lost its head and became so paralyzed by fear as the ISP which had itself paved the way for these events. Now these facts are proof that the Italian organization—and we should not forget that the party is not only ideas, a goal and a program but also an apparatus, an organization—this Italian organization could have secured victory by unswerving activity. September was the month of the great crisis for the proletariat and for the ISP. What were the consequences of these events for the proletariat? It is very hard to estimate this, in view of the fact that a class which breaks with its party loses immediately its sense of orientation. And the party—what conclusions has it drawn from this experience? For three years following the war, each and every comrade who arrived from Italy would tell us: "We have everything ready for the revolution." The whole world knew that Italy was on the eve of the revolution. When the revolution broke out, the party proved bankrupt. What then were the lessons of these events? What was done? We've been told: "We were unprepared because our organization was composed of elements which were manifestly incompatible and which acted to paralyze each other. To create certain conditions, insofar as this depends on our will, one must have the will to create them!" This, Comrade Lazzari,[21] is the crux of the matter; one must have the will to revolutionary victory! Only if such will exists can one then engage in discussion and undertake to analyze; because strategy is indispensable, because it is impossible to gain victory by means of a powerful will alone. Strategy is indispensable, but most indispensable is the will to revolution and to its victory! Turati and his friends are in this sense honest, because they declare daily, openly and repeatedly that they do not want the revolution. They do not want it and yet they remain members of the Socialist Party, even its prominent members.

You have lived through September. But what course did you pursue after this tragic month? You have moved further to the right. In your new parliamentary fraction, the reformists, that is, people who don't want the revolution, constitute the majority. Your central organ *Avanti* has turned the helm sharply to the right. This is the present state of affairs. It is impermissible to boast about one's past when the present situation is so clear and unmistakable. Between lip-service to the revolution and the cruel demands of the revolutionary situation there is a contradiction—which became manifest among you in September. Out of this contradiction flows one of two things: Either you will renounce that portion of your past which was revolutionary only in its lip-service, in other words, you will break with the reformists who hinder revolutionary action; or you must say: "Since we didn't want the September events we must likewise reject the methods that called them forth."

Turati will not hesitate to make use of the lessons of September; he is shrewd enough to single out the obvious contradictions which flow therefrom. So far as you, your party and your Central Committee are concerned, you are only adding to the lack of clarity which prepared and which predetermined in advance the failure of the September events and which has produced the ISP's shift to the right. Serrati was in favor of preserving a maximum concentration of forces; he wanted to keep the Communists, the centrists and the reformists together within a single party. In some specific instances this idea of concentration of forces might be justified by a hope of preserving the maximum of revolutionary forces in the party. He wanted to do this, he wanted to unite these three groups in order to be able later to say: "Here are the genuine bulwarks of our party; whatever and whoever stands outside our ranks is hostile to us."

You have gone through one of the bitterest, clearest and most tragic experiences. And only afterwards did this idea of concentration, which is somewhat abstract in and by itself, take on a definite political form. This idea became utterly reformist and not centrist, because the party's development has now definitely swung to the right.

Turati has declared: "In September the proletariat was not yet mature enough." Yes, it was not mature. But have you explained to the proletariat why the party was not mature? Did you say to the proletariat: "Yes, Turati is correct in this sense, that you, Italian workers, were not mature enough to cleanse your party, before engaging in decisive action, of all those elements who paralyze the party's work. Turati is correct in this sense, that the Italian proletariat by its failure to expel him from its ranks has thereby demonstrated that it was not mature enough for the decisive September actions." What is the present situation of the Italian proletariat? I am certain that it has become much more cautious after it was involuntarily betrayed by the party in which it had completely confided. Comrade Lazzari tends to interpret such expressions in a moral and personal sense. He said: "We are accused of treachery, but what did we get for it?" It is not a question of individual or venal treachery. It is a question of the bankruptcy of the party. And in political terms this is nothing else but a betrayal of the interests of the proletariat. I ask myself: What can the Italian proletariat possibly think? The party surely stands terribly discredited in its eyes. A new party has risen—the Communist Party. We are certain that it will continue to grow even were it to remain in the future as isolated as it is today. This party turns to the proletariat and offers it its revolutionary Communist program. Aren't you afraid that the Italian proletarians will say after listening to you: "But we've heard this melody before, we've already been duped in September." This is the whole gist of the extremely difficult situation that you have created in Italy for a period which, let us hope, will be a brief one.

The young Italian party must through energetic and audacious work conquer anew a genuine revolutionary reputation which is indispensable not only for parliamentary activity—which is something else again—but also for a new assault against the capitalist society. It is necessary to conquer anew the revolutionary reputation which the party has squandered through its activities, or better said, through its inactivity in September. You tell us that the followers of Turati submit to party discipline. Oh yes, the speakers were absolutely right who said that a plea had been delivered here in Turati's defense; it was a plea that was constructed in accordance with all the rules of juridical defense. What is the meaning of party discipline? There is formal discipline, and there is real discipline. It seems to me that there is a difference whether I act in a certain way because circumstances leave me no choice or whether I act of my own free will. We submit to the discipline of the capitalist state, we submit to capitalist legality—but how? Only to the extent to which we are compelled to do so. But at the same time we laugh at bourgeois legality, we create underground organs to circumvent such legality, and we utilize every avenue to break through bourgeois legality or to extend its framework. And what is Turati's attitude to your discipline? It's exactly the same attitude, Comrade Lazzari. He submits to your discipline as we submit to bourgeois legality. He creates his own illegal organizations, his own faction in your party. He carries on negotiations with the government, naturally on the sly and illegally. He does everything to extend and to break through the framework of this discipline and, over and above this, he mocks your discipline in his speeches and in his newspaper. He is therefore our conscious and methodical enemy, just as we are the enemies of bourgeois society and its legality. This is the true state of affairs.

You say: "But Turati hasn't given us any real grounds for expulsion. We haven't got enough facts." Yes, it can be flatly stated that even if we continue to wait indefinitely we shall still lack these facts inasmuch as Turati knows excellently just what he wants. Turati is no run-of-the-mill careerist, eager to become a minister in a capitalist government. Insofar as I can make him out, he has a policy of his own which he values highly and which he wants to carry through. He is not chasing after a ministerial portfolio. I can clearly visualize an interview between Turati and Giolitti. Giolitti says to him: "Here is a portfolio that belongs to you." But Turati replies: "Haven't you listened, my dear colleague, to the speeches of Lazzari? The instant I accept this portfolio, I shall supply him with very convenient data which he will not hesitate to use. I will be expelled from the party, and once expelled I shall lose all political importance so far as you and the preservation of the capitalist state are concerned. Since what is at issue is not so much the installation of one more Socialist minister but the support of democracy, *i.e.*, the support of capitalist society, I cannot accept your portfolio; for I do not intend to play into the hands of my severe colleague Lazzari. In the interests of bourgeois society let us leave things as they are."

You say: "Aren't we paying too much attention to Turati, his speeches, his books, his prefaces? Isn't this rather an isolated incident? It is a *quantité négligeable*! If that is the case, if so far as you are concerned all that's involved is a loss of one or more individuals, the loss of a *quantité négligeable* [a trifle], then why are you so upset? Let us imagine, dear comrades from Italy, that while we are discussing here Giolitti rings up Turati on the telephone to inquire: "Can it be that Lazzari left for Moscow to assume some obligations there?" And Turati answers: "No, no! This is purely an isolated incident." As you know, capitalist society holds to the principle of division of labor; and by breaking with the Communist International for the sake of safeguarding Turati, you are doing a great service to this society. You say that you are becoming more and more enthusiastic about the Russian Communist Party and about Soviet Russia. Permit me in this connection to speak quite freely, not only for the benefit of all the Italian comrades but for the benefit of all parties. When it comes to talking about us, it happens all too frequently that a very delicate tone is employed, as if to avoid picking a quarrel with us. As all of you know, our situation is an extremely difficult one. You were present on the Red Square and you have seen not only our soldiers and our armed Communists who are ready to come to the defense of the Third International; you've also seen our youth, our children, most of whom go around barefoot and undernourished. On visiting our factories each of you will see our economic and material poverty which beggars description.

Whoever arrives in Russia with the hope of finding a Communist paradise here will be cruelly disappointed. Whoever comes here with the aim of gathering impressions for eulogizing Russia is not a genuine Communist. But whoever comes here in order to collect facts pertaining to our poverty in order to employ them as an argument against Communism is an open enemy of ours. [Applause.] And here, comrades, is what Turati, a member of your party, has to say about Russia: "The Russians have invented the Soviets and the Communist International for their own profit and to further their own national interests." This is what he told the Italian worker who was dragooned into the war to defend fictitious national interests and who was duped like all the others. Today another bogey is being dangled before him—a national bogey. Today Soviet Russia, mind you, is seeking to further her own national interests through the medium of the Communist International. If you go through the German press for the period of the March events, you will find there the selfsame thought expressed about the position of the Soviet power. It says there that the Soviets found themselves terribly discredited at the time; and in order to save herself, Soviet Russia issued, through the Communist International, a command to launch revolutionary action in Germany. Today our perfidious and wily enemies are spreading a legend—one of whose most fervent disseminators is your Turati—a legend to the effect that to bolster up our domestic situation we are demanding of all other parties that they engage in revolutionary actions, which have no connection whatsoever with the political and social development of the respective countries. If we permit people who propagandize such ideas to remain much longer in our International, we can very well create a very difficult situation for the International.

Yes, comrades, we have erected in our country the bulwark of the world revolution. Our country is still very backward, still very barbaric. It unfolds before you a panorama of unheard-of poverty. But we are defending this bulwark of the world revolution since at the given moment there is no other in the world. When another stronghold is erected in France or in Germany, then the one in Russia will lose nine-tenths of its significance; and we shall then go to you in Europe to defend this other and more important stronghold. Finally, comrades, it is sheer absurdity to believe that we deem this Russian stronghold of the revolution to be the center of the world. It is absurd even to claim that we believe it is our right to demand of you to make a revolution in Germany or France or Italy, whenever this is required by our domestic policy. Were we capable of such perfidy, then all of us would deserve to be put against a wall and shot, one by one.

Comrade Lazzari! How can we remain in the same International with Turati who is a member of your party and who calls our International a "fantastic International"? These are his very words. Karl Liebknecht and Rosa Luxemburg are dead, but for this International they remain eternally alive. How can we combine within the cadres of our International Karl Liebknecht, Rosa Luxemburg and—Turati? Turati says that our organization is fantastic. And just think of it, even yesterday he himself was still a member of it. Well, that really is a fantastic episode in the life of the Third International. [Loud applause.]

23. Speech on Comrade Radek's[22] report on 'Tactics of the Comintern' at the Third Congress

Fourteenth Session, July 2, 1921

First, a brief formal comment. Comrade Thaelmann,[23] whose passionate speech we just heard, has complained that he was not allowed to take the floor after me. But, after all, the order in which speakers take the floor is determined by the speakers' list. Comrade Thaelmann also said that he is a very disciplined comrade. As such he ought to have accepted the discipline imposed by a speakers' list, instead of complaining about such an objective fact.

Comrade Thaelmann is likewise dissatisfied—once again unjustifiably—with Comrade Lenin who is quoted as having allegedly said that "We are here proposing our theses on tactics, and the other delegations have no right to present any amendments." This was not what Comrade Lenin meant, and Comrade Thaelmann's standpoint in this connection is absolutely false. Lenin said: "The theses we propose are not a product of the Russian delegation, nor were they elaborated in some quiet office in the course of an hour or so." Comrade Thaelmann can make the necessary inquiries among the members of his own delegation from whom he will learn that we held lengthy, exhaustive, and at times vehement negotiations and discussions over the theses, in which the members of the German delegation also participated and introduced their proposals; and that mutual concessions were made. And our theses are the result of this rather laborious process. Those of us who participated in elaborating them do not claim that they were approved by all the parties, groups and tendencies, but we do maintain that in our opinion the theses constitute a compromise, a concession to the leftist tendency. I shall presently try to analyze more closely just what the term "leftist tendency" signifies here. Right now I want only to underscore that we view these theses as a maximum concession to a tendency represented here by many comrades, including Comrade Thaelmann.

Comrades! Many delegates have privately expressed to me their impatience that so much of our time is being taken up by the German delegation to discuss its internal affairs. The impatience of these comrades is unwarranted, in my opinion. The main issue under discussion is the March action. Naturally, it is human, all too human for personal questions, personal antagonisms and emotions to become involved in such a purely political question. True, some comrades have needlessly sharpened the personal and emotional aspect of the question as, for example, Comrade Heckert did, whose speech was otherwise very interesting. But I think that we must single out here the essence of the question, and this essence, which is the main issue, is not a purely German issue but an international issue *par excellence.* In relation to Russia the German party is that particular Western European party which, after developing into an independent, definitive and large party, was the first to engage in independent action. And since the young, much too young Italian party, and the larger French party which is likewise young as a Communist Party, find themselves facing in this connection a similar situation, I believe that all the delegations, and especially the ones just mentioned, have a great deal to learn from this question.

I shall begin my discussion of the March action with an analysis of the amendments that have been submitted. For the Congress must choose between two tendencies. Of the stylistic and factual corrections and additions to the first draft of the theses I shall, naturally, say nothing. Well, we have to choose between two tendencies. Between the tendency which is represented here by Comrade Lenin, Comrade Zinoviev and particularly by the reporter Comrade Radek as well as by me; and the other tendency which is expressed in the amendments both as they stand now and as originally proposed. That is why it is important for us to take up these amendments. I shall confine myself only to the section dealing with the March action. Our theses state in this connection that we view the March action as forced upon the VKPD (United German Communist Party) by the government's attack upon the proletariat of Central Germany, and we recognize that by its courageous conduct "the VKPD has shown itself to be the party of the revolutionary proletariat of Germany." Then we go on to lay bare the chief mistakes committed during this action, and in conclusion we give the following advice:

> For the purpose of carefully weighing the possibilities of struggle, the VKPD must attentively listen to the voices which point out the difficulties of this or that action and carefully examine their reason for urging caution. But as soon as an action is decided upon

by the party authorities, all comrades must submit to the decisions of the party and carry out this action. Criticism of the action can commence only after its completion, and must be conducted only within the party organizations, giving due consideration to the situation wherein the party finds itself in the face of its class enemies. Since Paul Levi did disregard these obvious demands of party discipline and the conditions of party criticism, the Congress approves his expulsion from the party and declares it inadmissible for any members of the Communist International to collaborate politically with him in any way whatsoever.

Comrade Brand, however, is flatly opposed to any supervisory body whose admonitory voice the party is obliged to heed. We shall perhaps have further occasion to return to Comrade Brand who is so critical of admonitory supervision, statistics and many other things. What amendments do the German comrades and others propose to the foregoing paragraph? They propose to us that the Third Congress of the Comintern accept the March action of the VKPD as a step forward and declare the following:

> This action signifies that the strongest mass party of Central Europe has made the transition to real struggle; it constitutes the first attempt to realize in life the Communist Party's leading role in the struggle of the German proletariat—the role which the party had assumed in its founding program. The March action signifies the exposure of a victory over the open counterrevolutionary character of the USP (The Independent Socialist Party of Germany) and the masked centrist elements in the ranks of the VKPD itself. The March action, by disclosing in the very course of the strug-

gle numerous mistakes and organizational shortcomings of the party, has made it possible to clearly understand these mistakes and shortcomings and to begin liquidating them. This action revealed in the course of its development that the party's combat discipline is not strict enough and has aided to strengthen it. It attracted not inconsiderable masses of Social-Democratic workers and created a revolutionary ferment among these parties. This action, far from having impaired the organization, has, on the contrary, strengthened its fighting spirit. . . .

And so on and so forth.

When a demand is made of the Congress that it recognize that the March action was not only a mass action, imposed upon the working class (and thereby also upon the party), but that the party had also conducted itself stoutly; when a demand is made of the Congress that it likewise recognize that the party made an attempt to realize in struggle the leading role of the Communist Party—then the Congress should, after all, also be given the right to say whether this attempt was successful or unsuccessful. When we say that the March action was a step forward, we mean to say by this—at least that is how I understand it—that the Communist Party no longer stands before us as an opposition within the Independent Socialist Party or as a propaganda Communist organization, but as a unified, independent, firmly welded and centralized party, which has the possibility of independently intervening in the struggle of the proletariat; and that all this took place for the first time during the March action. In connection with the Second World Congress, I had many discussions with French comrades concerning the situation in the trade unions and in the party and I then told them: "Yes, you together with the syndicalists, the anarchists and the Socialists, you, too, represent nothing more than an opposition. As a result there are certain tendencies and nuances, and even potential stupidities. The instant you separate from the old organization and come out as an independent force, you will have made a big step forward." This has now been achieved in full [in Germany]. But it does not mean that the first action, this first attempt to play an independent leading role, has proved successful.

They tell us that they have learned a great deal from it and, moreover, precisely from their own mistakes. That is what their amendments say. I shall not stop to read them to you but they state that the major merit of the March action consists precisely in this, that it provided an opportunity of clarifying the mistakes committed therein, only in order subsequently to eliminate them. Isn't it a little too audacious to seek for special merits in this connection? In a private conversation with Comrade Thalheimer I told him that he reminded me of a Russian translator in the 'seventies who translated an English book and pointed out in his introduction that he had translated it solely to show the world how worthless this book is. [Laughter.] After all, one does not engage in an action simply for the sake of seeing what mistakes might arise therefrom and for the sake of eliminating them afterwards. These amendments are written in the spirit of self-justification, and not in the spirit of analysis.

In his interesting speech Comrade Heckert[24] has painted for us a picture of the March action showing that the situation was extremely acute at the time. The question of reparations, the occupation of the Ruhr, Upper Silesia, economic crisis, unemployment, big strikes. Under these circumstances the social contradictions became still further exacerbated and the final impulsion for the party's action came from the workers' movement in Central Germany. A truly beautiful, superb, economic picture! But another comrade defending this same action sketched for us an entirely different picture. When Comrade Thalheimer, thirty years from now, when his hair will already be grey, takes in hand the pen of Mehring[25] to write the history of the Communist Party, he will then find documents and books. . . . [Interjection by Radek: In my magic trunk. (Laughter.)] He will find documents and books in which an entirely different picture of the movement can be found, namely: that the international situation was quite confused and in general and on the whole, disclosed a tendency toward compromise. The Upper Silesian question hung suspended in midair. It could not exert any revolutionary influence. The disarmament question in Bavaria? *Rote Fahne* has consistently declared, contrary to Heckert's speech yesterday, that it was becoming more and more clear that this question would be solved by a compromise at the expense of the revolutionary workers of Bavaria and of all Germany; and besides, without any major clashes on an international scale, or any clashes between the German and Bavarian governments. And in this same connection Comrade Thalheimer will find, thirty years from now, articles proving that the crisis in Germany bore and bears an entirely different character from that in the United States or in England; that in Germany this crisis did not become aggravated so catastrophically as it did in those two countries; that Germany's entire economic life is in a state of decay and that under the existing economic conditions in Germany the crisis could not erupt with sufficient force. The number of unemployed in Germany is insignificant as compared to the United States and England.

So far as the internal relations are concerned, the Social Democrats are partly in the government, partly in the opposition. The same applies to the Independent Socialist Party, which keeps drawing closer and closer to the Social Democrats. The trade unions, their bureaucratic leadership, are all against us. And what conclusion must be drawn from this? After all, the same comrade tells us that incredible passivity reigns among the workers, and that it was necessary to make a breach in it through the revolutionary initiative of a resolute minority. Heckert, on the contrary, said that everything was in flux, everything was plowed up. Storm and stress. And then came the events in Central Germany. Another comrade said: "A stagnant swamp was everywhere. A wall of passivity was rising. We had to break through it at any cost." Each of these pictures is splendid as a finished logical unit but I hardly think they harmonize with one another. Still another comrade—Koenen—attested that an open insurrection reigned in Central Germany, while everywhere else there was a reign of passivity. Activity was implanted in a shell of passivity. From all this one gets the impression that the members of the German delegation still approach the issue as if it had to be defended at all costs, but not studied nor analyzed. And everything that we hear is, so to speak, a means toward an end—which is to defend the March action at any price before the International. But this will hardly succeed. The crux here, so far as I am concerned, lies in what Comrade Thaelmann has pointed out. He said that if we accept the theses or even the proposed amendments, "we shall carry out a reorientation in our country." I believe that our brave and staunch Comrade Thaelmann is correct in the given instance. He probably has very close ties with the masses. [Thaelmann interjects: Yes, indeed, the closest.] I don't doubt it in the least, especially when I take into consideration the frame of mind in which certain comrades have arrived from Germany or in which they published certain articles and pamphlets there. They have, after all, made a rather lengthy and uncomfortable journey to Russia in order to gain an opportunity to think over the situation somewhat more dispassionately. Then the theses appeared which met with stubborn opposition. Later came discussions with the other delegations, including the Russians, and the German comrades could not have failed to notice that the comrades in the International do not view things through German spectacles. And so they take the path, as it were, of strategic retreat.

It is, indeed, impossible to deny that the proposed amendments are dangerous, not so much in what they directly and immediately say, as in this, that they seek in a rather masked and misty form to express those ideas which were spread among the German workers and in the ranks of the German Communist Party in the name of the Central Committee during the hottest days of the struggle and after the struggle. Comrade Thaelmann and others say: "We must come back with theses which do not disavow us." We don't want this at all either; we don't want in any way to disavow the German party for it is one of our best parties. But the entire conception of the March offensive, the conditions of struggle and of victory are developed here in such a way that some of the articles, some of the speeches, some of the circulars of the German Central Committee and of its members must be understood as something that is very grave and dangerous. This is the main thing. They want to so influence the situation as to prevent the adoption of a thoroughly precise resolution, but to get instead an unclear, misty resolution into which they could gradually read a new meaning that they want and which they could imperceptibly interpret later on in an entirely different sense. This is the essential thing. This is inadmissible. For in our opinion the danger is far too great to allow so much scope for a gradual and imperceptible diminution of the spirit of the offensive. We shall never agree to this; it is excluded. Yes, you can clamp us down by a decision of the Congress majority, but even in that case we shall continue to fight within the framework, and only within the framework set for us by the Congress. I hope, however, that the resolution on tactics will be adopted as was the economic resolution. In the latter case the Left-Wing comrades of our German delegation also wanted to stage something in the nature of a demonstration; and after accepting these theses in principle, they nevertheless introduced a resolution which contained diametrically opposite views. But later it turned out that they decided not to insist on what they had previously wanted to say. And in the Commission almost nothing remained of the differences. It seems to me that exactly the same thing will happen with the tactical questions. I know from personal experience how unpleasant it is not to be recognized by a party Congress or a Congress of the International. However, comrades, I think that for your situation in Germany it is best to introduce clarity into this question. I don't believe what Levi has said, that is, that the party would perish from it. The Congress must say to the German workers that a mistake was committed, and that the party's attempt to assume the leading role in a great mass movement was not a fortunate one. That is not enough. We must say that this attempt was completely unsuccessful in this sense—that were it repeated, it might actually ruin this splendid party. [Thalheimer interjects: You know that this is excluded.] For you—yes; but not for thousands of organized workers who had assumed that the Congress would acclaim with ecstasy what we look upon as a blunder. [Hearty approbation.] The same applies to our young French friends. In the ECCI, we discussed the question of the 1919 draft and we asked whether the French party ought to advance the slogan not to obey this order. On that occasion I asked one of our young friends [Laporte]: "What is your opinion, should the draftees resort to armed or purely passive resistance?" And the comrade vehemently replied: "Naturally, with revolver in hand." He supposed that he was thus manifesting his complete agreement with the Third International; that he was thus giving the Third International the greatest revolutionary happiness and that he was fulfilling his duty by speaking as he did. He meant it quite seriously and he was unconditionally ready to fight the draft with revolver in hand. Naturally, we poured a bucket of ice water over him and I believe that the comrade will learn better. He has come into a new milieu here, something he does not see every day. The rough edges are being polished off little by little. But in Germany, France, Hungary! These 2–3 weeks during which we gather in the sessions of the Congress do introduce a few changes into our views. But there, in those countries, what has changed there? Nothing. And this famous philosophy of the offensive, absolutely non-Marxist, has arisen from the following propositions: "A wall of passivity is gradually rising; this is a misfortune. The movement is stagnating. Therefore, forward march! Let us break through this wall! It seems to me that a whole layer of leading and semi-leading comrades in the German party have been for quite some time educated in this spirit and they are waiting to hear what the Congress has to say on this score. If we now proclaim that we are throwing Paul Levi out of the window, while you utter a few muddled phrases about the March action, pointing out that it is the first attempt, a step forward, in short, if we smother criticism by phrase-mongering—then we shall have failed in our duty. It is our duty to say clearly and precisely to the German workers that we consider this philosophy of the offensive to be the greatest danger. And in its practical application to be the greatest political crime.

I am in complete agreement with Comrade Zinoviev and cherish, as he does, the hope that at this Congress we shall arrive at a unanimous verdict on the character of our activity; I also think that on this extremely important tactical question we do not have to make any major concessions to the so-called Left. A few comrades—among them, I believe, the French—have expressed concern over the struggle against the Left. Comrade Zinoviev has dealt with this. Fortunately, it is precisely in the French language that the word *"la gauche"* has a twofold meaning: *gauche*—that which stands on the left; and *gauche*—that which is helpless, awkward. [Interjection: *Linkisch!*] Yes, *linkisch*, but in the bad sense of the word. In German, by the way, it comes almost to the same thing. Well, I think that in conducting a struggle against the so-called Left, we do not at all feel that we are to the right of these "Lefts."

We see no party to the left of us, for since we are the Communist International, the Marxist International, it follows that we are the most revolutionary party there is. This means a party capable of utilizing every situation and every possibility, and able not only to lead the struggle but also to assure victory. That is the real goal. It is sometimes forgotten that we must learn strategy, must cold-bloodedly weigh the forces of our enemy as well as our own, must estimate the situation and not plunge into struggle in order to breach a wall of passivity or, as one comrade put it, to "activize the party." Therewith we are naturally obliged to also occupy ourselves a little with statistics, even though Comrade Brand has pointed out that opportunists spend a great deal of time over them.

In one of his speeches we heard him juxtapose the sword and statistics, while in a second speech we had the charge of opportunism flung at us. Such a position is dangerous for our Italian comrades, who have yet a great deal to do with statistics. If I had occasion to refer as did Heckert and Thalheimer to Italy, I might have said: "Here is a country ruined by war where the workers have seized the factories, where the followers of Serrati have perpetrated a betrayal, where the fascists are sacking labor printing plants and setting fire to working-class institutions. And if this party does not raise the cry: 'With All Our Forces Forward Against the Enemy,' then it is a cowardly party which will be condemned by world history." But if we look at things not from the standpoint of such phraseology but from the standpoint of weighing the situation cold-bloodedly, we would have to say what Comrade Zinoviev did, namely: they must gain anew the confidence of the working class since the workers have become much more cautious precisely owing to this treachery. They will say to themselves: "We heard the same phrases from Serrati. He said virtually the same thing and then he betrayed us. Where is the guarantee that the new party will not betray us, too?" The working class wants to see the party in action before going into the decisive battle under its leadership.

At this Congress we have three more or less clearly expressed tendencies, three groups, which have temporarily become converted into tendencies, and which must be borne in mind in order to evaluate correctly the interplay of forces at this Congress. In the first place we have the German delegation which has come almost directly from the fires of the March action and which expresses most sharply its attitude toward the philosophy of the offensive. That has, naturally, been discarded by some German comrades.

Then there are the Italian comrades, who are pursuing the same path. This is quite comprehensible if we bear in mind that their party has broken with the centrists. The Italian comrades say: "Now our hands are at last untied; now we can fulfill our duty, participate in the revolutionary actions of the masses and exact revenge for the treachery of Serrati." Nowadays you know, comrades, it is said—not only by Levi but also by the capitalist press and the "independent" press—that the March action was ordered by the ECCI and that Levi has been expelled for refusing to obey this order. Some comrades in the French and Czechoslovak parties have begun asking themselves—and this shows how little acquainted they are with the spirit of the ECCI—"What if I, too, should some day receive such an order in the name of the ECCI and if I fail to fulfill it will I then be expelled from the party?" These two different moods are represented here.

There likewise exists a third set of views which are expressed, we hope, in our theses. This third tendency holds that it would, of course, be senseless for the ECCI to accept the standpoint of a tactical philosophy which recommends that combat activity be raised through more or less artificial mass actions, and that we begin issuing such orders to the different countries. On the contrary, precisely because we have now become sufficiently strong and because as a result of this we are faced with the task of leading the mass movement as an independent centralized party, we are all the more obliged to analyze cold-bloodedly and with absolute thoroughness the situation as it exists in each country, and wherever it is possible and necessary, to attack and to assume the offensive with all our energies. This is just what our proposed theses say.

In France, one comrade said, there are no Lefts. Yes, there are none. The French party is in its moulting stage.

On reading its chief organ *l'Humanité*, you notice a rather confused, amorphous tone in agitation and speeches, which is dealt with quite definitively in our theses. Naturally, one can also find in *l'Humanité*, to borrow an expression from Comrade Bukharin, "the swinishness from the pen of Longuet and his closest friends." This newspaper is replete with Communist will, but this will is not adequately harnessed. Communist thought is neither sharp nor clear enough in it. One misses in it the will to continually expound and change the situation in a revolutionary sense. When this is missing in the party's central organ, then so far as I am concerned it is excluded for this party to summon forth a great revolutionary action and to lead it. The first precondition for it is a gradual crystallization of clear revolutionary thought and will in the party's paper and throughout its entire agitation and propaganda. This process of crystallization might take two, three or six months, perhaps a year, depending on the circumstances. And for many comrades all this will not take place fast enough. They do not take into consideration the internal import of this process—the revolutionary metamorphosis of a big party. They want to leap over this process and it seems to them that only a pretext is lacking for the launching of revolutionary action. And so they say: Frossard and others don't do this or don't do that. The 1919 draft—precisely in France where the anarchists and syndicalists are so strong, and, besides, with the French temperament and with the Parisian working class—here is an excellent pretext. And it is quite possible for a certain section of this working class—its best section, the one which will be of decisive importance in major battles—to be summoned and involved by younger, less experienced, impatient comrades in an action that might prove disastrous to the development of the revolutionary movement in France for many years to come. This is the situation. Naturally, the argument may be raised that: "You are singling out and attacking individual comrades. We'll grant you that this or another comrade delivered a bad speech, but that's not the issue." The issue, comrades, is this: that if everyone were able to arrive at a correct judgment, there would be no need of an International. The task precisely consists in sharply underscoring a danger (even the smallest one) the instant that it manifests itself; the task is to turn attention to it, to exaggerate it, if you please. That I or you exaggerate a danger, is not so important; it all comes down to how high you pitch your voice. But the other danger of being belated or of letting slip a situation, which enables this tendency to grow and to be trapped by provocation; the danger that this may burst into the conflagration of an adventure—this is a very great danger. This is the reason why some comrades get so heated in talking about it. Let me tell you that when I discuss this privately with this or that comrade I often notice that he does not understand me, that he is thinking to himself, that I am a little older while he is a little younger; that my hair is already grey but that he is bolder and that he approaches the question from the standpoint of temperament, then I say to myself: The greatest danger lies in this, that certain comrades are not aware that there is such a thing as dangerous soil, that they are politically inexperienced in a revolutionary sense, that they do not understand this counsel and how pertinent it is and they think, with their limited horizon, that someone is pulling them to the right. Not at all!

You have broken with the opportunists and you are moving forward, but look around you: there exist in this world not only opportunists, but also classes. There is the capitalist society, the police, the army, definite economic conditions; a section is for you, another section is more or less neutral, a third is against you. It is a whole complex world, in which it is a great and difficult task to correctly orient yourself. You must learn this when you answer me. You want me to fight the centrists? All the resolutions of the First and Second Congresses remain in full force, after all. And the entire activity in which we are engaged is, after all, nothing else but a slap in the face to opportunism. But our task does not lie solely in an interminable theoretical condemnation of opportunism. We must in practice overwhelm capitalist society, we must pin both shoulders of the bourgeoisie to the ground and strangle it to death. That is the task. And to solve this task—I must repeat this—one must combine the icy language of statistics with the passionate will of revolutionary violence. We shall learn this and we shall conquer! [Applause and cheers.]

24. Speech on Comrade Lenin's report: 'Tactics of the Russian Communist Party'

Seventeenth Session, July 5, 1921

Comrades! I don't get the opportunity to regularly read *Neue Zeit,* the theoretical organ of the so-called Social Democracy, issued by Heinrich Cunow, but from time to time an issue of this paper falls into my hands and in one of them I chanced to run across an article by Heinrich Cunow on the decomposition of Bolshevism, in which he deals with the question now before us. He formulates the question as follows: "How can one avoid a complete economic collapse, raise industrial and agricultural production, assure adequate food rations to urban workers, employes and men of education and eliminate the growing dissatisfaction among these circles?" The polemical barb of this formulation is aimed at us, but it is in essence correct. Then he lists the tendencies which presumably exist in our party and goes on to say: "Trotsky is supported by Bukharin, Rakovsky, Pyatakov, Larin,[26] Sholnikov...."

Who this Sholnikov is I don't know, unless, perhaps, it is a synthesis of Sokolnikov and Shlyapnikov.[27] Comrade Kollontai[28] is not mentioned, I don't know why.

The author adds: "and other Left Communists." Do you hear, Comrade Bela Kun[29]—Left Communists. [Laughter.]

> And other Left Communists in analyzing this question came to the conclusion that the only way out lies through a more rigid application of the Communist labor system. Factories and agricultural enterprises must be placed under even stricter control; economic organizations still retaining their independence must be likewise state-ized; the peasants must be compelled to deliver their surpluses to the needy urban population; and the laws against peculation and speculation in foodstuffs must be made more severe. It is on the whole necessary to energetically discipline and centralize the economic enterprises. But this goal can be achieved only when an end is put to the elections of the supervisory personnel by the workers since the workers frequently elect absolutely illiterate individuals. It is necessary to replace these functionaries by people appointed by the Soviet authorities. In order to raise productivity, Trotsky also wants to harness the trade unions which are predominantly non-Communist and to politicalize them, that is, place them under the control of the political organizations. Moreover, labor conscription must be introduced among the peasantry; the cultivation of the land must be decreed a 'state duty' and the peasants compelled under pain of stringent penalties to produce and deliver fixed amounts of the most essential food products. In addition to all this, Trotsky is conducting a fight against leasing large

areas to foreign capitalist companies, which he considers as anti-Communist.

In a word, this article paints a political portrait of our friend Kollontai—but under the pseudonym of Trotsky. In general this article, like everything concocted by its author, is a rehash of tritest Bernsteinism of the 'nineties. And these ideas now appear as the modern postwar doctrine, the spiritual sustenance of the German Social Democracy. Bernstein put all this together far more systematically, consistently and planfully than does Herr Heinrich Cunow. But this doesn't alter the gist of things. Let us, however, return to the Russian question. It is not solely Cunow's personal opinion that we have great differences of views among us, and that I personally belong to the opposition on the question of concessions and on the question of changing our economic policy. Not only the Social-Democratic press but also the capitalist newspapers harp on this. Every comrade in the least acquainted with our internal affairs is well aware that there are no serious differences among us, in the party, over these questions, except for a very small group whose representative, Kollontai, you heard today. If this question ever did come up among us, in the Central Committee, it was discussed only from the standpoint of whether this or that area, this or that concession should be granted or not, *i.e.*, from a purely practical standpoint. And it was precisely in these practical aspects that I happened to be in agreement with Lenin. Neither Comrade Bukharin nor Comrade Rakovsky, nor any of the comrades mentioned in Cunow's article has opposed concessions and the new agricultural or peasant policy in principle. This is an excellent illustration of the spiritual level of the German Social Democracy. For indeed, insofar as an individual really belongs to the

International—as was also the case in the heyday of the Second International—he is always greatly concerned in honestly following and understanding what takes place within a brother party, even if he has differences with it. When some lie used to be spread by Czarism it was a common saying that Czarism had broad shoulders and could bear up under anything. But from a theoretical representative of a party who is obliged to analyze events calmly, one could demand—not that he should understand and vindicate us, God forbid!—but that he should at least have some comprehension of the things about which he writes. But he lacks even this.

Well, the fact is, there are no differences among us over this question. The figure 99 percent would be a conservative estimate of the party majority on this issue. But how do matters stand with regard to the danger which the representatives of the Communist Workers Party and Comrade Kollontai depicted before us from two different sides—one from the side of Western European capitalism, and the other from the side of Russian Communism? This question also came up for discussion among us in the Economic Commission. One comrade set out to prove that to enable capitalism to unfold its activities "on the great Russian steppes" is to provide it with a road to salvation, with a way out from a difficult situation. But capitalism can move around only within limits offered it by our railroad network, our transport facilities, our open spaces, generally our entire economic culture. We have in mind not a business firm like Gerngross of Vienna which might very well be able to save itself at the expense of the Soviet Republic by becoming its supplier; we are talking of capitalism.

If capitalism could, by basing itself on Russia, restore its equilibrium in the course of the next decade, then this would signify that we have no need whatever of turning to Western European capitalism; for this would signify that we are powerful and strong enough to get along without the cooperation of Western European and American capitalism. But this is not the situation. We are not strong and powerful enough to be able to renounce capitalist technology, which is yet available only in its capitalist form; we are simply not strong and powerful enough to enable capitalism to heal all its wounds with Russia's assistance. This is the inner logic of the situation. In any case, those comrades who fear lest capitalism become strengthened by obtaining here a field for its activity, must take into consideration that in between this developing capitalism in Russia and the world revolution there stands Soviet Russia; and that long before Russian capitalism could start relaxing and regaining its strength "in the Russian steppes" it would have to crush the budding Communist economy. Yes, the first victim would be our budding socialist organization. In the Economic Commission I said that the key factor is still the circumstance that the power in our country belongs to the vanguard of the proletariat; that in our country the working class rules, being represented in political and state relations by this vanguard; and that is why we ought to grant concessions only to the extent that it benefits our cause. This premise requires no commentary. Had capitalism conquered militarily, the question of concessions would have never arisen. Capitalism would have arrogated to itself everything it needed. We would then have had no tactical question. But we do have this question today. Why? Because the power in our country belongs to the working class, *i.e.*, it conducts negotiations with capitalism; it has the possibility of granting concessions to some while refusing others; *i.e.*, it has the opportunity to make combinations, and to adopt this or that decision only after taking into consideration the general state of its own economic development and that of the world revolution. That is how things stand.

And I then drew the conclusion that those Western European and American comrades, who really fear lest capitalism regain its health in Russia, show thereby that they overestimate our technological and transport facilities and underestimate our Communist reasoning facilities. As I said, Comrade Kollontai, who belongs among comrades usually called Left Communists, was not mentioned in connection with the concessions question. But she has done so herself. She has the full right to do it. She puts the discipline of the International above the discipline of the party. I do not know, perhaps it also pertains to the question of concessions, but she wants to display the spirit of knighthood—I don't know how to put it in German—she wants to conduct herself like an Amazon . . . [Radek interjects: Like Valkyrie!] Like Valkyrie. I place the responsibility for this expression on Comrade Radek. [Laughter.] That is how Comrade Kollontai conducted herself in placing her name on the speakers' list, although it is customary among us to first take up the question with the delegation, with the presidium and with the Central Committee. I merely ask the comrades who are present here and for whom Comrade Kollontai is the spokesman how they regard the fact that no one raised any objections to it at the session of the Central Committee? We deemed it wholly natural for a politically insignificant and hardly noticeable minority on this question to acquaint the World Congress with its own views and its own tendency.

Let us now pass on to the essence of Comrade Kollontai's speech. Her main idea is this, that the capitalist system is outlived and that therefore it is impermissible, so to speak, to derive any benefits from it. That is her basic idea. Everything else is for her superfluous. This gives us an entirely adequate idea of Comrade Kollontai's historical and politico-economic approach. In the language of philosophy, this is known as a purely metaphysical outlook which operates with immutable, non-historical, dogmatic concepts. Capitalism has outlived itself and therefore it is not possible to get anything from it that can be of use to us. But, comrades, if it were actually true that capitalism has outlived itself, then should we be attacked by the English or French army, say, on the shores of the Black Sea, we could say to ourselves that since capitalism has outlived itself we can keep on sitting with hands folded. [Applause.] I believe that we would then all be sent to hell, with the permission of Comrade Kollontai. For capitalism will not stop to inquire whether or not it has outlived itself in accordance with Comrade Kollontai's dogmatic conceptions. It will run us through with bayonets manufactured in its capitalist factories; it will destroy us with soldiers rigidly trained under its capitalist discipline. But if an outlived capitalism is capable of slaughtering and murdering us, it shows thereby that it has plenty of power left. Why, the very fact that Comrade Kollontai, who belongs to an opposition in the Russian party, is compelled to present her oppositional views to the World Congress in Moscow is itself a bit of evidence that while capitalism is outlived in the great historical sense and cannot open up any new possibilities for mankind, it still remains powerful enough to prevent us from convening our congresses in Paris or Berlin. [Applause.] Or let us take capitalist technology, for example. What does Comrade Kollontai think of a good locomotive, an honest-to-goodness German capitalist locomotive? This is an interesting question. I am afraid that the German proletariat even after its conquest of power will have to travel across the country for a couple of years or so on genuine capitalist locomotives. After all, it will be very busy and I hardly believe that it will be able immediately in the very first months to begin building new locomotives. But comrades, is it permissible—from the standpoint of the ten commandments of Comrade Kollontai—to buy a new German locomotive from the firm of Ebert & Co.? I believe that Comrade Kollontai in answering this pointblank question would not deny us the right to buy a locomotive from Ebert. But if we buy a locomotive there, we must also pay for it there, and, besides, with gold. But, comrades, gold which flows from Russia into capitalist coffers tends to strengthen the latter. Of course the amount is far too small to pay the German debts. Fortunately we haven't got such a quantity of gold. [Laughter.] Hem and haw how you will, but if you want to remain steadfast in principle you dare not pay gold to capitalists. Or let us take another instance. Suppose we pay with lumber instead of gold. Comrade Kollontai will perhaps then say: I agree to permit trade between Soviet Russia and Germany or England, but concessions are out. What are concessions? To get locomotives, we must sell lumber. But we lack enough saws and other mechanical appliances and so we say: "The trees grow in a forest; let the English capitalist come with his machines and technical equipment, chop himself some trees and logs and give us locomotives in return. . . ." In short, I should very much like to know where Comrade Kollontai's principled opposition begins and where it ends. Is it with the purchase of locomotives or with the payment in gold, or with payment in lumber in the shape of forests? I am afraid that the opposition begins only with the chopping of trees. [Loud laughter.]

Comrade Kollontai furthermore asserts that we, in general, want to replace the working class with specialists and with other forces, *i.e.,* technicians. [Kollontai interjects: I didn't say that.] You said that the initiative of the working class is being replaced by other forces, that the vanguard of the working class is being compelled to cede its place to other forces. But these other forces are on the one hand the so-called technological intelligentsia, and on the other—the peasantry. The peasantry as a replacement is unconditionally excluded. But the class which holds the power in its hands does make a deal with the peasantry. As regards the technicians, over this question, too, we had a controversy in our party. The echoes of it still reverberate to this day. And perhaps we have heard if not the last then the next to the last echo from the lips of Comrade Kollontai. From the principled standpoint, Comrades, it is undeniable that more than ample power and initiative are inherent in the proletariat and we hope that all mankind will considerably change its aspects thanks to the power of the working class. But we never claimed that the working class is from its birth capable of building a new society. It can only create all the necessary social and political preconditions for it. More than this, through the direct seizure of power it is enabled to find all the necessary auxiliary forces, place them, wherever necessary, in the service of Communist economy, and thereby set the entire machine in motion. But we never said that a simple worker by becoming a Communist immediately acquired the ability to perform the work of a technician, astronomer or engineer. And when these technical forces are generalized and simply designated as "other social forces," and when the fact that these forces have been placed in the service of our cause is characterized as a lack of confidence in the working class, then I must state that such reasoning has absolutely nothing in common with Marxism and Communism.

Comrades! In that extremely simple field in which we have had to work up to now, in the military field, we were compelled from the beginning to resort to the aid of alien technical forces. A good deal of friction arose over this among us. The Central Committee committed not a few errors, and our military organization was upset on more than one occasion. We were told: "You are placing alien technical forces (the reference here was to the officers) in the service of the proletariat." Yet it later became obvious that had we based ourselves solely on the energy and self-sacrifice of our comrades, who were all sublimely fulfilling their duty, and had we been unable to utilize military forces alien to us, we could not have long survived in this world. This is absolutely clear. The Russian working class with its abilities and its capacity for self-sacrifice gave everything it had. It likewise evinced a great initiative in this, that after the seizure of power it proved capable, although it was backward and was living in a peasant country, to draw into its service officers, by employing sometimes force and sometimes propaganda. [Applause.] We had to have an army. But the working class did not possess sufficient experience and knowledge and we could not place officers from among the workers immediately and everywhere. Today we already have a great many Red officers who stem from the working class. They occupy the highest posts, and their number is increasing daily.

The very same thing applies to the technical field as well. The fact that we are still encircled by a capitalist world compels us to make concessions in the field of technology, too. But we have complete faith that our working class, which is becoming more and more cognizant of itself as a member of the great International, will also be able to withstand this breathing spell of capitalism and this unstable equilibrium which now prevails; and that during this selfsame breathing spell it will utilize alien forces and alien means alike, and place them in the service of its own cause. When we say to the Russian workers: "We are conducting negotiations with foreign capitalists, but we shall take all the necessary measures to stand on our own feet"; when we want the working class to survey its field of activity and say: "I can offer this or that concession to the German and American capitalists, but I want machinery in return"—is this then lack of faith in the forces of the Russian working class, of the Russian proletariat? If anyone is to be reproached with lacking faith in the forces of the working class, it is not us but the little group in whose name Comrade Kollontai has spoken here today. [Thunderous applause.]

VI

From the Third to the Fourth World Congress

Editor's note

The documents which appear in this section actually belong with the material of the Third Congress inasmuch as the discussion at the Youth Congress represented a continuation of the controversy which was resolved by the Third World Congress. This, incidentally, explains certain repetitions in Trotsky's speech and summary before the Youth Congress. The remaining documents appear in the second volume of this work.

25. The main lesson of the Third Congress

Classes are rooted in production. Classes remain viable so long as they can fulfill a necessary role in the process of social organization of labor. Classes begin losing the ground under their feet when the conditions necessary for their further existence come into contradiction with the growth of productive forces, *i.e.*, with the further development of economy. Such is the situation in which the bourgeoisie finds itself at the present time.

But this does not at all mean that a class, which has lost its living roots and has become parasitic, is by this very reason doomed to instantaneous death. While economy constitutes the foundation of class rule, the respective classes maintain themselves in power by means of the state-political apparatuses and organs, namely: army, police, party, courts, press, etc., etc. With the aid of these organs, which in relation to the economic foundation represent a "superstructure," the ruling class may perpetuate itself in power for years and decades after it has become a direct brake upon the social development. If such a situation endures too long, an outlived ruling class can drag down with it those countries and peoples over whom it rules.

Hence arises the necessity of revolution. The new class with living roots in economic development—the proletariat—must overthrow the bourgeoisie, must tear power out of its hands and convert the state apparatus into an instrument of economic reorganization of society.

The bourgeoisie had become a parasitic and anti-social class even prior to the World War. The incompatibility of bourgeois rule with the further development of economy, and even with the further preservation of economy, has been disclosed on a grandiose scale during the war. Furthermore, the war has not only laid bare this incompatibility but has also reinforced it in the extreme, bringing it to the highest pitch of intensity. The war has shattered the economic foundation of bourgeois society. At the same time the war has extraordinarily disorganized, weakened, discredited and paralyzed the political organs of bourgeois rule: the state, the army, the police, the parliament, the press, and so on. In the initial postwar period the bourgeoisie was in a state of extreme disorientation; it was fearful of the day of reckoning, had lost confidence in the old methods and usages of its rule, kept apprehensively probing the soil, kept wavering, and readily agreed to concessions. In the most critical year for the bourgeoisie, the year 1919, the proletariat of Europe could have undoubtedly conquered state power with minimum sacrifices, had there been at its head a genuine revolutionary organization, setting forth clear aims and capably pursuing them, *i.e.*, a strong Communist Party. But there was none. On the contrary, in seeking after the war to conquer new living conditions for itself and in assuming an offensive against bourgeois society, the working class had to drag on its back the parties and trade unions of the Second International, all of whose efforts, both conscious and instinctive, were essentially directed toward the preservation of capitalist society.

By employing this Social-Democratic shield, the bourgeoisie was able to take the best possible advantage of the breathing spell. It recovered from its panic, stabilized its state organs, supplemented them with counterrevolutionary armed gangs and started handpicking politicians who are specialists in applying combined methods in the struggle against the open revolutionary movement and who operate through intimidation, bribery, provocation, segregation, division, etc., etc. The basic task of these specialists is to engage isolated detachments of the proletarian vanguard in a series of battles, bleed them white and thus undermine the faith of the working class in the possibility of success.

In the field of economic restoration, the bourgeoisie has achieved nothing essential during the three years that have elapsed since the war. On the contrary, it is only today that the economic consequences of the war are unfolding in their full scope in the form of a crisis unprecedented in capitalist history. We thus have here a very graphic illustration showing that the political conditions of rule, although they are in the last analysis dependent on the economic conditions, do not at all run parallel to these economic conditions nor flow from them automatically. Whereas in the field of production and exchange the world capitalist apparatus has today fallen into such a state of complete disorganization that the situation in 1919 appears as the height of well-being in comparison with the present one, in the field of politics the bourgeoisie has in this interval succeeded to a very large degree in strengthening the organs and vehicles of its rule. The leaders of the bourgeoisie see all too clearly the economic abyss which yawns before them. But they are prepared and they will fight to the end. They approach the existing situation in terms of political strategy. Coolly and calculatingly they watch every move of the proletariat, seeking to emasculate it, especially in Germany, through a series of isolated bloody defeats.

During the last three years the workers have fought a great deal and have suffered many sacrifices. But they have not won power. As a result the working masses have become more cautious than they were in 1919–20. Throughout a series of spontaneous and semi-spontaneous offensives the workers have each time run up against resistance better and better organized and they were flung back. They have understood and sensed that the prerequisite of success is a firm leadership, that one must know how to calculate and plan, that revolutionary strategy is indispensable. If the working masses no longer respond today to revolutionary slogans so directly as they did in 1918–19, it is not because they have become less revolutionary but because they are less naive and more exacting. They want organizational guarantees of victory. Only that party will be able to lead them to decisive battles which reveals in practice, under all conditions and circumstances, not merely its readiness to fight, *i.e.,* its courage, but also its ability to lead the masses in struggle, its capacity to maneuver in attack or in retreat, its skill in leading them out of the line of fire when a situation is unfavorable, its ability to combine all forces and means for a blow, and, in this way, systematically to enhance its influence and its authority over the masses. It is unquestionable that the parties of the Communist International have not by far given sufficient consideration to this task. Herein is the main source of tactical errors and internal crises among the various Communist parties.

A purely mechanical conception of the proletarian revolution—which proceeds solely from the fact that capitalist economy continues to decay—has led certain groups of comrades to construe theories which are false to the core: the false theory of an initiating minority which by its heroism shatters "the wall of universal passivity" among the proletariat. The false theory of uninterrupted offensives conducted by the proletarian vanguard, as a "new method" of struggle; the false theory of partial battles which are waged by applying the methods of armed insurrection. And so forth and so on. The clearest exponent of this tendency is the Vienna journal *Communism*. It is absolutely self-evident that tactical theories of this sort have nothing in common with Marxism. To apply them in practice is to play directly into the hands of the bourgeoisie's military-political leaders and their strategy.

Undeniably these adventurist methods and theories arise as a reaction to the reformist and centrist tendencies within the labor movement, whose direct supplement they are. But while the reformist and centrist tendencies have been transformed into a force predominantly external and into an open enemy, the adventurist and subjective tendencies represent primarily an internal danger, whose gravity it would be completely inexcusable to underestimate. The trouble with revolutionary subjectivism, as Herzen[1] put it, is this, that it mistakes the second or fifth month of pregnancy for the ninth. No one has yet done so with impunity.

The Third Congress took note of the further falling apart of the economic foundations of bourgeois rule. But it has at the same time forcibly warned the advanced workers against any naive conceptions that from this flows automatically the death of the bourgeoisie through an uninterrupted offensive by the proletariat. Never before has the bourgeoisie's class instinct of self-preservation been armed with such multiform methods of defense and attack as today. The economic preconditions for the victory of the working class are at hand. Failing this victory, and moreover unless this victory comes in the more or less near future, all civilization is menaced with decline and degeneration. But this victory can be gained only by the skilled conduct of battles and, above all, by first conquering the majority of the working class. This is the main lesson of the Third Congress.

FIRST PUBLISHED IN
PRAVDA, NO. 150,
JUNE 12, 1921

26. Report on 'The Balance Sheet' of the Third Congress of the Communist International

Delivered at the Second Congress of the Communist Youth International, July 14, 1921

The Third Congress of the Comintern, if one were to express its significance in a succinct formula, will in all likelihood be inscribed in the annals of the labor movement as the highest school of revolutionary strategy. The First Congress of our Communist International issued the summons to rally the forces of the world proletarian revolution. The Second Congress elaborated the programmatic basis for mobilizing the forces. The Third International in its sessions already came in contact with these forces, consolidated them and was thus confronted with the most important practical questions of the revolutionary movement. That is why the Third Congress became, as I put it, the highest school of revolutionary strategy. From the outset the Third Congress raised the question of whether the fundamental position of the Comintern at its First and Second Congresses was correct. And after a deep-going and all-sided review of historical facts and tendencies—for facts as such, separate and apart from historical tendencies, are of no great significance—the Congress came to the conclusion that this position was correct, that we do find ourselves in the era of the development of world revolution.

After the war the bourgeoisie laid bare its utter inability to bring the factors of economic development, *i.e.*, the very foundations of its existence, back again into equilibrium. The entire attention of the bourgeoisie was centered on keeping the classes in equilibrium; and with great difficulty it did succeed for the last three years in preserving this unstable class equilibrium and that of its state superstructure. The Third Congress focused the attention of all fighters in the International precisely on the fact that in dealing with the question of tempo of development it is necessary to differentiate between economic factors, which are the deepest-seated foundations of society, and such secondary factors as politics, parliamentarianism, press, school, church, and so on. One must not delude himself that a class which is historically bankrupt in the economic sense loses instantaneously and, as it were, automatically the instruments of its rule. No, on the contrary, historical experience teaches us that whenever a ruling class, which has held power in its hands for centuries, comes face to face with the danger of losing power, its instinct for power becomes sensitive in the extreme; and it is precisely during the epoch of economic decline of the social order, which had been established under the rule of this class, that the ruling class reveals utmost energy and greatest strategical sagacity in maintaining its political position. This is deemed a contradiction by those Marxists who apprehend Marxism mechanically or, as the expression goes, metaphysically; and for them there really is a contradiction here. It is otherwise with those who apprehend history through its inner and dynamic logic, through the interplay of its different factors—through the interaction of the economic base upon the class, of the class upon the state, of the state, in its turn, upon the class and of the latter upon the economic base. For anyone who has not graduated from the school of genuine Marxism it will always remain incomprehensible just how the bourgeoisie on becoming transformed from a leading economic class, true, a class which exploits but which also organizes at the same time, into a completely parasitic class and into a force that is counter-revolutionary in the fullest sense of the word—just how this same bourgeoisie happens at such a time to be armed from head to foot with all the means and the methods of the class struggle, from the most hypocritical, democratic phrase-mongering to the most brutal and bloody suppression of the working class. Many of us imagined the task of overthrowing the bourgeoisie much simpler than it actually is, and as reality has now proved to us. Before us is a semi-decayed tree. Nothing would seem simpler than to simply pull it down. But with such an approach one cannot get very far in the swift flux of social events. By concentrating all its efforts during the last period not so much upon restoring the economic foundation as upon restoring class equilibrium, the bourgeoisie has scored very serious successes in the political and strategical sense. This is a fact, and it happens to be a fact that is quite gratifying to the revolution. For had the bourgeoisie succeeded in restoring the very foundation of its rule or had made even a single step forward in this direction, then we would have been compelled to say: Yes, the bourgeoisie has succeeded in restoring the mainstays of its class rule. The outlook for the future development of the revolution would in that case naturally be extremely dismal. But it happens that such is not the case; that, on the contrary, all the efforts of the bourgeoisie, all the energies expended by it in maintaining class equilibrium, manifest themselves invariably at the expense of the economic soil on which the bourgeoisie rests, at the expense of its economic base.

The bourgeoisie and the working class are thus located on a soil which renders our victory inescapable—not in the astronomical sense of course, not inescapable like the setting or rising of the sun, but inescapable in the historical sense, in the sense that unless we gain victory all society and all human culture is doomed. History teaches us this. It was thus that the ancient Roman civilization perished. The class of slave-owners proved incapable of leading toward further development. It became transformed into an absolutely parasitic and decomposing class. There was no other class to supersede it and the ancient civilization perished. We observe analogous occurrences in modern history too, for example, the decline of Poland toward the end of the eighteenth century when the ruling feudal class had outlived its day while the bourgeoisie still remained too weak to seize power. As a result the Polish state fell. As warriors of revolution, we are convinced—and the objective facts corroborate us—that we as the working class, that we as the Communist International, will not only save our civilization, the centuries-old product of hundreds of generations, but will raise it to much higher levels of development. However, from the standpoint of pure theory, the possibility is not excluded that the bourgeoisie, armed with its state apparatus and its entire accumulated experience, may continue fighting the revolution until it has drained modern civilization of every atom of its vitality, until it has plunged modern mankind into a state of collapse and decay for a long time to come.

By all the foregoing I simply want to say that the task

of overthrowing the bourgeoisie which confronts the working class is not a mechanical one. It is a task which requires for its fulfillment: revolutionary energy, political sagacity, experience, broadness of vision, resoluteness, hot blood, but at the same time a sober head. It is a political, revolutionary, strategic task. Precisely in the course of the last year a party has given us a very instructive lesson in this connection. I refer to the Italian Socialist Party, whose official organ is called *Avanti (Forward)*. Without subjecting to analysis the whole complex of tactical questions relating to the struggle and to victory, without any clear picture of the concrete circumstances of this struggle, the Italian party plunged into extensive revolutionary agitation, spurring the Italian workers—Avanti! Forward! The working class of Italy demonstrated that the blood circulating in their veins is hot enough. All the slogans of the party were taken by them seriously, they went forward, they seized factories, mills, mines, and so on. But very soon thereafter they were compelled to execute a terrible retreat and therewith became completely separated from the party for a whole period. The party had betrayed them—not in the sense that there are conscious traitors ensconced in the Italian Socialist Party, no, no one would say this. But ensconced there were reformists who by their entire spiritual makeup are hostile to the genuine interests of the working class. Ensconced there were centrists who did not and do not have any understanding whatever of the internal needs of a genuine revolutionary labor movement. Thanks to all this the entire party became transformed into an instrument of completely abstract and rather superficial revolutionary agitation. But the working class because of its position was compelled to accept this agitation seriously. It drew the extreme revolutionary conclusions from this agitation, and as a result suffered a cruel defeat. This means that revealed here was the complete absence of tactics in the broad meaning of the word, or, expressing the same idea in military terms, the complete absence of strategy. And now one can imagine—all this is, of course, pure theory and not an attempt to suggest such an idea to our splendid young Communist Party of Italy—it is possible, I say, to imagine that this party may proclaim: After such a terrible defeat, after such treachery on the part of the old Socialist Party, we Communists, who are really prepared to draw the most extreme conclusions, must immediately proceed to exact revolutionary revenge; we must this very day draw the working class into an offensive against the strongholds of capitalist society.

The Third Congress weighed this question theoretically and practically and said: If at the present time, immediately after the defeat consequent upon the treachery of the Socialist Party, the Comintern should set the Italian party the task of instantly passing over to an offensive, it would commit a fatal strategical blunder, because the decisive battle requires a corresponding preparation. This preparation, comrades, does not consist of collecting funds for the party treasury over a period of decades, nor of adding up the number of subscribers to the venerable Social-Democratic press, and so on. No, preparation—especially in an epoch such as ours when the mood of the masses quickly changes and rises—requires not decades, perhaps not even years, but only a few months. To forecast time intervals is, in general, a very wretched occupation; but at all events one thing is clear: when we speak today of preparation, it has an entirely different meaning than it did in the organic epoch of gradual economic development. Preparation for us means the creation of such conditions as would secure us the sympathy of the broadest masses. We cannot under any conditions renounce this factor. The idea of replacing the will of the masses by the resoluteness of the so-called vanguard is absolutely impermissible and non-Marxist. Through the consciousness and the will of the vanguard it is possible to exert influence over the masses, it is possible to gain their confidence, but it is impossible to replace the masses by this vanguard. And for this reason the Third Congress has placed before all the parties, as the most important and unpostponable task, the demand that the majority of the toiling people be attracted to our side.

It was pointed out here that Comrade Lenin had said in one of his speeches at the Congress that a small party, too, could under certain conditions carry with it the majority of the working class and lead them. This is absolutely correct. The revolution is a combination of objective factors which are independent of us and which are the most important, and of subjective factors which are more or less dependent on us. History does not always, or more correctly, history almost never functions in such a way as first to prepare the objective conditions, as, for example, you first set the table and then invite guests to sit down. History does not tarry until the corresponding class, in our case the proletariat, organizes itself, clarifies its consciousness, and steels its will, in order then graciously to invite it to accomplish the revolution on the basis of these socially and economically mature conditions. No, things happen in a different way. The objective necessity of revolution may already be completely at hand. The working class—we speak only about this class because we are now interested only in the proletarian revolution—may, however, not yet be fully prepared, while the Communist Party, may, of course, embrace only an insignificant minority of the working class. Comrades, what will occur then? There will occur a very prolonged and sanguinary revolution, and in the very course of the revolution the party and the working class will have to make up for what they lacked at the outset.

Such is the present situation. And therefore if it is true—and it is true—that under certain conditions even a small party can become the leading organization not only of the labor movement but also of the workers' revolution, this can happen only on the proviso that this small party discerns in its smallness not an advantage but the greatest misfortune of which it must be rid as speedily as possible.

Attending the Congress are certain comrades who represent the tiniest parties, for example, the Communist Workers Party of Germany (KAPD). This party is revolutionary, even very revolutionary, of this we have no doubt whatever. And if the revolution consisted in the KAPD's manifesting its superb revolutionary will in action, and if such a demonstration sufficed to bring the German bourgeoisie to its knees, the revolution would long have been an accomplished fact in Germany. But the demonstrative action of a single revolutionary sect is not enough. The representatives of the KAPD have said what Comrade Lenin, too, admitted, namely: that a small party can rise to the leading role. And that is really so. But in that event such a party cannot be a small sect, which engages in a struggle with a much bigger revolutionary party, the party of the working class, and which sees in its own small numbers a great historical superiority. Such a party can never become the leading party of the working class. This is the whole gist of the matter.

And so, the Third Congress proclaimed as the task of the hour—preparation. Coincident with this it was compelled to whisper to certain groups and certain comrades and sometimes also to shout at them to fall back a little, to carry out a strategic retreat, in order to undertake, by intrenching themselves on a certain political line, preparations for a real offensive. Now, Comrades, was this counsel which has become converted into an order really necessary? Or does it perhaps already mark the beginning of the Third International's downfall, as some claim? I believe that there was an urgent necessity to give this counsel to certain groups, certain organizations and certain comrades. For, I repeat, among certain groups—and I am referring not only to the KAPD but to much bigger parties and to tendencies within big parties—there was evident a genuine will to revolution, something which had not been discernible in Western Europe for a long while. In this respect we can register a great, a colossal step forward from the First Congress to the Third. We have big parties with a clearly expressed will to revolutionary action, and without such a will it is impossible to make a revolution—in the sense in which a party is able, in general, to make a revolution. But among certain groups, certain journalists, and even certain leaders, there prevailed views concerning the methods of this revolution that are far too simplified. You are probably aware that there was advanced the so-called theory of the offensive. What is the gist of this theory? Its gist is that we have entered the epoch of the decomposition of capitalist society, in other words, the epoch when the bourgeoisie must be overthrown. How? By the offensive of the working class. In this purely abstract form, it is unquestionably correct. But certain individuals have sought to convert this theoretical capital into corresponding currency of smaller denomination and they have declared that this offensive consists of a successive number of smaller offensives. Thus arose the theory, whose clearest exponent is the Vienna journal

Communism—the theory of pure offensive owing to the revolutionary character of the epoch.

Comrades, the analogy between the political struggle of the working class and military operations has been much abused. But up to a certain point one can speak here of similarities. In civil war one of the two contending sides must inescapably emerge as victor; for civil war differs from national war in this, that in the latter case a compromise is possible: one may cede to the enemy a part of the territory, one may pay him an indemnity, conclude some deal with him. But in civil war this is impossible. Here one or the other class must conquer at all costs. Soviet Russia was surrounded by the counter-revolution, and therefore our strategy had of necessity to consist in a victorious offensive. We were compelled to liberate our periphery from the counter-revolution. But on recalling today the history of our struggle we find that we suffered defeat rather frequently. In military respects we, too, had our March days, speaking in German; and our September days, speaking in Italian. What happens after a partial defeat? There sets in a certain dislocation of the military apparatus, there arises a certain need for a breathing spell, a need for reorientation and for a more precise estimation of the reciprocal forces, a need to offset the losses and to instill into the masses the consciousness of the necessity of a new offensive and a new struggle. Sometimes all this becomes possible only under the conditions of strategic retreat. The soldiers—especially if they are the soldiers of a class-conscious revolutionary army—are told this point-blank. They are told, we must surrender such and such points, such and such cities and areas and withdraw beyond the Volga, in order there to consolidate our position and in the course of three or four weeks or maybe several months, reorganize our ranks, make up our losses and then pass over to a new offensive. I must confess that during the first period of our Civil War the idea of retreat was always very painful for all of us and produced very depressed moods among the soldiers. A retreat is a movement. Whether one takes ten steps forward or ten steps backward depends entirely on the requirements of the moment. For victory it is sometimes necessary to move forward, sometimes to move backwards.

But to understand this properly, to discern in a move backwards, in a retreat, a component part of a unified strategic plan—for that a certain experience is necessary. But if one reasons purely abstractly, and insists always on moving forward, if one refuses to rack his brain over strategy, on the assumption that everything can be superseded by an added exertion of revolutionary will, what results does one then get? Let us take for example the September events in Italy or the March events in Germany. We are told that the situation in these countries can be remedied only by a new offensive. In the March days—and I say this quite openly—we did not have behind us one-fifth or even one-sixth of the working class and we suffered a defeat, in a purely practical sense, that is: we did not conquer power—incidentally, the party did not even set itself this task—we did not paralyze the counter-revolution, either. This is undeniably a practical defeat. But if we were to say today in accordance with the foregoing theory of offensive: only a new offensive can remedy the situation, what do we stand to gain thereby? We shall then have behind us no longer one-sixth of the working class but only that section of the former one-sixth which has remained fit for combat. Indeed, following a defeat there is always to be observed a certain depression, which doesn't, of course, last forever but which does last a while. Under these conditions we would suffer an even greater and much more dangerous defeat. No, comrades, after such a defeat we must retreat. In what sense? In the simplest sense. We must say to the working class: Yes, comrades, on the basis of facts we have become convinced that in this struggle we had only one-sixth of the workers behind us. But we must number at least four-sixths, or two-thirds, in order to seriously think of victory; and to this end we must develop and safeguard those mental, spiritual, material and organizational forces which are our bonds with the class. From the standpoint of offensive struggle this signifies a strategic retreat for the sake of preparation. It is absolutely unimportant whether one calls this going leftist or going rightist. It all depends on what one means by these words. If by leftism is understood a formal readiness to move forward at any moment and to apply the sharpest forms of struggle, then this, of course, signifies a rightward trend. But if the words "left party" or "left tendencies" are understood in a more profound historical sense, in a dynamic sense, in the sense of a movement which sets itself the greatest task of the epoch and fulfills it through the best means, then this will constitute a step forward in the direction of the left, revolutionary tendency. But let us not waste our time over such philological scholasticism. From those who cavil over words and who say the Congress has made a step to the right, from them we demand that they give us a precise definition of what they mean by right or left.

There is no need for me to dwell on the fact that some extremely clever comrades have advanced a hypothesis, according to which the Russians are chiefly to blame for the present "rightist tendency," because the Russians have now entered into trade relations with the Western State and are greatly concerned lest these relations be disrupted by the European revolution, and similar unpleasantries.

I did not hear this hypothesis myself, so to speak, firsthand but malicious rumor has it that there are also extant theoreticians of historical development who extend their loyalty to the spirit of Marx so far as to seek economic foundations for this rightist Russian tendency as well. It seems to me, comrades, that they have wandered into a blind alley. For even from a purely factual standpoint we would, of course, have to recognize that the revolution in Germany, in France, in England, would bring us the greatest benefits, because our rather tenuous trade relations with the West will never provide us with such aid as we could receive from a victorious proletarian revolution. The revolution would first of all free us of the necessity of maintaining an army of several million in our country which is so economically ruined; and this circumstance alone would bring us the greatest relief and at the same time the possibility of economic restoration.

And so, this hypothesis is entirely worthless. And in this respect it nowise differs from that other claim to the effect that the Russian Communist Party allegedly insisted on artificially provoking a revolution in Germany in March—so that Soviet Russia could cope with her domestic difficulties. This assertion is just as nonsensical. For a partial revolution, an uprising in any single country, can extend us no aid whatever. We are suffering from the destruction of the productive forces as a result of the imperialist war, the Civil War and the blockade. Aid can come to us only through shipments of large-scale auxiliary technical forces, through the arrival of highly skilled workers, locomotives, machines, and so on. But in no case from partial and unsuccessful uprisings in this or that country. That Soviet Russia will be able to maintain herself and to develop only in the event of the world revolution—this, comrades, you can read in literally everything that we have ever written. You can convince yourselves that fifteen years ago we wrote that by force of the inner logic of the class struggle in Russia, the Russian revolution would inescapably bring the Russian working class to power; but that this power can be stabilized and consolidated in the form of a victorious socialist dictatorship only if it serves as the starting point and remains an integral part of the world revolution of the international proletariat. This truth retains its full force to this very day. And for this reason Russia, like every other country, can be interested only in the internal logical development of the revolutionary forces of the proletariat; and not at all in artificially speeding up or retarding the revolutionary development.

Some comrades have expressed the fear that by formulating the question in the way we did, we are pouring water on the wheels of centrist and passive elements in the labor movement. These fears, too, seem to me absolutely groundless. In the first place, because the principles on which our activity is based remain those which were adopted by the First Congress, which were elaborated theoretically in detail by the Second Congress and which were confirmed, expanded and filled with a concrete content by the Third Congress. These principles determine the entire activity of the Communist International. If during the epoch of the First and Second Congresses we condemned the reformist and centrist tendencies theoretically, then this no longer suffices today. Today we must elaborate a revolutionary strategy in order to overcome in practice these tendencies condemned by us. This is the whole gist of the question. And in this respect, too, some Communists have an oversimplified, and therefore incorrect approach. They imagine that revolutionary results can be obtained by incessantly repeating that we remain irreconcilable foes of any and all centrist tendencies. Of course, we remain such. Every step toward reconciliation with the passive tendencies of centrism and reformism would signify the complete disintegration of our entire movement. The question lies not in this but rather in what course of action we ought to pursue to demarcate ourselves theoretically and organizationally from all centrist tendencies wherever they might appear. This is ABC. It would be ludicrous to engage in a dispute over this within the Communist International. Differences of opinion could arise only over the question of whether we ought to eject the centrist elements from this or that party right away, or whether it is more expedient to wait a while and give them the opportunity to develop in a revolutionary direction. Such practical differences of opinion are unavoidable in every vigorous party. But the principled recognition of the need to conduct a mortal struggle against centrism is the precondition for the revolutionary development of the forces of the Communist Party and of the working class. This is not in question. To consider this question to be on the same plane with practical questions of revolutionary strategy—this can be done only by those who have not yet fully understood just what constituted the core of the revolutionary questions at the Third Congress.

Our opponents in the centrist camp will, of course, try to turn to their own advantage what we have said. They will say: Look, in such and such places they advanced the slogans for a decisive offensive but now the Third Congress has proclaimed the necessity of a strategic retreat. It is natural and unavoidable for one side to seek to gain some advantage from every step taken by the other side. That is how matters stand in this war, too. When, during the Civil War, Denikin or Kolchak used to retreat we always wrote in our agitational leaflets: Look, instead of crossing the Volga, the enemy has withdrawn to the Urals.

We wrote it in order to raise the morale of the warriors. But if on the grounds that our opponents will interpret our move as a retreat, we were to conclude that we ought not to make this or that move, we would then sacrifice what is really essential for the sake of second-rate and formalistic considerations.

I have taken fully into consideration how extremely difficult it is to defend the strategy of temporary retreat at a Youth Congress. For if anyone is conscious of the right and of the inner necessity of waging an offensive, it is, of course, the young generation of the working class. If such were not the case, our affairs would be in a pretty bad shape. I believe, comrades, that it is precisely you, the young generation, who are destined to accomplish the revolution. The present revolution can continue to unfold for years and decades. Not in the sense that the preparation for decisive battle in Germany will last for decades. No, but the same thing can happen there that happened to us in Russia. By force of historic conditions we gained victory very easily, but then we were compelled for three years uninterruptedly to wage the Civil War. And even now we are not at all certain that war does not threaten us in the Far East with Japan; or, for that matter, in the West. Not because we seek war, but because the imperialist bourgeoisie keeps changing its methods. At first it fought us with military methods, then it entered into trade relations with us, but now it may again resort to implements of war. How the developments will unfold in Germany and France it is rather difficult to say. But that the bourgeoisie will not surrender suddenly is beyond any doubt. Nor is it subject to doubt that the revolution will one day conquer throughout Europe and throughout the world. The perspectives of the revolution are boundless, and the final phase of the struggle may endure for decades. But what does this signify? It signifies that precisely the young generation, you who are assembled here, have been summoned by history to bring our struggle to its conclusion. Some work will perhaps be left over even for your children. Let us not forget that the Great French Revolution and all of its consequences lasted for several decades.

Thus the tactical education of the Communist youth is a question of first-rate importance. In our time the young generation is bound to mature very early, because the wear and tear of human material is proceeding at an extremely rapid rate. We observe this in Russia; it is also to be observed in Germany; and in the future, this will manifest itself even more strikingly. For this reason it is of utmost importance for the Youth International to take—as is actually the case—an extremely serious attitude toward tactical questions. It is of utmost importance for the youth to review and criticize our tactics, and even, if need be, find them to be not leftist enough. It must not, however, view our tactics as a manifestation of some accidental moods within a single party or group but must analyze them in context with the aggregate tasks of the revolutionary movement as a whole. Concerning our resolution on the organization question someone might say: Mind you, it is stated here that the number of subscribers to Communist newspapers must be increased and that correspondents and collaborators for the Communist press must be recruited in the workers' districts. It is said here that it is necessary to concentrate on the work of expanding our organizations, and of consolidating Communist nuclei in the trade unions. Aren't all these piddling activities, activities which smack horribly of the Social-Democratic parties prior to the war? Yes, that is so, provided one tears this question out of its historical context, provided one fails to understand that we are living in an epoch that is revolutionary in its objective content and that we represent the working class which is every day becoming more and more convinced that it can secure the most elementary conditions of its existence only through revolution. But if one forgets all this along with the fact that we are engaged in a mortal combat with the Social-Democratic and centrist parties and groups for the influence over the working class, then, of course, one will get an entirely distorted conception of the tendencies, tactics and organizational principles of the Third Congress.

Today we are mature enough not to bind ourselves in all our actions by our formal opposition to reformists and centrists. The revolutionary task confronts us today as a practical task. And we ask ourselves: How ought we arm ourselves? What front should we occupy? At what line ought we intrench ourselves for defense? At what moment should we pass over to the offensive?

We are expanding our organizations. Whether this expansion takes place in the field of publishing newspapers, or even in the field of parliamentarianism, has meaning today only insofar as this creates the conditions for the victory of the revolutionary uprising. As a matter of fact, how could we possibly secure, in the stormy epoch of mass proletarian uprisings, the unity of ideas and slogans without an extensive network of correspondents, collaborators and readers of the revolutionary newspapers? And whereas newspaper subscribers and correspondents to its newspapers are important for a Social-Democratic party as a precondition for its parliamentary successes, for us Communists the selfsame type of organization is of importance as a practical premise for the victory of the revolution.

From this criterion, comrades, the Third Congress is a gigantic step forward as compared to the First and Second Congresses. At that time, especially in the era of the First

Congress, one could still hope that the bourgeois state apparatus had been so disorganized by the war as to enable us to overthrow the bourgeois domination through a single spontaneous revolutionary assault. Had this happened, we would, of course, have had occasion to congratulate ourselves. But this did not happen. The bourgeoisie managed to withstand the assault of the spontaneous revolutionary mass movement. The bourgeoisie succeeded in retaining its positions; it has restored its state apparatus, and has kept a firm hand on the army and the police. These are indisputable facts and they confront us with the task of overturning this restored state apparatus by means of a thought-out and organized revolutionary offensive—an offensive in the historical sense of the word, an offensive which includes temporary retreats as well as interludes for preparation.

The task of the Communist Party consists of applying all the possible methods of struggle. Were there no need of this, were the proletariat able to overthrow the bourgeoisie by a single tempestuous assault, there would be no need at all for the Communist Party. Both the fact that on a world scale this task is now posed as a practical task and the fact that the Third Congress has, after prolonged and rather heated discussion, arrived at a unanimous formulation of this task—this, comrades, is the supreme fact of our epoch, the fact that an International Communist Workers Party exists which is able to elaborate practically and adopt unanimously a strategic plan for the annihilation of bourgeois society. And if you are dissatisfied with some things—in my opinion unjustifiably so—you must in any case incorporate your dissatisfaction within the framework of this great fact, this great victory. If you do so, then criticism emanating from the Youth International will serve not as a brake but as a progressive factor.

It is possible that the greatest decisive battles may take place by next year. It is possible that the period of preparation in the key countries may endure until the next Congress. It is impossible to predict the date and duration of political events. The Third Congress was the highest school of strategic preparation. And it may be that the Fourth Congress will issue the signal for the world revolution. We can't tell as yet. But this we do know: We have taken a big step forward, and we shall all depart from this Congress more mature than when we came to it. This is amply clear, and not to me alone, I hope, but to all of us. And when the hour of great battles strikes, a very great role will be played in them by the youth. We need only recall the Red Army in which the youth played a decisive role not only politically but in a purely military sense. As a matter of fact, what is the Red Army, comrades? It is nothing but the armed and organized youth of Russia. What did we do when we had to launch an offensive? We appealed to the organizations of the youth, and these organizations would carry out a mobilization. Hundreds and thousands of young workers and peasants came to us and we incorporated them as nuclei into our regiments. That is how the morale of the Red Army was built. And if we get the same type of youth in the Communist International—as we shall—if in the days of decisive battles the youth streams into our ranks in organized regiments, then you will be able to use for the benefit of the labor movement that which now separates you from the "old" International—not so much in spirit as in maturity of mind.

Comrades, during the most perilous days of the Russian Revolution, when Yudenich stood beyond Petrograd, and during the hard days of Kronstadt, when this fortress almost became converted into a fortress of French imperialism against Petrograd, it was the Russian worker-peasant youth that saved the revolution. In the bourgeois newspapers you can read that we brought up Chinese, Kalmuk and other regiments against Yudenich and Kronstadt. This is, of course, a lie. We brought up our youth. The storming of Kronstadt was indeed symbolic. Kronstadt, as I said, was about to pass into the hands of French and English imperialism. Two or three days more and the Baltic Sea would have been ice-free and the war vessels of the foreign imperialists could have entered the ports of Kronstadt and Petrograd. Had we then been compelled to surrender Petrograd, it would have opened the road to Moscow, for there are virtually no defensive points between Petrograd and Moscow. Such was the situation. To whom did we turn? Kronstadt is surrounded by sea on all sides, and the sea was blanketed with ice and snow. Nakedly exposed one had to move on ice and snow against the fortress amply equipped with artillery and machine guns. We turned to our youth, to those workers and peasants who were receiving military education in our military schools. And to our call they staunchly answered, "Present!" And they marched in the open and without any protection against the artillery and machine guns of Kronstadt. And as before, beyond Petrograd, so now on the Baltic ice there were many, many corpses to be seen of young Russian workers and peasants. They fought for the revolution, they fought so that the present Congress might convene. And I am sure that the revolutionary youth of Europe and America, who are much more educated and developed than our youth, will in the hour of need display not less but far greater revolutionary energy; and in the name of the Russian Red Army, I say: *Long Live the International Revolutionary Youth—the Red Army of the World Revolution!*

27. Summary speech

Delivered following the report and discussion at the Second Congress of the Communist Youth International

The severest reproaches were leveled at the Third Congress by the Italian comrades. These reproaches were directed mainly against the Congress resolution on the Italian Socialist Party. Comrades Tranquilli and Polano[2] proceed from the assumption that this resolution muddles up the situation in Italy, that it will introduce confusion into the minds of Italian workers, without yielding any practical results in the future. In the opinion of Comrade Tranquilli, one can expect nothing from the Italian Socialist Party since not only its leaders—who are pacifists and reformists—but also the masses who follow these leaders are not revolutionary. I think that this approach to the Italian Socialist Party is false to the core. This party, hitherto united, has split, as you know, into three wings: the reformists who number about 14,000; the "unity" wing who number approximately 100,000; and the Communists—some 50,000. Comrade Tranquilli says that approximately 40,000 members dropped out of the Socialist Party and that it now counts in its ranks not more than 60,000 members, one-half of whom are members of municipal councils. I don't know just how exact these figures are; the last figure seems to me a little dubious.

I ask myself: Why has this party sent its delegation to Moscow? Its leaders are opportunists; the masses who follow it—likewise. True the party used to belong to the Communist International. But last September it took a reformist position. The ECCI has ruled that in Italy the Communist Party alone constitutes a section of the Third International. Thus the Socialist Party had itself expelled from the ranks of the Comintern. Serrati and his friends did not doubt that the Third Congress would uphold the decision of the ECCI, and yet they did send delegates to this Congress. To this it ought to be added that the reformists now play in the administration of the Socialist Party an even more important role than they did prior to the split. The reformist leaders, Turati and Treves,[3] are acquiring a strong influence over the Socialist Party. They enter into negotiations with Giolitti. In this period the Socialist Party has undergone a clear evolution to the right. Its parliamentary fraction becomes even more reformist than it was prior to the last elections. Turati, the genuine leader and inspirer of the party, begins baiting the Communist International with gibes and calumny.

How then to explain the fact that the representatives of this party appear in Moscow? The explanation offered by our young Italian comrades does not satisfy me. If the non-party masses regard the Communist International with such enthusiasm as to propel even Socialists to Moscow, then why don't these masses join the Communist International? I can't understand such super-circuitous politics on the part of the Italian workers. I believe that you are mistaken. The Italian working class is revolutionary, but its non-party masses are not sufficiently clear in their thinking, and it is precisely for this reason that they do not join the Communist Party. For this selfsame reason they do not exert sufficiently powerful pressure on the Socialist Party. The distance between Rome and Moscow is very great. And if the party leaders want to demonstrate that they are for Moscow; if they deem it necessary to lavish praise on Moscow, where, incidentally, they were not accorded a very warm reception; if they do all this, as you say, in order to deceive the masses, then it only goes to prove that the masses themselves have compelled these leaders to engage in such hypocrisy. Not the masses who are with the Communist Party, nor the non-party masses, but the rank-and-file members of the Socialist Party itself. You cite statistical data and you say that among 100,000 members of this party there are only 60,000 toilers, of whom some 30,000 are members of municipal councils or employes and so on. If this last figure is not exaggerated, one would have to admit that these employes who are shoving Lazzari and Maffi[4] to Moscow are not of the worst sort, and that we ought to try to attract them to us.

An assertion has been frequently repeated here to the effect that the doors have been left open to the Italian Socialist Party. Obviously the impression is that the doors are left wide open for anyone to enter. In reality the situation is somewhat more complex. We have stipulated that for two or three months the doors remain closed, and then the Italian Socialist Party must convene a party congress and discuss a number of questions publicly. First of all it must expel the reformists from its ranks. You may ask: Which ones? This is self-evident. Those who do not avow themselves as Communists, those who arranged the conference in Reggio-Emilia. This condition is quite specific. You know better than I do how great the influence of Turati and Treves is in the Italian Socialist Party. If our resolution compels the centrist and pacifist elements in the party to dissociate themselves from Turati and Treves, it would mean the complete capitulation of the party as a whole. The centrist elements have demonstrated that they lack any kind of policy. They can only be led by the nose—either by the Communists or by the reformists. Their most characteristic trait is their lack of character. And this is especially characteristic of Italy, where the revolutionary movement is very spontaneous in nature.

When parties who have been expelled from the Third International come to us and say: We wish to return to you; we reply: If you are prepared to accept our platform and to drive political saboteurs out of your midst, we shall not refuse to admit you. Does this really frighten you, comrades? Cite an instance, tell me of a different method whereby we can attract workers who still follow these leaders. You say that we ought to wait until the next action when the Socialist Party will expose itself by its periodic treachery, and then the masses will come over to us. You presuppose, therefore, that the Italian party is incapable of drawing any lessons from experience. There is no need of waiting for the next treachery in order to get rid of these creatures. We created the International precisely in order to safeguard the Italian proletariat against a new September ordeal, against new disillusions and new sacrifices. This, comrades, is precisely the meaning of the resolution of the Third Congress of the Comintern. We must expand the basis of our actions, of our activities.

Comrade Schueller[5] said that we need only dynamic actions, that only through them will we conquer the masses. He said that the masses have created the apparatus of revolution. This is correct, but in Italy there have been plenty of actions; all the recent years in Italy have been filled with political strikes, with uprisings in cities, villages and in the army, etc. The entire country seethed with rebellion. But it is not enough to interminably repeat the words "dynamic action." It is necessary to utilize these actions in laying the foundation of the revolutionary organization, in selecting the most resolute elements. It is necessary to center all efforts on the work of preparation. Which is precisely what was not done. There were actions, but there was no preparation for actions. This is what the comrades refuse to understand.

Comrade Polano said that it is necessary to break completely with reformist parties. But it was you, Comrade Polano, who told us that out of 100,000 members of the Socialist Party only 60,000 remained. Picture to yourself the fact that these 40,000, on dropping out of their party, did not join your party. The split that has occurred in the party has put them in a skeptical frame of mind, they are watching and waiting. And those who remained in the party have delegated Lazzari, Maffi and Riboldi[6] to go to Moscow. If we were now to say to them: We want no dealings with you; what impression, in your opinion, would this make upon the former party members, upon these 40,000 who have become skeptics? They inform us of their desire to join the International, but we tell them: No, we want no dealings with you. Will this facilitate your task of conquering the working masses for the Communist International? In no case! This would only reinforce the conservatism of the working masses and those selfsame members of municipal councils would form a bloc against you, against Moscow; because to refuse admittance into the International to those workers who wish to join is to deal them the cruelest insult. It is characteristic of a worker, in general, and of the Italian Socialist Party, in particular, that a worker always cherishes confidence in the organization which has awakened and educated him. This organizational conservatism has its positive as well as its negative side. If we repel a worker from us, we thereby strengthen the negative side of his organizational conservatism. No, by such a policy you will never gain the majority of the Italian proletariat. Never! Here you speak in the spirit of sectarianism and not in the spirit of revolution.

The same Comrade Schueller also said: Before us are theses on tactics; we accept them as disciplined soldiers of the proletarian army, but they were likewise accepted by Lazzari and Serrati and considerable satisfaction will be derived from them even by Levi. But comrades, what does this prove? We cannot reject these or other theses simply because they happen to please such and such an individual. If the theses are good, it remains for us only to congratulate ourselves that they were also adopted by Lazzari. And if they are bad, then it is first of all necessary to bring proof of that. Comrade Schueller said that we need actions, but if you read the theses over, you will become convinced that they express this same idea with a clarity of thought nowise inferior to Comrade Schueller's, even though he has expressed himself admirably. But Comrade Schueller is wrong in one thing. What we lacked was not actions, but the preparation of action.

I repeat, why are you so alarmed over the fact that Lazzari and Smeral[7] find our theses excellent? One of two things is possible: either Smeral has actually drawn closer to us, or he is a hypocrite. I don't believe in the latter supposition; I think that he is acting sincerely. But let us grant for a moment that he did approve our theses out of hypocrisy; if such were the case, why would he do it? Because he assumes that the masses who follow him are gravitating toward Moscow. As a matter of fact, let us suppose that Smeral is as much of a Machiavelli as Serrati—I can't say this of Lazzari, but in Serrati, why, there is a real Machiavelli for you—and so let us suppose that these Machiavellis say: Up to now we have reiterated that the Third International was making big mistakes, but now we must admit that it is acting correctly. What does this signify? This signifies that the masses who follow them are now for us. This signifies that they no longer have any arguments against us, that they can no longer hinder their masses from streaming into our ranks. You say that we have stripped them of all their weapons. Perhaps, but they themselves remain. Serrati remains. Smeral is coming to us. And don't we remain ourselves in the International, too? If Smeral demonstrates that he does not abide by the tactics of the Third International, we shall scarcely be scared of breaking with him after we have broken with the centrist and reformist parties. I cannot for the life of me understand what you are afraid of.

LAPORTE:[8] Since Smeral agrees with the theses, it follows that the theses are no good.

TROTSKY: Dear Comrade Laporte, this is precisely what you must first prove. You must prove that the tactics proposed by us are incorrect.

LAPORTE: I would prove it if I were granted the time.

TROTSKY: I would gladly listen to you on this question. But if it is really true that we, *i.e.*, the entire Communist Party, have advanced theses which are permeated with the spirit of opportunism, with the spirit of Smeral, then in that case it is impermissible to speak of our having left the doors open for Smeral and Serrati. After all, Smeral and Serrati will not be alone, they will be together with all of us. And if we are bad Communists, it means that our whole Communist family is bad and that there is no need of being afraid of these two.

A VOICE FROM THE FLOOR: The theses are not clear enough.

TROTSKY: It would of course be much simpler to throw all the vacillating elements out of the window and say: We shall remain a little sect, but by way of compensation we shall be absolutely pure. On the one hand, you always insist on revolutionary actions; but on the other hand, you want the party to consist of chemically pure elements only. These demands are contradictory. Because revolutionary actions are impossible without masses, but the masses do not consist solely of absolutely pure elements. This is beyond dispute. The masses are yearning for revolutionary action, but they have not yet lost faith in Smeral. Whether they are right or wrong is something else again, but the fact is they still continue to trust Smeral. We are consequently faced with the following alternative: either to reject Smeral together with the masses, or to accept him together with the masses. And since Smeral accepts the theses of the Third Congress, I assume, Comrade Laporte, that the mistake in this dispute is being made not by Smeral but by you. You are not striving to expand your base. Tactics cannot be unilateral, they must allow for maneuver, in order to attract the masses. It is a very complex task. But you say: No, I shall remain with my own family, the masses are not pure enough for me; I shall wait until the masses dribble into our party in little homeopathic doses.

Insofar as I am able to understand your tendency you are yearning for a more dynamic policy. If we were living in an organic epoch of slow and gradual development, I might perhaps agree that your tactic corresponds to the character of the epoch. But in our time, when the greatest events are taking place, the masses become educated through these events. And we must adjust ourselves to the situation, because a moment may arrive in Italy, perhaps on the morrow, when the Communist Party will be bound to act as a mass party. Serrati and Lazzari who have broken with the reformists will not have any personal or party influence and they will enter the Communist Party together with the masses that have compelled them to come to us. And should they then display anti-Communist tendencies, you would be able to throw them out of the party.

It seems to me that this exhausts all the objections which have been made here by certain comrades. No, they have accepted our theses not only as disciplined soldiers of the proletarian army, they have also accepted them out of inner conviction. This applies especially to the Italian comrades. The latest events in Rome demonstrate that the Italian proletariat is not completely disillusioned, that it still has revolutionary *élan*. On such foundations one can permit himself a bolder tactic, a tactic which does not flinch from embracing ever greater masses of workers. Furthermore, you ought not to forget, comrades, that the Italian party is not isolated, that there exists the ECCI which takes into consideration the experiences of all parties. If some Socialist group which has entered your party becomes a menace to you, even if you turn out to be in a minority—which incidentally is absolutely excluded—you could always appeal to the ECCI.

As regards the developments in Italy in the immediate future, I think that while our tactics in respect to the Socialist Party will not bring it completely into our ranks, they will nevertheless not remain unfruitful but will provoke a split. One thing is certain, namely: Within the Italian Socialist Party, the Left Wing will inescapably crystallize and demand the expulsion of the reformists. The Right Wing of the party will raise objections to this and as a result there will be a split in the party. You may say that the elements which split from the Socialist Party will not be pure enough for us. But in that case we could once again take up in the ECCI the question of admitting them into the Third International. You insist that between you and them there is nothing in common. But we would never have been a Communist Party if we had counted only on those workers who individually wanted to follow us. No, by such methods you will never attract the majority of the working class in Italy. The ECCI will help you to conquer a large faction of the Italian Socialist Party. We thus shall perhaps have in our ranks also some members of municipal councils. But they will only prove useful to you since, upon conquering power, you will need them in organizing food supplies, and so on. I hope that a few months from now I shall be able to congratulate you for having acquired several tens of thousands of workers and several hundred good municipal councilors.

Explanatory notes

(These notes are based on material collected by the Marx-Engels Institute under Ryazanov for the first edition of Lenin's *Collected Works*.)

Section I

1. The Federated Farmer-Labor Party was formed by the Workers (Communist) Party of the United States in 1924, the year capitalism finally succeeded in temporarily stabilizing itself following the First World War. Despite all of Trotsky's efforts, the ECCI, at that time under the domination of the *troika* (the triumvirate of Zinoviev-Kamenev-Stalin), refused to recognize the fact of capitalist stabilization until 18 months later. As a consequence 1924–25 were the years of pseudo-left policy, "leftist" mistakes and putschist experiments by the Comintern. The "farmer-labor" adventure of the American party was part of this false policy. Summing up this period in 1928, Trotsky wrote: "Finding itself in a cruel and constantly growing contradiction with the real factors, the leadership had to cling ever more to fictitious factors. Losing the ground under its feet, the ECCI was constrained to discover revolutionary forces and signs where there were no traces of any. . . . In proportion as obvious and growing shifts to the right were going on in the proletariat, there began in the Comintern the phase of idealizing the peasantry, a wholly uncritical exaggeration of every symptom of its 'break' with bourgeois society. . . . During 1924, *i.e.*, in the course of the basic year of the 'stabilization,' the Communist press was filled with absolutely fantastic data on the strength of the recently organized [in 1923] Peasants' International. . . . The representative of the Comintern (in the U.S.), Pepper-Pogany, in order to set the 'auxiliary mass'—the American farmers—into motion

at an accelerated tempo, drew the young and weak American Communist Party into the senseless and infamous adventure of creating a 'farmer-labor party' around LaFollette in order to overthrow quickly American capitalism." (*Third International After Lenin,* pp. 143–45.) [2020 printing] What predisposed the American party to this opportunist adventure was its previous ultra-left course. "Apparently no party can ever correct a deviation, it must over-correct it. The stick is bent backward. Thus the young party which a short time before had been concerned with the refinement of doctrine in underground isolation, having nothing to do with the trade union movement—let alone the political movement, the petty bourgeoisie and the labor fakers—this same party now plunged into a number of wild adventures in the field of labor and farmer politics. The attempt of the party leadership through a series of maneuvers and combinations to form a large farmer-labor party overnight without sufficient backing in the mass movement of the workers, without sufficient strength of the Communists themselves, threw the party into turmoil." (James P. Cannon, *History of American Trotskyism,* p. 49–50.) [2020 printing] By decision of the ECCI (under Trotsky's pressure), the American party later reversed its position. Less than one month after the St. Paul Convention of the FFLP where presidential candidates were nominated, the Central Committee of the CPUSA announced (July 8, 1924) that these candidates had been withdrawn, and that the CP would conduct its own campaign with its own candidates.

2. The Manifesto of the Communist International was adopted unanimously at the last (fifth) session of the First World Congress on March 6, 1919. It was published in the first issue of *Communist International,* organ of the Comintern which appeared in Russian, German, French and English, and which began publication in May 1919, with Zinoviev as editor.

3. The last pre-war Congress of the Second International took place in 1912 at Basle, Switzerland. Only one point was on the agenda of this Congress, namely, the struggle against

the war danger. After Jaurès delivered his report, a revolutionary resolution was adopted.

4. City—that section of London where the biggest English banks are located.

5. The term "theory of impoverishment" was invented by Bernstein, the father of revisionism, in 1890. Bernstein leveled his criticism especially against Marx's famous assertion that the poverty of the proletariat as a whole tends to increase with the development of capitalism. "Along with the constantly diminishing number of the magnates of capital, who usurp and monopolise all advantages of this process of transformation, grows the mass misery, oppression, slavery, degradation, exploitation. . . ." (Karl Marx, *Capital*, Vol. I, p. 836.) Marx and Engels first propounded this in the *Communist Manifesto* in 1848. Most of the theoreticians of the Second International made a concession to Bernstein by arguing that Marx had allegedly referred to the *relative* and not at all to the *absolute* impoverishment of the masses. "The proposition in the *Manifesto* concerning the tendency of capitalism to lower the living standards of the workers, and even to transform them into paupers, has been subjected to a heavy barrage. Parsons, professors, ministers, journalists, Social-Democratic theoreticians, and trade union leaders come to the front against the so-called 'theory of impoverishment.' They invariably discovered signs of growing prosperity among the toilers, palming off the labor aristocracy as the proletariat, or taking a fleeting tendency as permanent. Meanwhile, even the development of the mightiest capitalism in the world, namely U.S. capitalism, has transformed millions of workers into paupers who are maintained at the expense of federal, municipal, or private charity." (Leon Trotsky, introduction to *The Communist Manifesto*, Pathfinder, p. 9.) [2020 printing]

6. The League of Nations—the "thieves' kitchen" as Lenin called it—was created at the Versailles Conference convened by the victors of the first imperialist war early in 1919. At its inception and for many years thereafter the

League prohibited the entry of the conquered countries. It was one of the instruments which helped prepare the Second World War.
7. It was in this way that Czechoslovakia, Hungary, Poland, Yugoslavia and other countries were formed in 1919.
8. In 1916 uprisings occurred in Ireland against England which were crushed with typical imperialist brutality.
9. Madagascar, an island off the coast of Africa, is part of the French colonial empire.
10. Annam is a French colony on the eastern shore of the Indo-China peninsula.
11. Woodrow Wilson was President of the U.S. 1912–20. During the first imperialist world war Wilson offered to mediate between the Allies and Germany, proposing that a peace be negotiated without annexations or reparations, etc., etc. This pacifist program for world peace, along with the notorious "14 points" and League of Nations as a "world tribunal," etc., etc., were hailed by all the liberals and social-chauvinists. Every one of the Wilsonian ideas and "ideals" proved absolutely bankrupt and a complete fraud.
12. Algiers is a French colony in North Africa.
13. Bengal is the largest province in India. Within its borders are to be found Calcutta and other large cities of India.
14. Armenia was then a *de facto* protectorate of England.
15. Lloyd George, one of the authors of the Versailles Treaty, was the head of the English government during the First World War. Beginning his career as a liberal reformer, he came into prominence in 1908 as the sponsor of the 8-hour day for the miners. Thereafter he instituted (1909) arbitration bodies, comprising representatives of the government, labor and the "public," to regulate wages in the most backward branches of English industry; and in 1911, he sponsored laws covering unemployment insurance, sick benefits, etc. (compare Roosevelt's "New Deal"). Naturally, this record qualified him eminently to serve as the leader of the imperialist bourgeoisie during the First World War and in the critical period following this war. While propagandi-

zing the war as a "war for democracy" Lloyd George, hand in hand with the Tories, bolstered up the dictatorship of the English imperialist clique, undermined the previous conquests of the English working class, introduced conscription, crushed the uprisings in Ireland, and so on. In the postwar epoch, he resorted to compromise in order to restore capitalist equilibrium. After the Soviets had crushed all the attempts of the imperialist intervention and of the counter-revolution, he became one of the advocates of reestablishing economic ties with the Soviet Union. In November 1922, Lloyd George and his Liberal Party suffered defeat in the parliamentary elections, and the Tories took over the reins directly.

16. Clemenceau, chief inspirer of Versailles, was in his youth a radical, called himself a Socialist and was even for a time member of the French Socialist Party. Later he became the beloved leader of the French big bourgeoisie—its "Tiger." In the days of the Versailles Conference and during the era of the First World Congress of the Communist International, Clemenceau headed the French cabinet.

17. Bavaria—one of the autonomous states of the old German empire. Its population is predominantly rural, the largest section of this rural population consisting of the so-called "strong" or middle farmer.

18. Baden—a South German state with the same characteristics as Bavaria.

19. Up to the Franco-Prussian War (1870), Germany was divided into a number of independent states. The war with France and the victory over Napoleon III eliminated the chief opponent of their unification. The modern German empire was founded in 1871 with the Prussian King Wilhelm I at the head.

20. "The Socialist Center," or the Centrists in the labor movement—in 1914–18 and throughout the era of the first four Congresses of the Comintern constituted chiefly by the German and Austrian followers of Karl Kautsky. Kautsky preached that the basic task of the labor movement after the last war was to reestablish a *united* Second International;

and he pleaded with the Socialists of all countries that they mutually forgive and forget their respective sins.

21. Babeuf was the leader of the extreme wing of the French plebeian revolutionists at the end of the eighteenth century. Babeuf and his followers were the first ones in history to attempt a revolutionary overturn in order to establish the dictatorship of the toilers. Babeuf's conspiracy was discovered and, together with a number of his followers, he was executed in 1797.

22. Karl Liebknecht (1871–1919)—leader of the German revolutionary labor movement, founder with Rosa Luxemburg of the German Communist Party, founder of the Communist Youth movement. Long before the First World War, he earned revolutionary renown by his struggle against militarism. He was sentenced to 18 months in prison for writing his pamphlet, *Militarism and Anti-Militarism*. Liebknecht's name is a symbol of revolutionary internationalism and irreconcilable opposition to imperialist war. On August 3, 1914 he opposed voting for war credits at a session of the Social-Democratic parliamentary fraction; but under the pressure of party discipline he voted together with the entire party fraction at the Reichstag session on August 4, 1914. When the next vote was taken, on December 2, 1914, he was the only deputy who cast his vote *against*. But even before that, in October of the same year, he published, jointly with Rosa Luxemburg, Franz Mehring and Clara Zetkin, a statement against the official party position in the Swiss Social-Democratic press. In March 1915, when the Reichstag took a vote on war credits, 30 Social Democrats left the chambers and the only ones who voted against were Liebknecht and Otto Ruehle. In 1915 he began to organize the Spartacus League and started the publication of the famous "Spartacus Letters." When the Zimmerwald Conference convened, Liebknecht was drafted into the army and could not attend, but he forwarded a letter to this conference which closed with the following words: "Not civil peace, but civil war—that is our slogan." On January 12, 1916 the Social-Democratic fraction expelled him from its

ranks. On May Day 1916 he distributed anti-war leaflets in Potsdam Square in Berlin, was arrested and sentenced to hard labor. The victory of the Russian October found him in prison where he greeted the conquest of the Russian workers and peasants, and summoned the German workers to follow this great example. The November 1918 revolution in Germany freed him from prison, untying his hands for a direct struggle against the social-chauvinists and their centrist allies. Together with Rosa Luxemburg and Leo Jogiches (Tyshko) he organized the Communist Party of Germany which in December 1919 broke all connections with the Independent Social-Democratic Party, headed by Kautsky and Haase. As member of the revolutionary committee, he headed the uprising of the Berlin workers in January 1919. After this uprising was suppressed he was arrested by the Scheidemann government and on January 15, 1919 was assassinated together with Rosa Luxemburg by a gang of German officers, covertly abetted by the Scheidemannists.

23. Rosa Luxemburg (1871–1919)—the theoretician of German Communism and author of a number of theoretical books on economics, politics and other questions. She played a very prominent role in the labor movement before the First World War and was the leader of its left wing. She participated in the Polish and Russian revolutionary movements; and from 1910 headed the revolutionary opposition within the German Social Democracy. In 1918, together with Liebknecht, she founded the German Communist Party. Rosa, "our Rosa" as the old revolutionary movement knew her, was born in Poland. At the age of eighteen she was forced to migrate because of her revolutionary activities to Zurich, Switzerland. In 1893 she founded the Polish Social-Democratic Party (later known as the Social-Democratic Party of Poland and Lithuania). In 1897 she began participating in the German socialist movement. It was Luxemburg, Mehring and Plekhanov who initiated the struggle against revisionism within the Second International (Bernsteinism and Millerandism) and compelled Kautsky to take a position against it. At the 1907 London

Congress of the Russian party she supported the Bolsheviks against the Mensheviks on all the key problems of the Russian revolution. The same year, in autumn, together with Lenin she introduced at the Stuttgart Congress of the Second International the revolutionary anti-war resolution which was adopted in essence by that Congress. Long before the war she came into conflict with Kautsky and other Centrists in the German party. When the First World War broke out, she took an internationalist position from the outset. From jail—she was incarcerated in February 1915—she collaborated in the illegally published "Spartacus Letters," and in the work of the Spartacus League. In the spring of 1916 she wrote in jail, under the pseudonym of Junius, the famous pamphlet "The Crisis of the Social Democracy" in which she pointed out the urgent need of creating the Third International. After the November 1918 revolution in Germany she was freed and joined in the work of creating the Communist Party, being the founder and editor of *Rote Fahne,* the party's central organ. After the crushing of the 1919 uprising in Berlin she was arrested and murdered together with Karl Liebknecht.

24. Albert was the pseudonym of Hugo Eberlein, a prominent German Communist, who attended the First World Congress of the Communist International as a delegate of the Spartacus League. He was under instructions at the time to oppose the formation of the Communist International on the ground that the time was not yet ripe for it. Subsequently Eberlein became one of the leaders of the so-called "Center" in the German Communist Party.

25. Ebert was the first president of the German counter-revolutionary bourgeois Weimar Republic. He had been one of the closest collaborators of Bebel. During the imperialist war Ebert together with Scheidemann was the inspirer of the social-chauvinists. In the last days of the Hohenzollern monarchy Ebert entered the government in order to prevent the revolution and to save the monarchy. Failing in this effort the German Social Democrats then undertook—successfully—to restore capitalism in

Germany on the basis of the bourgeois republic. Ebert was elected president in 1919.

26. Scheidemann, another of Bebel's closest collaborators, was with Ebert the leader of the German Socialist traitors after Bebel's death. He, too, entered the cabinet of Prince Baden in order to save the monarchy. All his efforts, after the Kaiser's downfall, were directed to the crushing of the revolutionary movement. After the defeat of the Spartacists he became the head of a coalition government, succeeded in completely discrediting himself in the eyes of the workers and had to retire.

27. The Treaty of Brest-Litovsk was signed by the Soviet delegation on March 3, 1918 without even reading its predatory terms. The peace negotiations began on December 9, 1917 but were broken off, on the instruction of the Bolshevik Central Committee, by the Soviet delegation headed at that time by Leon Trotsky. The German Social Democrats supported throughout the imperialist policy of the Hohenzollerns and of the German bourgeoisie, under the pretext that the Bolsheviks had "agreed" to the peace and "wanted" it. Liebknecht throughout supported the Bolsheviks. Within the Russian Communist Party, the negotiations and the peace itself precipitated a sharp crisis, because of the opposition by the "Left Communists" headed by Bukharin who opposed the peace on grounds of principle. Lenin succeeded in carrying the day only because of the assistance rendered him in the crucial hours by Trotsky. But subsequently, the Stalinists tried to utilize the disputes of the Brest-Litovsk period in their struggle against Trotsky. For further details of this campaign of falsifications see: "Negotiations at Brest-Litovsk," Leon Trotsky, *My Life*. [2019 printing]

28. Karl von Clausewitz was the outstanding military theoretician in the first part of the nineteenth century. His best known work *Ueber Krieg und Kriegfuehrung (On War)*, three volumes, Berlin 1832–34, bears unmistakable evidence of the use of the Hegelian dialectic. Clausewitz participated in the campaigns against Napoleon and later served as the

head of the Prussian General Staff (1831). In 1812–13 he was in the service of the Russian army.

29. After the mutiny of the Czechoslovak troops in Penza, a White Guard-S.R. coup was accomplished in the summer of 1918 in Samara where all the members of the dispersed Constituent Assembly had assembled. These members of the Constituent Assembly organized a government in Samara and attempted to create a "People's Army." Toward the end of 1919 the initiative in the Civil War passed into the hands of the White Guard generals who dispersed this "People's Government" with the aid of the Czechs. The indignant S.R.'s—or more correctly their Left Wing, headed by Volsky—then sought refuge in the territories of Soviet Russia.

30. Kolchak was a Czarist admiral who after the Soviet power had been temporarily overthrown in Siberia came there as a puppet supported by the Allies. In November 1918 the Cossack *atamans* (chieftains) elected him supreme commander. When the counter-revolution suffered defeat he was left stranded by the Allies and was arrested during an uprising in the Irkutsk province. Kolchak was executed in February 1920 by the order of the Irkutsk Revolutionary Committee.

31. Kautsky was the outstanding theoretician of the Second International. From 1906 Kautsky, who had begun as a Marxist, started moving toward reformism. The war and the October Revolution transformed him completely into an avowed opportunist. In the last postwar period Kautsky, who no longer played a major political role, was the theoretician for the perfidious policy pursued by the Second International in the interval between the two world wars. After Hitler's coming to power he died an ignominious death in exile.

32. Order No. 83 is only one of the innumerable historical documents attesting that Lenin and his co-thinkers never viewed the Red Army otherwise than as the military arm of the world working class in its struggle for emancipation. In Lenin's day, the Congresses of the Third International

were invariably the occasion for great propaganda and agitational campaigns, especially in the ranks of the Red Army. Thus the day after the adjournment of the First World Congress, March 7, 1919, was proclaimed a public holiday, the Red Army paraded in Red Square and that evening great mass meetings were held throughout the country. Similar procedure was followed so long as Lenin remained alive.

Section II

1. Hegel—the greatest German philosopher of the first part of the nineteenth century. His outstanding achievement was the systematization of the dialectic character of development in nature and in society. The gist of Hegel's doctrine consists in recognizing that inorganic, organic and social formations arise, develop and are destroyed.

2. Kerensky—member of the Social Revolutionary Party, was elected deputy to the Fourth Duma. After the February Revolution of 1917 which overthrew the Czar, he became the outstanding representative of petty-bourgeois conciliationists. "Kerenskyism" has become a synonym for a transitional period between bourgeois democracy and the establishment of the dictatorship of the proletariat.

3. Tseretelli was one of the most prominent Russian Mensheviks from Georgia, deputy to the Second Duma. After the February Revolution he was one of the leaders of the so-called "revolutionary defensists" and entered as Minister of Posts and Telegraph into the coalition government.

4. Chernov was the founder and most prominent leader of the Social Revolutionary Party. During the first imperialist war he donned temporarily the cloak of Zimmerwaldism. After the February Revolution he served as Minister of Agriculture in the Kerensky government.

5. The reference here is to Kautsky's pamphlets: *The Motor Forces of the Russian Revolution* (an answer to a questionnaire sent out to prominent Socialist leaders by Plekhanov); *The Agrarian Question in Russia, The Russian and the American Workers, The Revolutionary Perspective,* and so on. In these

pamphlets and articles Kautsky supported the Bolsheviks. (See Note 31, Section I.)

6. On August 4, 1914 the Social-Democratic fraction in the German Reichstag voted credits for the war against which it had issued public statements only a short while before. (See Notes 22 and 23, Section I.)

7. Bernstein is the theoretician of opportunism, with whose name is linked the theoretical revision of Marxism which began in 1896–97. Bernstein served as the theoretician of reformism for 25 years. During the interval between the two world wars he did not play any significant political role. (See Note 5, Section I.)

8. The defeat of the German revolution, or more correctly the series of defeats (1918–19, 1921, 1923), which led to the crushing defeat of 1933 (the assumption of power by Hitler), was the most decisive single event in the interval between the two world wars. In his autobiography, Trotsky quotes from a letter he wrote to the Political Bureau, CPSU, in 1928: "The Lenin wing of the party has been under a hail of blows ever since 1923, that is, ever since the unexampled collapse of the German revolution. The increasing force of these blows keeps pace with the further defeats of the international and the Soviet proletariat as a consequence of opportunist [Stalinist] leadership." (*My Life,* Pathfinder, pp. 727–28.) [2020 printing]. The world working class, and mankind as a whole, has paid a frightful price for the defeat of the German revolution, and all the other catastrophes brought about primarily by the Stalinist leadership and its abysmal betrayals.

9. In October 1918 the military defeat of Germany led to the uprising of sailors in Hamburg, the proclamation of the Republic in Munich, etc. This series of events finally forced the Kaiser to abdicate his crown.

10. The reference here is to the famous demonstration of the Petrograd workers and soldiers on July 3–5, 1917. For further details see Trotsky's *History of the Russian Revolution,* Vol. II, Chapters I and II.

11. In 1876 the revolutionary intellectuals of Russia, who called themselves *Narodniki* (Populists), organized a party *"Zemlya i Volya"* (Land and Freedom) inside which contradictory political tendencies began to develop. In 1879 this organization split into two parties: *"Narodnaya Volya"* (People's Will) and *"Cherny Peredel"* headed by Plekhanov. The followers of *Narodnaya Volya,* known as *Narodovoltsi* (a contraction of the party's name) turned more and more toward methods of individual terror. After the assassination of Czar Alexander II (1881), their organization was smashed. Lenin's brother, A.I. Ulyanov, was a member of this party, and was executed together with others in 1887 after an unsuccessful attempt to assassinate Czar Alexander III. The Plekhanov group migrated abroad (1880) and evolved toward Marxism, forming the first Russian Marxist organization, "Emancipation of Labor Group," in Switzerland (1883).

12. The Stolypin epoch covers the period of reaction following the defeat of the 1905 revolution in Russia. Stolypin, one of the largest feudal landowners, headed the Czarist cabinet in this period until he was assassinated in 1911. His favorite formula was: "first pacification, then reform." "Pacification" meant the intrenchment of autocratic rule through suppression of the press, abolition of the trade unions, martial law, and large-scale application of firing squads. Stolypin's "reforms" came down to an attempt to stabilize Russian society through the artificial fostering of "strong" peasant economies (kulaks) in the country. All his attempts both at "pacification" and "reform" proved abortive.

13. Haase—one of the founders and leaders of the Independent Socialist Party of Germany (USP) formed in 1917. Before the First World War he was the first vice-chairman of the German Social Democracy. During the imperialist conflict, he headed the "moderate opposition" within the German party. On March 1, 1917, he became chairman of the Central Committee of the Independent Socialist Party of Germany. During the Spartacus uprising of January 1919, he

tried to play the role of "peacemaker." In October of the same year he was assassinated on the steps of the Reichstag by a Monarchist officer.

The USP withdrew from the Second International when the Comintern was formed and began negotiations concerning entry into the latter. In 1920 when the USP numbered 800,000 members, its Congress at Halle voted by two-thirds majority to accept the "21 conditions" for admittance into the Third International; thereupon the majority of the USP fused with the German Communist Party. The minority continued to exist as an independent organization adhering to the 2½ International until 1922 when the USP returned to the ranks of the official Socialist Party, with the exception of a small centrist group headed by Ledebour.

14. This article was written specially by Trotsky for the first issue of the *Communist International,* central organ of the ECCI, edited by Zinoviev and published in Russian, German, French and English. In the first years of the Comintern, it was the only printed organ of the ECCI, serving both as a theoretical magazine and as a means of publishing the documents of the CI. In 1921 the Third World Congress decided to supplement it with the publication of the *International Press Correspondence (Inprecorr)* and this served to push the *Communist International* into the background. The latter appeared irregularly until the end of 1924. With the launching of the campaign against Trotsky and "Trotskyism," its publication was regularized. From January 1, 1925 it appeared as a monthly; from September 15, 1926 it was issued as a weekly in Russian and German; and fortnightly in French and English. It was printed simultaneously in Moscow, Berlin, Paris and London. Once it had served Stalin's purpose its publication was discontinued.

15. This article was written by Trotsky while en route to the Southern front where Denikin had launched his offensive (May–August 1919). Many of Trotsky's writings in this period bear the title "En Route." They, together with innumerable other documents, orders to the various armies, etc., were written in the famous train. This train was organized

on August 7, 1918 at night, and the next morning it departed for Svyazhsk on the Czechoslovak front. The following information concerning it was compiled by Trotsky's secretariat during the Civil War: "Already in 1918 the train represented a mobile apparatus of administration. It was equipped with its own printing plant, telegraph, radio, electric power station, library, garage and bath. This train which steeled all wills and brought victory with it would appear in the most critical moments at the key sectors of the various fronts. During Yudenich's October offensive (1919) the train was sent to Petrograd. Out of its personnel was formed a detachment which manned the armored train named after Lenin, and another detachment which was incorporated in the Red Army in the region of Ligovo. For its participation in these battles the train received the order of the Red Banner. In the course of the Civil War the train fulfilled 36 missions, covering a total distance of 97,629 versts." (Leon Trotsky, *How the Revolution Armed Itself*, Vol. II, Book I, Page 463.)

16. Dan was one of the outstanding Menshevik leaders. The reference here is to the way in which the Mensheviks evaluated the campaign conducted by the German Social Democracy in 1909–10 against the three-class electoral system of Prussia, one of the remnants of the feudal-Junker rule.

17. Potressov—a prominent Menshevik who was really just a bourgeois liberal. Virtually throughout his Social-Democratic career Potressov was to be found in the Right Wing of Menshevism. At the time Trotsky wrote this article Potressov had left the political arena. He never returned to it.

18. Owing to the turbulent revolutionary ferment in Berlin, it was deemed most expedient to convene the Constituent Assembly, elected at the beginning of 1918, in the provincial city of Weimar in Thuringia.

19. Jaurès—one of the most prominent leaders of the pre-1914 Second International and a great orator. At the outset of his career he was simply a French radical. He entered the labor movement in 1890, founding the newspaper *l'Humanité*.

After the Dreyfus affair, Jaurès was instrumental in forming a political bloc between the Radicals and the Socialists to support Millerand when the latter entered the bourgeois government. By the middle 'nineties Jaurès began to play a major role in the Second International, supporting on almost all questions the reformist wing. As a sincere opponent of war, Jaurès conducted in the pre-1914 days a bitter campaign against war which resulted in his death. When the fumes of war filled the air in July 1914, Jaurès was assassinated by a French nationalist.

20. "Possibilists"—French opportunists of 1882–90 who tried to combine Proudhonism and Marxism, and who held that the tactics of the Social Democracy should be confined within the framework of what is "possible" in capitalist society. Hence the name—possibilists. The leader of this tendency was Brousse.

21. The wars of 1864, 1866, and 1871 were waged by Prussia against the main enemies of the unification of the German empire who were Denmark, Austria and France respectively. These brilliant diplomatic and military campaigns were conducted by Bismarck, the leader of Prussian Junkerdom, who had the active support of the industrial bourgeoisie. The seizure of industrial regions (Alsace-Lorraine, Silesia), the extortion of war indemnities and the creation of the national state gave a mighty impetus to the tempestuous industrialization of Germany.

22. Knopf was the head of a large English textile firm who built in Russia a number of textile factories whose technical equipment was far superior to the then existing Russian factories.

23. The reference here is to the controversy between the Populists *(Narodniks)* and the Marxists in Russia in 1880–90. The former maintained that capitalism in Russia came not as a result of the country's economic development but as an alien and artificial hybrid doomed to perish swiftly. So far as the internal conditions for capitalist development were concerned, the Russian Populists denied their existence, especially the domestic market. "For the develop-

ment of capitalism in Russia there are none such." The violent tempo of industrial development during the 'nineties dealt a death blow to the Narodnik theory.

24. "The Little Town of Okurov" is the title of a story by Gorki in which he describes a god-forsaken provincial town and its dull-witted citizenry, mired in the morass of day-to-day existence. The types depicted here by Gorki are all extremely negative, even revolting.

25. In the sphere of industry French capital was invested primarily in Donbas coal and in heavy metallurgy. French finance capital was exported to Russia chiefly in the form of loans to the Czarist government.

26. The 1919 parliamentary elections in France took place amid fanfares of victory and rabid agitation against the Bolsheviks. Promises based on German reparations and frequent alarms over the Red danger enabled the reactionary National Bloc to mobilize the petty bourgeoisie and to gain three-fifths of the seats in parliament.

27. Monatte—one of the leaders of the French Communist Party which he joined toward the end of 1922. Prior to the First World War Monatte stood in the ranks of the French revolutionary syndicalists, who constituted during the war years the core of the opposition in the labor movement to the social-patriots. After the war ended, Monatte continued his revolutionary work but did not immediately join the Communist Party. When the Frossard group split away in the winter of 1922, Monatte finally joined the Communist movement only to leave it subsequently.

28. Alfred Rosmer participated with Monatte in the revolutionary syndicalist movement. But in contradistinction to Monatte, Rosmer broke in 1919–20 with syndicalist prejudices and in 1920 attended the Second Congress of the Communist International serving as a member of its presidium. He actively defended the line of the Communist International within the French Communist Party and was one of the leaders of its Left Wing. Rosmer joined the Left Opposition (Trotskyists) in the early days of its existence, but subsequently became politically inactive. He is author

of one of the best histories of labor during the last war *Le Mouvement Ouvrier Pendant la Guerre (The Labor Movement During the War)* (1936).

29. July 21, 1919 was the date set for an international strike to protest against imperialist intervention in Russia, and as a demonstration of world proletarian solidarity. The strike was a failure owing to the treachery of the social-chauvinists and the passivity of the Centrists.

30. Jouhaux—secretary of the French General Confederation of Labor (CGT). Former revolutionary syndicalist who in the pre-1914 days was anti-patriotic and favored the general strike, but who betrayed his views when the war broke out, becoming a rabid chauvinist. One of the leaders of the Amsterdam Trade Union International. One of France's representatives in the defunct League of Nations.

31. Merrheim—French syndicalist; secretary of the Metal Workers Union. One of the authors of the 1906 Charter of Amiens. At the beginning of the First World War participated in Zimmerwald where he stood with the Right Wing. Subsequently became Jouhaux's comrade-in-arms.

32. Renaudel—leader of the extreme Right Wing of the French Socialist Party. A rabid jingoist.

33. Jean Longuet—French lawyer and Socialist who in the First World War held a pacifist position but invariably voted for war credits. Founder and editor of the newspaper *Le Populaire*. At the Strasbourg Congress in 1918 the majority of the French SP went over to Longuet's position. After the Tours Congress in 1920, where the Communists gained the majority, he split from the party, joined the 2½ International and returned later to the Second International. Grandson of Karl Marx.

34. Loriot—an old Socialist. During the closing years of the war of 1914–18 he was the leader of the extreme Left Wing in the French Socialist Party, supporting the Zimmerwald Left. In 1920–21 Loriot took active part in the split of the old French Socialist Party and the formation of the Communist Party of France, one of whose leaders he became.

Loriot attended the Third Congress of the Communist International and was elected to the presidium. A few years later he dropped out of the Communist movement.

35. Dumoulin—French syndicalist, colleague of Merrheim.
36. Any number of passages can be cited from Marx and Engels illustrating their contempt for parliamentarianism, bourgeois democracy, pure democracy, etc. We cite two instances from their correspondence: "The dogs of democrats and the liberal scoundrels will see that we are the only fellows who have not been stupefied by this appalling period of peace." (Marx to Engels, February 25, 1859.) "In any case our sole adversary on the day of the crisis and on the day after the crisis will be the whole collective reaction which will group itself around pure democracy, and this, I think, should not be lost sight of." (Engels to Bebel, December 11, 1884.)
37. Viviani—one of the galaxy of French bourgeois leaders who began their careers in the Socialist Party only in order to betray it for a government post. At the beginning of the First World War Viviani rose to the post of premier. He was replaced by Clemenceau.
38. Alsace-Lorraine was ceded to Germany by France in 1871 after her defeat in the Franco-Prussian War. The restoration of these territories was the favorite slogan of the French bourgeoisie in its 1914–18 war agitation.
39. Renan—French orientalist and scholar in the late nineteenth century. Author of *The Life of Christ*.
40. Vandervelde—leader of the Belgian Socialist Party and former leader of the Second International. Lawyer and professor. Throughout his entire career Vandervelde remained in the Right Wing of the Social Democracy. The war disclosed him as a complete traitor. He was among the first Socialists to enter the war cabinet, becoming His Majesty's premier. As Belgium's representative, he signed the Versailles Treaty. Participated in various coalition governments in the 'twenties.
41. Napoleon III, nephew of Napoleon Bonaparte, gained the imperial throne on the crest of French reaction after the

Revolution of 1848. Basing himself on the financial and industrial bourgeoisie, Napoleon III supported reaction in other countries. In the epoch of Napoleon III the corruption of bourgeois democracy was quite graphically revealed. See Karl Marx, *The Eighteenth Brumaire.*

42. Noske was the Social-Democratic executioner of the revolutionary movement of Germany in 1919–20. Noske came from the ranks of the labor bureaucrats who even prior to the First World War had openly supported the Kaiser's colonial policy. During the war he was one of the German government's lackeys. In the days of the 1918 revolution in Germany he served as the hangman of the counter-revolution. Together with Scheidemann, Noske was responsible for the shooting of tens of thousands of German workers. Later died in obscurity.

43. Barthou—one of the prominent political figures in the camp of the French bourgeoisie. Served in many cabinets and held the post of premier. Assassinated together with King Alexander of Yugoslavia in the autumn of 1935.

44. Briand—one of the outstanding examples of renegacy within the French Social-Democratic movement. In the 1890's Briand belonged to the Left Wing of the labor movement, being the chief agitator for the "Direct Action Group" a tendency which later fused with syndicalism. But even before 1914 Briand executed a right about-face, entered the ranks of the saviors of the French bourgeoisie, and made a career as one of the political leaders of French imperialism. In the middle 'twenties, *i.e.*, at the time this volume was published in Russia, Briand tried to resume his career as one of the conservative leaders of the "Left Bloc."

45. Millerand—president of the French Republic, like so many other leaders of the French bourgeoisie began his career as a Socialist. He worked together with Jaurès. In 1899 he joined the bourgeois government. Millerand's action precipitated a bitter controversy within the Second International. Millerand unswervingly evolved to the right, becoming in the end the outstanding leader of French reaction.

46. Foch—marshal of the French army. Commander-in-chief of the Allied forces in 1918. Resolute partisan of military intervention in the Soviet Union.

47. Gladstone—one of the prominent leaders of the Left Wing of the English bourgeoisie during the latter part of the nineteenth century. Gladstone was in favor of the peaceful assimilation of Ireland.

48. Campbell-Bannerman—a prominent English politician in the first half of the nineteenth century. In the 1840's he was the Lord Chancellor of Ireland. Also served as premier. Like Gladstone, Campbell belonged to the Liberal Party.

49. The Marne and the Somme are rivers in the northeastern part of France. During the war of 1914–18 they were the arena of gigantic battles in which hundreds of thousands were killed and wounded on both sides.

50. Bullitt was an attaché of the American delegation to Versailles. In February 1919 he was sent by Wilson to Soviet Russia to negotiate a peace between the White Guards and the Soviet government on the basis of the then existing frontiers. Bullitt was entrusted with the text of the Soviet counter-proposals. But inasmuch as Bullitt's return to Paris coincided with the first successes of Kolchak's offensive in the spring of 1919, the Allies decided to drop the matter. This created quite a scandal at the time.

51. Kuehlmann—Minister of Foreign Affairs of the German Imperial government who conducted the peace negotiations at Brest-Litovsk for Germany.

52. Czernin—Minister of Foreign Affairs of the Austro-Hungarian empire at the time.

53. The armies of the National Convention during the Great French Revolution were organized to meet the intervention of the counterrevolutionary armies of Austria and other feudal regimes who tried to base themselves on the forces of French reaction. Within a few years the armies of the National Convention not only repulsed the foreign enemy, but succeeded in extending the influence of the French republic far beyond its original frontiers. The

Convention sent into the armies its own emissaries who had dictatorial powers.

54. Turati—one of the founders of the Italian Socialist Party. Lawyer by profession. Except for the first few years when he was a Left Winger, the greater part of Turati's activity was devoted to the cause of Italian reformism. After Italy's entry into the First World War he voted against war credits, but supported Wilson's program. At the conclusion of the war, remained an opponent of the Russian Revolution and of the Communist International. After the split of the Italian party in 1922, he headed the party of reformists.

55. Albert Thomas—French Socialist and deputy, member of the coalition war cabinet in 1914–18. Extreme social-chauvinist. Chairman of the "Labor Bureau" attached to the League of Nations.

56. Varenne—a prominent French Socialist who was a chauvinist during the war of 1914–18 and who later became one of the most rabid proponents of the "Left Bloc," *i.e.*, a coalition between the bourgeoisie and the Socialists. Varenne and others of his stripe are Stalin's predecessors in the policy of the "People's Front."

57. Sembat—in the pre-1914 days one of the most prominent parliamentarians within the French Socialist Party. During the First World War Sembat became a chauvinist and entered Viviani's cabinet. He occupied an extreme right position in the French Socialist Party after the war.

58. Mistral—French Socialist who together with Longuet headed the "moderate opposition" during the First World War. Like Longuet, Mistral remained in the ranks of the Socialist Party, after the split at the 1919 Tours Congress.

59. Pressemane—another leader of the same tendency.

60. Huysmans—Belgian Socialist; secretary of the Second International. Professor of philosophy. Served in bourgeois cabinets. During the First World War Huysmans, a rabid chauvinist, attacked the Zimmerwald movement as the product of "Russian intrigues." He was very influential in the "party kitchen," *i.e.*, the inner circles.

61. Paul Boncour—a typical representative of French intellectual and parliamentary "socialism."
62. The outstanding representative of the tendency referred to by Trotsky is Jaurès.
63. *Clarté*—an organization of French intellectuals sympathetic to Soviet Russia, headed by Barbusse and others. Ideologically this group was a motley gathering, embracing various elements from Tolstoyans to Marxists.

Section III

1. Zinoviev's report on the role of the Communist Party in the epoch of the proletarian revolution was delivered at the July 23 session of the Second World Congress. Trotsky made his speech on July 26, 1920.
2. Paul Levi—at one time a co-thinker of Rosa Luxemburg. After the latter's assassination and after the murder of Jogiches (Tyshko), the chief organizer of the party, Levi became head of the Communist Party of Germany. In the autumn of 1920 Levi began to gravitate toward centrism. After the March action of 1921 Levi was expelled from the party. In 1929 he committed suicide by jumping out of a window.
3. Pestaña—leader of the Spanish syndicalists and delegate to the Second World Congress of the Communist International.
4. Serrati—an old leader of the Italian Socialist Party. For a long time Serrati was editor of the party's central organ *Avanti*. At the Livorno Congress of 1920 Serrati supported the reformists, thus being one of those who bear the responsibility for the defeat of the Italian workers in the autumn of 1920. In the middle of 1922 Serrati began moving to the left. He attended the Fourth Congress of the Comintern as a partisan of the fusion with the Italian Communist Party.
5. Syria, which had been a French protectorate, became in effect a French colony after the Versailles Treaty.
6. Monroe Doctrine—proclaimed December 2, 1823, by President Monroe; recognized foreign sovereignty only in

those American colonies securely held by European powers, pledged support of the United States to all colonies fighting for independence, and banned future American colonization by any European power. Several Spanish-American colonies were in revolt. Russia, coveting territory in the northwest, proposed joint European action against the uprisings. But England, having established a lucrative trade in the Spanish colonies after Madrid's monopoly was broken, refused aid to Spain and suggested Anglo-American cooperation in the controversy. Thus, backed by the British fleet, the then relatively weak United States could proclaim and enforce the Monroe Doctrine. By 1895, the United States had grown so powerful that President Cleveland, under threat of war, could force England to arbitrate a boundary dispute between British Guiana and Venezuela. Yankee imperialism had become supreme in the Western Hemisphere.

7. The reference here is to Czechoslovakia.

8. Denikin—a prominent Czarist general who became one of the leaders of the counter-revolution during the years of the Civil War. In the autumn of 1919 Denikin's troops almost reached Tula. After the annihilation of the Whites Denikin departed for Europe to write his memoirs.

9. Wrangel came to the fore during the Russian Civil War. After Denikin's defeat, Wrangel—as a "more liberal" general—was elected by the Whites to the post of Commander-in-chief. For almost a year Wrangel succeeded in remaining in Crimea. It was only in the autumn of 1920 that the heroic offensive of the Red Army liquidated Wrangel's rule in Crimea and he was compelled to flee with the remnants of his army to Turkey and the Balkans.

10. Soviet Hungary was proclaimed March 21, 1919, when the bourgeois government of Karolyi voluntarily ceded power to the Soviets. On August 1, 1919, this workers' government was overthrown by the intervention of the White Armies of the Little Entente. The power of the Soviets was replaced by the savage dictatorship of Admiral Horthy which maintained itself throughout the period between the two world wars.

11. In order to smash Turkey and establish her undisputed dominion over the Near East, the English imperialists embroiled their vassal state, Greece, in a war with Turkey. The struggle lasted from 1921 to the autumn of 1922. Supported by Soviet Russia and by France, who feared the complete entrenchment of English rule in Asia Minor, Turkey in the end succeeded completely in defeating the Greek army.
12. Samuel Gompers—ultra-conservative leader of the AFL bureaucracy who considered even the yellow Amsterdam Trade Union International as too "red." Gompers was the bitterest enemy of the revolutionary movement, and invariably aided the government and the employers in fighting against it.
13. Turgot—French nobleman, financier and minister of Louis XVI. He tried to resolve the contradiction between the reign of absolute monarchy and the needs of capitalist development by making some concessions to the bourgeoisie. The French autocracy in this epoch was hopelessly in debt.
14. Cadet Party, Cadets—the party of the Russian bourgeoisie, Constitutional Democrats. The term "Cadets" comes from the Russian letters in this party's name.
15. "Unionists"—an English political grouping, headed by Churchill and others, whose chief plank was the unification of the Tories and Liberals.
16. Giolitti—hoary leader of the Italian bourgeoisie who specialized in using reformists to avert the revolution following the First World War. He served as premier several times. After Mussolini's assumption of power, he passed into "opposition." Giolitti died before the Italian bourgeoisie could utilize him again after Mussolini's downfall, as it has one of his colleagues, Bonomi.
17. Mazziniists—followers of Mazzini, the leader of the Italian national revolutionary movement of unification during the first part of the nineteenth century. Mazzini's movement was aimed primarily against reactionary Austria.
18. Rothschild, Weir & Co. was at the time one of the largest banking firms in England.

19. Schneider—French industrialist, owner of the largest munition plants and other enterprises.

    Loucheur—another big French capitalist who often served as Minister of Finance in various cabinets.

20. Hugo Stinnes—the uncrowned king of post-Versailles Germany. During that period he controlled a vast industrial empire and the entire economic life of the country. His name became synonymous with the tendency of a single group to dominate a country's industry ("Stinnezation").

    Felix Deutsch—large German industrialist.

21. Rizello and Agnelli—large Italian industrialists and bankers. They financed Mussolini and his Black Shirts.

22. Lord Curzon—English Tory who specialized in foreign policy. In the pre-1914 days he served as Viceroy of India; in the 'twenties as Minister of Foreign Affairs. In the latter post he distinguished himself, together with his colleague Churchill, as the avowed and rabid enemy of Soviet Russia.

23. *Le Temps* (Paris *Times*)—organ of the French bourgeoisie, class sister of the London *Times* and the New York *Times*.

24. Winston Churchill—the most class-conscious representative of the English bourgeoisie, mortal enemy of the world working class. Churchill early displayed the greatest facility and flexibility in politics. From 1900 to 1906 he belonged to the Tory party and ran on the Tory ticket for parliament; from 1906 to 1922 he functioned as a member of the Liberal Party, and then resumed the Tory label. He held many cabinet posts. In 1910–11 he distinguished himself as Minister of Internal Affairs by calling out troops against the strikers in Liverpool and elsewhere. Churchill was Curzon's predecessor in the Ministry of Foreign Affairs and one of the chief inspirers of imperialist intervention in Russia after the October Revolution. He greatly admired Mussolini and just as thoroughly abominated Trotsky. His role as premier in the second imperialist world slaughter is a fitting climax to his lifetime career as watchdog of British imperialism.

25. Machiavelli, famous politician, diplomat, historian and writer of the early sixteenth century. He is recognized as the founder of political science. Marx considered his *History of Florence* a masterpiece. Machiavelli was a progressive and original thinker in his time. Organizer of the first popular militia and author of a treatise on war, he is credited with being the "first military thinker of modern Europe." He advocated the unification of Italy. Machiavelli favored a republic, but the "ideal" regime in his days was the centralized absolute monarchy. In his books, *The Prince* and *The Discourses*, Machiavelli demonstrated that for the preservation of class rule, any and all means are employed and justified by the spokesmen of the ruling class. Ironically enough, his name has become associated with the use of demagogy, deceit and ruthlessness in politics and the methods he probed into—the methods now utilized by the imperialist politicians to preserve dying capitalism—are termed "Machiavellianism."

26. Kapp-Luettwitz putsch occurred in 1920 and was the first attempt of the German counter-revolution to liquidate the Weimar Republic and its "democracy" by armed force. Despite the passivity of the Ebert-Scheidemann government, this putsch was crushed by the elemental resistance of the workers. This putsch served to discredit both Scheidemann and Noske.

27. Yudenich—Czarist general who in 1920 organized with Allied aid an offensive against Petrograd. There was some doubt in the Bolshevik Central Committee at the time as to whether Petrograd could be defended. At the beginning Lenin and the majority of the Central Committee favored evacuating the city, but on the intervention of Trotsky, supported by Zinoviev, the decision was finally made to defend Petrograd at all costs. Trotsky personally directed the counterblow by which Yudenich's offensive was crushed. This defeat removed Yudenich from the political arena.

28. Delacrois was Prime Minister of Belgium in the period of the Second World Congress of the Communist International.

29. Henderson—one of the leaders of the Labor Party of England. Henderson was all his life essentially a bourgeois liberal. Even in the pre-1914 days Henderson participated in the bourgeois government. He advocated war to the end. In the 'twenties Henderson served as Minister of Foreign Affairs in the so-called "Labor government" under MacDonald.

30. Tom Shaw—an old participant in the English labor movement. Class-collaborator. After the fusion of the Second and 2½ Internationals he was the secretary of the Executive Committee. In the 'twenties he held a post in MacDonald's cabinet.

31. Renner was the main leader of the Austrian Social Democrats. A typical representative of the Austro-Marxist movement; past master in combining revolutionary phrasemongering with the practice of reformism. During the war of 1914–18 Renner was a social-patriot. After the Habsburg dynasty was overthrown, he became Prime Minister in the coalition government. When the revolutionary wave subsided Renner, together with his colleagues, was booted out of the government.

    Seitz—premier of the Austrian government and one of the leaders of the reactionary Christian Socialist Party of Austria.

32. Niemetz—leader of the Czech conciliationists who at the time held a centrist position.

33. Troelstra—an old opportunist, leader of the Social Democracy of Holland, who was instrumental in expelling revolutionary Marxists from the Dutch party even prior to the war of 1914–18. During the First World War Troelstra was a Germanophile. At the termination of the war, he became one of the most active rebuilders of the Second International.

    Branting—one of the founders of the Swedish Social Democracy. Throughout his career Branting was a Right Wing leader. After the First World War Branting advocated fervently the participation of the Socialists in the government and succeeded in gaining the post of Prime Minister.

34. Dasczinski—one of the leaders of the petty-bourgeois Polish Socialist Party (PPS). Prior to 1914 he also played a prominent role in the Austrian Social Democracy, especially as deputy from Austrian Poland in its parliamentary fraction. After the formation of "free" Poland Dasczinski became one of the supporters of the anti-Soviet policy of Pilsudski and Co.

    Chkheidze—Georgian Menshevik who became prominent in the political life of the labor movement in Czarist Russia as deputy to the Fourth State Duma. After the February Revolution of 1917 Chkheidze was chairman of the All-Russian Central Executive Committee of the Soviets.

35. Pilsudski early in his career and as a youth was persecuted by the Czarist government. Leader of the petty-bourgeois revolutionary party—the PPS. After the First World War, when Poland was set up by the Allies as an independent state, Pilsudski became head of the government through a *coup d'état*. As ruler of Poland Pilsudski served as the executive agent of French imperialism.

36. August Bebel (1840–1912)—one of the founders of the German Social Democracy. For almost half a century Bebel was the leader of the German party, and at the same time played a dominant role within the Second International. Toward the end of his life, Bebel began drifting to the right, aiming his attacks not so much against the revisionists as against the extreme Left Wing in the party led by Luxemburg, Liebknecht, Tyshko, Mehring and others.

37. Among the signatories to the Manifesto of the Second World Congress were:

    Gregory E. Zinoviev (Radomylski) born in 1883; joined the Bolsheviks as a youth immediately after the Second Party Congress in 1903. During the 1905 revolution was active in Petersburg and then migrated abroad. At the Fifth Party Congress (1907) he was elected member of the Central Committee. Served on the editorial board of the Bolshevik newspapers *Proletari* and *Social Democrat*. During the war of 1914–18 he was Lenin's closest collaborator;

participated in the Zimmerwald and Kienthal Conferences; member of the Bureau of the Zimmerwald Left; co-author with Lenin of the famous volume, *Against the Stream*. Returned to Russia after the February Revolution. In October 1917, together with Kamenev and abetted behind the scenes by Stalin, he opposed the seizure of power. Served as chairman of the Petrograd Soviet after the conquest of power. Chairman of the ECCI in Lenin's lifetime. After Lenin's death, he became one of the triumvirate *(troika):* Zinoviev, Kamenev, Stalin, that usurped power in the Bolshevik Party. Broke with Stalin in 1925. In November 1927 he was expelled from the party together with the Left Opposition (Trotskyists). Capitulated to Stalin in 1928 and was readmitted into the party. In 1932 he was again expelled, and again capitulated. In January 1935, after the assassination of S.M. Kirov, he was sentenced to 10 years in prison on trumped-up charges. Again framed up and finally murdered in August 1936 in the first of the monstrous Moscow Trials.

N.I. Bukharin, another member of the Old Guard of Bolshevism, writer and economist, was born in 1888. In 1906 he worked as propagandist, agitator and organizer in Moscow. In 1908 he served as a member of the Moscow Regional Committee and as chairman of the Bolshevik fraction in the Duma. In 1911, after his third arrest, he escaped abroad. During the war of 1914–18 held an internationalist position, being arrested in Sweden for anti-militarist propaganda. Came to America where he participated with Trotsky in editing the Russian newspaper *Novy Mir.* On returning to Russia, after the February Revolution, he served on the Moscow Party Committee, the District Bureau, and the editorial board of the newspaper *Social Democrat.* At the Sixth Party Congress in July 1917, he was elected to the Central Committee, remaining in this body until the 17th Party Congress when Stalin broke his coalition with the Right Wing and demoted him to a candidate to the Central Committee. After the October Revolution Bukharin was the editor of *Pravda.* In the days of the Brest-Litovsk controversy, he headed the

"Left Communists" and issued a factional organ called the *Communist*. From 1923 to 1927 he worked hand in hand with Stalin in the struggle against the Left Opposition. In 1928 Stalin broke his coalition with the Right Wing (Bukharin-Rykov and others). In April 1929, Bukharin was removed as editor of *Pravda*, and from his post as chairman of the Comintern (in which he had replaced Zinoviev). In November 1929 he was removed from the Political Bureau. Upon capitulating to Stalin he was assigned to "educational work" for several years, until 1933 when he was appointed editor of *Izvestia*. Framed up and murdered by Stalin in the last of the public Moscow Trials, March 1938.

Ernst Meyer—an old member of the Spartacus League and one of the leaders of the German CP. Served on the ECCI as delegate of Germany.

J. Walcher—one of the oldest participants in the German Communist movement who at one time played an important role in the Red Trade Union International. He became a member of the Right Wing (Brandlerites) in the German Party, and was expelled from the CI in 1929 when Stalin broke with Bukharin-Rykov in Russia. Later Walcher headed a centrist movement in Germany (SAP).

Paul Levi, see Note 2, Section III.

A. Rosmer, see Note 28, Section II.

J. Sadoul was a chauvinist during the war of 1914–18, became a fervent Communist during his stay in Soviet Russia where he served as a military attaché to the French embassy. Subsequently became a lackey of Stalin.

H. Guilbeaux—one of the pioneers of French Communism; member of the Zimmerwald Left during the war of 1914–18.

T. Quelch—one of the leaders of the British Socialist Party who came over to the CI.

W. Gallacher—a Scotch labor politician who in 1920 was one of the typical representatives of "Left Communism" in England. Later evolved into a brazen chauvinist in the service of the Kremlin.

Sylvia Pankhurst—a colleague of Gallacher.

John Reed—American journalist, author of the famous book *Ten Days That Shook the World*. At the end of 1920 he contracted typhus and died in Moscow.

D.M. Serrati, see Note 4, Section III.

N. Bombacci—prominent Italian Communist who played a major role in the split of the Italian SP at the Livorno Congress and the resulting formation of the Italian CP.

Graziadei—one of the founders of the Italian Communist Party.

A. Bordiga—founder of the Italian CP who headed the Communist opposition while still in the Italian SP (Turin section). After the formation of the Italian CP, he became its leader and thereby head of the "Left Communist" majority. Bordiga remained a sectarian after his expulsion from the CI on the charge of "Trotskyism."

Wynkoop—old Dutch Socialist who together with Gorter, Pannekoek and others headed the so-called "Left Communists."

Varga—Hungarian economist who used to report on economic questions at the plenums and congresses of the CI. In the days of the Hungarian Soviet Republic, he was chairman of its Supreme Economic Council. Since Lenin's death, spineless flunkey of the Kremlin.

J. Markhlevsky—veteran of the Polish labor movement. Founder with Luxemburg of the revolutionary Social Democracy of Poland; also worked for decades in the German labor movement. Head of the University of the Peoples of the East in Leninist Comintern.

Stuchka—leader of the Lettish CP. Also worked in the Russian labor movement.

J. Rakhia—old Finnish Socialist. An opportunist and careerist.

Kabakchiev—one of the theoreticians of the Bulgarian CP.

Sultan-Saade—Persian Communist who participated in the Russian labor movement.

M.N. Roy—Indian revolutionist who became a Brandlerite after Lenin's death, and who ended up in the camp of British imperialism.

Maring—one of the leaders of the CP of the Dutch East Indies. Sponsor of the "two-class" party for China, later embraced by Stalin with such fatal results for the Chinese revolution of 1925–27.

Section IV

1. KAPD—initials of the Communist Workers Party of Germany, which consisted of "Left Communists" who split from the German Communist Party in 1920 because of principled differences over participating in parliament, over work in the trade unions, and so on. This tendency was strongly tainted throughout its existence with anarcho-syndicalism. Beginning its political life with a membership of several tens of thousands, the KAPD lost its best elements within two or three years and became transformed into a sect, which remained hostile to the Comintern and to Soviet Russia.

2. Gorter—Dutch writer and poet who for decades remained on the left wing of the labor movement. During the First World War Gorter held an internationalist position. In the years after the defeat of the German revolution (1918–19) Gorter, like the majority of the leaders of the Dutch Communist Party, fell incurably ill of sectarianism.

3. The reference here is to the Dutch Communist Party.

4. The Enlighteners-Rationalists of the eighteenth century were the cultural and political battering-ram by means of which the French bourgeoisie was able to breach the bulwarks of absolute feudal monarchy. The majority of the Enlighteners were materialists in philosophy and science (Diderot, Helvetius and others) but in politics, social sciences and history, they held that the decisive factor was knowledge and reason. They deduced the character of the political institutions from the prevalent ideas. Proceeding from this the Enlighteners came to the conclusion that it sufficed merely to change the opinion of kings, and of great people in general, in order to create the necessary preconditions for fundamental social and political transformations and reforms. Plekhanov's essays on Diderot, Helvetius and other representatives of this school are among the

best philosophical writings in Marxism. In English, *Essays on the History of Materialism.*

5. Hilferding—one of the outstanding representatives of the notorious Austro-Marxist school. In 1907, published his famous book *Finance Capital.* Throughout the First World War Hilferding was one of the leaders of the "moderate opposition" à la Kautsky. In 1918–20 Hilferding flirted with the idea of Soviets and elaborated political programs in which he fantastically combined parliamentarianism and the dictatorship of the proletariat. When the German "Independents" split at Halle, Hilferding headed the Right Wing of the Independents, and from then on proceeded to evolve in the direction of Scheidemannism. In 1923 Hilferding who had previously condemned the participation of Social Democrats in bourgeois governments entered the Streseman cabinet. He died in obscurity.

6. The United German Communist Party was the name assumed by the German Communist movement in 1920–21 after the merger with the Left Wing of the Independent Social Democratic Party.

7. The General Confederation of Labor (CGT) is the name of the largest trade union organization in France. In 1921 revolutionary elements actually had the majority in the French labor movement and in the CGT in particular. However, the movement was never won to the banner of Communism and therefore soon slipped back into the hands of Jouhaux and Co., where it remained up to the outbreak of the Second World War.

8. The Charter of Amiens was the programmatic resolution adopted by the French trade unions at their 1906 convention in the city of Amiens. The central point in this resolution was the affirmation of the independence of the labor movement (the trade union movement) and its non-political character.

9. Cachin—an old participant in the French labor movement. In the years before the First World War he was one of Guesde's closest collaborators. During the war of 1914–18 Cachin, like his teacher, became a jingoist. By 1919, owing to mass pressure, Cachin had already become one

of the Left Wing leaders of the French Socialist Party, out of which the French Communist Party later emerged. Despite the fact that in 1921-22 Cachin was a co-thinker of Frossard (see next note) he remained at his post when the latter deserted, thus saving for the party the central organ *l'Humanité*. This was one of the few acts of Communist loyalty on Cachin's part. Thereafter he became true to himself, or rather reverted back to his real nature. With the ascendency of Stalinism, he found himself in his native element, *i.e.,* among the case-hardened betrayers of labor.

10. Frossard came to the fore after the split with the followers of Longuet in 1919. In 1920-22 Frossard was the chief leader of the French Communist Party. Educated in the traditions of French parliamentary socialism, Frossard could never surmount this early training. During his brief stay in the French Communist Party he invariably supported centrist tendencies and after the Fourth Congress of the Communist International, when the latter turned the helm of the French Communist Party sharply to the left, Frossard together with a group of his co-thinkers left the party, and gravitated back to the Second International. He again joined hands with the Stalinists and with his former colleague Cachin when the People's Front policy was put through by the Kremlin in 1935-36.

11. Gallifet—French marquis and general who distinguished himself by his savagery in the suppression of the Paris Commune of 1871. Thousands of Communards were shot and tortured to death by his orders. In 1899-1900 the "Socialist" Millerand served in the same cabinet with Gallifet.

12. Prior to the First World War Caillaux was the Minister of Finance in the French government. He was one of the leaders of the French bourgeois Radical Party.

13. This letter was originally addressed to Lucie Leiciague—at that time member of the Central Committee of the French Communist Party and the representative of the French CP in the ECCI in 1922.

14. *Dissidents*—the name given to the followers of Longuet who, finding themselves in the minority at the Tours

Congress in 1919, split from the French party to form a party of their own.

15. Léon Blum—a prominent figure in the French Socialist Party. Blum was a wealthy man, a "boulevardier" who went into labor politics. Champion of the Left Bloc—and later of its Stalinist version, the People's Front, under which he became premier—and of participation in the bourgeois government. A typical French reformist-traitor.

16. Méric—a former anarchist. During the First World War he held an internationalist position inside the French Socialist Party. In 1919 took active part in the split at the Tours Congress. In 1920–23 he traveled the same road as Frossard and found himself shortly outside the ranks of the Communist movement.

17. H-P. Gassier—a very witty cartoonist who worked for a long time on *l'Humanité*, central organ of the French Communist movement.

Section V

1. Amsterdam—an abbreviation for the Amsterdam International Trade Union Federation also known as the Yellow Trade Union International.

2. Otto Bauer—the most prominent leader of the Austrian Social-Democratic Party. Prior to the war of 1914–18 Bauer was the secretary of the parliamentary fraction of the Austrian party. Author of a number of anti-Marxist books on the national and colonial questions. During the First World War Bauer held a centrist position which did not hinder him from becoming Minister of Foreign Affairs in the coalition government set up after the overthrow of the Habsburgs. Together with Friedrich Adler and others, Bauer participated both in creating the 2½ International and in burying the latter in 1923 through a fusion with the Second International.

3. Richard Calwer—at one time an eminent German economist. One of a legion of former German Social Democrats

who successfully underwent an evolution from Social Democracy to bourgeois democracy.

4. Alsace-Lorraine and the Saar basin were assigned to France by the Versailles Treaty. The Saar basin is one of the richest coal areas in Europe.

5. Albert Einstein—famous German physicist and mathematician. Einstein created a new epoch in science by supplying scientific grounds for the denial of the absolute character of time and space—a doctrine which had been advanced by Newton and which had been accepted for more than a century as one of the immutable laws of nature. Furthermore, Einstein has greatly advanced the natural sciences by supplying mathematical formulations to various processes in nature. In philosophy a materialist; in politics a pacifist.

6. Hughes—U.S. Minister of Foreign Affairs under the Harding administration. In the middle 'twenties he was violently opposed to the resumption of normal relations with Soviet Russia.

7. The reference here is to Engels' introduction to Marx's book *The Civil War in France*. In this introduction Engels wrote that the world crisis of 1847 was the real mother of the February revolution in France and of the March revolution in Germany.

8. Cunow—the theoretician of the Scheidemann school. Before the First World War Cunow considered himself an orthodox Marxist and fought consistently against theoretical revisionism. The war converted him into a social-imperialist. After perpetrating this treachery Cunow then proceeded to revise the theory of Marx.

9. Keynes—a prominent English economist. After the war of 1914–18 he became a member of the Allied Supreme Economic Council. In a number of books Keynes demonstrated effectively the economic senselessness of the Versailles Treaty. In 1919 he predicted that the Versailles clauses could not possibly be fulfilled. The reference here is to his first book *The Economic Consequences of Peace*. To-

day Keynes is among those who are now preparing a worse Versailles for Europe and the world.

10. Brand—a prominent Polish Communist, one of the delegates from Poland to the Third Congress.

11. This favorite quotation of Napoleon is taken from Voltaire's letter to a friend (1770): "It is said that God is always to be found on the side of the heaviest battalions."

12. Seemann—member of the KAPD (See Note 1, Section IV), whose delegation was seated with consultative votes at the Third Congress.

13. Sachs—another KAPD delegate.

14. Pogany—one of the leaders of the Hungarian Communist Party. At the Third Congress together with other Hungarian delegates, Pogany was among the "Lefts." Later with the Right Wing. Adventurer and careerist. Trotsky characterized him as "the consummate type of man who knows how to adapt himself, a political parasite." Representative of CI in USA where he used the name "Pepper." (See Note 1.)

15. Thalheimer—one of the closest collaborators of Rosa Luxemburg in the Spartacus League. After the formation of the German Communist Party Thalheimer became one of its leaders and the editor of the party's central organ *Rote Fahne*. In the early 'twenties Thalheimer with Brandler became one of the leaders of the Right Wing of the Communist Party—whose counterpart in America was the Lovestone group. The Brandlerites were expelled from the CI in 1929 and survived for a while as a centrist movement headed for the camp of the bourgeoisie (where they finally landed).

16. Koenen—one of the leaders of the German Communist Party; delegate to the Third Congress.

17. The reference here is to the coup in May 1921 through which the Far Eastern republican government in Vladivostok was replaced by a White Guard government. The coup was engineered with the support of the Japanese troops.

18. "The Triple Alliance" or the "Big Three" refers to the bloc formed in England by the three biggest unions—the transport workers, the railroad workers and the miners.

19. The Italian question was a special point on the agenda of the Third World Congress. The majority of the old Italian Socialist Party refused at the 1920 Livorno Congress to accept the "21 conditions." As a consequence, a split occurred. But inasmuch as the Italian Socialist Party still declared that it had no differences with the CI on all principled questions, and sent three delegates to the Third World Congress (Lazzari, Maffi and Riboldi), the ECCI voted to seat them in the Congress. This was done in order to help educate 100,000 workers who remained in the Italian Socialist Party and who were anxious to be members of the world Communist movement. Seating these three delegates exposed the Italian Centrists who had split with the Communists for the sake of unity with the reformists under the cover of the argument that the Communists were dictatorial.

20. The reference here is to the Italian Socialist Party and its central organ, *Avanti*. In the 'twenties *Avanti* temporarily passed into the hands of the trade union movement of Italy. It was suppressed by Mussolini. Since the latter's downfall, it has reappeared in Rome edited by Pietro Nenni and other Italian Socialists.

21. Lazzari—veteran of the Italian labor movement, one of the founders of the Italian Socialist Party. In the pre-1914 days and during the First World War Lazzari remained with the Left Wing of the Socialist Party but when the split occurred at the Livorno Congress he remained with Serrati. After the Third World Congress Lazzari loyally fulfilled the promises he had made to agitate for the fusion of the Italian Socialist Party with the Communist Party.

22. Karl Radek—one of the leaders of the Communist International in Lenin's day. In 1910 Radek began active work in the ranks of the German revolutionary opposition. In the years of the First World War Radek joined the Zimmerwald Left from the outset. After the death of Luxemburg and Liebknecht, Radek became the leading politician of the German Communist Party. In the 'twenties Radek worked in the Communist International as a member of the presidium of the ECCI. After Lenin's death Radek belonged

for a number of years to the Left Opposition. But in 1929 he capitulated to Stalin, serving the latter zealously until January 1937 when he was framed up in the second Moscow Trial and sentenced to jail. His final fate remains a secret of the Kremlin.

23. Thaelmann—a Hamburg worker who became prominent in the German labor movement in the 'twenties. For a number of years Thaelmann headed the Left Wing within the German Communist Party, only to swing over in later years to the extreme Right Wing, *i.e.*, to Stalinism. He unquestioningly and docilely carried through the Kremlin's fatal policy in Germany from 1929 to 1933 when the Stalinists kept the ranks of the working class divided and thus permitted Hitler to come to power without even a battle. Thaelmann was caught by the Nazis as he was about to leave the country and was imprisoned. His subsequent fate is unknown. The rumor is that he was executed with others by the Nazis.

24. Heckert—a prominent German Communist who participated in a number of the Congresses of the Red Trade Union International and of the Comintern. Like the other German leaders he obediently accepted Stalin's orders, remaining prominent in the German party and in the Stalinized Comintern. During the purges after the Moscow frameups, it was reported that he together with other foreign Communists had been executed by the GPU.

25. Franz Mehring—great Marxist publicist, famous historian of the German Social Democracy. Coming into the labor movement from the camp of bourgeois democracy, Mehring remained for decades in the Left Wing of the Socialist movement. At the very beginning of the differences with Kautsky, Mehring openly joined the opposition. During the First World War despite his old age he worked actively as a publicist in the Spartacus League. The tempestuous days of the German revolution, imprisonment and the death of his closest friends—Luxemburg and others—drained Mehring's failing health. He died in 1919 after spending approximately 40 years at his revolutionary post.

26. Christian Rakovsky—old revolutionist, participant in the labor movement of a number of countries and especially prominent in the pre-1914 days in the Balkans. Like Mehring, Rakovsky was a member of the bourgeoisie who broke with his class, sacrificed his fortune and devoted his entire life to the labor movement. After the October Revolution, Rakovsky was chairman of the Council of People's Commissars of the Ukraine and performed there great and important work in consolidating the Soviet power. Rakovsky later served the Soviet Republic as ambassador. One of the leaders of the Left Opposition who was finally broken after years of exile. He capitulated to Stalin only to be framed up like the rest of Lenin's closest co-workers during the infamous Moscow Trials.

    Yuri Pyatakov worked in the ranks of the Russian Bolshevik Party for approximately 40 years. During the First World War Pyatakov together with Bukharin conducted internationalist propaganda in the Scandinavian countries. During the first years of the Civil War Pyatakov worked in the Ukraine. In the middle 'twenties he served as Rykov's deputy in the Supreme Economic Council of the USSR. Member of the Left Opposition who capitulated with Radek, was framed and shot by Stalin.

    Larin—a veteran worker in the Russian Social Democracy. For a number of years he was a prominent Menshevik. After the July days in 1917 he joined the Bolsheviks. In the 'twenties he worked chiefly as an economist. Toward the end of 1921 he headed the movement of the so-called "Communist reaction," who demanded a return to the methods of War Communism. This former Menshevik who became so radical in Lenin's lifetime joined without hesitation in the hunt against Trotskyism. Died in 1932.

27. Gregory Sokolnikov—an old Bolshevik who in the 'twenties served as People's Commissar of Finance. Although never a member of the Left Opposition he was framed up with the others in the second Moscow Trial (January 1937).

    A.G. Shlyapnikov—an old Bolshevik who was especially active in the illegal organization in Russia during the First World War. One of the heroes of the Civil War. In 1921–23

Shlyapnikov headed the so-called "Workers' Opposition" and later the group of "22" who were very sharp in their criticism of the New Economic Policy. He was jailed by Stalin. His fate is unknown.

28. A. Kollontai—prior to the First World War she was a Menshevik. In 1917 she joined the Bolshevik Party and in the days of Kerensky became prominent as a popular agitator. In 1921–23 Kollontai became extremely radical, heading together with Shlyapnikov in the days of the Tenth Party Congress the so-called "Workers' Opposition," an obvious deviation toward syndicalism. In the 'twenties Kollontai became ambassador to Norway and has served in various ambassadorial posts since then. Her former leftism was later supplemented by subservience to Stalinism in the declining years of her life.

29. Bela Kun—leader of the Hungarian Communist Party. In the days of the Hungarian Soviet Republic, Bela Kun was chairman of the Council of People's Commissars. Ultra-leftist at the Third Congress. Later a rabid anti-Trotskyist. Reported among those shot by the GPU during the monstrous purge in the USSR. Also reported still alive.

Section VI

1. Herzen—a revolutionary democrat in the middle of the nineteenth century, founder of Russian *Narodnikism* (Populism). In the reign of Czar Nicholas I, Herzen was compelled to migrate to Europe (London) where he issued the famous revolutionary magazine *Kolokol*.

2. Polano—leader of the Italian YCL; member of the Executive Committee of the Youth Communist International. Polano and Tranquilli represented the youth at the Third Congress.

3. Treves—an Italian reformist who played an important role in the split of the Italian Socialist Party. Colleague of Turati.

4. Maffi—prominent Italian Socialist, delegate of the Italian Socialist Party to the Third World Congress. After that Con-

gress, Maffi returned to Italy and advocated unconditional acceptance of the CI's decisions.

5. Schueller—one of the leaders of the German YCL who worked in that period in the Executive Committee of the Communist Youth International as its secretary.
6. Riboldi—leader of the Left Wing of the Italian Socialist Party who was one of its three delegates to the Third World Congress. Like Maffi, Riboldi became a staunch advocate of entry into the Communist International.
7. Smeral—leader of the Czechoslovak Communist Party. An old participant in the labor movement. Congenital Right Winger. Under the pressure of the Czech workers, Smeral joined the Communist Party together with the Left Wing of the Czech Social Democracy. Smeral even in Lenin's day (1920–23) did not hesitate to avow his opportunist tendencies. He received full scope for his proclivities when Stalin usurped power.
8. Laporte—leader of the French YCL who criticized the policies of the Comintern from the "left" in that period. Laporte like most of the youth leaders at the time suffered from the disease of leftism.

Index

Acharia, 199
Adventurism, 333, 427, 434–35
Afghanistan, 159
Africa, 44, 149, 289, 348
"Against Imperialist Peace—For Revolutionary Russia!" (Jean Longuet), 119
Agnelli, 175, 486
Agriculture, 187, 270–71, 276, 278–79, 285, 312, 351, 354, 360–62, 364
   decline of, 270–71, 278, 285, 312, 351, 354, 361–62, 364
   European, 187, 270–71, 278, 285, 312, 351, 354, 360–62, 364
   French, 278, 354
   German, 187, 276
Albert (Hugo Eberlein), 33, 51, 63–64, 67, 468
Algiers, 43, 464
Allen, R., 199
Allies, 33, 42, 149, 163–64, 292–93, 358–59, 372, 441
   blockade Soviet Russia, 33, 149, 165, 292–93, 359, 441
   imperialist oppression, 42
   standard of living, 372
   See also Entente
Alsace-Lorraine, 120, 123–24, 278, 479, 497
American Communist Party. *See* Communist Party of the United States

American Federation of Labor, 169
Amsterdam International Trade Union Federation, 49, 255, 265, 343, 368–69, 496
Anarchism, 87, 102, 140–41, 153, 236–37, 244–45, 247, 394, 403
   anti-parliamentarian, 247
   errors, 140–42, 247
   French, 87, 102, 153, 236–37, 244–45, 247, 394, 403
   theories, 140–41, 247
Anarcho-syndicalists, 244–45
   French, 244–45
Angell, Norman, 326
Anglo-American rivalry, 160–61, 164, 316–19, 336, 339, 342, 365–67
Annam, 43, 464
Arabs, 43, 125–26
   self-determination, 125–26
   war role, 43, 125
Argentina, 362
   small farmers ruined, 361–62
Armenia, 43, 162–63, 198, 464
   war role, 163
Asia, 43–44, 149, 289, 318, 348
   coal, 289
   U.S.-Japanese rivalry in, 318

505

Asia Minor, 163
Australia, 89, 149, 312, 357, 362
  capitalism, 89, 357
  crises, 357
  decline of farmers, 312, 361–62
  immigration, 362–63
  wartime development, 357
Austria, 33, 47, 79, 82, 162, 198, 229, 284, 369
  currency stabilization, 369
  economic decline, 284–85, 369
  proletarian revolution, 47, 79, 229
Austria-Hungary, 42, 47, 88, 157, 163, 260, 272, 300, 347, 358, 464
  broken up, 42, 315, 358
  foreign trade, 300
  monarchy falls, 347
  national wealth, 272
  revolution, 47, 260
Avanti (Forward), 379, 381, 433, 499

Babeuf, 49, 466
Baden, 44, 465
Baku, 39, 166
  oil, 39, 166
  seized by England, 166
Balkan Federation, 33
Balkans, 95, 161–63, 272, 284, 300, 315, 369
  currency stabilization, 369
  foreign trade, 300
  national wealth, 272
  ruined, 161–62, 284
Balkan war, 95

Barcelona, 180
Barthou, 123, 243, 480
Basle Congress, 36, 462–63
Bauer, Otto, 266, 496
Bavaria, 44, 61, 81–84, 395, 465
  proletarian revolution, 81–84
  Soviets established, 61, 83–84
Bavarian Soviet Republic, 61, 83–84
Bebel, August, 192, 489
Belgian Social Democracy, 122–23, 342–44
Belgium, 88, 158, 163, 198, 281, 284, 354
  economy, 281, 284, 354
  war role, 158, 163
Bengal, 43, 464
Berlin, 72, 230
Berne Conference, 33
Bernstein, 38, 67–68, 121–22, 409, 463, 472
Bernsteinism, 409
Bible, 250
Bidégarrey, 112
Black Friday, 307
Black Reichswehr, 13
Bloody Sunday, 74
Blum, Léon, 249, 496
Bohemia (Czechoslovakia), 162, 484
Bolshevism, 25–28, 174, 262, 407
  feared by bourgeoisie, 174, 262–63
  struggle against *Narodnikism*, 25–26
Bombacci, N., 198, 492
Bombay, 43
Boncour, Paul, 138, 249, 483

Booms, 259, 293–329, 335–41,
  349–55, 360–61, 376
  analyzed, 259, 293–98, 302–
    11, 328–29, 337, 375–76
  European, 299, 303–4, 311–
    12, 360–61
  German, 297–98, 354–55
  postwar, 293–98, 302–3,
    328–29, 350–52, 354–55,
    376
  prewar, 349–50
  relation to revolution, 303–
    12, 328–29, 335–41, 377
  Russian, 307–8
  United States, 297–301,
    324–25
Borderes, 108
Bordiga, A., 198, 492
Bourgeois democracy, 33,
    44–46, 66, 90, 116–17,
    139–40, 173–81, 190–98,
    213–14, 216–17, 326
  collapse of, 44–46, 173–81,
    190–98, 326
  English, 117
  French, 90, 116
  See also Parliamentarianism
Bourgeoisie, 10, 16, 19–22,
    28–29, 82–87, 90, 92–93,
    96–97, 115–16, 136, 139–
    40, 157, 168–81, 190, 194–
    95, 197–98, 218–19, 241,
    262–66, 278, 298–99, 306,
    313–14, 320–22, 325, 334–
    38, 343–44, 348–52, 355,
    361–63, 367–70, 373–75,
    383–84, 423–26, 430–33,
    444, 447
  American, 19
  anti-Soviet, 367

Bourgeoisie *(continued)*
  cartelized, 314
  colonial, 325–26, 363
  composition, 176–77
  corruption, 168–69, 175–79
  counter-offensive, 320–22,
    325–26, 336, 348
  Danish, 19
  English, 19, 37, 85–86, 97
  European, 10, 19, 262–66,
    344
  fails at economic
    restoration, 425–26
  fears revolution, 177–79,
    262–63, 320–21, 348,
    350–52
  French, 20–21, 85–87, 96–97,
    115–16, 135–36, 170–71,
    177–80, 278–79, 335
  gains appeasement, 262–66
  German, 16, 19, 28–29, 82,
    87–88, 218–19, 241, 335,
    426
  imperialist, 444
  Indian, 363
  Italian, 263, 335
  legality under, 383–84
  maintains equilibrium,
    334–35, 447
  middle, 313–14
  neutral countries, 355
  objectives, 173, 430
  parasitic and anti-social,
    423–24, 431–32
  petty, 25–27, 44, 82, 90, 92–
    93, 242, 313–14, 360–61
  postpones postwar crisis,
    298–99, 321–22, 337–38
  postwar victory, 373
  regains confidence, 178,
    262–66, 299, 348, 350–52

Bourgeoisie *(continued)*
  relies on peasantry, 172
  resorts to threats and force, 178–80, 190
  restores political and social equilibrium, 425, 431
  restores state apparatus, 363–73, 447
  rural, 361
  Russian, 96–97, 173
  survives postwar ferment, 10, 447
  tactics, 19–20, 85–87, 92–93, 173–75, 262–66, 298–99, 321–22, 325–26, 337–38, 367–68, 375–76, 425–26, 430
  United States, 19, 174–75
  urban, 361
  wage-cutting, 306, 321
  world, 367–68
  See also Capitalism; Economic equilibrium; Social equilibrium
Bourse, 123, 126
Boycotts, 186
Branting, 191, 488
Brest-Litovsk Treaty, 10, 51, 67, 126, 156, 344, 469
Briand, 123, 243, 480
Briand-Barthou Act, 243
British Labor Party, 22, 29, 149, 190–93
  entry of Communists into, 149
  routinism of leaders, 192–93
  victory, 22
Bukharin, N.I., 33–34, 149, 198, 255, 403, 407, 409, 490–91

Bulgaria, 180, 198
Bullitt, 126–27, 481
Bureau of the Communist International, 33
Bureaucracy, 17, 189, 213–14, 322–23, 340, 370–71, 424–25
  party, 323
  trade union, 17, 189, 213–14, 322–23, 424–25

Cachin, 241–42, 494–95
Cadet Party, 173, 485
Caillaux, 242, 495
Calwer, Richard, 276–77, 496–97
Campbell-Bannerman, 125, 481
Canada, 312, 357, 362
  crises, 357
  decline of farmers, 312, 362
  wartime development, 357
Cannan, Edwin, 298–99
"Can the Revolution Be Made on Schedule?" (Leon Trotsky), 12
Cape Colony, 159
Capital, 39–40, 96–97, 176, 272–73, 298–99, 311, 313–14, 335, 351, 360, 363, 477
  accumulation of, 334
  cartel, 314
  concentration of, 176, 311, 360, 362
  fictitious, 273–74, 298–99, 351–52
  finance, 39–40, 96–97, 477
  productive, 351
Capitalism, 16, 44–45, 81–82, 84–97, 113–15, 124,

Capitalism *(continued)*, 159–60, 165–71, 179–80, 184, 203, 208–9, 228–32, 259–329, 334–40, 344–45, 348–58, 362–72, 375–76, 395, 409–14, 416–17, 425, 476–77
American, 411
automatic disintegration, 339
booms, 259, 293–329, 335–41, 349–50, 376
Chinese, 289, 308, 344–45, 363
contradictions, 272–74, 351
crises, 170–72, 259, 274–75, 290–328, 336, 338–40, 350–58, 363–64, 372, 376, 394–95, 425
cyclical character, 294–95, 299, 303–5, 353
division of labor under, 267–85, 289, 357
English, 81, 84–86, 88–89, 91, 93, 97–98, 207–8, 232, 281–84, 295–98, 302, 364–67
Entente, 340
European, 361–62, 369–70, 410–11
evolution of, 88–91
finance, 45, 96, 208, 477
French, 86–87, 96–97, 124–25, 477
German, 302, 354–55, 364–66
Indian, 344–45, 357, 363
international character, 163–64, 266–68, 314–15
Japanese, 159, 289–90, 325, 344
main curve, 295–96, 301–5, 328, 349–53, 375–76

Capitalism *(continued)*
preserves rule, 232, 348–49
pre-war rise, 349
proletarianizes masses, 184–85
Russian, 88–91, 96–97, 208–9, 260, 410–12, 476–77
United States, 114–15, 355–57, 362–63, 365, 411
wartime degeneration, 165–68
Capitalist equilibrium, 16, 94–95, 203, 228–29, 259–329, 334–35, 339, 353, 356, 368, 373–76, 410–11, 416
analyzed, 259–329
disrupted, 94–95, 259–64, 267–69, 334–35, 356, 373
resistive power, 259–60
restoration of, 203, 228–29, 339–40, 353, 368, 376, 410–11, 416
Carron, 108
Cartels, 314, 349
Cattle, 270–71, 278–79, 287, 354, 361
European, 271, 361
French, 278
German, 354
United States, 287
Central America, 161
Central Empire, 42
Central Europe, 162–63, 165, 183, 273, 282, 297, 300, 305, 342, 361, 364, 366, 372
proletariat, 372
Centrism, 48–49, 237–38, 381–82, 402, 405, 427, 433, 442–46, 465–66

Centrism *(continued)*
  French, 237–38
  Italian, 381, 402, 433
  struggle against, 442–46
CGT. *See* General
  Confederation of Labor
Chablin, 198
Charter of Amiens, 235–36, 494
Chavenon, Léon, 281, 305
Cheka, 326
Chernov, 64, 471
Chicherin, 34
China, 199, 289, 308, 325, 344–45, 357, 363, 366
  bourgeoisie, 363
  capitalism, 289, 308, 344–45, 363
  crises, 357
  peasantry, 345
  proletariat, 325, 345, 363
  U.S.-Japanese rivalry in, 366
  wartime development, 289, 308, 357
Chkheidze, 191, 489
"Christianity and Socialism," 249–50
Christian Socialism, 250
  French, 249–50
Churchill, 177, 486
City, 188, 463
Civil war, 47–48, 53, 71–76, 79, 95–96, 329, 369, 376, 438–39
  Austrian, 79
  Communist policy in, 47
  European, 79, 369
  German, 71–76, 79
  Hungarian, 79
  imposed on proletariat, 47

Civil war *(continued)*
  relation to capitalist culture, 95–96
  requirements for, 329
Civil War (Russia), 53–54, 61, 292–93, 359, 439, 441, 443–44
  effect on labor force, 292–93
Clarté, 143–44, 483
Class equilibrium. *See* Social equilibrium
Class struggle, 47, 71, 192–96, 311–14, 320–22, 339–40, 430–32
  in ancient Rome, 432
  bourgeois methods of, 430–31
  in feudal Poland, 432
  sharpens, 194–96, 320–22, 340
Clausewitz, Karl von, 52, 469–70
Clemenceau, 43, 102, 113, 115–16, 123–27, 176, 465
Clerical Party, 190
Coal, 39, 124–25, 166, 271, 278–79, 282–89, 293, 315–17, 354–56, 364–65, 497
  Asiatic, 289
  Donbas, 39
  Donetz, 166, 293
  English, 282–83, 288, 317, 354, 365
  European, 271, 285
  French, 278–79, 364
  German, 124, 279, 285, 315–16, 354, 364
  Russian, 39, 166, 293
  Saar, 124, 278, 364, 497
  United States, 286–88, 317, 356, 365

INDEX / 511

Colonial question, 22, 42–44, 97, 125–26, 138, 149, 158, 187–90, 207–10, 250–51, 325, 344–45, 363
  in England, 22, 42–43, 97, 125, 187–89, 207–8, 251, 344
  in France, 42–43, 125–26, 138, 250–51
Colonies, 42–44, 125–26, 164, 207–8, 289, 325, 344–45, 348, 357, 363
  bourgeoisie, 325, 363
  capitalist development, 344–45, 357, 363
  crises, 357
  industrialization, 289, 325, 344–45, 357, 363
  insurrections, 43, 164
  peasantry, 208, 325, 345, 363
  postwar struggles, 348
  proletariat, 325, 344–45, 363
  strikes, 43
  war role, 42–43, 125, 481
Comintern. *See* Communist International
Communism, 102–5, 107–8, 116–17, 121, 141–46, 181, 236–38, 255, 348, 407–17, 426–27, 432–49, 451–60
  creative force, 181–82
  feared by bourgeoisie, 348
  French, 102–5, 107–8, 116, 141–46, 236–38
  German, 121
  Left, 255, 407–17, 426–27, 432–49, 451–60
Communism, 427, 438

Communist International, 9–11, 20, 28, 33–34, 131–40, 149, 156, 194–98, 205, 227–28, 232, 245, 255, 257–58, 331–45, 367, 373–77, 385–87, 389–405, 427–49, 451–60
  compared with Second International, 373–74, 377
  educational role, 195
  entry conditions, 131–40, 149
  Executive Committee, 20, 28, 33, 134, 149, 205, 228, 245, 255, 399, 402, 452, 459–60
  greeted by Red Army, 257–58
  methods, 194–97
  organizational structure, 132, 255
  statutes, 34
  tactics, 10–15, 323–24, 331–45, 389–405, 429–60
  tasks, 193–97, 347, 372–77
  See also First to Fifth World Congresses
Communist International, 77–79, 225, 474
Communist Manifesto (Marx-Engels), 35, 151, 209, 216
Communist parties, 29, 149–56, 255, 322–24, 326–28, 338, 372, 376–77, 382–83, 427, 445–47, 483
  attitude toward bourgeois legality, 383
  internal crises, 426–27
  methods, 255
  organizational structure, 255

Communist parties *(continued)*
  postwar immaturity, 322–24
  role, 149–56, 483
  tactical errors, 426–27
  tasks, 328, 376, 445–47
Communist Party of the
  Soviet Union. *See* Russian
  Communist Party
Communist Party of the
  United States (Workers
  Party), 25–27, 194, 461–62
  supports Third Party, 25–27,
  461–62
Communist Women, 227
  Second World Conference,
  227
Communist Workers Party of
  Germany (KAPD), 205–25,
  255, 410, 436–37, 493
  policies, 205–25
  sectarian, 437
Communist Youth
  International, 421, 429–60
  Second Congress, 421,
  429–60
Conciliationism, 19–29, 49,
  102–4, 107–8, 139, 142,
  325, 377
  Danish, 19, 22
  English, 19–22, 29, 49
  European, 19–25, 28–29
  French, 19–23, 28–29, 49,
  102–4, 107–9, 139, 142
  German, 49
  Italian, 19–20
  Japanese, 19, 22
  relation to revolution, 19–21
  Russian, 49
  struggle against, 107–10
  United States, 19, 22, 25–28

Confederation of Labor. *See*
  General Confederation of
  Labor
Congo, 190
Congress of Paris, 48
Consortiums, 39, 349, 352,
  360
  wartime expansion, 360
Constituent Assembly, 53, 66,
  83, 470
Convention, 127, 481–82
Convention of Lyons
  (Syndicalist), 112, 115, 142
Cooperatives, 255
Cost of living, 170, 185, 350,
  372
Council of People's
  Commissars, 154–55
Counter-revolution, 116,
  162–63, 177–81, 190, 194,
  261, 303
  concept of, 194
  German, 261
  Hungarian, 162–63, 180
  relation to boom and crisis,
  303
  role of parliaments, 116
Craft unions, 185
Crises, 169–72, 259, 274–75,
  289–329, 336, 338–41, 349–
  55, 357–60, 363–64, 366,
  372–73, 376, 394–95, 425
  analyzed, 259, 289–329
  economic, 259, 351–53
  English, 297, 299, 306,
  353–54, 358, 395
  European, 291, 297–306,
  351–53, 357–61, 363–64
  French, 299, 301, 305, 353
  German, 300–301, 353, 395

Crises *(continued)*
 Indian, 357
 Italian, 299, 353
 Japanese, 289–90, 299, 353, 357, 366
 neutral countries, 353, 355
 Norwegian, 172
 political, 352
 postwar, 288–93, 296–329, 352–54, 424–26
 pre-war, 349, 351
 relation to revolution, 303–29, 334–37, 340–42
 Russian, 307
 United States, 171, 290–91, 324–25, 351–53, 356–58, 395
Cunow, Heinrich, 309, 407–10, 497
Currency. *See* Money
Curzon, Lord, 176, 486
Czechoslovak Communist Party, 402
Czechoslovakia (Bohemia), 42, 162, 198, 261, 348, 464, 484
 anti-soviet role, 162
 strikes, 261, 348
Czernin, 126, 481

Dahlstroem, K., 198
Dan, 82, 475
Dasczinski, 191, 489
Delacrois, 190, 487
Democracy, 33, 44–45, 66, 90–91, 117, 140, 173–81, 190–97, 214, 216, 326, 480
 bourgeois, 33, 44–45, 66, 90–91, 117, 140, 173–81, 190–97, 214, 216, 326, 480
 workers', 44

Democratic Party, 175
Demonstrations, 110, 328
 Communist participation in, 328
 French, 110
Denikin, 61, 163, 182, 443, 484
Denmark, 19, 22, 198
 bourgeoisie, 19
 conciliationism, 19, 22
Depression. *See* Crises
Deutsch, Felix, 175, 486
Dissidents (Socialists), 24, 248–49, 495–96
Donbas, 39
Donetz, 166, 293
Dresden, 72
Dumoulin, 111, 139, 237, 479
Dutch Communist Party, 205–25, 493
 sectarian, 205–25
Dutch East Indies, 199
Dzerzhinsky, 149

Eastern Europe, 297, 300, 361, 364
Eastern Prussia, 51, 55, 68
Eastern question, 255
Eastern Siberia, 164, 166
East Indies, 289
 wartime growth, 289
Eberlein, Hugo. *See* Albert
Ebert, 51, 55, 134–36, 176, 190, 224, 261, 276, 326, 414, 468–69
Economic equilibrium, 16, 28–29, 268, 305, 308–11, 321–22, 334–35, 339–40, 358, 430
 disrupted, 357–58

Economic equilibrium *(continued)*
  English, 322
  European, 28–29
  German, 16–17
  restoration of, 28, 305, 309–10, 321–22, 334–35, 339, 357–59, 430
  See also Capitalist equilibrium
Economics, 16–17, 39–40, 165–73
  basic character of, 16–17
  postwar, 39–40, 165–73
Economist, 290
Egypt, 159, 164, 187–88, 357
  crises, 357
  uprising, 187–88
  wartime development, 357
Einstein, Albert, 284, 497
Engels, Frederick, 35, 209, 303–4, 497
England, 19–22, 28–29, 33, 37–38, 43, 49, 68, 81, 84–86, 88–89, 91, 93, 97–99, 113, 117, 125, 149, 152, 156, 158–66, 173–80, 187–88, 192–93, 198, 203, 207–8, 212, 219, 223, 232, 251–52, 260–61, 270, 275, 281–84, 286–89, 291, 295–99, 302, 305–6, 315–19, 322, 324, 326, 336, 339, 342, 344, 347–48, 353–58, 362, 364–67, 372, 375, 395, 441, 449, 464–65, 485–86, 498
  bourgeois democracy, 116–17
  bourgeoisie, 19, 37, 84–86, 97
  bourgeois revolution, 86

England *(continued)*
  capitalism, 81, 84–86, 89, 91, 93, 97, 208, 232, 281–84, 295–97, 302, 364–67
  coal, 282–83, 288, 317, 354, 365
  colonial question, 22, 42–44, 97, 125–26, 187–89, 208, 251, 344
  conciliationism, 19–23, 28–29, 49
  conservatism, 223, 232
  Continental policy, 158, 315–17, 342, 364–66
  counterrevolutionary role, 177–79
  crises, 296–99, 305–6, 352–54, 357–58, 395
  decline in world status, 316–17, 324
  decline of, 281–84, 316–17
  economic equilibrium, 321–22
  economic position, 165–71, 270, 281–84, 287–89, 291, 295–98, 315–17, 324, 353–54, 364–65
  effects of February Revolution, 260
  foreign trade, 28–29, 203, 282–84, 286–89, 357–58, 365
  French alliance, 367
  general strike, 283
  housing, 274–75
  imperialism, 37–38, 42–43, 68, 156, 158–64, 166, 174, 187–88, 449, 464–65, 485
  Japanese alliance, 318, 365, 367

England *(continued)*
  labor government, 19–22, 173
  Labor Party, 22, 29, 149, 192–93
  labor productivity, 282, 316–17, 354
  living standard, 372–73
  military budget, 318–19
  money market, 288, 317
  national debt, 283
  national income, 282–83, 354
  navy, 160–61, 164, 318, 365
  parliamentarianism, 152, 176
  peasantry, 207–8
  prices, 298
  proletarian revolution, 22, 81, 84–85, 223–24, 441
  proletariat, 84–85, 97–98, 173, 207–8, 223–24, 375
  rivalry with United States, 160–61, 164, 316–19, 336, 339, 342, 365–67
  Russian intervention, 449
  seizes Baku, 166
  shipping, 287, 291
  social equilibrium, 344
  strikes, 188, 260–61, 283, 306, 326, 347–48, 354, 375
  trade unions, 113–14, 212–13, 375, 498
  unemployment, 395
  wages, 306
  war cost, 281–82
  war role, 37
English Communist Party, 193

Entente, 33, 36–38, 68, 97, 105, 157–58, 163, 165–67, 173–74, 318, 340, 449, 478
  capitalism, 340
  debts, 317–18
  hatred of Bolshevism, 174
  imperialism, 157–58
  intervenes in Russia, 97, 105, 157–58, 162, 165–67, 182–83, 449, 478
  postwar plans, 157–58, 167
  Supreme Economic Council, 173
  war guilt, 36–38
Essen, 72
Esthonia, 159, 162, 180, 182, 198
Étatism, 169
Europe, 9–25, 28–29, 35–44, 61, 66, 77–99, 149, 157–73, 183, 185–89, 208–9, 229, 241–42, 262–89, 291, 297–319, 324, 334–35, 337–39, 342–44, 349–74, 410–11, 437, 440, 444
  agriculture, 187, 270–71, 278–79, 285, 312–13, 351–52, 354, 360–61, 364
  Balkanized, 161–64, 315, 364
  booms, 297–98, 303–5, 311, 360
  bourgeoisie, 10, 19–20, 262–66, 344
  bourgeois tactics, 19–20, 87, 173–75, 298, 320–22, 325, 337–38
  capitalism, 360–62, 369–70, 410–11
  cattle, 270–71, 361

Europe *(continued)*
  Central, 162–63, 165, 183, 273, 282, 297, 300, 305, 342, 361, 364–66, 372
  civil war, 77–79, 369
  coal, 271, 285
  conciliationism, 19–25, 28–29
  crises, 291, 296–306, 350–53, 357–58, 360, 364
  currency, 272–73, 358, 369
  debts to United States, 288, 317–18
  Eastern, 297, 300, 361, 364
  economic decline, 28–29, 36–40, 165–73, 269–85, 299–303, 308, 311–12, 324, 334, 344, 349–54, 356–64, 369
  economic equilibrium, 28–29
  emigration, 362–63
  foreign trade, 267, 284–86, 291, 300–301, 321, 352–53, 358
  housing shortage, 274–75
  militarism, 318–19
  national income, 271–74, 284–85, 311, 360, 369
  national struggle, 161–62
  national wealth, 270–74, 311–12
  neutral countries, 353, 355
  "organization" of, 158–61
  peasantry, 208–9, 312–13, 360–61
  perspectives, 308–9
  population, 271
  proletarian revolution, 9–20, 41, 61, 66, 77–99, 369–70, 440–41, 444

Europe *(continued)*
  proletariat, 162–63, 183–85, 189–90, 209–10, 241–42, 344, 372–74
  role of France, 16, 342
  role of Germany, 354–55
  social equilibrium, 308–9, 324, 334–35, 344, 362, 368–70
  social gains lost, 38
  Southern, 297
  state debts, 273, 288, 298–99, 317–18, 321–22, 351–52
  strikes, 61, 369
  wages, 306
  Western, 9, 209, 229, 299, 305, 437
Executive Committee of the Communist International (ECCI), 20, 28, 33, 134, 149, 205, 228, 245, 255, 399, 402, 452, 459–60
  composition, 33
  elections to, 149, 255
  elects Bureau, 33

Far East coup, 367–68, 498
Farmer-Labor Party (Minnesota), 27
Farmer-Labor Party, 25–28, 461–62
Fascism, 12, 19–20, 264, 401
  German, 19–20
  Hungarian, 19–20
  Italian, 19–20, 264, 401
February Revolution, 71, 260, 471
Feudalism, 159, 325
  Japanese, 159, 325

Fictitious capital, 272–74,
 298–99, 351–52
 defined, 273–74
Fifth World Congress, 10–11
Finance capital, 39–40, 96–97,
 477
Finance capitalism, 45, 96–97,
 208
Finland, 159, 162, 180, 182,
 198
First International, 48–49, 77
First World Congress, 9, 31–58,
 227, 232, 405, 429, 437,
 442, 446–47
 agenda, 33
 evaluated, 429, 446–47
 Manifesto, 9, 35–50
 representation, 33
Flynn, 198
Foch, 124–25, 164, 167, 176,
 481
Foreign trade, 29, 203, 267,
 270–71, 276–89, 291, 300–
 301, 321, 349–50, 355–58,
 365, 367, 410–14, 441
 Balkan, 300
 disrupted by war, 280–83
 English, 28–29, 203, 281–84,
 286–89, 357–58, 365
 European, 267, 285, 291,
 300–301, 321, 349–50, 358
 French, 29, 279–80
 German, 28, 276–77, 285–86,
 300, 358
 Russian, 203, 270, 300, 358–
 59, 367, 410–14, 440–41
 United States, 285–89, 291,
 355–57, 365
Fourth World Congress, 11,
 20, 448

Fraina, A., 198
France, 16, 19–25, 28–29,
 33, 37, 43, 49, 61, 68,
 81, 86–87, 90, 93, 96–99,
 101–29, 135–46, 152–53,
 158–59, 161–80, 190, 192,
 198, 212, 218–19, 235–52,
 260–61, 263–64, 270, 274,
 276–81, 284, 288, 297–
 301, 305, 310, 315–16,
 335, 342, 347–48, 353–56,
 362, 364–67, 369, 386–87,
 393–94, 402–3, 441, 444,
 448, 477–79
 agriculture, 278–79, 354
 alliance with England, 367
 anarchism, 87, 102, 140–41,
 153, 236–37, 244–45, 247,
 394, 403
 anarcho-syndicalism, 244–45
 anti-clericalism, 174
 bourgeoisie, 20–21, 86–87,
 96, 115–16, 136, 170–71,
 177–80, 278, 335
 bourgeois revolution, 86–87
 budget, 280–81, 354
 capitalism, 86–88, 96–97,
 124, 477
 cattle, 278
 centrism, 237–38
 Christian Socialism, 249–50
 coal, 278–79, 364
 colonial question, 42–44,
 125–26, 138, 250–51
 conciliationism, 19–23,
 28–29, 49, 102–3, 107–9,
 139, 142
 Continental role, 16, 342
 counter-revolution, 180
 crises, 299–301, 305, 353

France *(continued)*
  currency, 280–81, 305, 310, 354, 369
  currency stabilization, 310, 369
  demonstrations, 110
  economics, 165–72
  financial leadership, 270
  foreign trade, 28–29, 279–80
  general strike, 261, 264
  housing, 274–75
  imperialism, 43, 68, 119–23, 138, 158–59, 161–62, 166, 190, 250–51, 448–49
  iron, 315–16, 364
  Left Bloc, 19–20, 28–29
  loots Germany, 279–81, 297, 310, 354, 368–69
  militarism, 354
  money market, 311–13
  National Bloc, 21, 61, 242–43
  national debt, 29, 281
  parliamentarianism, 101–7, 119–29, 140–41, 144, 152–53, 175–76
  peasantry, 242, 279, 354
  petty bourgeoisie, 90, 242
  "possibilism," 87
  postwar role, 158–59, 161–62
  postwar tension, 261
  prices, 280, 298
  proletarian revolution, 20–21, 81, 86–87, 92–93, 101–17, 241–45, 260–61, 347–48, 386–87, 441, 444
  proletariat, 86–87, 96–99, 102–4, 112–14, 174
  reformism, 247–48
  relief, 170
  ruined by war, 354

France *(continued)*
  Russian interests, 88–89
  sectarianism, 243–45
  Social Democracy, 23–25, 236
  social equilibrium, 315–16, 334–35
  Socialism, 110–12, 116, 127–28, 249–50, 393–94
  strikes, 104–5, 170, 178, 260–61, 264, 478
  syndicalism, 21, 102–16, 139, 140–45, 152–54, 192, 235–39, 243–45, 251–52, 394
  trade unions, 102–9, 112–14, 139, 144–45, 153–54, 178, 180, 211–13, 235–39, 244–45
  wages, 335
  war role, 37
Franco-Prussian War, 48–49, 465
French Communism, 102–8, 116, 142–46, 236–39
  tasks, 143–46
French Communist Party, 23–25, 145–46, 192, 237–39, 243–44, 247–52, 391, 399–405
  attitude toward church, 249–50
  centrist tendencies, 237–38
  electoral power, 23–25
  fusion with syndicalists, 237–39
  growth, 24–25
  press, 247–52
  trade union tasks, 244
French Revolution (1789), 86, 445

French Socialism, 111–12, 116–17, 127, 242, 393
French Socialist Party, 23–25, 49, 102–5, 110, 134–39, 191–92
  class-collaborationist, 140
  conciliationist, 49
  electoral power, 23–25
  unification, 102
French syndicalism, 21, 102–16, 139, 140–45, 152–54, 192, 235–39, 243–44, 251, 394
  anarchist theory, 140–45, 152–53
  Convention of Lyons, 112, 115, 142
  fusion with Communists, 237–39
  revolutionary, 235–39
Fries, J., 198
Frossard, 241, 249, 403, 495

Galicia, 198
Gallacher, W., 198, 491
Gallifet, 242, 495
Gassier, H-P., 252, 496
General Confederation of Labor (CGT), 104, 145, 180, 235–36, 494
  outlawed, 180
Georgia, 162, 180, 198
German Communism, 121
German Communist Party, 9–19, 63, 134, 203, 216, 221, 224–25, 241, 264, 386–87, 389–401, 439–41
  electoral successes, 14–19
  Left Wing, 11–12, 15, 398–402

German Communist Party *(continued)*
  March action, 9–10, 18–19, 203, 241, 263–64, 386, 390–400, 439–41
  1923 defeat, 11–16
  Right Wing, 11–12
German Communist Workers Party (KAPD), 205–25, 255, 410, 436–37, 493
  policies, 205–25
  sectarian, 436–37
German Independent Party. *See* Independent Socialist Party of Germany
German Independent Social Democracy. *See* Independent Socialist Party of Germany
German Social Democracy, 13, 17, 64, 66, 72–73, 88, 134–37, 152, 184, 189–90, 192, 342–44, 373–74, 395–96, 407–9, 472
  blocks revolution, 189–90
  split, 134–35
  votes war credits, 66, 472
German Socialism, 121
German Socialist Party, 342
Germany, 9–21, 28–29, 33, 36–38, 41–42, 47–48, 51–52, 61, 66–76, 79, 82–84, 87–88, 93–99, 117, 120–21, 124, 152–53, 156–58, 163–64, 166–67, 170–71, 174–79, 187, 192, 198, 203, 212, 215–19, 224–25, 229–31, 241, 260–64, 270–81, 284–86, 293, 297–302, 310–11, 315–16, 323–24,

Germany *(continued)*, 335,
340–43, 347–48, 353–56,
358–60, 364–67, 369, 374,
386–87, 390–401, 426,
438–41, 444–45, 465–67,
472, 476, 487
  agriculture, 187, 276
  booms, 297–98, 354–55
  bourgeoisie, 16, 19, 28, 82,
    87, 218–19, 241, 335, 426
  bourgeois revolution, 82, 87,
    218–19
  capitalism, 302, 354–55,
    364–66
  cattle, 354
  Central, 261, 324, 348, 391,
    395–96
  civil war, 71–76, 79
  coal, 285, 315–16, 354, 364
  conciliationism, 49
  Continental role, 355
  counter-revolution, 261
  crises, 299–301, 353, 395
  currency, 276–77, 310, 369
  currency stabilization, 310,
    369
  economics, 166, 270–81
  foreign trade, 28, 276–77,
    285, 300, 358
  housing, 274–75, 277, 335
  imperialism, 68, 156–58
  industrial decline, 297–98
  Kapp-Luettwitz *putsch*, 61,
    179, 261, 343, 347–48, 487
  living standards, 16–17, 355
  looted by France, 279–81,
    297, 315, 354, 364
  March events, 9–11, 18–19,
    203, 241, 263, 324, 386,
    390–400, 438–41

Germany *(continued)*
  militarism, 37, 260
  national debt, 276–77
  national income, 275–78,
    355
  national wealth, 272–76,
    355
  parliamentarianism, 176
  prices, 297–98, 310, 355
  production, 355
  proletariat, 11–19, 66–76,
    83, 87–88, 98, 174, 323–24,
    340, 355, 374, 391, 426
  relief, 170
  reparations, 21, 167, 276,
    340, 342–43, 366, 394
  revolution, 9–20, 47, 61,
    71–76, 79, 81–84, 88, 116–
    17, 203, 215–16, 218–19,
    224–25, 229–31, 260–61,
    374, 426, 441, 444–45, 472
  social equilibrium, 335
  Stinnes question, 360
  strikes, 72, 170, 192, 260,
    341, 394
  trade unions, 17, 212–13,
    374, 396
  transport, 355
  unemployment, 394–95
  uprisings, 192, 348
  wages, 335
Gerngross, 410
Giolitti, 174, 384–85, 452,
  485
Gladstone, 125, 127–28, 481
Gold, 286, 288, 310, 356, 358
Gompers, Samuel, 169, 194,
  292, 485
Gorki, 91
Gorter, 205–25, 492

Gradualism, 26, 38–40, 82, 370
Graziadei, 198, 492
Great Britain. *See* England
Greece, 163, 485
Guilbeaux, H., 198, 491
Gula, 198

Haase, 75, 473–74
Habsburgs, 37, 228
Harding, 318, 365
Heckert, 255, 390, 394–96, 401, 500
Hegel, 63, 471
Henderson, 190–91, 193, 488
Herzen, 427, 502
Herzog, 198
Hilferding, 224, 308, 333, 494
Hoetzch, Professor, 305
Hohenzollerns, 37, 48, 67–68, 72, 228, 230, 326
Holland, 198, 205–25
  sectarianism, 205–25
Housing, 274–75, 277, 335
  English, 274–75
  European, 274–75
  French, 274–75
  German, 274–75, 277, 335
  postwar, 274–75
Hughes, Secretary of State, 292–93, 497
Humanité, l', 243, 247–52, 403
  weaknesses, 243, 247–52, 403
Humbert-Droz, 198
Hungary, 20, 33, 42, 61, 79, 81–84, 154, 162–63, 168, 180, 186, 193, 198, 260, 347, 369, 399, 464, 484
  civil war, 79

Hungary *(continued)*
  counter-revolution, 162–63, 180, 186
  currency stabilization, 369
  proletariat, 83–84, 162–63
  raided by Rumania, 168
  revolution, 47, 61, 79, 81, 83–84, 162–63, 193, 260, 347
  Soviet Republic, 61, 79, 83–84, 162–63, 260, 347, 484
  White, 180, 186
Huysmans, 136, 482

Imperialism, 36–39, 41–43, 46–47, 68, 78, 90, 94–97, 105, 114, 119–22, 138, 156–64, 166–68, 172–75, 182–84, 187–90, 314–15, 325, 359, 363–64, 367, 444, 448–49, 463–65, 478, 483–85
  aggravates want, 171–72
  Allied, 42
  Balkanizes Europe, 161–64, 364
  colonial struggle, against, 325, 363
  contradictions, 363–65
  economic foundations, 314–15
  English, 37–38, 42–43, 68, 156, 158–64, 166, 174–76, 187–88, 449, 464–65, 485
  Entente, 157–58
  financial, 364
  French, 43, 68, 120–21, 138, 158–59, 161–62, 166, 190, 448–49
  German, 68, 156–58

Imperialism *(continued)*
  industrial, 364
  intervention in Soviet
    Russia, 97, 105, 158, 162,
    165–67, 182, 448–49, 478
  provokes war, 94–96
  United States, 159–61
Impoverishment, 38, 463
  theory of, 38, 463
Independent German
  Social Democracy. *See*
  Independent Socialist
  Party of Germany
Independent Labor Party, 49
  conciliationist, 49
Independent Party. *See*
  Independent Socialist
  Party of Germany
Independent Socialist Party
  of Germany (USP), 49, 67,
  75–76, 133–37, 192, 215,
  221, 225, 265, 327, 374,
  392–93, 396, 473–74
  conciliationist, 49
  split, 215–16, 221, 225
India, 42–43, 159, 164, 187–88,
  199, 208, 325, 344–45, 357,
  363
  bourgeoisie, 363
  capitalism, 344–45, 357,
    363
  crises, 357
  industrialization, 325, 357
  peasantry, 208, 345, 363
  proletariat, 345, 363
  revolution, 164, 187–88,
    208, 344–45, 363
  strikes, 43
  war role, 42–43
Indo-China, 250

Information, l', 281
Intelligentsia, 143–44, 313–14
  discontent, 313–14
  role, 143–44
International Communist
  Party. *See* Communist
  International
International equilibrium,
  269–70
International situation, 347–77
  theses of Third World
    Congress on, 347–77
Ireland, 43, 125, 128, 164,
  188, 464
  revolution, 43, 188
Iron, 286–87, 315, 364
  French, 315, 364
  United States, 286–87
Italian Communist Party,
  382–83, 391, 401–2, 434,
  452–54
  tactics, 434
Italian question, 379–87,
  451–60, 499
  speech on, 379–87
Italian Socialist Party (ISP), 33,
  193, 203, 261, 263, 374,
  379–87, 401–2, 433–34,
  451–60
  bankruptcy, 380–84
  centrists in, 381–82, 402,
    433, 453–54
  Communists, 381–83
  composition, 380–82, 453–54
  conditions of reentry, 453–54
  expelled from Comintern,
    452
  impotence, 374
  opportunism, 374
  pacifists, 451, 454

Italian Socialist Party (ISP) *(continued)*
  reformists in, 380–82, 433, 451–54, 458–60
  resolution of Third World Congress on, 451–60
  sabotage by Right Wing, 193
  split, 451–52, 455, 459–60
  treachery, 203, 261, 263, 374, 379–84, 401–2, 433–34
  verbal revolutionary, 379, 433–34
Italy, 19–20, 37, 159, 164–65, 170–71, 174, 187, 193, 198, 203, 255, 261, 263–64, 281, 284, 299, 313, 335, 348, 353–54, 369, 374, 379–87, 401–2, 433–34, 438–39, 451–60
  agricultural workers, 187
  bourgeoisie, 263, 335
  centrism, 381–82, 402, 433, 454
  conciliationism, 19
  crises, 299, 353
  currency stabilization, 369
  economics, 159, 164, 170, 281
  fascism, 19–20, 264, 401
  hostile to France, 164
  pacifism, 451, 454
  petty bourgeoisie, 313
  proletarian revolution, 193, 203, 261, 263, 348, 374, 379–83, 433–34, 438
  proletariat, 174, 374, 379–82, 433–34, 452–53, 459–60
  reformism, 381–82, 433, 451–55, 459

Italy *(continued)*
  relief, 170
  ruined by war, 354
  sectarianism, 456
  September days, 203, 261, 263, 348, 379–83, 433, 438–39, 454
  social equilibrium, 335
  Socialist Party betrayal, 203, 255–63, 374, 379–84, 401–2, 433–34
  strike of functionaries, 313
  strikes, 170, 313, 454–55
  wages, 335
  war guilt, 36
  workers seize plants, 203, 261–63, 348, 433
Izvestia, 20, 58, 99, 258

Janson, 198
Japan, 19, 22, 159, 164, 166, 231, 260, 268, 272, 289–91, 299, 318, 325, 344–45, 350, 353, 357, 365–68, 444
  budget, 366
  capitalism, 159, 289–90, 325, 344–45
  conciliationism, 19, 22
  crises, 289–90, 299, 353, 357, 366
  in Eastern Siberia, 164, 166, 367–68
  emigration, 366
  English alliance, 318, 365, 367
  enriched by war, 289–91, 350, 357, 366
  Far East coup, 367
  feudalism, 159, 325
  national wealth, 272

Japan *(continued)*
  navy, 318
  proletariat, 231, 289
  revolution, 159, 260
  rice disorders, 260
  rivalry with United States, 318, 366–67
  silk industry, 290
  trade unions, 289
  war economy, 268
  women workers, 231, 289
Jaurès, 86, 90, 177, 475–76, 483
  murderer acquitted, 177
Joergenson, O., 198
Jouhaux, 105–6, 108–9, 112, 116, 139, 192, 237, 478
July days, 71, 472

Kabakchiev, 198, 492
Kaiser-Socialism, 136
Kamenev, 255
Kapp-Luettwitz *putsch*, 61, 179, 261, 343, 347–48, 487
Kautsky, Karl, 54, 64–67, 75, 94, 117, 151–52, 156, 191, 224, 333, 470–72
Kautskyites, 131, 333
Kerensky, 64, 471
Kerenskyism, 242
Keynes, 315, 497–98
Kiev, 61
Kin-Tulin, 199
Knights of Liberty, 179–80
Knopf, 88, 476
Koenen, 342, 396, 498
Kolchak, 53, 61, 163, 182, 443, 470
Kollontai, A., 408–17, 502

Korea, 199
Krastyn, 198
Kronstadt, 203, 448–49
Krupskaya, 149
Kuehlmann, 126, 481
Kun, Bela, 408, 502

Labor, 165–67, 170–71, 182–83, 267–85, 289–90, 309–10, 316–17, 320–22, 339–40, 354, 356–60, 365, 368–72, 408
  bureaucracy, 322–23, 340, 370–71
  conscription, 182, 408
  division of, 165, 267–85, 289, 356–60
  intensity of, 170, 276, 309–10, 369
  productivity, 170, 282, 309–10, 316–17, 321–22, 354, 365, 372, 408
Labor Party. *See* British Labor Party; Farmer-Labor Party
LaFollette, Senator, 22–28
Laou Siu-chau, 199
Laporte, 399, 457–58, 503
Larin, 407, 501
Latvia, 159, 162, 180, 182, 198
Launat, 249
Lazzari, 380–87, 453–57, 459, 499
"Leader cult," 221–25
League of Nations, 40, 138, 160–63, 190, 326, 367, 463–64
Left Bloc, 19–21, 28–29
Left Communism, 255, 407–17, 426–27, 433–60

Left Communism *(continued)*
  German, 436–37
  Italian, 433–60
  Russian, 407–17
  tactical theories, 427
Leiciague, Lucie, 495
Lenin, V.I., 10, 33–34, 120, 122, 128, 149, 198, 255, 292, 389–91, 407–9, 435
Lepetit, 115
Letonmyaki, 198
Levi, Paul, 151, 198, 392, 398–402, 456, 483, 491
Levitzky, 198
Liberalism, 39–40, 190, 194
Liberals, 85, 173
Liebknecht, Karl, 49, 69, 79, 121–23, 128, 177, 192, 218–19, 387, 466–67
Ligue Civique, 180
Lithuania, 162, 198
Lloyd George, 43, 115, 168, 173–74, 176–80, 190, 464–65
Loans. *See* National debts
Lockouts, 259
London *Times,* 295, 326
Longuet, Jean, 105–6, 108–9, 114, 116, 119–29, 135–36, 141–42, 242, 403, 478
Longuetism, 128, 249
Longuetists, 131, 134–37
Loriot, 110, 116, 139–41, 478–79
Loucheur, 175, 486
Loyal American League, 179
Luxembourg, 250
Luxemburg, Rosa, 49, 64, 69, 79, 121, 123, 128, 177, 192, 387, 467–68

Lyons Convention (Syndicalist), 112, 115, 142

MacDonald, 22, 29
Machiavelli, 177, 456–57, 487
MacLaine, 198
Madagascar, 43, 464
Madsen, A., 198
Maffi, 453, 455, 502–3
Manchester Guardian, 298
Manifesto of the Communist International (First World Congress), 9, 35–50, 462
Manifesto of the Communist International (Second World Congress), 9, 149, 157–99
Manner, K., 198
March events, 9–10, 18, 203, 241–42, 263, 324, 386, 390–400, 438–41
Maring, 199, 493
Markhlevsky, J., 198, 492
Marx, Karl, 35, 67, 89, 91, 119, 128, 209, 303–4, 478–79
Marxism, 26, 66–67, 85, 217, 333, 415, 427, 430–31
Maximov, 198
May Day, 264
Mazziniists, 174, 485
Mehring, Franz, 395, 500
Menshevism, 26, 49, 82, 267
Merchant marine. *See* Shipping
Méric, Victor, 250, 496
Merrheim, 105–6, 108–9, 112–16, 139, 237, 478
Mesopotamia, 317
  oil, 317

Metal Workers Convention, 107–8
Metal Workers Union, 107–8, 112
Mexico, 199, 317
  oil, 317
Meyer, Ernst, 198, 491
Middle estate, 313–14, 360, 362
  decline of, 313–14, 360, 362
  discontent, 362
  proletarianization, 360
Militarism, 37–38, 46–47, 160–61, 164, 260, 318–19, 354, 363–68
  French, 354
  German, 37, 260
  Japanese, 366
  United States, 161, 164, 318–19, 365
Military Revolutionary Council, 58
Milkich, 198
Millerand, 124, 168, 171, 177, 480
Mistral, 136, 482
Mitskevich-Kapsukas, 198
Mohammedans, 188
Monatte, 102, 104, 110, 115–16, 139, 141, 153, 235–39, 477
Money, 39, 167–68, 272–74, 276–77, 279–81, 283–84, 288, 298, 305, 310–12, 317–18, 321, 326, 334–35, 341, 351–55, 358, 360–61, 369
  Balkan, 369
  credit, 273–74

Money *(continued)*
  depreciation of, 39, 167, 310, 313, 321, 326, 334, 341, 351–52, 354–55, 358, 360, 369
  English, 283–84, 288, 317–18
  European, 273–74, 357–58, 369
  French, 279–81, 305, 310, 354, 369
  German, 276–78, 310, 369
  Hungarian, 369
  Italian, 369
  market, 288, 317
  neutral countries, 353, 355
  paper, 272–74, 276–77, 280, 283, 298, 310, 312–13, 321, 326, 341, 351–52, 354–55, 358, 360–61
  stabilization, 310, 321, 334, 369
Monopolies, 39, 162, 349, 352, 360, 372
Monroe Doctrine, 160–61, 483–84
Morgan, 175
Moscow, 52, 54–55, 63, 149, 208
Munich, 61, 72

Napoleon, 332, 498
Napoleon III, 123, 479–80
Narodnikism (Populism), 26, 73, 473
Narodovoltsi, 73, 473
National Bloc, 21, 61, 242–43
National debts, 29, 273–77, 288, 298–99, 317–18, 321, 351–52, 354–55

National debts *(continued)*
  European, 273–74, 288, 298–99, 317, 321, 351–52
  French, 29, 281
  German, 276–77
  neutral countries, 355
National defense, 40, 190
National income, 273–78, 284–85, 311, 314, 354–55, 360, 369
  European, 271–74, 284–85, 311, 360, 369
  German, 275–78, 355
Nationalism, 47–49, 93–94
Nationalization, 139, 142, 168–69
National question, 41–43, 149, 161–64, 187–89
National Security League, 179
National wealth, 271–76, 311–12, 351–52, 355
  Balkans, 272
  European, 269–74, 311–12
  German, 272–77, 355
  Japanese, 272
  mobilized for war, 351–52
  Russian, 272
  United States, 271–72
Nazarityan, 198
Nazis, 17
Near East, 165
Negroes, 42–43
Neue Zeit, 407
Neue Zuercher Zeitung, 263–64
Neutral countries, 353, 355
  crises, 353, 355
  currency, 355
  debts, 355
  enriched by war, 355

New Economic Policy (NEP), 203
Niemetz, 191, 488
Nikhad, 198
Nilsen, M., 198
1905 Revolution, 64–66, 73–75, 307
  defeat of, 307
North America, 158, 271, 302
  capitalism, 302
  coal, 271
Norway, 159, 172, 198, 261
  crises, 172
  economics, 172
  general strike, 261
Noske, 123, 135–37, 190, 480
Nuremberg, 72

October Revolution, 64–68, 71–73, 79, 81–84, 89–91, 97–98, 116–17, 120, 184–85, 227–28, 325, 347
Oil, 39, 166, 287–88, 317, 356, 365
  Baku, 39, 166
  Mesopotamian, 317
  Mexican, 317
  Rumanian, 39
  United States, 287–88, 317, 356, 365
Okurov, 91, 477
Opportunism, 27–28, 36, 38, 78, 98–99, 108, 155–56, 308, 333, 369, 374, 400–401, 404–5
  defined, 155, 308, 333
  French, 107–9
  Italian, 374
  Socialist, 38, 77–78

Opportunism *(continued)*
  United States, 26–27
Ossinsky, 33–34

Pacifism, 115, 326, 368, 451, 454
Pak Djinshoun, 199
Pankhurst, Sylvia, 198, 491
Paris, 25, 177
Paris Commune, 87
Parliamentarianism, 39, 48, 73, 78, 101–7, 115–16, 119–29, 138, 140–41, 144, 149, 152–54, 175–76, 184–85, 196–97, 211–14, 216–20, 247–48, 446
  anarchist opposition to, 140–41, 247
  compared with Soviets, 196–97
  counterrevolutionary, 116
  English, 152, 176
  fear of, 217–20
  French, 101–7, 119–29, 140–41, 144, 152–53, 175–76
  German, 176
  revolutionary use of, 219–20
  Russian, 73–74
  syndicalist opposition to, 140–41, 144
  United States, 176
Particularism, 315
Peasantry, 25–27, 44–45, 65–66, 73, 155–56, 187, 207–9, 242, 279, 312–14, 325, 345, 354, 360–63, 408–9, 415–16
  Argentina, 362
  attitude toward socialism, 187

Peasantry *(continued)*
  Australian, 312, 362
  bourgeois reliance on, 172
  Canadian, 312, 362
  Chinese, 345
  colonial, 208, 325, 344–45, 363
  economic decline, 312–14, 361
  European, 208, 312, 361
  French, 242, 279, 354
  Indian, 208, 345, 363
  political role, 25–28, 44–45, 65, 172, 187
  poor, 361
  Russian, 65, 73, 155–56, 207–9, 408–9, 415–16
  South African, 362
  underestimation of, 25–26
  United States, 312, 361–62
  West European, 207–9
People's militia, 52–54, 470
Persia, 43, 159, 164, 187, 198
Pestaña, 154–55, 198, 483
Petrograd, 52, 61, 74, 149, 208, 448–49
  imperialist campaign against, 448–49
Petty bourgeoisie, 25–28, 44–45, 82, 90, 92–93, 242, 313–14
  discontent, 242, 313–14
  economic decline, 44, 92, 213–14
  French, 90, 242
  Italian, 313
  political role, 26–28, 44, 92–93, 242
  United States, 25–27
Peuple, Le, 342–43

Pilsudski, 191, 489
Platten, 33
Poegelmann, G., 198
Pogany (Pepper), 335–39,
   461–62, 498
Pokrovsky, 149
Poland, 41–42, 61, 65, 154,
   162, 182, 186, 198, 264–65,
   369, 432, 464
   anti-Soviet role, 162, 182
   currency stabilization, 369
   feudal-capitalist struggle, 432
   war with Soviet Russia, 61,
     154, 162
   White, 186
   Workers' Soviets, 264–65
Polano, 451, 502
Polish Communist Party,
   264–65
Polish Socialist Party (PPS),
   191, 265
   breaks with Second
     International, 191
   helps destroy Soviets, 265
Political equilibrium, 269,
   310, 425–26, 431–32
"Political Perspectives" (Leon
   Trotsky), 20–22
Populaire, 24
Populism. *See* Narodnikism
"Possibilists," 87, 476
Postal and Telegraph Workers
   convention (France), 108
Potressov, 82, 475
Pravda, 23, 428
Pressemane, 136, 482
Prices, 280, 296–98, 310, 337,
   341, 351–52, 355, 360–61,
   369
   English, 298

Prices *(continued)*
   fall, 337
   French, 280, 298
   German, 297–98, 310, 355
   regulation of, 352, 369
   rise, 341, 352, 360–61
   United States, 298
Proletarian revolution, 9–22,
   40–42, 45–47, 50, 61, 64–
   67, 71–76, 78–117, 132–33,
   149, 162–63, 183–84, 193–
   94, 203, 218–19, 223–25,
   228–30, 241–45, 260–62,
   303–29, 335–42, 347–49,
   369–70, 373–77, 386–87,
   416–17, 426–28, 432–34,
   437–39, 444–45
   Austrian, 47, 79, 229
   Bavarian, 61, 81, 83–84
   English, 22, 81, 84–86, 223
   European, 9–20, 41, 61, 66,
     77–99, 369–70
   French, 20–21, 81, 86–87,
     93, 101–17, 241–45, 260–
     61, 348, 386, 441, 444
   German, 9–20, 47, 71–76,
     79–84, 218–19, 374
   Hungarian, 47, 61, 79–84,
     162–63, 193, 260, 347
   Italian, 193, 203, 261, 263,
     348, 374, 379–84, 433–34,
     438
   main curve of, 375–76
   related to boom and crisis,
     303–29, 334–42, 375–76
   role of party, 149
   role of peasantry, 65
   Russian, 73–74, 79–83, 89–
     91, 97–99, 183–84, 347,
     415–17

Proletarian revolution *(cont'd)*
  Socialist conception of,
    92–93
  tempo slows down, 375–76
  West European, 9
Proletariat, 9–19, 27–28, 40,
    67–76, 79, 82–88, 92–93,
    96–99, 102–3, 105–6, 110–
    14, 117, 132–33, 162, 171–
    75, 184–89, 193–96, 207–
    10, 222–25, 230–33, 242,
    289, 314, 320–25, 327–29,
    333–34, 336–40, 344–50,
    355, 361–63, 367–83, 391,
    413–17, 424–28, 432–33,
    441–42, 454–60
  Bavarian, 83–84
  Central European, 372
  Chinese, 325, 345, 363
  colonial, 325, 344–45, 363
  defensive struggles, 336, 376
  dictatorship of, 117, 133,
    374
  effects of booms on, 328–29
  English, 84–85, 97–98, 173,
    207–8, 223–24, 375
  European, 162, 184–86,
    188–90, 209–10, 241–42,
    343–44, 372–74
  French, 86–87, 96–99, 102–3,
    112–14, 174
  German, 11–19, 66–76, 83,
    87–88, 98, 174, 323–24,
    340, 355, 374, 391, 426
  growth, 91–93
  Hungarian, 83–84, 162–63
  Indian, 344–45, 363
  international, 442
  Italian, 174, 374, 379–83,
    433–34, 454–60

Proletariat *(continued)*
  Japanese, 231, 289–90
  leadership, 320–23, 374–75,
    426
  living standards, 313–14,
    355
  postwar defeats, 9–10,
    425–26
  postwar movement, 337–38,
    347–50, 368–72
  role, 424
  rural, 187, 361
  Russian, 65–66, 73–75, 79,
    91, 96–99, 207–9, 347
  share in national income,
    314
  strata, 230–32, 370–71
  struggle for power, 322–25
  technology of, 413–17
  United States, 27–28, 171,
    325
  West European, 209
  woman, 231–33, 289, 371
Propaganda, 210–11
Prosperity. *See* Booms
Pyatakov, Yuri, 407, 501

Quelch, T., 198, 491

Radek, Karl, 149, 255, 389,
    391, 395, 412, 499–500
Radicals, 116, 174, 242
Radical-Socialist Bloc, 242
Radical-Socialists, 116
Railway Workers Federation
    (France), 112
Rakhia, J., 33, 198, 492
Rakoszy, 198
Rakovsky, Christian, 407, 409,
    501

Rationalism, 211, 493–94
Red Army, 48, 51–58, 61, 68–69, 181–82, 203, 257–58, 261, 331, 348, 359, 416, 448–49, 470–71
  greets Comintern, 257–58
  report on, 51–55
  role of youth, 448–49
  Warsaw campaign, 261, 348
Red Guard, 51–52
Red Navy, 57–58
Red Trade Union International, 255
Reed, John, 198, 492
Reformism, 48–49, 140–42, 169, 186, 196–97, 216–18, 247–48, 305, 313–14, 325–26, 427, 433–34, 442–43, 445–46, 451–54, 459
  bourgeois agency, 197
  class base of, 313–14
  French, 247–49
  Italian, 380–83, 433–34, 451–54, 459–60
  national base, 48–49
  nationalization program, 169
  parliamentary, 140–41, 196–97
  struggle against, 140–41, 196–97, 216–18, 247–48, 442–43, 446
Reggio-Emilia conference, 453
Reichswehr, 13
Renan, 120, 122, 125, 128, 479
Renaudel, 105–6, 108–9, 116, 135–37, 141, 153, 478
Renner, 191, 488
Reparations, 21, 167–68, 276, 340, 342–43, 366, 394

Republican Party, 25, 169, 174–75
Revolution, 9–22, 41–43, 45–50, 61, 64–67, 71–99, 116–17, 132–33, 149, 159, 162–64, 183–85, 187–88, 192–95, 203, 207–11, 215–16, 218–19, 222–33, 241–45, 259–64, 303–29, 332–42, 344–48, 362–63, 368–70, 373–83, 386–87, 415–17, 423–24, 426–28, 431–42, 444–49, 471–73
  Austrian, 47, 79, 229
  Bavarian, 61, 81, 83–84
  bourgeois, 82–83, 85–86, 218–19
  causes, 340–42
  English, 22, 81, 84–86, 223–24, 441
  epoch of, 259
  European, 9–20, 41, 61, 65–66, 77–99, 369–70, 440–41, 444
  fluctuations, 320
  French, 101–7, 241–45, 441, 444–45
  German, 9–20, 47, 61, 71–76, 79–84, 87–88, 117, 203, 215–16, 218–19, 224–25, 229, 260–61, 374, 426, 441, 444–45, 472
  Hungarian, 47, 61, 79, 83–84, 162–63, 193, 260, 347
  Indian, 164, 187–88, 208, 344–45, 363
  inevitability, 332–33
  Irish, 43, 188–89
  Italian, 193, 203, 261, 348, 380–84, 433–34, 439

Revolution *(continued)*
  Japanese, 159, 260
  national-agrarian, 210
  objective factors, 332–34, 336–38, 345, 434–36
  proletarian, 9–22, 40–42, 45–48, 50, 61, 64–67, 71–99, 116–17, 132–33, 149, 158–59, 192–94, 203, 208–12, 219, 222–25, 260–64, 303–29, 336–42, 347–48, 370, 373–83, 386–87, 415–17, 426–28, 431–42
  relation to boom and crisis, 303–29, 335–41, 376
  role of Communist parties, 435–37
  role of economics, 16–17, 303–29, 335–37, 339–42
  role of youth, 444–45
  Russian, 64–66, 71–84, 89–91, 97–99, 116–17, 120, 182–84, 229, 307, 325, 347, 385–87, 448–49
  sources, 324–26, 340–41, 344–45, 423–24
  subjective factors, 16–19, 332–34, 336–39, 345, 434–38
  United States, 344
  world, 232–33, 335, 363, 441–42, 444
Revolution of 1848, 296, 303–4, 328
Revolution of 1905, 64–65, 73–75, 307
  defeated, 307
Riboldi, 455, 503
Rizello, 175, 486
Rockefeller, 175
Romanovs, 37
Rome, 432
  class struggle in, 432
Rosmer, Alfred, 102, 104, 109, 139, 141, 153, 198, 477–78, 491
Rote Fahne, 395
Rothschild, Lord, 175, 485
Rouger, 112
Roux, Victor, 108
Roy, M.N., 199, 344, 492
Royalists, 174
Rudnyansky, A., 198
Rudzutak, 149
Ruhr, 10–11, 124–25, 315–16, 342–43, 364, 366, 394
Rumania, 39, 168
  oil, 39
  raids Hungary, 168
Russia, 25–26, 33–34, 37–39, 46–47, 49, 52–53, 61, 64–66, 68–84, 88–91, 93–94, 96–99, 105, 149, 154–58, 162, 165–66, 173, 182–84, 198, 207–9, 227–28, 260, 270–73, 292–93, 300, 307, 325, 333, 347, 358–59, 385–87, 407–17, 438, 440–44, 448–49, 476–78
  blockade, 33, 149, 292–93
  booms, 307
  bourgeoisie, 96–97, 173
  capitalism, 88–91, 96–97, 208, 260, 410–12, 476–77
  Civil War, 52–53, 61, 292–93, 359, 438–39, 441, 443–44
  coal, 39, 166, 293
  conciliationism, 49
  crises, 307

INDEX / 533

Russia *(continued)*
  Czarism overthrown, 347
  Czarist, 77–78
  economic decline, 292–93
  Entente intervention in, 97, 105, 157–58, 162, 165–66, 448–49, 478
  February Revolution, 71, 260
  foreign trade, 270, 300
  national wealth, 272
  1905 Revolution, 64–65, 73–75, 307
  October Revolution, 67, 73, 79–84, 89–91, 97–98, 116, 120, 183–84, 227–28, 325, 347
  parliamentarianism, 73
  peasantry, 65, 73, 156, 207–9, 408–9, 415
  proletariat, 65, 73–74, 79, 91, 96–99, 207–8, 347
  strikes, 73–74
  war role, 37
  See also Soviet Russia
Russian Bolshevik Party. *See* Russian Communist Party
Russian Communist Party, 51–55, 64, 79, 149, 154–56, 209, 255, 385, 407–17, 441
  Central Committee, 155
  leadership, 209
  Left Communism, 408–17
  report on, 51–55
  role, 155–56
  tactics, 51–55, 64–67, 255, 407–17, 441–42
Russian Soviet Federation. *See* Soviet Russia

Ryazanov, 149, 461
Rykov, 149, 255

Saar, 124, 278, 364, 497
  seized by France, 124
Sachs, 332–34, 498
Sadoul, J., 198, 491
Samuelson, 198
Saumoneau, Louisa, 110
Saxony, 230
Scandinavia, 33, 171–72
  postwar economics, 171–72
Schefflo, 198
Scheidemann, 51, 55, 72, 134–37, 151–52, 190, 224, 468–69
Schneider, 175, 486
Schueller, 454–56, 503
Seaman, F., 199
Second Congress (Communist Youth International), 429–60
Second International, 36–37, 48–50, 66, 73, 77–78, 93, 132, 136–37, 140, 178, 189–92, 197, 213–19, 265–67, 332, 342–44, 374, 407–10, 425, 462–63, 470
  anti-socialist role, 189–92
  Basle Congress, 36, 462–63
  bourgeois agency, 19, 49, 178, 197, 343, 373–76, 425–26
  class-collaboration, 139–40
  collapses, 48–49, 66, 77–78
  compared with Comintern, 373–74, 377
  conception of proletarian revolution, 93
  conciliationist, 49

Second International *(cont'd)*
  contempt for theory, 140, 266, 332–33, 343–44, 407–10
  counter-revolutionary, 189–92
  nationalism, 48, 93–94, 132, 140, 342–43
  opportunist, 48–49, 132
  parliamentarianism, 48, 140–41, 214, 216–20
  reformist, 48–49, 196–97, 213–20
  splits, 136–37
  See also Social Democracy
Second World Congress, 9, 61, 99, 149–99, 229, 348, 405, 429, 442, 446
  agenda, 149
  evaluated, 429–30, 442
  Manifesto, 9, 157–99
  Sectarianism, 205–25, 243–44, 436, 455
  Dutch, 205–25
  French, 243–44
Seeckt, 14
Seemann, 332, 335, 498
Seitz, 191, 488
Self-determination, 42–43, 120, 124–26
Sembat, 135, 482
September days, 203, 261–63, 348, 379–83, 433–34, 438, 454–55
Serbia, 163
Serrati, D.M., 155–56, 198, 381, 401, 452, 456–57, 459, 483, 492
Shaw, Tom, 191, 488
Sheffik, 199

Shipping, 286–87, 291, 356, 365
  English, 287, 291
  United States, 286–87, 291, 356, 365
Shlyapnikov, A.G., 408, 501–2
Sholnikov, 408
Siberia, 164, 166, 308
Sirola, 33
Smeral, 456–58, 503
Social Democracy, 19–20, 22–25, 33–37, 64–65, 72–73, 88, 98, 121–23, 133–37, 152, 175, 184, 188–92, 213–19, 236, 265–66, 269, 332–33, 342–44, 368, 370–71, 373–74, 377, 395–96, 407–10, 445–46
  Belgian, 121–23, 342–44
  betrayals, 188–90
  bourgeois agency, 188–91, 269, 342–44, 373–75
  French, 23–25, 236
  German, 13, 17, 64–65, 72–73, 88, 134–37, 152, 184, 188–90, 192, 342–44, 374, 395–96, 407–10
  maintains political equilibrium, 269
  See also Second International, Socialist parties
Social equilibrium, 96, 268–69, 298–99, 308–15, 321–23, 334–35, 339–40, 344, 349, 362, 368–70, 372–74, 430–32
  disrupted by war, 268–69, 298–99
  English, 344

Social equilibrium *(cont'd)*
  European, 308–9, 324, 334–35, 344, 349, 362, 368–70
  French, 315, 335
  German, 335
  Italian, 335
  postwar, 308–13, 321–23, 334–35, 349, 430
  related to capitalist culture, 96
Socialism, 121, 182–83, 193, 249–50
  Christian, 249–50
  German, 121
  planning under, 182–83
  United States, 193–94
Socialist center (Two-and-a-Half International), 49, 266, 465–66
  composition, 49
  conciliationist, 49
Social-patriotism, 36–37, 49, 140–41, 269
Social revolution, 91–94
  See also Revolution
Social Revolutionaries (S.R.'s), 26, 333
Sokolnikov, Gregory, 408, 501
South Africa, 362
  small farmers ruined, 361–62
South America, 161, 289, 308, 312, 357
  crises, 357
  decline of farmers, 312
Southern Europe, 297
Soviet Hungary, 61, 79, 83–84, 162–63, 260, 347, 484
Soviet Russia, 10, 33, 48, 51–55, 61, 68–69, 97–99, 105, 126–28, 149, 154–55,

Soviet Russia *(continued)*, 157–58, 162, 165–67, 176, 179, 181–86, 188, 191, 203, 241–42, 250, 257–58, 260, 262, 292–93, 331–32, 335, 348, 358–59, 367, 384–87, 407–17, 438–45, 448–49, 478
  Allied blockade, 33, 149, 165–66, 292–93, 359, 441
  attitude toward church, 249–50
  Civil War, 53, 61, 203, 292–93, 359, 438–39, 441, 443–44
  concessions, 411–14
  economic policy, 407–11
  economics, 165–68, 182–83, 358–59, 385–86, 407–12, 441–42
  Entente intervention, 97, 105, 157–58, 163, 165–67, 181–82, 448–49, 478
  foreign trade, 203, 358–59, 367, 410–14, 440–41
  labor conscription, 182, 408
  peasantry, 408–9, 415
  proletariat and technology, 414–16
  Red Army, 48, 51–58, 61, 68–69, 181–82, 203, 257–58, 261, 331–32, 348, 359, 416
  Red Guard, 51–52
  Red Navy, 57–58
  relations with European proletariat, 186, 188, 241–42
  revolutionary role, 386–87
  role of émigrés, 179

Soviet Russia *(continued)*
  state-ization, 407–12
  trade unions, 408
  treaties, 367
  war with Poland, 61, 154, 162
  See also Russia
Soviets, 45–46, 114, 145, 149, 187, 195–96
  compared with parliaments, 196
  organization of, 145, 149
  role of, 45–46, 114, 145, 195
  Workers', 45–46, 50
Soviets of Deputies, 114
Soviets of Workers', Soldiers' and Peasants' Deputies, 45–46
Spain, 152, 154–55, 172, 180, 198, 340
  demonstrations, 172
  economics, 172
  revolution, 340
  strikes, 172
  syndicalism, 152, 154
Spanish Communist Party, 155
Spartacists, 63, 71–72, 76
Spartacus League, 63
Stalin, 149
Standard of living, 16–17, 170, 290, 307, 313–14, 340–41, 355, 369, 372
  in Allied countries, 372
  Central European, 372
  effect on revolution, 306–8, 341–42
  English, 372
  German, 16–17, 355
  middle estate's, 313

Standard of living *(continued)*
  proletarian, 314
  United States, 290–91, 372
State-ization, 39–40, 408
  Soviet Russian, 408
Statistics, 331–33
  role of, 332–33
Stauning, 22
Steinhardt, K., 198
Stinnes, Hugo, 175, 276, 360, 486
Stolypin, 73, 473
Strasbourg resolution, 137
Strategy, 442–43
  See also Tactics
Strikes, 43, 61, 72–74, 104–5, 170, 178–79, 185–89, 192, 259–61, 264, 268, 283, 306, 313, 326, 328, 341, 347–48, 354, 369, 375, 394, 478
  Communist participation in, 328
  Czechoslovakian, 261, 348
  English, 188, 260–61, 283, 306, 326, 347–48, 354, 375
  European, 61, 369
  French, 104–5, 170, 178, 261, 264, 478
  general, 73, 261, 264
  German, 72, 170, 192, 260, 341, 394–95
  Indian, 43–44
  international, 105, 478
  Italian, 170, 313
  Norwegian, 261
  Russian, 73–75
  United States, 261, 347
Stroemer, 198
Stuchka, 198, 492

Stuttgart, 72
Sultan-Saade, 198, 492
Supreme Economic Council, 172
Sweden, 159, 198
Switzerland, 33, 171, 198, 263
  economics, 171
Syndicalism, 21, 102–16, 139–45, 152–55, 235–39, 243–45, 251–52, 394
  American, 152
  anarchist theory, 140–42
  conciliationist, 141–42
  Convention of Lyons, 112, 115, 142
  French, 21, 102–16, 139–45, 152–54, 192, 235–39, 243–45, 251–52, 393
  revolutionary, 21, 140–41, 235–39
  Spanish, 152, 154–55
Syndicates. *See* Trade unions
Syria, 158, 483

Tactics, 10–16, 18–20, 51–55, 64–67, 84–88, 92–93, 173–74, 255, 262–66, 298–99, 320–25, 331–45, 367–68, 375–77, 389–417, 425–60
  adventurist, 427–28, 433–35
  bourgeois, 19–20, 84–87, 92–93, 173–75, 262–67, 298, 321–22, 325–26, 337–38, 367–68, 375–76, 425–26, 430
  Russian Communist Party, 51–55, 64–66, 255, 407–17, 441–42
  sectarian, 436–37
  united front, 10, 324

Taylor system, 183
Teachers Union (France), 112–13
  Tours Convention, 112–13
Temps, Le, 177, 264, 280, 486
Thaelmann, 389–90, 396–97, 500
Thalheimer, 339, 394–95, 398, 401, 498
Third International. *See* Communist International
Third Party, 19, 25–28, 461–62
Third World Congress, 9–11, 203, 255–417, 421–60
  Economic Commission, 410–13
  evaluated, 10, 421–60
  Left Wing, 398–400
  theses of, 347–77
Thomas, Albert, 135–36, 138, 153, 190, 482
Tomann, K., 198
Tomsky, 149
Tories, 85, 173
Trade unions, 17, 39, 45–46, 102–9, 112–14, 139–41, 144–46, 149, 153–54, 169, 178–80, 185–89, 192–94, 210–14, 218, 235–39, 243–45, 251, 255, 268, 289, 323, 328, 370–71, 374–75, 396, 408, 424–25, 498
  bureaucracy, 17, 45–46, 189, 213–14, 322–23, 425
  Communist participation in, 211–14, 243–45, 251–52, 327–28
  compared with Soviets, 45–46

Trade unions *(continued)*
  composition changes, 184–87
  conservatism of leaders,
    189–90
  craft, 185, 210
  effect of war on, 39
  English, 113, 212, 375, 498
  French, 101–9, 112–14,
    139–41, 144–45, 153–54,
    180, 212, 235–39, 243–44
  German, 16, 212, 374, 395
  industrial, 210
  influx into, 113–14, 186–87
  Italian, 374
  Japanese, 289–90
  pre-war, 268
  Red, 255
  role of, 141, 145–46
  Soviet Russian, 408
  United States, 169, 194
Tranquilli, 451
Treves, 452, 454, 502
Triple Alliance (Big Three),
  375, 498
Troelstra, 191, 488
Trotsky, Leon, 33, 58, 149,
  198, 255, 258, 391, 407–9,
  421
Trusts, 39–40, 162, 349, 352,
  360, 372
  wartime expansion, 360
Tsakhaya, M., 198
Tseretelli, 64, 471
Tunis, 125
Turati, 133, 193, 380–87,
  452–54, 482
Turgot, 171, 485
Turkey, 163, 198, 484–85
Tuzar, 191

Two-and-a-Half International.
  See Socialist center

Ukraine, 39
Unemployment, 290, 321,
  325, 328, 335, 338, 340,
  371–72, 394–95
  English, 395
  German, 394–95
  insurance, 325
  relief, 321
  rise in, 371–72
  United States, 290, 395
Unionists, 173, 485
United Communist Party
  (Germany), 225, 391–401,
  494
United front, 10, 324
United German Communist
  Party (VKPD), 225, 391–401,
  494
  Left Wing, 398
United States, 19, 22, 25–28,
  33, 37–38, 88, 114–15, 149,
  152, 158–61, 164, 167, 169,
  171, 174–76, 179–80, 193–
  94, 198, 261, 267–68, 270–
  72, 275, 285–92, 297–303,
  305–9, 312, 316–19, 324–
  25, 335–36, 339, 342, 347,
  350–53, 355–58, 361–62,
  365–67, 372, 395, 411
  booms, 297–301, 324–25
  bourgeoisie, 19, 175
  capitalism, 114–15, 356–57,
    362, 365, 411
  cattle, 287
  coal, 271, 286–88, 317, 356,
    365

United States *(continued)*
  concentration of capital, 362
  conciliationism, 19, 22, 25–28
  counter-revolutionary groups, 179–80
  crises, 171, 290–91, 299, 303, 305–6, 324–25, 351–53, 357, 395
  economic rise, 269–71
  economics, 167, 169–71, 285–89
  economy, 267–68
  emigration, 171
  enriched by war, 286–89, 291, 300–301, 308, 350, 356–57
  European debts to, 288, 317–18
  farmers, 25–28, 312, 361–62
  foreign trade, 288–89, 291, 300–301, 308, 356–57, 365
  gold, 286, 288, 356
  housing, 275
  immigration, 171, 362–63
  imperialism, 160–61
  iron, 286–87
  labor productivity, 316–17, 365
  living standards, 290–91, 372–73
  loses European market, 303
  militarism, 318–19
  money market, 288
  national wealth, 272
  navy, 161, 164, 318–19, 365
  oil, 287–88, 317, 356, 365
  parliamentarianism, 176
  peacetime conversion, 297

United States *(continued)*
  petty bourgeoisie, 25–28
  prices, 298
  proletariat, 27–28, 171, 325
  repressions, 261
  revolution, 344
  rise in world status, 316–17, 344
  rivalry with England, 160–61, 164, 316–19, 336, 339, 342, 365–67
  rivalry with Japan, 318, 366–67
  shipping, 286–87, 291, 356, 365
  strikes, 261, 347
  syndicalism, 152
  trade unions, 169, 194
  unemployment, 290, 395
  wages, 306
  war economy, 268
  war role, 37–38, 366–67
Upper Silesia, 364, 394–95
USP. *See* Independent Socialist Party of Germany

Vandervelde, 121–22, 128, 190, 479
Vanek, 198
Van Leueven, 198
Van Overstraaten, 198
Varenne, A., 135–36, 138, 482
Varga, 198, 297, 336–37, 492
Vatican, 174
Verdier, 244
Versailles Peace Treaty, 61, 115, 120–22, 126, 157, 164–66, 191, 358, 364
Vie Ouvrière, La, 102, 104, 107–10, 236–37, 244

Villaine, Senator Gaudin de, 166
Viviani, 119, 128, 479
VKPD. *See* United German Communist Party
Vorovsky, 34
Vorwaerts, 342–44

Wages, 306, 321, 326, 335, 338, 341, 350, 352, 369
  English, 306
  European, 306
  French, 335
  German, 335
  Italian, 335
  postwar rise, 350–52
  regulation of, 369
Wakmann, R., 198
Walcher, J., 198, 491
Wall Street, 115
War, 46–47, 52–55, 71–76, 78–79, 94–96, 184–85, 329, 350–52, 368–69, 376, 438–39
  Balkan, 95
  civil, 47–48, 53, 71–76, 79, 95–96, 184, 329, 369–70, 376, 438–39
  imperialist, 45–47, 350–52
  See also World War
Warsaw, 61, 332, 348
  campaign, 61, 332, 348
Weimar Republic, 61, 83, 575
  See also Germany
Weir, Lord, 175, 485
Western Europe, 9, 207–9, 229, 299, 305, 437
  proletarian revolution, 9, 298–99, 305, 437
  proletariat, 207–10

White Guards, 69, 162, 166, 179
White Terror, 178, 190
Williams, 198
Wilson, Woodrow, 38, 43, 114–15, 120, 122, 126–28, 160–63, 177, 180, 261, 318, 365, 464
Winberg, 198
Wolfstein, R., 198
Women's movement, 231–33, 255, 289, 371
World Federation of Soviet Republics, 57, 184
World War, 9, 36–43, 49, 78, 85, 94–96, 109, 113–14, 125, 157–73, 176, 180, 184–86, 228–29, 259–60, 266–86, 289–90, 292, 297–303, 308, 311–19, 324–26, 334, 339–40, 344, 347–62, 366–69, 372–74, 424, 441, 481–82
  casualties, 164–65
  causes, 302–3, 314–19, 366–67
  colonial role, 42–44, 125–26, 481
  consequences, 424–26
  cost, 165–73, 270–74, 280–82
  destroys bourgeois democracy, 180–81
  destroys old balance of power, 157–60
  disrupts economy, 267–68, 349–51, 359–61
  disrupts equilibrium, 268–69, 298–99
  disrupts trade, 282–83

World War *(continued)*
  effect on division of labor, 165–66, 267–85, 289, 355–59
  enriches Japan, 289–91, 350, 357, 366
  enriches neutral countries, 355
  enriches United States, 285–89, 291, 300–301, 308, 350, 355–57
  impoverishes Europe, 36–40, 165–73, 269–85, 299–303, 308, 311–12, 334–35, 344, 349–50, 353, 355–57, 361–62
  increases concentration of capital, 176
  kills Second International, 48–49, 78
  revolutionary influence, 114, 185, 266, 347–48, 424
  role of Belgium, 158, 163
  roles of Armenia, Serbia, 163
  roles of England, France, Italy, Russia, 36–37
  ruins farmers, 312–13

World War *(continued)*
  ruins France, Belgium, Italy, 354
  ruins middle estate, 313–14
  undermines Russian economy, 292, 441
  United States' role, 37–38, 366–67
Wrangel, 163, 174, 182, 484
Wynkoop, 198, 492

Yellow International, 369
Youth movement, 255, 444–45, 447–49
  tactical education, 445
  See also Communist Youth International
Yudenich, 61, 182, 448–49, 487
Yugoslavia, 42, 161–62, 198, 464

Zapototsky, 198
Zetkin, Clara, 255
Zimmerwald, 112
Zinoviev, Gregory E., 34, 149, 151, 198, 205–6, 255, 391, 400–401, 483, 489–90

THE COMMUNIST INTERNATIONAL IN LENIN'S TIME

To See the Dawn
Baku, 1920—First Congress of the Peoples of the East

How can peasants and workers in the colonial world achieve freedom from imperialist exploitation? By what means can working people overcome divisions incited by their national ruling classes and act together for their common class interests? These questions were addressed by 2,000 delegates to the 1920 Congress of the Peoples of the East. $17

Workers of the World and Oppressed Peoples, Unite!
Proceedings and Documents of the Second Congress, 1920

The debate among delegates from 37 countries takes up key questions of working-class strategy and program and offers a vivid portrait of social struggles in the era of the October Revolution. Two volume set. $45

Lenin's Struggle for a Revolutionary International
Documents, 1907–1916; The Preparatory Years

The debate among revolutionary working-class leaders, including V.I. Lenin and Leon Trotsky, on a socialist response to World War I. $30

Other volumes in the series:

The German Revolution and the Debate on Soviet Power (1918–1919). $27

Founding the Communist International (March 1919). $25

ALSO BY LEON TROTSKY

The History of the Russian Revolution

How, under Lenin's leadership, the Bolshevik Party led millions of workers and farmers to overthrow the state power of the landlords and capitalists in 1917 and bring to power a government that advanced their class interests at home and worldwide. Unabridged, 3 vols. in one. Written by one of the central leaders of that socialist revolution. $30. Also in French and Russian.

The Third International after Lenin

Leon Trotsky's 1928 defense of the Marxist course that had guided the Communist International in its early years. Writing in the heat of political battle, Trotsky addresses the key challenge facing working people today: building communist parties throughout the world capable of leading workers and farmers to take power. $20. Also in Farsi.

The Revolution Betrayed

What Is the Soviet Union and Where Is It Going?

In 1917 workers and peasants of Russia were the motor force of one of the deepest revolutions in history. Yet within ten years a political counterrevolution by a privileged social layer, whose chief spokesperson was Joseph Stalin, was being consolidated. The classic study of the Soviet workers state and its degeneration. $17. Also in Spanish, Farsi, Greek.

PATHFINDERPRESS.COM

COMMUNIST CONTINUITY AND PROGRAM

New!
The Fight against Jew-Hatred and Pogroms in the Imperialist Epoch
Stakes for the International Working Class

V.I. LENIN, LEON TROTSKY
FARRELL DOBBS, JAMES P. CANNON
JACK BARNES, DAVE PRINCE

Jew-hatred and pogroms—like Hamas carried out on October 7, 2023—are now part of the permanent social convulsions and wars of the imperialist epoch. That's why fighting Jew-hatred is of decisive importance to the working class and oppressed nations of the entire world. The authors answer the all-important question: *What is to be done to end it*—for all time. $10. Also in Spanish, soon in French.

The Low Point of Labor Resistance Is Behind Us
The Socialist Workers Party Looks Forward

JACK BARNES, MARY-ALICE WATERS, STEVE CLARK

The global order imposed by Washington after its victory in World War II is shattering. A long retreat by the working class and unions has come to an end. The bosses and their government are stepping up attacks on our wages, conditions, and constitutional rights. This book highlights opportunities for building a mass proletarian party able to lead the struggle to end capitalist rule, opening a socialist future for humanity. $10. Also in Spanish and French.

Are They Rich Because They're Smart?
Class, Privilege, and Learning under Capitalism

JACK BARNES

Exposes growing class inequalities in the US and the self-serving rationalizations of well-paid professionals who think their "brilliance" equips them to "regulate" working people, who don't know what's in our own best interest. $10. Also in Spanish, French, Farsi, Arabic.

Malcolm X, Black Liberation, and the Road to Workers Power
JACK BARNES

The conquest of state power by a class-conscious vanguard of the working class is the mightiest weapon working people can wield against racism and Black oppression, as well as Jew-hatred and every form of human degradation inherited from class society. $20. Also in Spanish, French, Farsi, Arabic, Greek.

In Defense of Marxism
Against the Petty-Bourgeois Opposition in the Socialist Workers Party
LEON TROTSKY

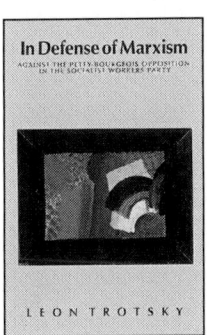

A reply to those in the revolutionary workers movement in the late 1930s buckling to bourgeois patriotism during Washington's buildup to enter World War II. Trotsky explains why only a party fighting to bring workers into its ranks and leadership can steer a communist course. In the process, he defends the materialist and dialectical foundations of Marxism. $17. Also in Spanish and French.

The Struggle for a Proletarian Party
JAMES P. CANNON

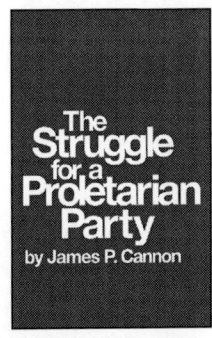

"The workers of America have power enough to topple the structure of capitalism at home and to lift the whole world with them when they rise," Cannon asserts. On the eve of World War II, a founder of the communist movement in the US and leader of the Communist International in Lenin's time defends the program and party-building norms of Bolshevism. $20. Also in Spanish and Farsi.

PATHFINDERPRESS.COM

The truth about the Moscow Trials

THE CASE OF LEON TROTSKY
TESTIMONY BEFORE 1937 COMMISSION INVESTIGATING CHARGES MADE AGAINST HIM IN MOSCOW TRIALS

Was the regime of Joseph Stalin and his heirs a continuation of the Bolshevik-led workers and peasants government established by the October 1917 Revolution?

No! says Bolshevik leader Leon Trotsky in testimony before a 1937 international commission of inquiry into Stalin's Moscow frame-up trials. Reviewing forty years of working-class struggle in which Trotsky was a participant and leader, he discusses the fight to restore V.I. Lenin's revolutionary internationalist course and why the Stalin regime organized the Moscow Trials.

He explains working people's stake in the unfolding Spanish Revolution, the fight against fascism in Germany, efforts to build a world revolutionary party, and much more. $28

Companion volume **NOT GUILTY**
FINDINGS OF THE 1937 COMMISSION

"The Moscow Trials were a frame-up" said the 1937 commission of inquiry into charges leveled against Trotsky in Stalin's kangaroo court. Full text of report. $23

My Life
Leon Trotsky
A leader of the Russian Revolution, Red Army, and the fight to maintain Lenin's continuity recounts lessons from battles he took part in from the early 1900s to his forced exile in 1929 from the Soviet Union by Stalin's counterrevolutionary regime. $27

CUBA'S SOCIALIST REVOLUTION

New Edition!
Che Guevara on Economics and Politics in the Transition to Socialism
CARLOS TABLADA

It's essential for working people to win state power, said Ernesto Che Guevara. "Then there's the second stage, maybe more difficult than the first"—the transition from dog-eat-dog capitalism to socialism. That includes moving from work as a condition for survival, to voluntary social labor through which we express our common humanity. Includes Fidel Castro's 1987 speech "Che's Ideas Are Absolutely Relevant Today." New edition with substantially expanded selections from Guevara's writings. $17. Also in Spanish, coming in French.

Women in Cuba:
The Making of a Revolution within the Revolution
VILMA ESPÍN, ASELA DE LOS SANTOS, YOLANDA FERRER

The integration of women in the ranks and leadership of the Cuban Revolution was intertwined with the proletarian course of the leadership of the revolution from the start. This is the story of that revolution and how it transformed the women and men who made it. $17. Also in Spanish, Farsi, Greek.

Colombia: Fidel Castro on the Debate around Revolutionary Strategy and Lessons of the Cuban Revolution
FROM THE PAGES OF THE *MILITANT*

Fidel Castro describes the Cuban leadership's efforts to end decades of war between the FARC guerrilla movement and Colombia's brutal regime. He explains why Cuban revolutionaries, unlike FARC leaders, rejected taking hostages and organized Cuba's working people to win state power, not pursue a "prolonged people's war." $5. Also in Spanish.

PATHFINDERPRESS.COM

REVOLUTIONARY LEADERS IN THEIR OWN WORDS

Cuba and the Coming American Revolution
JACK BARNES

This is a book about the example set by the Cuban people that revolution is not only necessary—it can be made. A book about the struggles of workers and other exploited producers in the imperialist heartland, and the youth attracted to them. About the class struggle in the US, where the revolutionary capacities of working people are as utterly discounted by the ruling powers as were those of the Cuban toilers. And just as wrongly. $10. Also in Spanish, French, Farsi.

Thomas Sankara Speaks
The Burkina Faso Revolution, 1983–87

Under Sankara's guidance, Burkina Faso's revolutionary government led peasants, workers, women, and youth to expand literacy; to sink wells, plant trees, erect housing; to combat women's oppression; to carry out land reform; to join others worldwide to free themselves from the imperialist yoke. $20. Also in French.

Maurice Bishop Speaks
The Grenada Revolution and Its Overthrow, 1979–83

The triumph of the 1979 revolution in the Caribbean island of Grenada under the leadership of Maurice Bishop gave hope to millions throughout the Americas. Invaluable lessons from the workers and farmers government destroyed by a Stalinist-led counterrevolution in 1983. $20

Teamster Politics

FARRELL DOBBS

How Minneapolis Teamster Local 544, guided by a class-struggle leadership in the 1930s, organized the unemployed and truck owner-operators, deployed a Union Defense Guard to stop a membership drive by fascist Silver Shirts, campaigned against Washington's war drive, and won workers to the need to break from the bosses and organize a labor party based on the unions. $16. Also in Spanish.

Lenin's Final Fight

Speeches and Writings, 1922–23

V.I. LENIN

In 1922 and 1923, V.I. Lenin, central leader of the world's first socialist revolution, waged what was to be his last political battle—one that was lost after his death. At stake was whether that revolution, and the international communist movement it led, would remain on the revolutionary proletarian course that brought workers and peasants to power in October 1917. $17. Also in Spanish, Farsi, Greek.

Malcolm X Talks to Young People

"The young generation of whites, Blacks, browns, whatever else—you're living at a time of revolution," said Malcolm in 1964. "And I for one will join with anyone, I don't care what color you are, as long as you want to change this miserable condition that exists on this earth." Four talks and an interview in the last months of Malcolm's life. $12. Also in Spanish, French, Farsi, Greek.

PATHFINDERPRESS.COM

DEFENDING CONSTITUTIONAL FREEDOMS

50 Years of Covert Operations in the US
Washington's Political Police and the American Working Class
LARRY SEIGLE, FARRELL DOBBS STEVE CLARK

How class-conscious workers have defended constitutional freedoms and fought the capitalists' drive to build the "national security" state essential to maintaining their rule. $10. Also in Spanish and Farsi.

Socialism on Trial
Testimony at Minneapolis Sedition Trial
JAMES P. CANNON

The revolutionary program of the working class, presented in response to frame-up charges of "seditious conspiracy" in 1941, on the eve of US entry into World War II. The defendants were leaders of the Minneapolis labor movement and the Socialist Workers Party. $15. Also in Spanish, French, Farsi.

FBI on Trial
The Victory in the Socialist Workers Party Suit against Government Spying
MARGARET JAYKO

The record of a historic victory in the fight for political rights, including the 1986 federal court ruling against government spying and excerpts from trial testimony by SWP leaders Farrell Dobbs and Jack Barnes. $17

THE WORKING CLASS AND THE FIGHT AGAINST JEW-HATRED

The Jewish Question
A Marxist Interpretation
ABRAM LEON

The battle against reactionary forces aiming to exterminate the Jews remains central to world politics, as shown by the genocidal October 2023 pogrom in Israel. Why is Jew-hatred still raising its ugly head? What are its class roots? Why, as Abram Leon explains, is there no solution "independent of the world proletarian revolution"? Revised translation, new introduction, and 40 pages of illustrations and maps. $17. Also in Spanish and French.

Imperialism's March toward Fascism and War
JACK BARNES

"There will be new Hitlers, new Mussolinis. That is inevitable. What is not inevitable is that they will triumph. The working-class vanguard will organize our class to fight back against the devastating toll we are made to pay for the capitalist crisis. The future of humanity will be decided in the contest between these contending class forces." In *New International* no. 10. $14. Also in Spanish, French, Farsi, Greek.

The Founding of the Socialist Workers Party
Minutes and Resolutions, 1938–39
JAMES P. CANNON

At founding gatherings of the Socialist Workers Party in 1938–39, revolutionists in the US codified two decades of experience in building a communist party. They charted a working-class course in resisting the coming imperialist war, fighting fascism and Jew-hatred, the struggle for Black rights, forging an alliance with exploited farmers, and the battle to transform the unions into revolutionary instruments of struggle by working people. $23

PATHFINDERPRESS.COM

EXPAND YOUR REVOLUTIONARY LIBRARY

Labor, Nature, and the Evolution of Humanity
The Long View of History
FREDERICK ENGELS, KARL MARX
GEORGE NOVACK
MARY-ALICE WATERS

Without understanding that social labor, transforming nature, has driven humanity's evolution for millions of years, working people are unable to see beyond the capitalist epoch of class exploitation that warps all human relations, ideas, and values. Only the revolutionary conquest of state power by the working class can open the door to a world free of capitalist exploitation, degradation of nature, subjugation of women, racism, and war. A world built on human solidarity. A socialist world. $12. Also in Spanish and French.

The Turn to Industry
Forging a Proletarian Party
JACK BARNES

A book about the working-class program, composition, and course of conduct of the only kind of party worthy of the name "revolutionary" in the imperialist epoch. A party that can recognize the most revolutionary fact of this epoch—the worth of working people, and our power to change society when we organize and act against the capitalist class. It's about building such a party in the US and in other capitalist countries. $15. Also in Spanish, French, Greek.

The Communist Manifesto
KARL MARX AND FREDERICK ENGELS

Communism, say the founding leaders of the revolutionary workers movement, is not a set of ideas or preconceived "principles" but workers' line of march to power, springing from a "movement going on under our very eyes." $5. Also in Spanish, French, Farsi, Arabic.

The Clintons' Anti-Working-Class Record
Why Washington Fears Working People
JACK BARNES

What working people need to know about the profit-driven course of Democrats and Republicans alike over the last three decades. And the political awakening of workers seeking to understand and resist the capitalist rulers' assaults. $10. Also in Spanish, French, Farsi, Greek.

Tribunes of the People and the Trade Unions
KARL MARX, V.I. LENIN, LEON TROTSKY
FARRELL DOBBS, JACK BARNES

A tribune of the people uses every example of capitalist oppression to explain why working people, in class battles, will break from the bosses' parties, organize a revolutionary fight for state power, and lay the foundations of a socialist world of human solidarity. $12. Also in Spanish, French, Farsi, Greek.

Pathfinder Press **accessible e-books** for the blind, those with low vision, or other challenges reading print books

For a list of current accessible titles, go to: pathfinderpress.com/collections/books-for-the-blind.

Visit bookshare.org for information on how to sign up.

PATHFINDERPRESS.COM

WOMEN'S LIBERATION AND SOCIALISM

Cosmetics, Fashions, and the Exploitation of Women
JOSEPH HANSEN, EVELYN REED MARY-ALICE WATERS

How big business reinforces women's second-class status and uses it to rake in profits. Where does women's oppression come from? How has the entry of millions of women into the workforce strengthened the battle for emancipation, still to be won? $12. Also in Spanish, Farsi, Greek.

The Origin of the Family, Private Property, and the State
FREDERICK ENGELS

The emergence of class-divided society gave rise to repressive state bodies and the oppression of women to enable the ruling classes to pass along wealth and privilege. Engels discusses the consequences for working people of these class institutions—from their ancient forms to their modern versions. $15. Also in Spanish and Farsi.

The Emancipation of Women
V.I. LENIN

Women's emancipation, Lenin wrote, begins "only when an all-out struggle begins, led by the proletariat wielding state power," to draw women as equals into productive social labor. And as cooking, childcare, and other housework are transformed into social tasks of "a large-scale socialist economy." $7

New International
A MAGAZINE OF MARXIST POLITICS AND THEORY

NEW INTERNATIONAL NO. 7
Opening Guns of World War III: Washington's Assault on Iraq
JACK BARNES

The murderous assault on Iraq in 1990–91 heralded increasingly sharp conflicts among imperialist powers, growing instability of capitalism, and more wars. Also includes:

1945: When US Troops Said No!
by Mary-Alice Waters

Lessons from the Iran-Iraq War
by Samad Sharif

$14. Also in Spanish, French, Farsi.

NEW INTERNATIONAL NO. 12
Capitalism's Long Hot Winter Has Begun
JACK BARNES

Today's global capitalist crisis is but the opening stage of decades of economic, financial, and social convulsions and class battles. Class-conscious workers confront this historic turning point for imperialism with confidence, Jack Barnes writes, drawing satisfaction from being "in their face" as we chart a revolutionary course to take power. $14. Also in Spanish, French, Farsi, Arabic, Greek.

NEW INTERNATIONAL NO. 11
U.S. Imperialism Has Lost the Cold War
JACK BARNES

The collapse of regimes across Eastern Europe and the USSR claiming to be communist did not mean workers and farmers there had been crushed. In today's sharpening class conflicts and wars, these toilers are joining working people the world over in the struggle against capitalist exploitation. $14. Also in Spanish, French, Farsi, Greek.

PATHFINDERPRESS.COM

PATHFINDER AROUND THE WORLD

UNITED STATES
(and Caribbean, Latin America, and East Asia)
  Pathfinder Books, 306 W. 37th St., 13th Floor
  New York, NY 10018

CANADA
  Pathfinder Books, 7107 St. Denis, Suite 204
  Montreal, QC H2S 2S5

UNITED KINGDOM
(and Europe, Africa, Middle East, and South Asia)
  Pathfinder Books, 5 Norman Rd.
  Seven Sisters, London N15 4ND

AUSTRALIA
(and New Zealand, Southeast Asia, and the Pacific)
  Pathfinder Books, Suite 2, First floor, 275 George St.
  Liverpool, Sydney, NSW 2170
  Postal address: P.O. Box 73, Campsie, NSW 2194

JOIN THE PATHFINDER READERS CLUB
BUILD YOUR LIBRARY!

$10 / YEAR
25% DISCOUNT ON ALL PATHFINDER TITLES
30% OFF BOOKS OF THE MONTH
Valid at pathfinderpress.com and local Pathfinder book centers

Go to: pathfinderpress.com/products/pathfinder-readers-club

Pathfinder
pathfinderpress.com